THE ANTHROPOSOPHIC APPROACH TO MEDICINE

Volume II

The Anthroposophic Approach to Medicine

An Outline of a Spiritual Scientifically Oriented Medicine

Volume 2

Established by
FRIEDRICH HUSEMANN

Edited and revised by
OTTO WOLFF

With contributions by Otto Wolff, Margarethe Hauschka-Stavenhagen, Gudrune Wolff-Hoffman, Johannes Ziemann, Guy van der Bie, and Andreas Rohen

Translated by Lisa Davisson

MERCURY PRESS
Chestnut Ridge, NY

This volume is a translation by Lisa Davisson of *Das Bild des Menschen als Grundlage der Heilkunst Band II, Halbband 2* (first half) published by Verlag Freies Geistesleben, Stuttgart. It is published with the kind permission of the German publisher.

Wolff, Otto
Husemann, Friedrich
The anthroposophic approach to medicine

Translation of: *Das Bild des Menschen als Grundlage der Heilkunst.*
Includes bibliographical references.
1. Anthroposophic therapy – Collected works.
I. Davisson, Lisa. II. Wolff, Otto, Dr. med. III. Title
RZ409.7.H8713 1982 615.5'3 82-24309

Library of Congress Control Number: 2014954793

First printing by Anthroposophic Press, Inc.

ISBN 978-1-935136-12-5

Mercury Press
The Fellowship Community
241 Hungry Hollow Road
Chestnut Ridge, NY 10977

Printed in the United States of America.

Table of Contents

SPECIFIC PATHOLOGY AND THERAPY

GENERAL PATHOLOGY AND THERAPY

Anamnesis and Diagnosis

A sick person often senses that something is "not in order"—a simple but appropriate expression since an illness is a deviation from "ordinary" physiological behavior. Among other things, he experiences a certain undefined deficiency, causing him rightly to say that he *lacks* something. The physician, however, establishes the reverse condition. He finds that the patient *has* something—an infection, an ulcer, a neurosis, etc. This seeming contradiction illumines the medical situation in which the patient's element of feeling expresses something other than what the modern doctor discovers; he would prefer to consider what can be measured, weighed and counted, which is the scientific way of proceeding. Both the subjective experiencing of the patient and the objective facts found by the doctor are, however, equally justified; they cannot replace, but ought to supplement, each other. The contemporary over-evaluation of the doctor's findings results from the scientific approach to medicine; this tends to turn the patient into an object. A concern with the subjective symptomatology, the evaluation of which grasps the situation and the structure of the personality, is, in contrast, an art that is neglected to a large extent. It is the goal of this book to indicate directions that lead the physician to practice and develop this art without sacrificing the achievements of science.

The rapid development of technology has made technical possibilities available to medicine that have been used especially in diagnosis. Consequently it has progressed, but therapy has been unable to keep pace. A massive accumulation of technical equipment is frequently the status symbol of the modern physician, impressing the patient with the plethora of diagnostic procedures to which he is subjected and thus with the "thoroughness" of the physician.

The resulting discrepancy between clinical and therapeutical practices is also apparent today:

> While there is often a disproportionate emphasis on diagnosis in the clinics as compared to therapy—which even becomes an end in itself, like art for art's sake—in many private practices it is almost exactly the reverse. Here, simply expressed, the most evident symptoms that arise from the complaints of the patient are treated.[1]

This difference makes the "gulf between the practicing physicians and the clinicians grow ever wider" ("Hiatus scientificus," in Bock's expression).[1] Critics speak of a "number-credulous laboratory medicine," estimating that 88 percent of all medications are of a symptomatic nature; moreover, their therapeutic value is asserted to be smaller than "we had assumed in the tumult of medicine's great and unquestionable victories."[2]

It is quite evident, of course, that the experience of the clinician must be different from that of the practicing physician; the latter often takes care of the patient throughout his life, whereas the clinician usually sees him for only a few days. Many minor illnesses and disturbances are rarely seen by the clinician, and so he cannot properly evaluate their significance to the patient or to the course of an illness. Essentially, however, the manner of thinking is different. The clinician with a clinic at his disposal that is fitted out with extensive technical equipment may, because of specialization, make more exact "diagnoses" and develop a "more specific therapy," though often at the expense of the totality of the organism. The ensuing consequences for therapy will be elaborated later. In any case, thought models can be developed through clinical practice that will not be applicable to the conditions of the office practice of medicine, which, nevertheless, must be considered as scientifically established and generally valid.

Of course, the refined diagnostic methods that are available today must be used and, in some cases, they must be dealt with completely. However, they should never be used at the beginning of an examination, but rather at the end! One ought also to be aware that the physician is in danger here of neglecting his empathic ability or "clinical view." Because of the profusion of clinical findings, he fails to create for himself a picture of the patient and his illness—something that is often considered to be "subjective" where only objective "hard" data are valid. Thus, much more than in earlier times, the physician today is in danger of subjecting himself completely to laboratory findings, which means he relinquishes establishing a diagnosis to the apparatus, thereby replacing his abilities by them. If the laboratory findings show nothing, then the patient does not "have anything." He must either be healthy or a psychopath. That he can nevertheless feel that something is missing or lacking is a reality that is independent of the findings.

To a large extent, then, diagnosis has become a technical problem. The physician is pressed ever more into a passive role. As an unavoidable counterbalance to these technical possibilities, however, it is necessary first to get hold of the constitution, the total situation, the disposition, etc., of the patient. This means to create for oneself an image of the patient.

Anamnesis would be an essential contributing factor here, but the brief period in which the physician must learn the patient's history is undoubtedly an obstacle. What matters, however, is the artful ability to sense what is important in the many details the patient presents, and to pursue this by asking things the patient does not consider important or has "forgotten" or suppressed.

How long the condition has existed, what brought it about, what value it has for the patient, etc., are all important considerations for the evaluation of the findings. Time belongs just as much to the factors of development as the substantial or spatial occurrences.

Living organisms possess a "time form" as well as a space form. The temporal occurrence of events is part and parcel of the nature of the life in which the ether body manifests. This, according to Rudolf Steiner, can also be called the life or time body.

Familiar hereditary connections are also significant. The changeable apperance or metamorphosis of cradle cap, hay fever, asthma, and neurodermatitis, for example, is of the greatest importance in therapy. Occasionally one can find a kind of "family constitution" displayed. In these cases a constitutional treatment with a particular remedy is indicated for a whole family, since various manifestations of an illness have the same disturbances as their basis.

The psychological atmosphere in which the patient grew up can be similarly revealing. How a child develops and is influenced by his environment and education was described in the first volume. If, for example, the outbursts of his father's rage were unleashed in the child's presence, or if he continually put the patient down and did not acknowledge his worth, then this will have left a deep effect on him also.

Experiences of shock especially can bring forth a lasting alteration of the constitution that may result in illnesses decades later. In particular, a shock of a psychological nature results in a loosening of the higher members of man's being, including a partial loosening of the ether body. If reintegration does not occur, the constitution is then "shifted." Organs or organ systems—in serious cases, the whole body—are no longer taken hold of and structured properly. This can result in a feeling of coldness or strangeness in certain areas of the body or in the formation of deposits and circulatory problems among others. Even the birth of an individual can be a shock in this sense, so that following it a completely new constitution can appear. Rudolf Steiner pointed to this metamorphosis of psychological shock experiences into bodily processes, particularly in connection with diseases that manifest deposits.

The Constitution

To gain a valid picture of the patient, it is important to understand his constitution correctly. This applies especially to chronic illnesses.

The age of the patient can be most revealing. The critical question is whether the patient is prematurely aged or has possibly remained too young. Premature aging can indicate processes expressed in a tendency to sclerosis, or, in contrast, the predominance of an inflammatory tendency. This evaluation is particularly important in the management of an illness. The pairs of concepts, inflammation–sclerosis and youth–age, may be related but they are not the same. Time as well as space and place play roles in their working together. It is necessary to recognize the dynamics here; that is, the nature of the process behind the symptomatology.

The anamnestic question in relation to childhood illnesses is more important than is generally realized. If, for example, a patient did not have the measles in childhood, it could have been because his ego-organization was too weak or disturbed. This is by no means an "advantage" as it is frequently considered to be today, but especially when it is disclosed that other feverish illnesses have not occurred, it is an indication of a kind of anergic reactivity. This means that the inflammatory capacity, which is a constitution-building and integrating aspect of the human being, is poorly developed in these individuals. This deficiency, which is not recognized today, can become manifest decades later in circumstances in which it will be expressed in an increased tendency to tumorous or cancerous illnesses. If the adult patient has not had these earlier developmental illnesses, the physician will rarely be dealing with a healthy human being.

In this connection, the question of the tendency to febrile reactions and inflammations in general, such as abscess and pus formation, is important. The tendency to heal wounds is also related to this. It is, for example, particularly good in carcinoma patients because they lack the inflammatory factor.

The visual capacity of the patient is also revealing. Rudolf Steiner has indicated that near-sighted people have "retention in relation to the physical body, a certain retention of the ego in the astral body." This will be described in detail in the chapter on ophthalmology.

The reaction of the individual to the elements is also important for his constitution. Is he subject to cold, or is he usually too warm (not equivalent to sweating)? These factors give an indication of his warmth organism and say something indirectly of the conditions of his incarnation, particularly of his ego. This is, however, a question of the metabolism of iron. Anemic individuals have an inadequately or weakly developed warmth organism, but the warmth organisms of some people today are so disturbed that they may no longer experience a deficiency of warmth and are unable to be cold. One can frequently find a lowered body temperature, an anergic reactivity with the attendant serious consequences, but the distribution of warmth is independent of that. Ice cold hands and feet, in the presence of a normal or even slightly elevated temperature or blood collected in the head show the incapacity of the organism to distribute warmth. While warmth formation is primarily an iron (and sulphur) process, here it is a disturbed copper process. Here, too, many individuals, women in particular, have become so accustomed to cold extremities that they even deny having them when questioned.

An insight into the regulation of the air organism can be obtained by observing the patient and by questioning him as to how he responds to air; whether, for example, he becomes slightly nauseated in bad air or whether he has an extraordinary need for fresh air. This is as important as observing the breathing rhythm. Repeated sighing may not only point to an occasional unconscious psychological depression, but also to a disturbance in breathing, which constitutionally points to the kidney system since the proper pervasion of the breath is a kidney problem; it can be approached therapeutically with Carbo (D15,20). As the conditions of warmth are more an indication of the ego and its workings in the organism, so the conditions of the air organism permit an insight into the working of the astral body. This is not connected intensively enough with the body in these disturbances, and it therefore doesn't take hold enough, or it works in the wrong way; this can lead to cramping. To what extent the kidneys play a role in these events is described in a later chapter.

Disturbances in the water organism are frequently much easier to notice. Often one is dealing with collections of fluid. The whole organism may appear watery and thus too cold, since water, having the greatest capacity to hold warmth, absorbs it. The rate at which a liquid is excreted can be a most revealing factor.

Here, a primary relationship with the liver is established; this will also be described in detail later. Often there is an inability to enliven the water properly and to take it up into the ether body. Thus, particularly in the morning or before menses, fluid congestion is often clearly evident. Here, Calcium carbonicum is indicated. Of course, the events occurring in the water organism are ruled by the function of the kidney system, in which the kidneys have a more operational character. By way of the adrenal glands, however, they work together with the liver (aldosterone). Typical kidney edema is well-known (sacks under the eyes, whereas liver congestion affects the upper lid more), but the easy sweating, which indicates a pathological excretion that should actually occur in the kidneys, points to their involvement in the functional realm. This means that the sweating manifests without clinical findings. In these conditions Equisetum, Carbo, Apis, and Mercury are indicated. Of course, such sweating must be distinguished from neurasthenic sweating, which favors the head and upper body. Finally, the function of the heart also plays an essential role in the water organism. The edemas dependent on heaviness point immediately to the heart and the corresponding therapy with Digitalis, Scilla, and Cardius-peonia, and others.

The physical body, in an extended sense, all substances but particularly all solid substances are an expression of the earth elements. The relationship to these other elements, however, is decisively important here. The tendency of the organism to become permeated with solid substances needs to be recognized. Salt is an essential physical substance, and man's relation to it can be most revealing. He can fluctuate between exceptional craving for it and a complete refusal of it. When a person's need for salt is considered in relation to his other symptoms, Rudolf Steiner's indication that the higher members (ego and astral body) of those who crave salt have a strong affinity with the physical body will be confirmed. The increased requirement of salt at the time of puberty is quite remarkable.

Not only the example of the need for salt, but also the other tastes—sweet, sour and bitter—as well as certain appetites and anti-appetites are most revealing and offer insight into the being of the patient.

A strong craving for sweets is frequently encountered today;

this can even be addictive. It was pointed out in the previous volume that sugar forms a foundation for the ego-organization and that the "ego feeling" is strengthened by sugar. Especially with children, this is a new experience that is brought about too early, enhancing a more egotistical way of life. On the one hand, this excessive craving for sweets is certainly an educational problem and often only a bad habit; on the other hand, there could be a real experience underlying it that something is "lacking"—perhaps insufficient motherly warmth, or inadequate nutrition such as a deficiency of suitable minerals. The sweets then become a replacement for a psychological or bodily deficient state. Since the sugar does not really correct and balance the deficiency, the situation tends to worsen and can, as with alcohol and drugs, become an illness. The final result is a weakening of the ego. The enhanced ego feeling provided by sweets offers only a seeming increase in strength. Therefore, through nutrition, therapy will also straighten out the psychological spiritual situation, thus providing a suitable foundation for the activity of the ego in the body.

The quality of sourness is related to the astral body. A need for sour food expresses the demand of the astral body to incarnate more strongly. Frequently, anemic individuals have an exceptional craving for lemons and vinegar, a pure feeling that initiates therapy (vitamin C and fruit acids favor the resorption of iron). One can also find a clear preference for sour foods in disturbances of the stomach and liver, which is a correct perception of low acidity. Acids help in the digestion of food. Higher organic acids, particularly the lactic and orotic acids found in sour milk products, are physiological substances for the liver and have a high dietetic value. Often one can see a diagnostic indication in a preference for one or another of the acids.

The need for bitter substances is most rare; yet there are some people who passionately love them. The bitter taste works far stronger than the sour in enhancing consciousness, activating and incarnating it. It is not by chance that gall is bitter. Bitter substances help the individual to overcome the outer world, to penetrate and assert himself in his environment; this is also true of digestion. Here is certainly an indication of an inadequate or insufficient iron impulse, but the disturbance lies more in the digestive metabolic region than in the blood, as it does in the need for sour substances. Through such indications one can more narrowly differentiate the many sides of the iron process and its disturbances.

In this way, one can arrive at the starting points relative to the members of man's being. Certainly one will also attempt to interpret other clinical findings in this sense. An overly powerful or insufficiently active astral body, or an unruly or excessively weak ether body can all be behind the manifold appearances that have developed in the course of a life.

Although it is essential to understand clearly the fundamental constitution of man's being, it may, under certain circumstances, be more significant to recognize a dynamic disturbance as being within the threefold organism. Examples of this are mentioned in volume I. Under other circumstances it is only possible to gain a satisfying insight into a disturbance if one finds, for example, that there is a typical metal disturbance in an individual. Among the numerous metals there are seven that can be distinguished by their special significance for man. To recognize an insufficient or excessive lead process in a person, for example, can be of the greatest significance for his well-being and therapy. The members of man's being, the dynamics of threefolding, and the processes of the seven metals are realities that are not mutually exclusive, but rather are various aspects of man's many-sidedness.

Man's life in sleeping and dreaming is an expression of the relationship of his physical and ether bodies to his higher members. Sleep occurs when the astral body withdraws from its connection with the nerve-sensory system and works unconsciously through the metabolic system into the organism. It alternates the direction of its activity from downward in the waking state to upward in sleep. During the day, it serves consciousness, and at night, anabolism. Upon waking, the astral body reunites with the nerve-sensory system, and with it the ego, the individuality of man, also enters the organism. The ego centers the consciousness that is mediated through the astral body into ego consciousness.

The events of sleep are most significant. Light sleep, difficulty in falling asleep, rapid or difficult awakening, all point to the relationship that man has with the spiritual and physical worlds. Dream life between waking and sleeping is also significant. For example, there can be organ dreams in which the individual experiences as a picture the formative forces at the basis of an organ that is not taken hold of properly by the members of man's being, thereby he frees the formative forces. Or perhaps the astral body and ego work inadequately into the lower members. Then the state just prior to awakening, when the astral body first touches the ether body, is retained longer than usual, and the events of the astral body are "mirrored" in it and appear as images. This also explains how one can awaken with the solution of a problem. Many people find it difficult to "come to themselves" in the morning because the constructive processes are carried over into the day, which may require Lachesis or Belladonna to facilitate awakening, or there may be an inadequate tendency to incarnate, which may be treated with iron or phosphorus.

One must not forget to ask whether and in what form children have been given vitamin D. The problems connected with it will be discussed later. One must also note the course of birth and teething, and whether the child was breast-fed.

The acquisition of learning, speaking and thinking are typically human activities that give an indication of the structuring of the organism by the ego. Delays and premature development both require strictest attention; the latter are often evaluated positively but erroneously so. School conditions, too, are most significant for later health. If memory and intellect are over-developed, the child will be quite pale. The educator who is truly trained in the knowledge of man will attempt to balance a predisposition to pallor by stimulating the child's fantasies. This is a fundamental motif of Waldorf education. The evaluation of memory and fantasy in a child is, therefore, a problem for the school physician. An abnormally early intellectual development must almost always be evaluated negatively, and it is up to the physician, the parents, and the educator to determine a balance. Because of the false pride this "special capacity" creates, it is often most difficult to do so.

The condition of the child's teeth gives important indications. If they are abnormally soft, it could be due to an inadequate or one-sided period of nutrition. This is, however, a question of the proper balance between magnesium and fluorine, which is most important in childhood. The change of teeth indicates the development of the independence of the ether body.

Seasonal disturbances are of great significance. If, for example, a patient notes that his condition or even his whole general life experience reaches a high point in autumn and a low point in spring then this indicates the therapeutic application of iron. Fall is the physiological iron time. Fruiting and the transformation of vitality that occur in autumn correspond in man to an iron or gall process (see the chapter on the liver in volume I). In spring, however, there is a renewed process of incarnation that is difficult for this particular person.

If a patient is unable to tolerate summer, then the light or heat could be responsible. In the case of intolerance for light, the therapeutic application of Hypericum (D4) is indicated, in that for heat Hypericum may also be indicated but more so quartz.

It should be pointed out here that the classical homeopaths were admirable masters in the discovery of modalities—the forms of reaction of an organism. With an exceptional gift of observation and a capacity for loving empathy they studied the remedial pictures which showed numerous revealing symptoms. Even though an art of healing that is extended through spiritual science does not arrive at remedies through this method but rather through images of a substance's essence in its relation to man, nevertheless, the exact observation and vast amount of study material of the homeopaths can be admired. It is possible to use these remedy images because they are worked out over a long period of time. Homeopathy, which will be discussed thoroughly later, ultimately is a method of healing, the basis and spiritual content of which can become comprehensible through and dignified by anthroposophical medicine. It remains a deep tragedy that official medicine does not want to utilize the often irreplaceable therapeutic possibilities of homeopathy; indeed, it even denies them.

It is only through an inner image of the patient, hence an imaginative process, that intuition can become active through inspiration; a therapeutic idea encompassing man and natural processes develops that thus allows the recognition of the remedies that the patient needs. The concepts imagination, inspiration, and intuition are used here in the sense of the spiritual science of Rudolf Steiner, i.e. not according to today's vague usage of these words for an idea or hunch, etc., but referring to the result of an exact path of inner schooling which R. Steiner has described at length.

Imagination is the image-like grasping of what lies at the basis of the organism as a super-ordinate principle of activity; it can be perceived spiritually and is not the abstract sum of separate observations. In human development, consciousness evolved from the picture-like experience of archetypal wisdom to ideas and concepts that become progressively more abstract. In order to grasp the working and creating archetypal forces active in life, it is necessary that this procedure be reversed; that is, that thoughts are again transformed into pictures or images. The first step in this process, which was mentioned as an example, allows the recognition of the inner properties of beings. Training in this area is to be found in the fundamental works of Rudolf Steiner.[3]

Aspects of Therapy

It is important for the physician to be aware of the profound significance of every encounter with a patient. Something noble and unique always occurs at such meetings. A human being goes to another to ask for advice and help. The patient is ready to grant trust from the outset, something that otherwise only develops from long experience. In every moment that a person trusts another, the forces of childhood awaken in him, and he tries to begin life anew as he was as a child. These forces of childhood are, however, the forces of growth and healing, and the physician should use them quite objectively. In a certain sense, a situation that has been left behind by the patient must be lived through again. This unusual destiny in which the physician finds himself in relation to the patient obligates him to treat the patient with the utmost respect, even if he may reveal things that would cause others to form a negative judgment. Here lies the profound justification for the physician's silence. The patient reveals intimacies, and the physician is for him, though perhaps unconsciously, more than a human being. He represents a profession whose beginnings were found in all cultures in religion.

In order to avoid hubris, the physician will do well to be aware that the patient's trust is only partially to be attributed to him as a personality. Nothing would be more damaging to true success in healing than to neglect this danger of conceit. Self-assurance based on a thorough knowledge of one's field is of course necessary in establishing a basis of trust; nevertheless, overestimation of oneself or one's achievement and a feeling of superiority represent the greatest occupational hazards for the physician. He must always bear in mind that he himself does not heal, but "only" influences the healing forces present in the patient: *medicus curat, natura sanat* (the doctor treats, nature heals). Until the dawning of the scientific age, healing forces were always seen as an expression of divine creative powers, and the doctor was aware of himself as their mediator (*medicus*). The remedy (*medicamentum*) then becomes the mediator of the therapeutic intention, as in the word's original sense.

The establishment of a proper contact with the patient is an absolute precondition to gaining his trust. This can occur when the patient feels that the physician understands him. The latter must set aside his own point of view and accommodate himself to the world of the patient. He must "understand" him and never play the role of "objective" observer. In the psychological realm measuring, weighing, and numbering are without significance because they apply only to physical events. The patient's fear, illness, even pain, etc., cannot be objectively evaluated; the significance of the symptom to the patient is what matters. Thus, a true understanding is not possible without inner activity and personal engagement.

Illness and Healing

Contemporary medicine has achieved much in recent times and has even brought about triumphal successes in the battle against illnesses. It must, however, be clearly realized that these successes are not to be attributed to the art of the physician, however much that may have progressed, but rather to the results of technology, chemistry and physics, that is, to science. It is certainly necessary to make use of these results, but in subjecting itself increasingly to these disciplines, medicine has negated its own being. The gigantic hypertrophy of technical possibilities makes the art of the physician expendable and will gradually stifle it. It causes the physician to become uncertain, and he then considers as significant only what can be verified, proved in an external way as "statistically significant." The inner experience and engagement of the physician means little compared to all that is therefore hardly practiced anymore.

The consequence of this position is the conscious exclusion of specific capacities and activities of the physician in a controlled clinical trial. He becomes a director of studies or a diagnostician for the clinical pharmacologist.

It is easy to see that this development has led people to be unable to find an inner relationship to illness. They see no sense in illness and consider it to be only a technical problem, a functional defect or disturbance brought about apart from themselves, and something that similarly ought to be repaired by the physician without their help. Psychosomatic medicine, however, attempts to point out the significance of the psychological life in the development of illness, but it exists at best parallel with the predominant medical viewpoints—for example, psychotherapy and internal medicine—and the patient is "referred" from one specialty to another. The method of psychotherapy, though, is oriented toward natural science, but the nature of spirit and soul and the difference between them also demand a method appropriate to them.

We live in an age of specialization. Without doubt the great progress medicine has made can also be attributed to this development, but the danger in it is naturally a loss of the view of the total man. As a counterbalance to specialization, Rudolf Steiner spoke of the "socialization of specializing physicians."[1] By working together in an integrated way, they can overcome specialization without giving up its achievements. The first steps toward this goal can be found in group practices and to a certain extent in therapeutics.

A discrepancy is apparent in the development of medicine. On one side, life expectancy has been lengthened, but it does not take deep insight to see that this trend cannot continue forever. On the other side, the increased life expectancy does not reflect an improved state of health. It is an undeniable fact that humanity has become increasingly ill. This can be seen in the progressive constitutional weakness that can, for example, be observed in beginning school children who show a general connective tissue weakness with the corresponding consequences of skeletal illnesses, increase of chronic and degenerative illnesses of the muscular-skeletal system, increase of chronic and degenerative illnesses, increased use of drugs, etc. This forces us to question the fundamental goal of this approach. This is especially demanded by the so-called iatrogenic illnesses and problems that are produced as side effects of pharmacology. The term "iatrogenic" is deceptive in that it is not the physician who causes the damage but the inadequate methodological application of a drug. This does not occur in the context of healing but based on a concept of success that is merely directed toward an effect.

The question of purpose and that of the meaning of a symptom is not asked. Here we touch on the basic question of medicine in general, namely, what is illness and healing? Being impregnated by science, which can comprehend neither illness nor healing, modern medicine as a consequence finds it impossible to answer this question. This reveals the absence of a concept of illness in contemporary medicine. "Although the bases of modern medicine are the manifestations of illness, it has not been able to give a satisfying and generally valid and acceptable definition of what illness actually is."[2]

These phenomena, as well as the general explosive increases in the cost of medicine that have had far-reaching effects in society, can be considered corrective. Through them the chemical and technical possibilities of medicine are beginning to be delimited and a return to fundamental questions demanded.

It is evident from the considerations presented in volume I that the physical events are only one part of reality and can be understood only through the higher members of man's being, which use substances as instruments. It was also described in volume I how illness is deeply connected with the being of man and can never be understood when isolated from his totality. In a higher sense, every illness is a stage of development for the human being, and without the potential possibility for illness, man's development would be impossible. He must be able to become sick to realize his being. This is inseparably connected with the question of freedom. On a spiritual plane, man's freedom was bought with the possibility to err. On the psychological plane, this corresponds to the loss in man of instincts which direct the animal with certainty but not in freedom. On an organic plane, it is the possibility to become ill that brings with it the achievement of freedom.

There are transitions from one plane to another. As long as one limits oneself to one plane, the phenomenon of illness cannot be understood. Psychological causes of organic illnesses are well-known today, particularly in gastric or duodenal ulcers. But "psychological accompanying symptoms" are also frequently considered to be possible causes in the serious intestinal disturbances of ulcerative colitis. The fact that one methodically considers only one organ and because of scientific thinking fails to penetrate its essence inhibits a true understanding that would go beyond mere statistical relationships. The essence of an organ is of a supersensible nature and can therefore be comprehended only with concepts adequate to it. In the chapters on the various organs, an attempt will be made to develop images of the specific organs and of the forces underlying them.

In the final analysis the capacity for illness is a spiritual problem. What begins in the spirit metamorphoses in the course of time into the organic. Thus, illness manifesting in the organic realm is not only a consequence of events on higher planes but also a remedy to overcome and solve something on a lower plane which could not be dealt with in a higher realm. In this light, illness gains a totally different dimension; it is not only a consequence of the deviations of the soul-spiritual life, but it also helps in the development of the spirit.

This touches on the problem of destiny, which is deeply connected with illness. One of the most important results of spiritual science is that it makes possible an insight into the relationship of illness and destiny with the human individuality. Here, however, the recognition and acceptance of an after-life, as well as a life before birth—that is, the recognition of the reincarnation of the spiritual being of man—is necessary. Only in this way does illness gain real meaning as a help in the development of man's higher being and as a step in the process of individuation. This question is amply touched upon in vols. I and IV.

The recognition of the polar nature of the two tendencies of inflammation and sclerosis is most significant for the fundamental conception of illness. It has been pointed out that in the absence of one or the other of these tendencies life would be impossible and that health consists of a balance between the two.

Illness is considered today only as an intellectual abstraction that does not exist in itself, and it is said that one treats sick people, not illnesses. As correct as it is natural to treat a human being and not an abstraction, it must nevertheless be said that to accept only the results of observation as real is a nominalistic viewpoint. The recognition of an active being does not come from mere observations, nor does a concept of illness arise therefrom. Behind the inflammatory and sclerotic illnesses there are, however, polar world forces, the activity of which is as real as that of warmth and cold. But warmth and cold are also considered only quantitatively and physically and are not experienced as the polar forces Goethe showed them to be.

Like the realm of life, illnesses are not abstractions of physical or chemical events but concrete reality on a plane above them. Their effects may reach into the sensory world but their nature cannot be comprehended on this level. It requires a recognition of the spirit and spiritual science to gain access to these higher realms.

As an example, we may mention cancer. Here, there is a unified disturbance that finally manifests as a proliferation of cells, a tumor. Whether one is dealing with a stomach, genital, or other tumor and no matter what its course, its form is quite individual. Along with individual variation, there is a unified occurrence; this may be treated with a unified remedy, mistletoe. It must be applied individually, however, and be supported by measures that take hold of the individuality, such as a constitutional therapy without which it may not be effective. In the sense of the considerations above, the cancer would be an abstraction. If one treats it instead of the illness that stands behind the tumor, one bypasses the illness and the human being. Since illness belongs to the being of man, it is of necessity as many-sided as he.

A primary phenomenon of becoming ill can be experienced when a person no longer understands someone with whom he is closely united. He must now forego the basic experience of soul-spiritual community which he recognizes as an enhancement of his own soul life. There are thousands of events that can lead an individual to feel separated from his community, i.e. to feel—or even become—ill. In such cases, a single word can make a person ill; similarly, a single word may often suffice to remove the disturbance, thereby re-establishing inner health and the higher life. But the proper word spoken out of insight is certainly only effective in healing when it arises from the deeper layers of the soul rather than from loveless contentiousness. When the soul has become purified, it can meld the broken circle, thereby uniting the separated souls again. Healing is reconciliation, overcoming the duality of separation.

If the estranged person fails to find the way to reunite with the world, or if the world rejects him, the ensuing conflict becomes chronic; he becomes resigned to the situation and his ego withdraws even further. An inner wasting right down to bodily desiccation can be the consequence when the physical organism is no longer illumined and permeated by the ego. The astral body will become overly powerful and unruly, directing its activity inward rather than outward. These basic problems of the soul, behind which stands the failure of the ego, are the primary causes of ulcers in the gastro-intestinal tract. Auto-aggressive illnesses can also be mentioned here. However, even in therapy it is insufficient to consider only psychological causes. Rather, the ruling function of the ego or the inadequate functioning of it in bodily events must be considered here. A first step in this direction is the singular insight into the nature of the ego as a spiritual entity clearly differentiated in the soul. It is a problem of the spiritual history of humanity that this distinction was extinguished, with the result that today the corresponding concepts and insights related to it are lacking. Rudolf Steiner's inauguration of the knowledge of man, which is the basis of this book, works specifically with the differentiated higher members of man and their working in the physical body, its organs and substance.

The Nature of Healing

A central aspect of Rudolf Steiner's presentation of evolution is that humanity during its earliest development was guided directly from the spiritual worlds. In those early stages the ego could not yet be very independent. Man possessed a child-like innocence that kept him from deviating from cosmic laws and from becoming ill from within. This dull consciousness did not permit a significant individualization and separation.

From this point of view, the evolution of humanity appears to be a path to ever-increasing independence of the ego, which is thus progressively divested of spiritual guidance. In exchange, however, it becomes possible for it to deviate further from the immanent laws of life. Here it can again be understood that the physician was also a priest in earlier times and that healing could only be achieved through catharsis. But the art of healing unavoidably had to accommodate itself to the evolution of humanity by gradually relinquishing its earlier mystery character.

Psychotherapy has existed since the beginning of culture, and the further back we look, the more is this therapy practiced by the priest. In place of abstract concepts we discover freely selected images that developed from the living connection of man with nature. They appeared in his soul like fruit and encompassed nature and spirit. This healing occurred throughout antiquity, particularly in the Asclepian sanctuaries where the image of Asclepius served everyone. He was portrayed as an upright human form carrying a staff with a snake wound around it. This image can be found earlier in the Old Testament. It represents the overcoming of the fall into sin, the descent into matter. The snake has developed the horizontal position most perfectly, and since it does not lift itself from the earth with legs, one can say it is excessively bound to earthly conditions and forces. It is especially these forces that Asclepius compels into a vertical position. The presentation of this image has a profound effect on the patient's ego organization. As one of the inaugurators of Greek culture, Asclepius had to prepare the independence of the ego and its control over corporeality, all of which was destined to be achieved in the course of Greek culture. Thus, the art of healing of the Aesclepians formed the transition from the old Egyptian medicine, which utilized sleep in the temple, to one more in accord with Greek culture.

In the course of time it became less possible for the spiritual, in the form of mystery pictures or ritual acts, to take hold of the physical. This was related to the necessary progressive densification of the body. As a result, the therapist came to use external methods to influence pathological bodily conditions; thus, the transition from priest to physician was completed.

The continuing increase in the independence of the ego was related to the change in the bodily constitution and brought about the decline in healing by purely spiritual means. Although Christ directed His disciples to heal, Christian culture has been unable to develop a specific Christian art of healing. For example, what lives as the impulse for healing in the care of the ill and in religious orders has no inner connection to contemporary medicine, which is governed by the thinking and actions of scientists.

The overcoming of separation that was described as a primitive image at the basis of all illness and healing can be traced through all illnesses. Even in a fractured bone we have the same phenomenon in the physical events. A bone is split in two. Healing consists in reestablishing a unity that will be stronger than before. This occurs on the level of the ether body and is entirely unconscious. Yet, from this kind of healing to that previously described as "purely spiritual," transitions can be discovered.

Frequently a complex of problems is suppressed and then appears one or two stages lower on the corporeal level. If a symptomatic or substitution therapy is applied only on these lower levels, the problems often persist and the patient produces a "new illness." Then, especially if the slide down to lower levels does not proceed far enough to result in clinical manifestations of organic disturbances, the patient is termed neurotic or psychopathic, and the disturbance is merely covered up with psychopharmalogical agents.

Today, many more patients than is commonly recognized experience the psychological and spiritual aspects of their illnesses. Often, however, they do not trust their physicians enough to express the true nature of their problems.

In times of psychological needs, few patients turn to their priest or minister. (C.G. Jung reports that eight per cent of his

Protestant patients and fifty-eight of his Catholic ones turned first to their clergyman.) After having been to their clergyman, most of them go immediately to their physician so that he, too, is pressed into the role of caring for the soul. But C.G. Jung also admits that he is unable to respond to his patient's questions about the meaning of life because he does not know the answer himself. He believes that this confession induces the patient's trust in his physician, but in the long run he cannot be helped merely with that. Jung is also convinced that no one can be healed who is not religious.

Contemporary medicine has lost its connection with religion and every spiritual view of the world. It has fallen away from a holistic view of the world and thus has become ill. The same applies to the physician who acknowledges only the validity of contemporary medicine. Of course, he wants to help his patients as much as possible, but the often torturing questions of life that are related to the meaning of illness and destiny are bypassed. In the patient who has a true religious connection, the question of life's meaning rarely develops to such a degree that severe suicidal crises occur. To feel truly satisfied, modern man demands insight into the nature of his existence, into illness, and into destiny.

Such insights can be found by the physician as well as by his patients in the image of man presented in Rudolf Steiner's anthroposophy. It demands not simply belief, of which the man of today is less and less capable, but directs the ego by means of clear thinking to insights that have been closed to him. The circle between man and God that in earlier times had to be closed with acceptance and faith remains open today when it is not understood how this unification is possible in the present. Because man takes hold of his ego in clear thoughts today, he cannot leave himself behind when he wants to encounter God.

Every true insight into the order of the world has a healing effect because it helps one to reintegrate and orient oneself with supra-personal harmonies; thus, the human being can again reflect them. Healing is bringing oneself into harmony with the divine creative force, and one who does not nurture spiritual life is bound eventually to become ill. A spiritual orientation in life works in a therapeutic and healthy way.

Such thoughts seem to be contradicted by the fact that a materialist or atheist may be most robust and healthy, whereas an individual striving spiritually may be quite weak and susceptible to illness. It must, however, be realized that these are only superficial observations. Life in its entirety—the physical earthly as well as that after death—must be taken into consideration; they cannot be separated. To consider only one is to view only half of reality. Inheritance and environmental damage offer other influences on a man's state of health as well as the natural endowments of the individual. A dull person is certainly much less susceptible to illness than a sensitive person whose capacities often bear an enhanced susceptibility. So, to consider only immediate problems and conditions is not always helpful because one is actually dealing with a hygienic problem that encompasses all of humanity. Considering the rapid deterioration of the physical constitution that can be observed today, this hygienic problem is of the utmost significance.

Education, to which the constitution is related in the most comprehensive way, is also part and parcel of this hygienic question. Thus, an indication of Rudolf Steiner becomes comprehensible; he says that a person can be healed much more easily when he has been accustomed from youth to sense-free mental pictures.[3] He refers, of course, to a true healing and not to remedies that simply affect symptoms. This applies to everyone. Through these mental pictures healing can be helped or hindered according to the appropriateness of the application. In the following, two exercises are given that have a general hygienic character for the soul.

Rudolf Steiner gives "the path of devotion" as the first exercise. (Goethe had already described the exercise of threefold devotion as the basis of every human path of training or education.) Contemporary man has an inadequate capacity for devotion and instead is capable of much criticism. His criticism, however, weakens and empties his soul and in the long run makes it ill. When he practices seeing the positive in others, forces awaken in his soul that can unite him with the world and finally with God. Healthful sources are thus opened up. This brief summary should be taken as a mere indication that cannot replace Steiner's original presentation.[4]

The second exercise, which we will mention only briefly, is reviewing the events of the day in reverse. In the evening one reviews in one's mind the day's happenings, beginning with the last and proceeding back to the first. This exercise is immeasurably valuable in cultivating a hygiene of the soul. We know how many impressions a person takes in and forgets throughout the day. Because they have not been worked through in consciousness, they can produce disturbances in the subconscious. In extreme cases the individual who experiences such disturbances will seek to have his difficulties uncovered by a psychotherapist through psychoanalysis. It is understandable that such an exercise prevents repression through this overview of daily experiences and is thereby prophylactic against a later disturbance. In practicing it, however, there is a danger that one may get caught up in isolated experiences. Therefore, one should practice this exercise as an observer; that is, he should look at himself as though observing another person's actions. It is also necessary that the review should be filled with images rather than intellectually abstract. The point of the exercise is to lift the subconscious impressions again into consciousness so that they can be taken hold of by the ego. Being thus relieved of the organic, they will not irritate its activities. Hence, the exercise works a retroactive metamorphosis. It must also be noted that practicing it should at first be limited to ten or fifteen minutes.

The two exercises briefly described here as examples work therapeutically for the soul life of everyone who practices them. The activity brought about by them strengthens the ego. Since this is training in self education, immediate beneficial results cannot be expected.

This is so in every true healing. Illness makes a demand on the organism that activates and transforms the ether or astral body and finally also the ego. Once this has been achieved, the illness is overcome and the patient has been strengthened.

A contradiction to this thought seems to occur in illnesses that produce healing but with resulting defects. This is valid only when the physical aspect alone is considered. One can often see that a physical defect frequently causes a soul-spiritual aggravation that makes possible a new step in development that would be impossible without the defect of the illness.

The same phenomenon can be observed on the organic plane in the immunity brought about through the treatment of an infectious disease. Thus it can be understood why Rudolf Steiner called illness life's great teacher,[5] and described how healing educates just as educating heals. Therefore, healing without the participation of the human being—without a transformation of the higher members of the patient's being—is not possible. Naturally, this can occur on various levels.

This approach must also be considered when a person is deprived of undergoing an illness, something that is certainly possible today. Every illness is a crisis that an individual can take on or circumvent, but such problems can be approached satisfactorily only when one looks behind the pathological phenomena to the patient's individuality and to how he is handling the illness.

Here, the activity of the physician in relation to the so-called "incurable illnesses" must be considered. For the individuality or spiritual being of a person it is most significant that the healing measures are continued even when no recognizable effect can be seen or even expected. It is decisive for man as a spiritual individuality to support his attempts to handle his illness, which may bear fruit only after he has left his body.

It is here that the importance of a spiritual image of man for the practice of medicine becomes evident. If death is seen merely as the end of life, then it must appear justifiable to shorten a seemingly "senseless" life. However, if death is seen as the gate to a spiritual life free of the body, then earthly life gains meaning. Life on earth thus serves to prepare for another form of existence into which earthly experiences flow. When one sees man in his spiritual reality, then all measures taken, even in treating an unconscious, moribund individual, have a far-reaching significance.

The inner activation that was discussed as a precondition to healing is not to be taken to mean still *more* activity. What is essential lies much more in a change, a transformation, a reversal, of the existing condition. This is not possible without catharsis, which occurs on various levels throughout the course of an illness, as was known by knowledgeable people throughout the ages. An integral part of this is a kind of relinquishing, a certain restraint, a sacrifice. Only thus will a transformation become possible that will lead to a new stage of development, the overcoming of separation, and the reestablishment of a new unity, indicating that healing is possible. This basically is the sequence of sacrifice, transformation and communion; as an event of the ancient mysteries, it is an archetype of healing.

Hence, in all cultures the beginnings of the physicians' calling are to be found in the realm of religion. As an expression of his mercurial activity, the physician ought to mediate between spirit and matter, between the earthly and divine from which the forces of healing emanate. He is the keeper of the healing forces, which are always experienced as divine. To use a statement by Rudolf Steiner: In healing, man is the helper of the gods. *Healing is the restitution of the divine archetype of man. Illness is the path to this.—Restitutio ad integrum* does not mean restoration of the earlier state; it means the regaining of the integrity of the archetype, but now in a new order which includes the achievements of individual activity in overcoming the disease.

Uniting with the objective forces of healing demands the active participation of the physician, that is, the courage to heal, to which Rudolf Steiner attributed as much significance as to the knowledge of healing. In no way does this refer to the suggestive working of an unfounded optimism, but rather to the activity that is necessary to penetrate to the process of illness from within by uniting with the natural processes so that a therapeutic idea can develop. The passivity into which the physician is pressed today permits him to proceed only on the physical plane where the nature of illness cannot be comprehended. With therapeutic courage and the will to heal, the physician makes access to the forces of healing possible to the patient; these forces reach right into the new ordering of destiny. The encounter between a patient and his physician today is pushed into the realm of chance. However, it is actually a meeting that occurs in the realm of destiny.

The courageous effort of the physician is an objective procedure through which new facts are produced. In his personal participation, man is creatively active. He reshapes the world. But here it is the physician who helps to reshape the life of the patient in accordance with his individuality. Without an actively courageous intervention, however, it is not possible to find either new or individual paths. Here lies a danger of modern medicine, which by virtue of the standardization of therapy through an excessive evaluation of statistical means makes it impossible to reach the individuality. This is to a large extent an unconscious attack on the personality of the patient and his development as well as a massive blocking of the physician's real activity. The courage to heal is an essential aspect of his nature. Through it there is an appeal to the patient on the plane of the ego; it is an inner activity and enhancement in which, in the final analysis, the meaning of the events of illness is to be found.

Today when one speaks of "self-healing" or auto-immune processes, etc., one knows only abstract facts of the independent healing process. But when Paracelsus speaks of the "inner physician," he shows that he still had a concrete experience of the self-healing forces. These forces *in toto* are an expression of the ether body that governs growth and regeneration. An unequivocal penetration and conceptual understanding of its rightful activities makes possible a comprehension of the healing process and also a path to practical applications. Paracelsus used the word *archaeus* to designate the ether body; contained in it is the word *archae*, which means origin. This refers not only to the starting point of man's physical evolution, but also to the fact that in healing, an appeal is made to the original forces.

Methodology

The image of man that underlies medicine is an important guide for therapy. Today an entirely one-sided evaluation of therapeutic measures prevails. Apart from surgery and radiation, only medicamental therapy is recognized. Everything else is looked upon as second or third degree and as expendable. Modern "treatment" is considered, particularly by the patient, to be equivalent to writing a prescription. Actually, treatment really includes the activity of the physician, but with the exception of surgery that is degraded almost to an undesirable activity. What physician today still does massage or teach the patient an exercise? For a long time a "special form of treatment," that is, chiropractic was appraised negatively, and it has only gradually come to be recognized. The evaluation of therapeutic measures is quite bound to time and fashion. In the Middle Ages, for example, surgical measures such as opening abscesses or pulling teeth were unbecoming to the physician and were left to the overseers of the baths. Today there is a lack of understanding of the significance of other extra-medical measures.

Therapeutic procedures aiming to heal will always start with the totality of the human being. This means that the effects of every measure undertaken in the treatment of a child must be considered right into his old age. The decisive practical consequences of this have already been mentioned. The recognition of the polar character of inflammatory and sclerotic illnesses is of fundamental significance here, as is the importance of fever. This certainly does not mean that fever ought not to be influenced, but when its meaning for the organism and the whole course of man's development is recognized, then it will not be suppressed but rather guided. This means simply to dampen overshooting reactions and to support the organism in the illness so that a dangerous symptomatology does not occur. Then the symptom dissolves almost of itself. Thus, one does not simply attack a symptom but always brings in the activity of the organism, which brings about an "indirect" resolution of the symptoms (Brauchle).

If an illness is not healed but rather suppressed or prevented so that the underlying disturbance persists, it can reappear in another deeper area and the tendency progresses (progressive metamorphosis). One is then often dealing with an illness that has become more serious. This problem of "pathomorphosis" (Hellpach) is frequently seen today in the "transformation of the classical symptoms of illness" (Doerr) and in the change of "the time form of illnesses" (Bock); yet this way of looking at illness is concerned primarily with the transformations that occur only in one aspect of an illness. The change in the direction of an illness, which is discussed in detail in the chapter on the lung, is far more significant.

Illnesses can tend to be progressive. As examples, we could name the "sliding down" of a cold in the upper respiratory track to pneumonia, and also the change from hay fever to asthma. Further examples were mentioned in the chapter on childhood illnesses. Illnesses can also tend to fluctuate. We can name here the vicarious occurrence of eczema and hepatic dysfunction.

In order to heal, one always strives to bring about a regressive metamorphosis, a "rolling up" of the illness. In doing so, lesser, more hidden illnesses can recur. They should certainly not be treated symptomatically or suppressed but should be permitted to "live themselves out" so that the tendency becomes dissolved and can be healed. Frequently, this is accomplished by bringing chronic illness such as inflammations to an acute state, thereby making it more accessible to healing through the participation of the ego.

This process is set in motion by every remedy which takes hold at a higher level. The same ends can also be achieved through a diversion to the skin, for example, or through so-called non-specific transforming measures. Since the concept of illness in earlier times was concerned more with the beginning of an illness rather than with its end, the therapeutic measures were general, functional and comprehensive, that is, non-specific. It can be understood that the contemporary narrow viewpoint brought about by the advent of the microscope makes it impossible to consider this past approach with understanding. Specialization corresponds to the abandonment of the whole for its parts and to the accumulation of isolated details; yet the view of the whole should not be lost. In more recent times, however, a renewed interest in the non-specific reactions, valuing and dignifying their therapeutic significance, has occurred.

Contemporary therapeutic measures are considered to be eternally valid and exclusively effective, as if a "true" therapy began only with the age of science, and more exactly with the advent of chemotherapy. Earlier measures arose from a different thinking and feeling, from a different historical milieu, and also from different aims. An understanding of these aspects is important for an insight into therapeutic principles. Thus, various measures will be discussed here even though they are to a large extent not in use any more.

It is true that in the course of time illnesses have changed. From the Middle Ages to the last century phlebotomy was one of the most frequently used therapies and justifiably so because people were more full-blooded and illnesses were predominantly inflammatory. That this measure was finally applied too frequently is a human problem. This has happened at all times with favored treatments—even today with the highly valued drug therapy, for example. The neglect of phlebotomy today is a consequence of this one-sidedness. Properly used, it is still a valuable measure, primarily relieving the head. When the metabolic system predominates, phlebotomy often helps immediately to relieve the condition because the ego and astral body cannot be active in a stronger formative way. Phlebotomy also provides favorable conditions for remedies such as quartz and stannum that help from the direction of the head. The same applies to full-bloodedness and pulmonary congestion in which therapy is only successful when the organism is temporarily relieved of the oppressive predominance of the anabolic processes. Such a situation can occur, for example, in menopause or delayed menstruation when astralization cannot occur because of an over-riding metabolism. When about 50 to 100 cc of blood are removed, the period often will immediately begin.

In all these cases one must naturally remember that phlebotomy is not a healing but only creates a “space” for healing and that phlebotomies repeated at short intervals can well be a stimulus to increased blood formation.

Bloodless phlebotomy, as practiced in the application of tourniquets by tying off an extremity to decrease the blood flow into it, works differently. In pulmonary edema, for example, it is still a justifiable measure, especially in emergency situations. Since it can save life in a most simple way, it ought not be forgotten.

The application of leeches enjoys even less popularity and understanding; yet their proper application can bring about a rapid, extensive and often irreplaceable effect that extends beyond the removal of blood. In this, it differs from phlebotomy. Their application is indicated in localized inflammatory congestion and also peripheral vascular and climacteric disturbances, retention, apoplexy and anuria, among others.

The application of leeches brings about a diversion of the astral body through the astral animal principle that initiates a metamorphosis of the formative forces. The most favorable effects therefore are in relieving the pain, temperature, tension, etc., of congestions.

The opposite principle is applied in the use of suction cups, which with modern pumps can easily create a vacuum. In this way, a local hyperemia can be produced that can induce healing since the blood brings the etheric forces to such active areas. The indicated remedy can be particularly efficacious when it is injected into the hyperemic area. A spinal or gynecological treatment can thus be significantly intensified. A milder application is furnished by Bier's treatment, which primarily permits a successful suction massage.

The bloodless suction cups present a transition to the injection of the patient's own blood. This is done by taking one to ten cc of venous blood and immediately injecting it intra-muscularly. The blood then dies, releasing its etheric forces which stimulate the ether body. In principle, every remedy used to work on the ether body can be combined with the patient's blood; for example, Argentum D6, Argentum nitricum D20, Magnesium phosphoricum D6, or Aurum D20 in depressions if the specific ampule is drawn up with the venous blood. This is one of the most effective treatments in cases of fatigue.

In febrile states of unknown origin, and in lengthy suppurations, the blood can be citrated, radiated with ultraviolet light and then injected intra-muscularly. The relatively healthy organism becomes involved with this blood that is breaking down and in many cases it will lead to a successful overcoming of the illness. A further development of this principle is the HUVC-treatment (HOT = hematogenic oxydation therapy), in which blood is suffused with an O_2/O_3 mixture and then irradiated with short-wavelength (filtered) ultraviolet rays.

The measures used by physicians in the past were much more broadly based than today; now isolated symptoms are treated, and this is why the older measures are no longer understood. The application of hundreds of emetics that continued into the nineteenth century is considered by modern physicians to be sinister quackery. Actually, the old physicians were interested in stimulating a physiological process that defends the organism against overwhelming outer influences. The physical emesis of the content of an overburdened stomach or of bad food is only an expression of what was achieved more widely through the use of various emetics, that is, the stimulation of self-assertion against foreign influences. Thus it can be understood that in asthma, for example, the application of emetics can have a beneficial influence. Today this might be called “a vegetative retuning.” In any case, the old physicians were more interested in the transformation of the patient’s illness than in emesis itself, which is seen today only as an effect and is thus misunderstood.

The prescriptions of the great physicians of former times, such as Paracelsus, or of the alchemists, must remain totally incomprehensible to the contemporary frame of mind because it approaches them with false presuppositions. Isolated substances are never found in these prescriptions, but rather highly differentiated preparations that can be understood only on the basis of alchemy and never through chemistry. It was then the goal to find a universal remedy, a “polychrest theriac,” a panacea having a generalized effect that would work more comprehensively, encompassing many illnesses, even contrasting ones. Actually, such a preparation would be an archetypal remedy having a completely non-specific effect that would include the total organism.

Such remedies were the ideal of the physicians in the past. They are exactly the opposite of what is striven for today in the various therapies, which are highly specific and disregard the total reaction of the organism. Certainly this specific way of proceeding can also be necessary, but the neglect of the older approach is a negation of healing.

The so-called remedies for typical illnesses were developed from insight into these connections. For the most part they go back to Rudolf Steiner. They do not work specifically against an illness, but rather work toward establishing an archetypal image of healthy functioning. The universal character of a comprehensive reorientation also underlies the "Solutio alcalina" mentioned previously.

For a long time, even until today, certain non-specific measures have been retained, but in earlier times they were used in a more comprehensive way and for other indications. The necessity, for example, of an intestinal cleansing to relieve and detoxify is recognized today, but in earlier times purging was considered to be a total cleansing of the body that was completely independent of constipation. Differences in illnesses and the personalities and types of patients were carefully noted. A differentiation was also made between intestinal relief and that of the kidneys or skin. In extreme cases, a fontanel or artificial suppuration was established.

Every period has its views, its stages of development and corresponding methods. In principle, it is not possible to take over old customs, no matter whether they happen to be Indian paths or medieval or Chinese medicine. Yet, it is important and appropriate to come to a true understanding of past and other measures, and to gain an insight into those principles that may be made use of today. Here we can mention the works of B. Aschner, whose goal it was to make the fruits of old medical experience beneficial to our time.

As the transformation of medicine progressed and the earlier comprehensive consciousness of the physician declined, various healing measures were dropped. The most that is granted these measures today, usually pejoratively, is to summarize them as "natural" methods of healing. To look at these measures again, to recognize their inner connection, and to educate the physician anew to a more comprehensive awareness of the total human personality is a necessity for medical training that has not yet been recognized. There is the added difficulty of the technical development and discoveries of chemistry and physics that have been used in medicine not having yet been adequately permeated with consciousness. All these things are applied according to the criteria of their effectiveness but without considering the subsequent results. This is so especially in relation to man, concerning whom animal experiments give no information.

The more universal a measure the "higher" the level on which it intervenes in bringing about a transforming, a retuning, and healing. The more specific an effect, the more obvious and evident it is, even in producing a symptom that does not have much to deal with healing. Since healing that encompasses the total human being must be striven for, certain therapeutic measures will be discussed here that proceed from the more general to the specific.

The Healing Effects of the Elements

The controlled use of elements in the old categories of earth, water, air and fire or light has a profound influence in reorienting the members of man's being in chronic illnesses. The healing process has already been described as a reorientation of man and the reestablishment of his connection with the environment. Here the elements play an essential role since in nature they are what has become independent in man in his warmth, air, and water organisms.

The earthly sphere plays an essential role in all climatic cures. There is a significant difference between living on a calcitic or granitic soil, or even in moving to a new place. Subtle observations show that some people are healthier or recover from an illness faster on one type of soil, whereas others will benefit most from another type. In general, calcitic soil has a more solidifying and dulling effect, while granitic soil produces a wakeful effect that can cause insomnia. This earthly influence, of course, is modified by the elevation above or below sea level and by the conditions of the air and by the relative humidity.

For individuals such as asthmatics who are most open to climatic influences, a change of climate can sometimes be the only way to a bearable life. Water is frequently a possible treatment. The organism developed in a watery environment, and until birth this was its life-giving element. When applications of water are used, this primitive relation of man to water is appealed to. The treatments are basic to regenerative processes after the ether body has been weakened by the environment.

Ever since antiquity healing springs have been known as areas in which special etheric streams are concentrated. In the old days these waters were experienced by people as being permeated with etheric forces, and they perceived them as beings whom they designated as nymphs, undines, water women, etc. Many old mysteries such as Eleusis, Delphi, and especially those of Asclepius were connected with these waters. The recognition of nature permeated by spirit has disappeared from modern consciousness, and one now seeks for the physico-chemical constitution of remedial water to explain its effect. But many studies show that water treated artificially with physico-chemical means does not produce the same biological effects in plant and animal experiments as natural spring water. It is possible that similarly composed remedial waters can have quite different effects and vice-versa. These effects are produced by the large quantities of substances in solution. This is particularly true of bitter waters containing Glauber's salts ($NaSO_4$) and bitter salts ($MgSO_4$), which stimulate the formation of bile and the intestines.

The waters of salt springs bring the skin into an intensive connection with sodium chloride, whose significance for the organism and the processes of consciousness was described in volume I. Salt incorporates the earthly element within water and hence salt baths bring about a consolidation of the constitution. They are primarily indicated in children with lymphatic constitutions.

Spring waters containing clear silicic acid work on the nerve-sensory organization, strengthening the formative effect and inhibiting the inflammations in the kidney area. Thus, Wernarzer water from Bad Brückenau works strongly to effect diuresis and is also indicated in illnesses of the kidneys.

In a bath the body is lifted and removed from gravity and

thereby returned to the conditions of embryonic existence. Quite apart from the substances in solution, bathing acts deeply on a person's consciousness and he experiences himself as removed from earthly forces. The being of the water carries and takes him up, and he becomes again child-like. Primitive human and childhood experiences are activated, and afterward he feels almost "new-born." This is the physiological background of baptism, and it "reminds" the person undergoing it. In an earlier time, rebirth was still experienced in baptisms. All baths actually work on the rhythmic system and the circulation. Physically the peripheral vasculature is somewhat compressed, but the central circulation is enhanced. The effect on the rhythmic system is increased when the water contains carbonic acid. This deepens respiration and brings about relaxation.

Stahl baths containing iron intensify the effect of baths, particularly on the heart and circulation. Iron produces a clear tonus, causing the weakened astral body to be more active. It is particularly indicated in hypotonicity. Levico water must also be mentioned here.

Waters containing sulphur work on the metabolic system. Through the sulphur they effect a stimulation of the entire metabolism and are indicated in all rheumatic and gouty illness, as well as in illnesses of deposition—arthroses, arteriosclerosis, etc. In contrast to an ordinary water bath, a definite rise in body temperature is noted after a sulphur bath, along with improved skin circulation. Thus, recently healed inflammations, which really should not be bathed at all, should not be treated with sulphur baths.

A spring's temperature is of special significance. In Central Europe it is well-known that the temperature of the water increases one degree centigrade for every thirty-three meters it rises from its source. It is possible that biological research will someday discover that this warmth streaming upward in the water from the deeper regions of the earth is different from externally added warmth, and that the water should be used as it comes from the earth.

The *Akratothermen* or warm springs have maintained their reputation as healing baths for thousands of years. For the most part, they do not contain significant minerals, but it does not seem to make any difference. When amenorrhea and dysmenorrhea caused by uterine hypoplasia can be cured by *Akratothermen* and climacteric disturbances can be influenced beneficially by them, etc., it is obvious that these waters truly contain "rejuvenating" forces. To some extent the etheric forces of the earth can fill the human ether body with new life. These springs have been designated as "fountains of youth" ever since ancient times. Because they stimulate the ether body and growth forces, these springs are absolutely contra-indicated for carcinoma or sarcoma since they would obviously increase tumorous growth.

The effect of healing water, such as Gasteiner water, is enhanced by radioactivity. Generally, following a cure a so-called bath reaction can be detected consisting in a worsening of the symptoms of the illness and in the recurrence of past complaints combined with a generalized ennui, fatigue, and even depression. At times, this may be the consequence of excessive bathing. Nevertheless, it shows that the bath brings about a deep-reaching biological influence, which is true of all stimulative therapies. It also demonstrates that the rejuvenation does not arise from turning backward but rather brings about a new orientation and restructuring of the members of man's being so that a crisis may be overcome.

This phenomenon is known in homeopathy as the initial exacerbation. It occurs following a correct remedy and also due to an excessively intense dose. In both cases, one is dealing with a positive reaction; the activation of the organism is brought about by a necessary or transient overburdening. Thus, such reactions must be carefully recognized and evaluated.

Baths with Additives

In general practice one must be satisfied with baths with added substances. If there are no other indications, such medical baths ought to be rather cool; that is, about 35° C. From the plethora of additives and indications, we will mention only a few.

Arnica essence 20%, 10 gms in a full bath in multiple sclerosis and muscle rheumatism; arm baths with increasing temperature for angina pectoris.

Valerian root as a sedative and also in insomnia.

Oak bark (Quercus Dec. 20%) in dermatoses, moist eczemas, vaginal discharge, parametritis, prostatitis, etc.

Iron bath, Levico with the possible addition of Ferrum sulfuricum.

Equisetum (a handful of Herba boiled for 20 minutes), Equisetum Dec. 10% externally in chronic nephritis; hot sitz baths in pyelitis.

Pine needles in mental or physical fatigue, generally to refreshen and strengthen.

Formica 5% for asthma and adiposity.

Hayflowers for diaphoresis; in arthritis, rheumatism, hot sitz baths in cystitis and adnexitis.

Chamomile as a sedative and in inflammations.

Chestnut (Aesculus 10%) in rheumatic illnesses.

Wheat in dermatoses.

Carbonic acid baths in asthma and hypertension.

Copper baths (Cuprum sulphuricum 20%, 1 to 2 tablespoons) in hyperactivity and kidney illnesses; also as arm baths of increasing temperature and hot foot baths in hypertension and peripheral arterial vascular disturbances.

Dwarf pine (for example, Mabex), in chronic bronchitis, strengthening of the respiratory organs.

Levico (Starkwasser 50 ml) for incarnation weakness, anemia, hypotonia.

Nourishing bath to stimulate metabolism (½ litre fresh milk, 1 egg yolk, 1 cup sugar, 1 lemon and 1 spoonful of honey).

Oil baths using the oil dispersion apparatus developed by Junge to stimulate the warmth organism. For additives, see the Wala list.

Prunus bath to stimulate vitality.

Rosemary (Emulsio Rosmarini 5 ml) refreshing, stimulates circulation; also for various disturbances of peripheral vasculature; hypotonia, and as an additive to the morning wash water.

Sulphur bath (Kalium sulphuratum 30%, 1 to 2 tablespoons per bath, or coloidal sulphur baths) in all illnesses with deposits; arteriosclerosis, arthrosis deformans, asthma, rheumatoid arthritis and dry eczemas.

Mustard flowers as an additive to footbaths in amenorrhea and insomnia.

Silver bath with Argentum coloidale 2%, 2 ml; in multiple sclerosis.

Soda baths (30 to 50 gms) to stimulate nerve function in poliomyelitis, post-syphilitic conditions and detoxification.

Salt bath (5 handfuls of sea salt) in adenoidal lymphatic constitutions, chronic otitis.

Thuja (2 ml) to revitalize in a tendency to suppuration, sties, pyodermia, otitis cystopyelitis.

Lemon bath for patients unable to sweat, and also for adiposity (3 or 4 lemons grated, squeezed and added to the bath).

The Healing Effects of Air and Light

Meteorological events can work on man through his internal air organism, which is part of the airy envelope of the earth. Watery activities are subject to the ether body, whereas the air organism is ruled by the astral body. When there is excessive sensitivity to weather changes, this membering is incomplete; the astral body is incarnated inadequately so that part of it is free and active perceptively in the atmospheric region. Scorodit D10 is to be used here. This mineral compound of iron arsenic affects the astral body and has an incarnating effect. At higher elevations the air pressure and humidity are lower and the effects of light are more intense; these conditions can be used therapeutically. Asthmatics are almost always relieved at higher elevations because the effect of air is weakened, thereby lessening the astral body's intervention. A stay at a higher elevation also brings about an immense increase in the working of ultraviolet light that stimulates the skeletal system and increases the formation of blood and bone. All in all, to live at a higher elevation stimulates the light metabolism. Along with the positive effects in anemia, developmental disturbances, rickets, lymphatic diathesis, some forms of tuberculosis and asthma, one must however also consider that it can lead to an excessive hardening. In carcinoma, any beneficial effects will be misdirected, as was described for the baths.

The Therapeutic Significance of Warmth

Today one can find a weak, almost atrophic, warmth organism in many people that plays an important role in anamnesis, giving one the impression of numerous foci of "coldness" in them. These form the points of inflammatory development since the organism attempts to dissolve them with focussed warmth. Such cold foci remove the organs they afflict from the total organism. Thus, many disturbances of menstruation, adnexitis, cystitis, etc., originate in this way. When the unfolding warmth of the organism is not strong enough to permeate the affected region completely, "nests of coldness" then form. These are the points at which chronic inflammations followed by tendencies to proliferation will occur because the etheric forces are here removed from the total organism. An antiphlogistic therapy, as it is frequently practiced in such cases, can give temporary relief, but usually the symptoms recur, which shows that the organism is still capable of defending itself. When this no longer happens, the tendency to proliferation can then go over effectively to new formations. The speed at which freedom from the disturbance is achieved is not decisive in such cases, but rather the grasping and dissolving of the disturbance through the principle of wholeness. Local applications of warmth are certainly indicated—sitz baths, Fango, and possibly diathermy.

An atrophic warmth organism can be most beneficially stimulated by a "salt." Here Silicia D60 injected approximately once every four weeks has proved useful. The stimulating effect of warmth to produce further warmth has already been mentioned in volume I (salt fever). When the water organism predominates, this must be treated first because the higher capacity of water to hold heat overburdens the warmth organism.

It is also possible to stimulate a weak warmth organism with mistletoe. A disturbed warmth organism can always be found in cases of carcinoma. One can find local cold spots as well as a general inadequate warmth production and even a decreased body temperature. With an injection of Iscador, the tumor is surrounded by a warmth mantle that can be most significant for therapeutic effectiveness. All Iscador cures should result in a temperature reaction, and if this does not occur, it can be improved by local applications of heat or with baths. After the Iscador injection, it is also necessary for these patients to stay in bed as long as the enhanced temperature reaction persists. At least they should avoid any cooling.

If at all possible, one should strive to have the organism itself become capable of forming and regulating warmth. Supportive measures of adequate clothing and living habits must also be taken.

It is certainly justified to apply external warmth insofar as possible not as a substitute but more as a stimulant. The alternating foot bath is an example. It can be taken hot (up to 45° C for one minute), and then cold (about 15° C for one-half minute). This is repeated three to five times. The effect can be enhanced by adding one teaspoonful of 2% copper sulphate solution to the warm water. Such changing foot baths regulate the vasculature and should be continued for weeks, allowing a brief pause approximately every four weeks. The treatment can be helped and supported by walking.

When there is inadequate skin activity, congestion in the water organism, and in the general metabolism, a hot air bath in a sauna is most valuable. The addition of one or two applications of Ferrum phosphoricum D6 one-half to one hour before the bath to aid the warmth processes and sweating has proved useful.

One of the strongest effects of warmth is achieved with the hyperthermic bath of Schlenz, Lampert, et al. Properly administered, the body temperature can be increased to more than 40° C without harming the patient. Since a hyperthermic bath is almost the same as an operation, it must be emphasized that its administration requires skilled supervision and post-bath treatment. Adequate information is provided in the literature.

Finally, we wish to indicate the possibility of an iatrogenically produced fever by autolytic bacteria (Vaccineurin) or plant products (Echinacin). These measures are particularly useful in raising the general body temperature and strengthening the patient's defense in Iscador therapy when the production of warmth is inadequate. This therapy is particularly indicated when the course of a chronic disease has more or less come to a standstill; that is, when the ego cannot intervene in an orderly or guiding way. The fever produced by the hyperthermic bath gives the ego a new opportunity to intervene.

The application of cold water as previously described by Kneipp, the physicians S. and J. Hahn, et al., must be considered as a stimulating therapy in which the reaction of the organism is the significant factor that must be recognized in improved warming and circulation. If the organism is unable to react in this way, then the application of cold water is inappropriate. Here, too, ministration by an expert who takes into account the reactive capacity of the organism is a precondition for therapeutic success.

When an individual's warmth organism is hypertrophic or if too much warmth is continuously produced, he will feel too warm, particularly in the head where coldness is more the physiological state, and also in the feet. Since sulphur represents internal warmth, one uses Sulphur D12, D20, D30 and even D200 here in order to relieve the organism of the heat. Hyperthyroidism may also be possible, and this must be treated with copper.

Apis has a special connection to warmth and can be used in lower potencies for local warming and fighting cold spots. It is indicated in local inflammations with belladonna; Erysidoron I, for example. Here, too, it brings about a better warming so that the inflammation becomes unnecessary.

If the warmth organism is inadequate, warmth dissipates into the periphery. These patients may well have warm hands and feet but will have a tendency to catch cold since their warmth organism cannot withstand the penetrating coldness. By enclosing it with lead, the warmth organism can be limited and can be brought to concentrate inwardly.

However, when this concentration is excessive and congestion develops causing the patient to complain of cold hands and feet, then an attempt is made to dissolve it to allow the warmth to stream into the periphery. Copper, which has an anti-spasmodic, dissolving effect, is indicated here.

Since healing applies to the whole organism, it is always generalized. Nevertheless, particular attention can be given a specific member of man's being. Regeneration is governed by the ether body, so we can mention some non-specific measures that it activates.

Nutrition is of fundamental significance for the ether body; this has already been described in detail, but in illnesses today it is relegated to a subordinate, dietetic role; its far-reaching significance for general health is yet to be understood. It takes a long time for the effects of malnourishment on the ether body to become manifest. It is most significant, however, that there are numerous people who have had chronic illnesses and have regained their health by changing their nutritional habits. At times they have become reformers who have urged others to experience their enormous success, and it is interesting to note the most varied diets that have been used successfully by them. Their successes could not be reproduced in others, however. Obviously, nourishment that is in keeping with the laws of nature and that retains the formative forces is better than artificial modern foods in contributing to health. The basis of success, however, lies in the transformation and consequences of maintaining a diet chosen by oneself. In denying habitual food, even the effort made to prepare a diet chosen by oneself and prepared in the right way, demands an exceptional inner activity that is most beneficial to the ether body. This is at the basis of every healing. Rudolf Steiner indicated that to form a new habit has a lasting influence on the regeneration of the ether body. This can be brought about, for example, when a person consciously alters his handwriting or gives up other habits. Since habits reside in the ether body, what really matters is the change. The continued practice of habits brings about a weakening and rigidification, the learning anew, a vitalization and expansion.

Sleep is of special and natural significance for the regeneration of the ether body. It is the primal phenomenon of healing and regeneration and in it the astral body, through which the destructive impulses of the nervous system work, is set aside. True healing, therefore, must allow for adequate sleep and rest. This may well be taken as a matter of fact, but most hospitals pay it little heed.

Sleep Disorders

Because of the significance of sleep for generalized regeneration, we will speak briefly about disorders of sleep and their therapy. The length of time one sleeps is not decisive; this can differ from one individual to another. A person may experience insomnia, but the real fact is that he simply manages with less sleep. It is much more important to know whether the duration of sleep—or better said, the period of rest—is adequate for regeneration. Thus, even a "bad" sleep can be quite positive for one who manages to utilize the experiences of intermediary states. This can be founded in one's destiny. Rudolf Steiner noted that inability to fall asleep can point to positive future forces. Not every symptom requires treatment.

In general, however, insomnia today indicates an excessive hold on the nerve-sensory system and the inability to let it go. This is also a constitutional problem in the widespread neurasthenic pattern of illness.

A constitutional tendency to disorders of sleep can occur in neurasthenics, in whom through excessive mental exertion or constitutional problems the astral body clings too strongly to the nerve-sensory system. Here, Phosphorus D6 or D5 given in the morning and at about 2:00 p.m. have been used quite succesfully in particular when the patient cannot readily awaken in the morning and therefore stays up late. Phosphorus in a lower potency brings about a more intensive and rapid incarnation in the morning. In children and adolescents there occurs a more astral awakeness, manifesting itself in unrest, excitement, a feeling of being driven, symptoms, in other words, which show that the astral body is not sufficiently controlled by the ego. In this case Phosphorus D6 c. flor. malvae is indicated; it is best administered towards 4 or 5 o'clock in the afternoon. The opposite, encouraging the ego to leave the body, can be achieved with Phosphorus in a higher potency. Phosphorus D25 with mallow blossoms given in the evening has proved effective. If applications of Sulphur are indicated, as in warmth deficient constitutions, Phosphor/Sulphur D25 given in the evening is better.

Cold is a more banal cause of disturbed sleep. In accordance with its nature, this belongs to the nerve-sensory pole of catabolism. Thus, cold feet as well as a cold bed inhibit sleep quite considerably. This is often not noted. The rational way to relieve it, of course, is to supply adequate covering and insulation from the mattress. Alternating footbaths can also be applied.

An age-old soporific is a glass of sugar water before going to bed. It is an absolutely rational therapy. The ego is bound gently to the blood thereby and can separate from the nerve-sensory system. Sleeping tea with honey is even better; a sweet meal in the evening or an apple can give the same effect.

A seemingly purely neurasthenic insomnia can also be caused by unrecognized pathological processes in the head. A middle-aged woman, apparently in good health, suffered from a resistant insomnia. Neither organic nor psychological causes could be found. Finally, a slight reddening of the conjunctiva of the left eye pointed to the answer. An X-ray showed a granuloma in the left upper canine tooth. After the granuloma was removed, normal sleep immediately returned. Insomnia can easily be understood in this case. The granuloma radiated into the head region causing conjunctivitis. The astral body had to fight the inflammation, but it became too firmly fixed. This led to a lasting state of wakefulness, even during the night.

Insomnia in children prompts us to search for rickets. A similar treatment with Phosphorus is then indicated. Excessive wakefulness can also be observed in children today. Argentum per Bryophyllum or Bryophyllum argentum cultum, which stimulates and reorders the regenerative processes, are indicated here. Magnesium phos. D6 has a similar effect but acts through the light ether. In Pavor nocturnus the sluggish astral body is addressed most beneficially with Datura stramonium

D6, D15 or Aconite D30 if Bryophyllum argentum cultum failed in the regenerative processes.

Severe cases of insomnia can also develop from neglecting the rhythmic processes. Here, Cardiodoron and Aurum, especially as an ointment to be applied to the region of the heart, can be considered. Among other symptoms, palpitations or being aware of the beating of the heart point to a disturbance of this nature.

Constitutional weakness of the nervous system that is continuously overburdened by the individual's profession has been beneficially treated with Argentum Nitricum D20 injected between the shoulder blades.

Some people fall asleep easily but awake soon after and then can fall asleep again only toward morning. Here, for the most part, there will be a weak ether body. Falling asleep occurs from exhaustion, but actual sleep arises only toward morning. In these patients Sulphur D6 or Argentit D6 are indicated, and also warm sulphur or oxalis compresses on the body. When sudden starting up or jerking sets in already during the process of falling asleep, this can be an indication for zinc (Zincum val. D3, D4). This is particularly indicated when the patients concerned have a strong iron impulse whose activity does not allow the organism to come to rest. (On zinc, see volume I.)

Another group of sleep disorders is related to the metabolic system. Migraine is the basic disorder. The underlying disturbance, however, can appear in the most refined forms. The pathological metabolic products can lead to a slight dullness in the head as well as to disturbance of sleep. For patients who recall having had migraine Kephalodoron could possibly be of help.

Stimulation of the metabolic forces can also be helped with Plumbum D20. The combination of Plumbum D20/Cardiodoron D3 has frequently been used successfully as an injection.

When the general metabolism predominates as, for example, in a plethoric condition, phlebotomy could be considered or a cool bath with cold compresses on half the body.

Disorders of the liver-gall rhythm lead to typical disturbances such as awaking at about 3:00 a.m. This problem is discussed in more detail later.

Insomnia can also indicate a predisposition to cancer. Here prophylactic Iscador is indicated.

It is not necessary to explain that many disorders of sleep have psychological causes, such as fear, grief, and suffering. These demand specific care and also practice in the ability to shut them out. Refer to the section ***The Nature of Healing*** for the appropriate exercises.

Spiritual causes, too, can lead to disorders of sleep, since the soul is then immersed in the living spiritual world. If it does not have the necessary organs to perceive that world and does not bring adequate concepts with it, it experiences a falling into nothingness and awakens from fear. The exertion of spiritual cognition can again create forces for the soul to make it possible to cross the threshold to the world it enters in sleep.

Drug Therapy

The preference of contemporary medicine for a one-sided medicamental therapy has already been discussed, and it has been shown how it considers others methods to be more comprehensive and neglects the transformed approaches to dietetics, climatic change, artistic therapy, etc., and even claims they are ineffective.

The same situation prevails in medicamental therapy. In accordance with contemporary molecular thinking, an attempt is made with a single chemical substance to intervene directly to produce a chemical reaction. Thus, bacteria or proliferating cells are destroyed by an active substance that blocks a reaction or replacing a missing substance.

This procedure is considered to be the most effective and only way worthy of development. With this direct intervention, however, the organism and its reactions are bypassed, but this is ignored since only effects are considered.

Contemporary therapeutic thinking is limited and beclouded by the rapid and intensive effects of medicaments. These are taken as a standard of comparison. The reactive capacity of the organism is taken into account as little as the question of purposefulness. Physician and patient alike let themselves be blinded too easily by momentary successes without thinking of the consequences that may follow a suppressed illness. Simply because it is possible to do something, however, ought not to mean that it actually must be done.

With such rapid and manifold therapeutic possibilities at their disposal, today's physicians feel the urge to be sure they have "done everything"—often out of fear of committing malpractice by failing to do all they can. The principle of *primum nil nocere* is given less weight here, which results not only in a polypragmasy, but also in iatrogenic damages, in the blunting of the most potent weapons (antibiotics for trivial illnesses, see below), and also in dependency particularly on psychotropic drugs, which are called into play even for indispositions, when an inner exertion on the part of the patient would represent a causal therapy. Similarly, it is a result of today's one-sided linear thinking when the principle for selection and development is based on the question, whether a substance is "more effective" and hence better than another—and naturally, preference is given to the one with the stronger effect in terms of time and intensity. This choice does not reflect reality, however, since the notion that the preparation more effective in this sense is also the better one is simply an altogether unfounded postulate of this very frame of mind.

Only under the most favorable conditions can a single symptomatic effect be thought about in this way. In the biological realm an isolated maximum principle is not valid. It is rather a problem of method, which, in such studies, ignores the wholeness of the organism in favor of testing an isolated reaction.

Since in all tests only the significant parameter is usually evaluated, a less active substance must naturally not do as well. Nevertheless, such a substance can cause effects that are much more comprehensive and can even work synergistically. It is well-known, for example, that along with the "primary active substance" of a plant, there are constituents working synergistically, which explains why whole extracts have stronger physiological effects than isolated substances. Antagonistic substances also occur together in nature and make it possible to avoid the damages of one-sidedness. Thus, vitamin D always occurs in nature with vitamin A, its antagonist, thereby avoiding the dangers of hypervitaminosis D.

It was described above how it is the signature of a remedy to work on the broadest, supra-ordered basis. Thus, the principle of preferring the most highly active substance is actually a renunciation of a remedy. It can result only in a highly specialized effect that neglects the whole organism. Therapeutic interventions should proceed according to this principle: they should work protectively and intervene as little as possible. This is not a question of dosage but rather of method!

If highly active medicaments successfully destroy bacteria, subdue inflammations, lower blood pressure, etc., then these results generally occur without considering the effects on the rest of the organism. It does not make sense merely to be careful about dosages to avoid side effects, nor is it sensible to "shoot sparrows with cannons." This is not a question of dosage but of principle. "Careful cannon shots" are a *contradictio in adjecto* and therapeutical nonsense.

In illness and healing there is a conflict and reordering of the relationship to the environment. Therefore, the same applies here as for interpersonal relations. To insure survival, it may be necessary to battle the opponent with highly effective weapons, but this step should be taken only after other methods are exhausted. Even in successful cases, however, the conflicts are not removed and the real problems will still have to be faced.

So it is obviously wrong to begin by treating simple, even banal, illnesses with antibiotics, and it ought not take the development of resistant bacteria with the consequent problems to be able to see through this procedure. It is also unsound practice to administer antibiotics in too small amounts or for too long.

In principle, successfully handling interpersonal conflicts as well as illnesses cannot occur on the basis of warlike battling and disruption. War is just as little the continuation of diplomacy as destruction in therapy is healing.

This warlike procedure has arisen from the coining of the term "the struggle for existence." Such a struggle does exist in a limited framework, but it is unsuitable to speak here of the background and impulses of evolution since it is inadequate in providing a basis for treatment in social and therapeutic areas.

The same principle is used in agriculture today to destroy pests and weeds. It is becoming evident, however, that the problems are by no means solved this way but only shifted. The imbalance of nature, which is expressed in the proliferation of pests and weeds, is enhanced by their destruction, while the development of resistant pests and the increasing sensitivity and susceptibility of plants to disease show the reactions of nature to a purely symptomatic approach. A new way to heal in this area must emanate from an overview that considers the whole biome. And along with that, there must be a proper respect for the laws of the living, granting them preference over economic aspects.

The consequence and goal of this warlike way of comprehending illness is the extinction and prevention of all illnesses. This is not only an illusion but a negation and circumvention of the meaning of illness.

To influence a symptom directly can certainly be necessary, which is where analgesics, spasmoledics, etc., have their place. This approach can be designated symptomatic therapy. Certainly a medicament that works symptomatically can initiate healing, perhaps by temporarily relieving the organism of an activity until it has "learned" it by itself. There is an ever-present danger, hwoever, that the organism, having been relieved of the reaction, will avoid learning it. Borderline cases of these effects will be discussed later.

Substitution, that is, the replacement of a substance or glandular product is another therapeutic procedure. The application of insulin in diabetes is an example.

Surely symptomatic and replacement therapies have their justification. Both practices can save and prolong life and, in fact, do so frequently in the treatment of coma with insulin, shock therapy with cortisones, etc. Narcotics also should be mentioned. Without them, operations would not be possible, and their use cannot be avoided. But it ought to be understood that these measures have nothing to do with healing. If healing occurs as a consequence of their use, then it is only because an emergency has possibly been handled with a substitution, or because the reactions of the organism have been temporarily relieved until self-healing can take place.

The decision as to whether or not a medicament is necessary is not made by considering the medicament and its possibilities however, but through an understanding of the illness. Here the question arises as to what the value of a symptom is; that is, what value is it given in the totality of the illness? Many reactions such as fever, allergies and polar illnesses can present not only potential dangers to the individual but also to his entire development, constitution, and disposition toward illness.

The therapeutic procedures used, then, should fundamentally be such that the attempt is made to make do with measures that least disturb the individual's own regulation, thereby most closely approximating healing. Naturally, this cannot always be achieved. We have discussed this before; yet this healing ought to be striven for in every case. That the path to healing is a struggle demanding much time of the physician and patient and taking much more time and effort than a rapid improvement must be understood. Seen over a long period of time, however, it is in every respect the appropriate way to lead man further. In addition, this approach is the socially more responsible one.

Principles of Healing

Fundamentally, the various possible therapeutic procedures can also be found in Hippocrates. "The physician ought to replace the *physis*[1] when it fails completely, support it when it does not achieve its goal alone, and delimit and change it when it errs." In "replacement" one can recognize substitution therapy that is limited to the complete "failure." "Support" corresponds most closely with symptomatic therapy, while "delimiting and changing" depends on the understanding of where it errs, that is, on the significance that must be attributed to the symptom. Undoubtedly, this evaluation was made in ancient times from much more comprehensive points of view than those of contemporary science. Therefore, it is especially the guiding and leading—the changing—of an organism during an illness that is the art of the physician, for which quantitative substitution or symptomatic suppression should often only form the foundation.

It has been shown that to fight or destroy fever, high blood pressure, bacteria, etc., with antibiotics, antihypertonics, antipyretics, zytostatics, etc., are justifiable but one-sided therapeutic principles. In more simple cases, an inflammation and increased warmth are treated with cold, excessive acid formation is neutralized with alkalis or bases. This approach goes back to the Galenic principle, *contraria contrariis curari*, which can also be found in Hippocrates who saw it working together with other principles. It was Galen who first presented it with an almost dogmatic one-sidedness.

One is dealing here with an especially old principle. Along with it, phytotherapy also persisted but worked in an entirely different way. Plants certainly contain bactericidal substances such as ethereal oils, enzymes, etc. Nevertheless, plant preparations primarily affect the organism by stimulating reactions, not by relieving it of them. Bitter substances, for example, stimulate rather than replace glandular activity; nor do they work directly on an enzyme substrate but rather indirectly by stimulating the organism to form these enzymes itself.

A principle that works indirectly on the organism encompasses it; it takes hold of it on a higher level and when properly selected, comes closer to healing. An appropriate remedy, properly conceived, encompasses the various components contributing to an illness. Mistletoe can be mentioned as an example. It is strongly anti-cytogenic and also stimulates the immune system. It is well-known that in a carcinoma there is cellular proliferation and also an anergic immune system. When a medicament is given that affects only one of those aspects, the illness may be improved but is not properly treated. It is better to apply both therapeutic principles; then, along with the anti-cytogenic effect, the immune system is also stimulated. The reactive principle of customary anti-cytogenics is also suppressive through the immune system and this may strengthen the disturbed principle. Ideally, both disturbances ought to be grasped with one remedy. This we have in mistletoe; it is active anti-cytogenically and also as a stimulant of the immune system, and thus it is a remedy for cancer. That the possible uses of mistletoe are not exhausted is a problem of development and does not affect the fundamental principle.

As a further example, Gencydo was developed to treat hay fever. Here there is a predominance of the water organism and an enhanced tendency to inflammations. Gencydo works by drawing the watery activities together and also works in an anti-inflammatory way. As a remedy, its takes hold of the two main disturbances of hay fever. Related problems are discussed in more detail in the chapter on the lung.

However, a remedy is not simply arrived at by adding together two or more various medicaments. It is the sum of active substances and is itself an organism, an artistic creation, which the pharmacist must protect and maintain just as nature has created it. He may complete it, however, by preserving its organismic unity rather than its "constituents" in its preparation. As a basic principle, however, with each therapeutic measure one should be aware whether it aims at the symptom or the illness. To fight directly against bacteria, fever, etc., is to take away from the patient a confrontation to be met; the symptoms disappear and the patient quickly feels relieved. This can be necessary when dealing with a weakened organism. However, in this way the disease has not been overcome, i.e. healed, but only put off until later (chronic illness or relapse) or to another area (suppression).

The aim of therapy, however, should be to support the organism in its own attempt to master the challenge posed by the disease.

Therefore, the measures taken in an acute phase will often be different from those in a chronic one or in a relapse. The latter are often an expression of a weakness in coping with a stress. Strengthening can be brought about primarily through a correct program of exercises. Measures of this nature are best applied in intervals, i.e. precisely when the patient is "doing well." These will include all "reattuning" measures, desensitization, hardening ("toning up"), etc., all of which represent a training, a challenge to the organism. In the same way that these measures can represent an overtaxing during the acute phase, so on the other hand is a long-term treatment senseless whose only effect is to relieve the organism of something. However, since today's therapeutic approach is almost exclusively directed at the "pathogenic agents" (see chapter on Infectious Diseases), long-term antibiotic therapy (for example) is applied in the hope of preventing relapses, an approach which by its nature must lead to a further weakening of the organism.

Before we speak of other healing principles, the problem of

poisons must be considered since they, too, belong to the therapeutic equipment of the physician.

The Use of Poisons

One of the fundamentals of the spiritual scientific image of man is that his spiritual life can unfold only through destructive processes that are related to the effects of poisons. "In all thought activity and psychological development, we affect the body with the influence of poisons."[2]

Man naturally forms poisons within himself, and it may also be necessary to administer them therapeutically. In the last analysis, it is not an accident but rather from an inner necessity that most remedial plants are poisonous.

The knowledge that *dosis sola facit venenum* goes back to Paracelsus. In applying this maxim, however, the dose ought not to be an abstract concept but should be directed to the healing of the patient since a fatal dose for a healthy person might actually heal somebody who is ill. In the same way, in cases of extreme sensitivity a minimal dose can set off allergic reactions. Both cases point to the problematic nature of toxic doses, normal values, maximum tolerance limits, etc., which may well be valid in a collective sense yet can be meaningless in the individual case.

Rudolf Steiner emphasized that it is nonsensical to speak of a medicine that is free of poison. The activity of the astral body reveals itself in poisons. When they are given in an appropriate form, the influence of the astral body is strengthened. The particular poison to be used determines the focus of activity; where it should be applied is revealed by the knowledge of the nature of man or by the remedial picture. It is understandable that in this relationship of nature and man, only natural substances are referred to here. Even synthetic substances that have intense effects do not have inner connections to the nature of man's organism. Therefore, the immediate and delayed side effects of their activity are not predictable, and they can be determined only after they have occurred. It is for this reason that the results of studies with animals cannot be extrapolated to include man. At most, this can only be done with isolated data or single parameters.

An understanding of the fundamental differences in the activities of various poisons can be gained from a statement of Rudolf Steiner. "Mineral poisons cause the astral body to pull itself into the ether body; plant poisons cause the ether body to pull itself into the astral body; animal poisons cause the astral body to pull itself into the ego."[3] It must be understood that even though the effects of poisons are referred to here, it is not their therapeutic effects that are meant. For these, other approaches, such as preparations, are necessary.

The application of appropriate poisons in therapy is necessary. They are like food for the astral body, which can thereby be diverted from a particular place. Nevertheless, healing proceeds from the ether body, which is stimulated by other events. This is actually a higher art; that was the goal to be achieved through the universal non-specific remedy.

It was an alchemical ideal to make a true remedy non-toxic or free of poison. To do this, various processes of "sweetening" were carried out to overcome astrality so that a universal remedy, a panacea, elixir, etc., could develop. Poisons were certainly not excluded but their limited therapeutic possibility was realized.

Poisons can be administered in various ways. When a person drinks coffee, he uses the characteristic stimulating effect of the "poison" caffein on consciousness.

Although in the customary use of digitalis, for example, one is certainly dealing with the administration of a substance whose dose determines the effect—that is, apart from the patient's sensitivity and individual requirements—it is not limited to material results. If, for example, a rheumatic person whose organism deposits metabolic substances because of a lack of formic acid is given Formica, it stimulates his organism to produce its own formic acid. Through this medicament the astral body takes a stronger hold on the physical body thereby producing more formic acid. This is an "activating substitution"; that is, the remedy relieves the organism of a functioning long enough to "show" it what it lacks, and it has learned again to form the substance.

Formic acid, however, is not meant to be used only as a substance, but it should also be administered in potentized form even in extremely high potencies in which, as is well-known, not one "molecule" of formic acid is present. Particularly in potentized substances one is no longer dealing with a pure substitution but rather with an activity of forces that stimulate those of the organism.

The direct opposite of influencing an illness or pathological appearances with substances, and certainly not the use of a molecular biological method, is present in the active principle of homeopathy. An extended medicine must come to terms with its fundamentals.

Homeopathy

A therapeutic principle was introduced into medicine almost two hundred years ago by Samuel Hahnemann. It later became known as homeopathy, and is based on the statement, *similia similibus curentur*; that is, likes heal likes. This is the opposite, in fact, of the Galenic principle, *contraria contrariis curari*. In customary usage today, the homeopathic concept is applied to remedies that are prepared by a process of potentization. A similar principle underlies every immunization, desensitization and therapy involving training and practice. In immunization the organism is given a product similar to that produced in illness—an inactivated pathological agent, for example—or the organism is made to undergo a lesser illness to protect it against a more severe one. Here, one speaks justifiably of an active immunization in contrast to a prepared, finished product, the antibody, used in a passive immunization. In desensitization the noxious agent is administered in relatively low doses to allow the organism to deal with it. More accurately we should call this "isopathic," since it is the same, rather than a similar, substance. Fundamentally, every therapy that uses irritating substances as well as many cathartic procedures belong in this category since most of them cause small stresses intended to activate and strengthen the organism to overcome difficulties. The Biersch congestion belongs in this category, and also the reactive excessive blood supply of the brief application of a tourniquet. Biersch himself was aware of the connection of this procedure with the homeopathic principle.

The most appropriate remedy is equal to the picture of the illness; that is, a specific therapy on the highest plane. The organism receives a remedy that is a modified, diminutive form of its illness, and this in a specially potentized form can heal it. It is no longer the substance but rather an activity of forces that is applied. Thereby, in overcoming the organism "learns" exactly the forces it lacks; it "learns to rule the illness" and to overcome it.

The epitome of the art of homeopathy consists in administering exactly that remedy that can potentially call forth the manifestations of the illness; it should, however, be given in a specially prepared or potentized form rather than as a substance. The step-wise dilution or rubbing processes of potentizing are merely the outer aspect. Hahnemann clearly pointed out that the essential part of the process is the "dynamization," the liberation of spirit-like forces. These are the active principle and not the diluted substance with which the process is begun. The word "dilution" is possibly justified in lower potencies in which the substance plays a role; in higher potencies, however, the substance of the initial material no longer plays a part. In high potencies, at least from D23 on and higher, it is exclusively dynamization, which means that a principle of force is active whose qualities are determined by the initial substance. Thus, one is dealing with a liberation and metamorphosis of the constituent forces of the substances. The difficulty in understanding these processes and in accepting the method of preparation lies in the one-sidedness of contemporary therapeutic thinking that accepts only chemical reactions, and in the concept that considers substance only as matter and not as a carrier of forces.

Modern man justifiably demands comprehension of and insight into his actions. Through spiritual science it is possible to recognize the connection of matter with spirit and to understand through a corresponding concept of substance the activities of high potencies. In addition, there are now comprehensive statistical findings that should dispel all doubts concerning the effects of these remedies.

The ideal of a purely homeopathic procedure consists in the application of *one* remedy. When this "fits," the process of the illness regardless of its nature is specifically addressed. Finding the remedy and the remedy itself are not based on pathological and anatomical concepts and symptoms but rather on the appropriate remedy picture, which may well encompass and include all the various customary designations of the illness.

Our contemporary comprehension and designation of illness, which goes back to cellular pathology, is based primarily on pathologic anatomical diagnoses. Other considerations such as humoral and functional pathology, and diagnosis and therapy based on the members of man's being, are not similarly justified but involve other aspects of illness, that is, of the reality of life. The over-evaluation of pathologic anatomical concepts is necessary in our times and has been determined by historical development. No objection can be made against them as long as they are not exclusive.

Homeopathy starts from the picture of a remedy and its similarity to the picture of an illness. For that reason, the classical homeopath correctly designates an illness with the name of a remedy. The diagnosis is identical with the remedy; an illness is, for example, Stannum or Belladonna, etc., whereby the clinical diagnosis, though still essential, is secondary.

Since man is actually a microcosm encompassing all realms of nature, isolated natural processes can be found that correspond to specific activities in his organism. Homeopathy with its many proven remedies has masterfully established this connection in the past two hundred years. Thus, when an appropriate remedy has been found, its application can heal an illness.

However, such healings are possible only when the remedies are used in high potencies. Their application demands a most exact knowledge of the remedy pictures, or a corresponding insight into the relation of man to nature.

This process can be compared to setting a railroad switch; that is, the measure can be immediately successful, thereby avoiding a possible catastrophe. This is called constitution therapy. Whichever of these two possibilities applies depends on the organism and the situation. Homeopathic, potentized remedies are in no way limited to chronic illnesses or less serious disturbances. In seriously acute states these remedies bring about decisive turning points most rapidly. Those who have experienced such therapeutic effects will admit that they can be achieved in no other way.

The homeopathic demand for a single remedy is partly justified when one considers its theoretical bases. This procedure can be designated as an ideal, which cannot always be achieved nor applied. The reason for this is not only the limitation of available remedies and the difficulty of finding the exact one, but it depends above all on the fact that there are various active principles that also strive for healing with similar justification. One can attack an illness from various sides. In this sense, appropriate remedies could meaningfully supplement one another. This is especially so if one does not start only with proving a remedy to be the right one but with the picture of a substance's being; this makes it possible to experience how, for example, Apis and Belladonna, or copper and zinc, supplement each other. The process of an illness can also be considered to limit an excessively strong activity and strengthen a weaker one. Similarly, an external application can be supplemented by an inner one. Here, the so-called combination preparations or complex remedies find their justification when their use arises from a related conception and is not simply giving the patient substances that are similarly active. Furthermore, the homeopathic "proving" picture of a remedy and the picture of a substance arrived at through spiritual science, both of which are necessary for diagnosis, can complement one another in a remarkable way. The former describes minute details, such as the particular time of a change in condition, specific sensations, etc. (modalities); the imaginative picture of a substance, on the other hand, makes it possible to understand its effect on the basis of a recognition of its essential nature and to perceive this in meaningful connection with the nature of the disease. When properly dealt with, detail and overview can work together.

The Discovery of Remedies

A knowledge of the healing forces of the Word and of plants was common throughout all earlier cultures. It was based on a different state of consciousness than that of today, and to the extent to which it was transformed into our contemporary more conscious and abstract thinking the possibility of directly perceiving the formative forces of plants disappeared correspondingly. Thus, today there is a lack of understanding of the way in which the healing forces of plants were previously discovered.

It is believed that this discovery simply happened through trial and error, but were this the case, how much easier would it be today. However, modern pharmacy and the search for remedies show how difficult it is to find them. Men in earlier times certainly were unable to make exact observations, but they possessed another consciousness that could be called "clair-sensing." They were acquainted, for example, with all kinds of plants that contained caffeine and that produced a stimulating effect. Chemical analysis has not been able to discover a single plant containing appreciable quantities of caffein that did not previously belong to folk knowledge!

This is true also of almost all of the hallucinogenic plants. It is complete nonsense to assume that all this was discovered by trial and error. When looking at a remedial plant, people then had experiences and sensations that were similar to the states of illness in which a plant was effective. With the rise of the enhanced consciousness of modern times, this instinctive capacity was gradually lost. Modern consciousness then fixed these direct insights into permanent recipes and they have since become traditional. This is how folk and natural medicine originated. The original experiences of earlier people have in the last few centuries become traditional and half-knowledge. The introduction of Digitalis and Strophanthin goes back to these sources and so does practically all of phytotherapy, therapeutic baths and much else.

The way to new remedies—except through searching out old traditions—is naturally closed today. It is certainly justifiable to take up old traditions and to carry them further with new methods as phytotherapy attempts to do by analysis, extraction of active ingredients, etc. In keeping with the customary thinking that is directed to material aspects, however, only the so-called active substances are considered, and these are isolated and enriched to have the greatest possible intensity. In two earlier chapters on pharmacodynamics and remedial plants it was described how, through modern spiritual science, it is possible to analyze the material aspects of a plant and also to come to know its formative forces, to preserve them, and to carry them further.

With the rise of the new scientific thinking, all bodily processes were considered from a chemical point of view and separated from the supra-ordered principle of life and the spirit. Consequently, attempts were made to intervene directly in these processes through molecular biology. This led to the development of chemotherapy. It is based on diagnoses of pathological and anatomical symptoms and makes use of substances that are formed naturally—salicylic acid, for example—or whose effects are enhanced by being chemically modified as in salicylamide.

This path led to the use of substances that are purely synthetic, such as phenacetin, pyrazolon, and phenothiasin derivatives, etc. Since these are substances whose effects on biological organisms were unknown and could not be determined from their formulas, it became necessary to test them on animals. Apart from chance discoveries, these tests are considered to be the only way of demonstrating the pharmacologic effects of the substances.

The impossibility of determining all the effects of a substance is inherent in matter and is not a question of exact methods of experimentation. Therefore, it is not possible to predict the effects on man of substances that may affect only one species of animal or none at all. The thalidomide catastrophe is an example. Thalidomide was well-tested and proved in animal studies before it was applied to humans and was shown to be exceptionally effective and tolerable except for the resulting malformations. It is inherent in such endeavors that only isolated parameters of animal studies can definitely be applied to humans, that is, only the symptomatic effects on blood pressure, sleep, etc.

A completely different approach to finding remedies lies at the foundation of homeopathy. It starts from the remedy picture that is called forth by a substance. This is then given in a potentized form for the corresponding illness. In preparing these remedies a process of potentizing is used, based not on a direct influence of the process or of the action of substances—certainly not in a molecular biological sense. It is rather "spirit-like" (Hahnemann) effects that matter. Modern thinking, oriented as it is only to material procedures, can have no comprehension of these remedies that do not contain "one molecule" of the initial substance. Thus, they are declared to be ineffective by official medicine and, to the detriment of the patient, they are not used. The remedial effect of these homeopathic remedies cannot be achieved in any other way.

The spiritual scientific method of discovering remedies differs from all of these. The connection of man with nature is fundamental to it. In earlier chapters on plant, animal, and mineral remedies a process in man was described that can be discovered to correspond clearly to a process in nature.

One of the fundamental results of spiritual scientific investigation is that man has undergone a common evolution with the realms of nature and that a recognizable, essential relationship exists between him and them. Step by step he has removed the natural realms from himself—a view that is part of the oldest wisdom and is revealed in mythologies; it can also be found in the works of Goethe, Oken and Carus. Man is a composite of the animal realm or, expressed differently, the world of animals portrays the human being spread fan-like over the earth (Rudolf Steiner). The plant world developed correspondingly; that is, formative impulses of specific plants can be rediscovered in the formation of certain human organs. Because of this inner, essential relationship, these plants can act as remedies for related organs and functions.

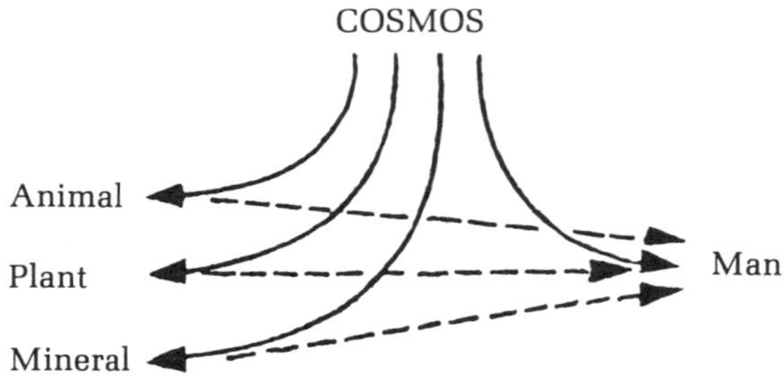

Evolution is not a chance occurrence, nor is it based on purely material processes. It is an expression of a process that is induced by creative spiritual powers. The investigation of these relationships in a modern manner was made possible by Rudolf Steiner.

When an ill person is given a natural process as a suitable remedy, he regains a specific connection with nature and the cosmos that was lost to him as described above.

In summary, one can say regarding the various ways of finding remedies that they are fundamentally different and can be compared only conditionally. The use of natural remedies is based primarily on experience and tradition that goes back to an earlier state of human consciousness. The contemporary school of medicine is based on pathological anatomical diagnoses and the direct influencing of these states. Homeopathy uses the remedy picture as the basis from which the remedy is derived. In anthroposophical medicine a knowledge of and insight into the disturbances of the connection between man and nature form the foundation for therapy. It is self-evident that these possibilities are not exclusive but can be mutually complementary.

A new principle of forming remedies goes back to Rudolf Steiner. In these remedies for typical illnesses, such as Bidor, Cardiodoron, etc., that at first glance look like combinations of substances, opposing processes are usually held in balance and united by a third element so that a new organism results. These remedies work by presenting a picture of healthy functions making it possible for the diseased organism to become oriented toward the harmonious image. Thus, the warlike principle used to fight an illness mentioned above is rejected. These remedies are not directed against an illness but rather toward creating a healthy function whose prototype they represent.

These new remedies correspond in a modern way to the old idea of polychrests. They stimulate the ether body and work non-specifically on organs and functions as opposed to the principle of fighting an illness, which naturally is directed against it and uses primarily specific poisons or antidotes. It has already been emphasized that the two procedures are not mutually exclusive and the use of poisons can be therapeutically necessary. The principle of remedies for typical illnesses is, however, more comprehensive and fundamental.

This method of healing works by indicating a direction rather than by compulsion, and it allows the organism the freedom to react; it is a truly pedagogical therapy. Included here is the original principle of healing that consists of the physician pointing the way with the help of an adequate remedy through an understanding of the process of the illness. An example of the effectiveness of these remedies will now be described in the action of Bidor in the treatment of migraine.

Migraine

Bidor is the preparation indicated for the treatment of migraine, but it cannot be compared with customary remedies. It is not directly analgesic nor does it contain vasomotor substances such as ergotomine derivatives or caffeine. Since the therapy ought to arise from the pathology, an understanding of the nature of migraine is thus a pre-condition to treatment.

It should be mentioned parenthetically that there is no comprehensive definition of migraine today. The criteria can be more or less limiting. The minimal symptoms are described as periodic attacks of severe headaches, occurring more or less infrequently. The unilaterality of the headache, nausea, vomiting or neurological losses are not always part of the process. Certainly there are also transitions to other forms of headache, of which ophthalmic migraine along with vasomotor migraine, the symptomatic migraine with serious neurological changes, *migraine accompagnée* (Charcot), complicated migraine and the Bing-Horton syndrome are typical.

It is remarkable that despite intensive research no cerebral organic basis has been found for this illness. The frequent neurological symptoms are completely reversible. It is also undeniable that neither encephalitis nor meningitis lead to the development of migraine, which should indicate that the cause of migraine does not lie in a disturbance of the nervous system. Undoubtedly, however, a pathogenic relationship exists between the vascular system and migraine. Although there is no vascular disease, the disturbance is of a functional nature. It is also known that there is a clear relationship to the various organs; the French school quite early presented the theory of toxic migraine (Bouchard and Charcot).

Linking the attacks with the menstrual cycle occurred so frequently that one came to speak of menstrual or ovarian migraine, and the connection with other organs noted earlier is indicated by gall bladder migraine, abdominal migraine, etc. Many migraine sufferers know that certain foods will set off attacks (alimentary-dietetic migraine). Frequently metabolic illnesses such as diabetes, alcoholism, gout, etc., occur in the hereditary backgrounds of migraine sufferers. It is revealing that it is thirty times more frequent among women, in whom the formative impulses of the metabolic system predominate, than in men, whose formative impulses are of the nerve-sensory system. The tendency to migraine is passed on more frequently by the mother than by the father. Furthermore, infant colic can be an early form of migraine, which also speaks for a metabolic genesis.

Most commonly, a migraine attack begins in the morning after waking. Thus, the formative impulses of the nervous system were not active during the night and the metabolic system was necessarily predominant during the phase of regeneration. Many patients notice a change on the day prior to the attack, complaining of lack of appetite, fatigue and general malaise. All these symptoms clearly show that migraine is a process that encompasses the entire organism and that localization in the head is only the final phase of the process. The vascular reaction is most noticeable, and it is usually attacked directly with vasomotor substances today.

It is made clear by these conditions that the causes of migraine must be looked for in the metabolic system. The symptoms in the areas of the nerve-sensory and vascular systems are to be considered merely as side effects.

Recent investigations confirm this view that the deeper causes of migraine are metabolic. The significance of metabolic products can be recognized, for example, in that alimentary migraine is initiated by chocolate and cheese, in which tyramine is generally considered to be the activating factor. This was first related to migraine when the monoaminooxidase inhibitors were used extensively in the treatment of depressions. Chocolate and cheese contain a high tyramine content, or it is released in their breakdown, and by giving it to sensitive patients it has been possible to set off migraine attacks.

Besides tyramine, still other catecholamines and protein products have have been found to have a clear connection to the development of migraine. Serotonin and its breakdown product, indolacetic acid, should be mentioned. "Pain substances" such as neurokinin, bradykinin, and the catecholamines are included under the rubric of "vasoneural active substances." With these substances one is dealing with metabolic breakdown products of protein. Here it is clearly evident that tissue hormones are active as biogenic amines. These frequently show clear vascular activities.

It can be assumed that not one but several substances can elicit the specific reactions. It is also probable that the same symptoms can be elicited by diverse substances as in allergies in which the reaction is the same regardless of the allergen.

With the role of metabolic substances in the development of a migraine attack thus established, the humoral theory of the development of migraine, which is possibly the oldest, gains a certain support.

The fluid organism also participates in the development of the illness. Frequently there is congestion, water retention and increased edema prior to an attack. Thickened eyelids or swelling in the temporal regions also point to this tendency. Often the water retention is relieved at the beginning of the attack, but it can precede or even follow it; then there is a flood of urine with diarrhea or profuse sweating. Here, too, one can see that only when the metabolism is properly worked through by the astral body are the pathological metabolic processes liberated. This is the basis of the therapeutic discovery (Gerson) that an absolute no-salt diet can "cure" some forms of migraine. Sodium is the carrier of the astral body within the water organism. Deprived of its instrument, it is no longer able to intervene—pathologically—and to produce cerebral edema, for example.

The nausea and vomiting can also be understood from the metabolic condition. They can be understood as a consequence of intoxication and are intended to relieve the metabolism. Thus, vomiting frequently brings relief.

Accordingly, the deeper causes of migraine must be sought in pathological metabolic processes. Quantitatively excessive or qualitatively modified substances press forward or upward from the metabolic system by way of the rhythmic system into the nerve-sensory region. As a first line of defense, the rhythmic system attempts to deal with these dynamics. At the beginning of an attack there is vasal constriction of the cerebral vessels; this can be considered an attempt of the organism to defend itself against the attack of the metabolism. If constriction is not successful, a dilation of the cerebral vessels follows; permeability is widely disturbed and a perivascular edema develops. This is the phase of resignation. The initial vasoconstriction is a reaction to the vaso-active substances. These can be formed either in greater quantity or they can appear in a pathological modification, thereby shifting the emphasis of the causal events to the metabolism. This is neither qualitatively nor quantitatively governed properly.

In 1924 Rudolf Steiner pointed out that uncontrolled metabolic processes that flood the brain and elicit pathological reactions there lie at the root of migraine. These relationships can be understood through the threefolding of the human organism. It is possible to follow this process step by step with modern scientific investigations.

When one's starting point is founded in a spiritual scientific perception of illness, a causal therapy results. In accordance with our discussion, this therapy ought to begin with a treatment of metabolism. Thus, it is actually possible to influence or even heal migraine by treating the metabolism. This can be done, for example, by excluding certain allergens, by changing the diet and by treating disturbances of the liver, ovaries, etc. The basic constitutional situation, which was described as the predominance of the metabolism over the nervous system, has not yet been touched, however. According to customary thinking and acting, an attempt should be made to bring this under control, but Rudolf Steiner introduced a new therapeutic principle that is far more encompassing. Based on his suggestions, a remedy, Bidor or Kephalodoron, appeals to the entire threefold nature of the organism. As has been said, this illness may well manifest in the nerve-sensory area, but at the same time the rhythmic system is also a participant, as can be noted from the vascular reaction. Yet, the starting point lies in the metabolic system. Hence, it is important to delimit not only the metabolism, because vitality would thereby be withdrawn from the nervous system; rather, this vitality must be brought into the organism in the proper form. To accomplish this, this remedy is also structured in a threefold way. The three constituents of it are not simply mixed but are put together according to a special procedure.

The stimulation of the nervous system is achieved with silicic acid or quartz, which in the extra-human realm of nature corresponds to the dynamics and function of the nerve-sensory system.

Silica represents the nerve-sensory system and sulphur the metabolic. As is well-known, sulphur plays a dominant role in protein metabolism and its detoxifying action is recognized.

Iron, whose connection with the blood is well-known, is the mediator between these two systems and substances. It has also an outstanding detoxifying function. How certain substances, particularly those derived from protein metabolism, are specifically bound or detoxified by iron is evident even in their chemistry. Here we need only be reminded of the detoxification of cyanide by iron. The behavior of porphyrins in hemoglobin is also quite characteristic. In themselves, they can bring about severe disturbances, and they only fulfill their physiological function through iron. When these three substances are properly united through a pharmaceutical process, the effect which would occur only in one system if the substances were given separately is coordinated. Thus, it is evident that the effect of a remedy made in this way cannot be symptomatic, nor is such a claim made for it. Its point of attack lies more in the disturbed relationship of forces of the three systems of the human organism; they are harmonized with the help of the remedy.

This explains in a way the frequent observation that patients who take Bidor regularly feel a greater vitality. Because of the harmonization of the metabolic and nervous systems, the nervous system gains the necessary vitality, the loss of which can generally be attributed to a constitutional disturbance. Finally, migraine attacks can be considered a frustrated attempt to increase the vitality of the nervous system. This is why some patients feel essentially better before or after an attack.

In the way Bidor works, we are dealing with a true remedy. The illness is not suppressed or displaced but corrected by dissolving the pathological processes that led to its development.

Although Bidor is indicated for migraine, it goes somewhat beyond such a simple designation. Rather, it could be said that through Bidor the displacements in the threefolding of the organism are harmonized again. Since these displacements can bring about the most varied states of illness, we have in the conception of Bidor an archetypal healing principle, the basis of which is not yet recognized today and is therefore too infrequently applied therapeutically.

This, it must be noted, is a constitutional principle of medicaments that harmonizes the originally disturbed dynamics. To be effective in migraine, however, it may also be necessary to treat a disturbed organ. These disturbances are often refined and not clinically evident, however, and occasionally may be difficult to find. Furthermore, it could be necessary to exclude such exogenous noxious agents as chocolate, sweets and cheese and also to change the patient's life style to help establish the harmonization striven for with the remedy.

Occasionally the indications for an organ are easily found; for example, in ovarian migraine, Cimicifuga given in homeopathic doses and silver treatment could be indicated. If the liver or the gall bladder is involved, one must think especially of Chicorium and Oxalis. With a strongly "radiating kidney," Camomilla radix is specifically indicated. Often the intestines or metabolic deviations within them play a primary role (with or without obstipation). In these cases, enteroclysis or even an enema can help—even in an acute phase. As medication in these instances, Digestodoron is recommended over a long period of time and Pancreas D4–6, possibly with Ferrum sidereum.

At times there can be a "weakness" or an unnoticed chronic inflammation in the metabolic area. These can be treated locally with injections of Apis/Belladonna, which works through warming, release of cramps and proper ordering of the astral body. Occasionally, treatment of the cervical spine (Migraine cervicale) can be necessary here; Disci preparations (Wala) are used.

In many cases it is possible to find a suitable remedy in the homeopathic pharmacopoeia through a refined observation of symptoms. The use and therapeutic success of such remedies in no way contradict what has been said. The basic remedy and individual variations always complement one another. In a certain way the grain fungus, Secale, actually corresponds in nature to the basic pathological process. As is well-known, it is a parasite that grows on rye, depriving it of etheric forces. The resulting metabolic products (ergotamine derivatives) produce a penetrating effect that works from the metabolism into the nerve-sensory region via the vascular system. Thus, in more or less modified, active substances (ergotamine derivatives), Secale is used in homeopathy and pharmaco-therapy in the treatment of migraine. The combination of Secale/Quartz (Wala) has proved to be most useful.

The dosage of Kephalodoron is quite important. Occasionally a few tablets of Bidor work prophylactically in migraine as well as in other forms of headache. This, however, is no measure of effectiveness in healing. As in every basic remedy, it is much more important to apply the medication over prolonged periods. It is suggested to take one or two tablets of Bidor three times a day for seven weeks, to be followed by a pause of approximately five weeks.

The effect of Ferrum (quartz capsules), whose basic substance is prepared in the same way as Bidor is much more intensive. A thorough study of this remedy has been made.[4]

Forty-two practicing clinicians in four clinics studied Ferrum/quartz capsules in 415 patients with headaches. The preparation was most successful in the treatment of migraine and vasomotor headaches, with a positive effect of 75.4 percent in migraine and 84.6 percent in vasomotor headaches. One capsule daily, best taken in the morning and given over a long time, is generally adequate to achieve a high rate of success. An application lasting only two to four weeks shows hardly any influence. In acute attacks the repeated application of one capsule at half hour intervals proved to be quite effective. Good results were also evident in patients with pains from concussion, while cervical headaches did not respond.

In more sensitive individuals and children a potentized remedy in a D3 strength may be indicated. Here, too, the dose should be as sparing as possible but as strong as necessary.

Concerning Medication

The use of potentized remedies is not a question of dosage. The claim that lower potencies contain more and higher ones less "active" substances is irrelevant for therapy since the initial substance in the various potencies, especially the higher ones, is not significant. It is rather the dynamization, the force effect that was discussed above, that is important.

A key to understanding the use of potencies is given by the threefolding of the organism. This was discussed in volume I in the chapter on pharmacodynamics. In general, one will use the lower potencies D0–6 to work on the metabolic system, the middle potencies D8–15 to work on the rhythmic system, and the higher potencies D20–30 to work on the nervous system. Young patients are treated with lower potencies and older ones with higher. This meets the shifting dynamics that occur during the course of life.

In acute cases one will prefer low potencies and tinctures and choose plant before mineral remedies. The more chronic the illness the higher the potency, and the higher the potency the more infrequent the application. Extremely high potencies such as D200 often need only be given once, especially when given as an injection, or at most about 7 drops once a day for a week, when the effect will either be noticed or, if not, the remedy will not be indicated. In either case, further use is not necessary. It must be mentioned here that by ordering potencies in this way, a schema is provided that can be modified by other processes; thus, under different circumstances it may be necessary to deviate from it.

Among the plant remedies, the blossom shows the more rapid effect while the root works slowly and more constitutionally.

If a remedy has caused an illness to deteriorate, one must then wait for the reaction to subside before applying the next remedy, which is first given in the same potency.

If a remedy has produced a good effect that has then subsided, one then gives the same remedy in a somewhat higher potency. In general, it is good to let an effect die away and then stabilize it through a higher potency.

By combining one active principle with another, one can guide the effects more specifically. For example, a generalized astralization can be achieved with arsenic, but by combining it with copper, as in olivenite, the effect can be directed to the copper area in man, especially the kidney system. If one wants to affect the inner aspect of man, then carbonates are preferred; to work on the stomach, malachite, natural copper carbonate, is used. Siderite, natural iron carbonate, works on the pancreas or gall bladder. When combined with silicic acid, however, the substance becomes active peripherally.

The type of constitution of the patient can also contribute to the selection of the combination of substances. Blond, light-eyed patients are more "sulphuric." Thus, one would want to avoid combinations containing sulphur in this type, but they would be especially preferred in dark-haired patients. Chalcocite, which is natural copper sulfide, would be given to dark-haired hyperthyroid patients, for example, but sulphur types would get cuprite, cuprous oxide.

One ought to take into consideration the physiological and

rhythmical processes of the organism in the application of remedies. Thus, it is more meaningful to give iron and phosphorus in the morning since both work on the incarnating process. Silver and copper work better on the physiological anabolic processes when they are given in the evening. To support the physiological warmth rhythm, Iscador, which causes a warmth reaction, is best applied in the morning. In chronic illnesses of the liver and gall bladder it is advisable to use the gall bladder medication in the morning, but corresponding to its physiological rhythm, the medication for the liver should be given in the evening.

Naturally it could be necessary to give a remedy several times a day quite independently of what has been said. Nevertheless, the customary dosage "three times a day" is justified because it is related practically to before and after meals. The patient's daily rhythms must also be taken into consideration.

It is perhaps not necessary to mention that the application of 3 × 10 drops is not the same as 1 × 30 drops, or even 5 × 6 drops. Besides the practical aspects of taking remedies, it must not be forgotten that a therapy is not intensified by increasing the dosage, but rather by the way and frequency it is given.

Application of a remedy over months or years may be necessary to achieve a constitutional transformation, and giving it rhythmically is more favorable than uninterruptedly. Bidor, for instance, is given for seven weeks and then withheld for five, etc. Scleron or other lead remedies may not be given for years without pause. A guided interruption is part and parcel of therapy, just as a pause is meaningful in music. Such intervals can either be free of therapy or a complimentary remedy can be given. Frequently, prolonged medication with iron can be necessary, and then it is advantageous after a few weeks to appeal again to the basis of the illness. Insofar as the interaction of gall bladder and liver is concerned and depending on the constitution and type of the patient, this could be done with magnesium. With the blood, however, copper is the metal that is polar to iron, and it could also supplement iron therapy for short periods.

Finally, the iron process is also based on all vitalizing processes that must lead further. Thus, silver can also supplement iron therapy.

Correspondingly, copper following a lead medication will give permanence to the latter's positive effects. Calcium can also be used here as a supplement. Even after the application of a remedy has begun, a change is advisable. Thus, one can begin silver therapy with Argentum per Bryophyllum, for instance, and change this after four weeks to Argentum Prep. D6; after four more weeks it can be changed to Argentit or Argentum Nitricum, etc.

It has already been indicated that oral applications work more on the metabolism, injections on the rhythmic system and the circulation of body fluids, and external applications work more on the nerve-sensory organization. It has been shown repeatedly that injections achieve a more rapid and intensive effect than can be achieved with the same remedy given orally. A middle stage occurs when the remedy is given perlingually; here, ampules can also be used.

With potentized remedies, particularly those of higher potencies, the effect is dynamic and the initial substance is not of much significance. Nevertheless, the quantity of the dynamic carrier plays a role. Thus, it has been shown that often several ampules—three to five, possibly even ten—may be more effective than 1 ml. An example here is the hemostatic effect of Stibium D6, which is therefore also available in 10 ml ampules.

It is not a matter of indifference whether drops or globules are taken with or without water. Substantial doses (tinctures up to about D3) work better when given directly (perlingually). It appears that higher potentized remedies work better when taken with or dissolved in water.

Injections are generally given subcutaneously above the affected organ or in corresponding locations. For example, to affect the metabolism, the injection is given in the upper thigh; to affect the heart, in the left upper arm; to affect the head, in the arm or neck. Under certain circumstances an intravenous application can be more effective. Low potencies of plant preparations such as Cardiodoron 5 percent ought not be given intravenously because of possible allergic reactions. An exception here is Ampelon 10 and 20 percent (grape *juice*, not grape sugar), which was developed particularly for intravenous injection. Intracutaneous injections are a modified version that may significantly enhance the remedy. Here, 1 to 2 ml is injected 5 to 10 times into the head zones or the neuro-therapeutic areas.

To understand the various effects it must also be pointed out that there may be something like a "genius loci" in therapy, which means that certain tried and proved remedies do not work actively enough. This has been experienced frequently and can be understood when one considers that to bring about a true healing the totality of man's members is addressed. They depend, however, on where the patient is located geographically in the ether body of the earth. The study of climate and of whether the geographic areas are composed of soils of calcium or silica is helpful. Also, in many areas certain remedies are more frequently indicated and more active than elsewhere.

Finally, it must be mentioned that a correctly indicated and properly applied remedy can remain without effect because the organism inhibits it. In these cases one must look for foci in the teeth, tonsils, etc., and clear them up. But an auto-intoxification can disturb and bar the way to healing, too. Here an intestinal cleansing, along with a detoxification of liver and kidneys, must precede the actual therapy. Adequate production of body heat, the body temperature, and heat distribution should also be noted. Along with correct stimulation of the organs, a reaction remedy can be given; Sulphur D30, for example, can bring about the necessary change. An acute detoxification via the intestine can be achieved with an enema, but as a temporary measure a laxative can be given such as Clairo Tea. Practically every chronic illness goes hand in hand with a bacterial imbalance that in turn is an expression of an inadequate metabolism. This is a nutritional problem, and it may be necessary to deal with it by giving a brief low-protein or protein-free diet. The problematic substances in intoxications originate primarily through protein metabolism that is expressed in extreme formation of indole and skatole (the indican test). But the biogenic amines, such as the inadequate detoxification of histamine, also come into consideration here. These problems were discussed earlier. Digestodoron is often used to master the intestinal metabolism; an adequate dosage is 3 × 10–25 drops given over several months. Special preparations to modify the intestinal flora can also be most helpful.

The detoxification of the liver will be discussed later. The remedies to be considered in this connection are Hepatodoron, Carduus marianus, Sulphur D6 or Antimonite D6 (directing the action of the protein metabolism) and, in general, Argentite, which stimulates excretion.

Detoxification via the kidneys can be achieved with a copious fluid intake and by Solidago virg. 30 percent; Equisetum with Sulf. tost. D3–6 can also be used.

To divert a substance to the skin can be immensely effective in various depositional diseases of the joints and in regressive metamorphosis. The stimulation of an inflammation and the diversion of the disturbance are decisive here. These can be achieved by Cantheride plasters (irritating ointments based mostly on Capsicum), and also by mechanical irritations. The Baunscheidtieren process is a combined application. The application of mustard plasters and compresses must also be mentioned here; they can be understood from the previous discussion. Even sweating signifies an increased excretion that is often not possible elsewhere. The humoral approach to relief of metabolic waste products may certainly be correct to some extent, whereas customary thinking that starts from anatomical pathological events is unable to deal with the phenomena. Thus, these applications, which can be highly effective and often irreplaceable when correctly indicated, are rarely used and even less understood. These effects are based on the diversion of the astral body, and they thereby prompt it to correct its activity from the inside out; then the illness can be overcome without danger and can be dissolved. The skin in particular is a stage where the conflict with an illness can be overcome, but the role of its significance and function is not given proper attention today.

It is of utmost importance for the physician to be aware of the various possibilities of healing so that he will be able to choose in freedom the necessary treatment for the patient.

Physical Therapy

Artistic Therapy

Profound healing forces lie hidden in art. It is not so much merely the passive submission and opening of oneself to a world lying above earthly needs in which the spirit can be experienced that is effective here, but much rather a person's own activity, especially in a new, unfamiliar area.

The possibilities for artistic therapy comprise the entire realm of art—music, painting, sculpture, speech formation and especially eurythmy, the art form created by Rudolf Steiner, with its special modification, curative eurythmy. What in the form of a thought touches the soul of one who is ill only superficially, can through the imagery, rhythm, and harmony of artistic activity speak directly to the depths of his soul.

Throughout the presentation of the results of his spiritual scientific investigations and in all areas of practical cultural life, Rudolf Steiner introduced the artistic element as something essential to them. Thus, the artistic element permeates all branches of science, especially pedagogy and the new medicine, that can be fructified by spiritual science, that is, all fields that are concerned with the human being and with the Creator's greatest work of art, his body. Art, which man above all other beings is able to practice, flows as a creative activity from his innermost being. As Schiller explained in his letters on the aesthetic education, art is sustained by the freely breathing middle, by the man within man who can reconcile and harmonize the contrast between the necessity of reason (formative drive) and the compulsion of the sensory nature (material drive) through the free play of his forces. Thus, man can heal contrasts in the world through art. Just as in our individual lives we carry the health-giving middle in our breathing and circulation, so art flows like a vivifying breath and warming stream through our culture.

Is it not then possible to conceive of unknown healing forces slumbering in this artistic element? It is different, however, when to develop an art of healing the artistic element is carried into the more limited healing realm. In this way, curative eurythmy developed from the basic elements of eurythmy. Here one turns away from the work of art toward the patient who wants only to be stimulated to do artistic exercises related to his condition. Eurythmy as an art is thus sacrificed to some extent for curative eurythmy. It is the same with every art that is transformed for healing, but it is nevertheless always possible to have both. Through a healing art the patient experiences an enhancement of his life processes and even more so through experiencing great art, but the transforming therapeutic exercises that he can do on a small scale can be individually structured for him from the art of healing.

In our contemporary culture, intellect and will (Schiller's formative impulse and material impulse) dangerously threaten to fall apart. The formative impulse is overly powerful. Science, technology and mechanization rule the life of the soul. The will is pressed back and either asserts itself in one-sided achievements of power or is pervaded by a noticeable weakness. The middle requires specific care and nurture since even the life of art seems to be ruled by the analyzing, abstracting forces of the head. For this and many other reasons, Rudolf Steiner has permeated the Waldorf School curriculum from the first to the last grade with a gradual, transforming artistic element that is appropriate to the age of the child. Here he has created a grandiose prophylaxis for our damaging age. And when Rudolf Steiner began to give suggestions for the more narrow realm of medicine, he introduced the artistic element into therapy right from the start.

A healing effect is hidden in the nature of each of the arts. Only when one understands the interaction of the members of a man's being, be it ever so complicated, can it be possible to understand the deeper effects of art on him. Only a few indications can be given here though the subject calls for in-depth study. Whoever wants to devote himself to artistic therapy must learn to trace the artistic process in human beings; for example, what forces become active in human beings when they make music, or paint, or sculpt? Every art contains all elements —form, rhythm, and material—but they all bring these elements into activity on different levels.

Music is an entirely non-spatial art that uses tone, an etheric sound element, ordered in accordance with the laws of the heavens. It is the echo of the music of the spheres that was experienced in different states of consciousness until the time of Plato. The twelve tones and seven steps of the scale mirror the zodiacal and planetary relationships. Spiritual laws are active here and true music opens the way for the spirit to take hold even of the physical body. Music contains the laws of the ego that are ordered above the astral body. It can harmonize the soul and also throw it into chaos. It can tame the "animal" in us, and when they hear certain music, animals may try to stand upright, a posture the ego makes possibly only to man. Thus, with selected elements of music, one can attempt to work toward ordering the ego into the physical body, even into the bones, via warmth. Music spiritualizes the entire human being with the laws of his entelechy. It penetrates him as does the warmth element. The spinal column is a special structure of ego activity, and today it is subject to many injuries. Besides the many shocks it receives through walking on concrete, through means of transportation and machines, through the immense influence of the counter-rhythms of modern music and its dances, it experiences a loosening of the ego-organization. This can gradually bring about a predisposition to organic damages that appear in the soul as an undermining of deliberate reason, thereby opening the gates to deeply hidden destructive urges. One must also mention the widespread mechanical production of sound, which paralyzes rather than heals.

Thus, music works between spirit and substance, filling and inspiring us from above downward. Our skeleton is a musical creation of cosmic motifs metamorphically transformed. Rudolf Steiner once called man a "frozen sonata." An intimate knowledge of these various connections can result in an extensive application of musical exercises of varying effects, depending upon whether a melody, an isolated tone, an interval, or the harmony of a chord is used. It should not be forgotten that we are only at the beginning of the development of the artistic therapies that will form a new profession.

The nature of painting lies a stage lower than that of music. Man ensouls himself by living in color. It is a direct expression of his world of feeling. Just as colors originate between light and darkness, so the colorful scale of his feelings develops between the joyfulness of light and the suffering of darkness. Sympathy and antipathy, like joy and suffering, can also be considered as the profound polarities of soul life. The soul is healthy only when it can live in a breathing alteration between these possibilities in which its place as mediator between the inner life and the outer world lies. The soul is impressionable and receives impressions from outside. It breathes everything in, but it also needs to breathe out, for it is also capable of giving expression. It must be able to bring the inner outward. In colors are now mirrored the laws of the soul world, of the astral body, that produces images in the ether body. There, the soul becomes a picture in "the body of formative forces." What radiates outward, the element active outwardly, lives in shades of yellow-red; in blue-violet is the soul element that is directed inwardly. When we truly live with colors and do not only stare at them, colors become paths of the soul.

Again an intimate study is needed to comprehend the relationships between color and soul in their full extent. As a therapeutic activity, painting is therefore beneficial in all disturbances that concern the breathing contact between astral and ether bodies. Where this life of breathing is disturbed, painting can be a decisive help. This is true in psychological disturbances in which there is difficulty establishing contact with the environment and in tendencies to cramping and hardening, causing such bodily symptoms as asthma, angina pectoris, etc. It also includes the area of the anti-social behavior of the soul and the widespread loss of interest in a world that no longer satisfies because of its materialism.

Working with colors brings courage to our sensory life and

enables it to carry new experiences. It awakens interest in a newly perceived world, and when we make a picture of something that shows we are united in love and understanding with our environment, it mediates a deeper comprehension of it. Fixed thoughts can be loosened and blurred thoughts can be meaningfully formed. Therapeutic exercises can be developed toward both sides. Therapeutic painting, which can be applied widely, is also of great importance in pedagogy.

Something different is activated when a person models with clay. Here, the person has the substance of the earth in his hands and must impregnate it with living form. The ether body is the sculptor in us, structuring and modifying the form. Again we have descended a stage lower in the connection of the members of man's being to his physical body.

1. Music—impregnates the astral body with the laws of the ego.
2. Painting—impregnates the body of formative forces with the laws of the soul.
3. Modeling—impregnates the physical body with the laws of the body of formative forces, the living form.

Modeling exercises those forces with which we take hold of the physical body directly from within. We place ourselves in the forces of space; the senses of touch and balance play a special role. Here, too, there must be a balance between solidification that tends to rigidity and sclerosis and an inadequacy of formative forces that leaves everything undetermined and undifferentiated. Here, the metamorphosis of form assumes a special role—for example, a platonic form or other motif—because a continuous metamorphosis of processes rules a healthy physical body that is securely grasped by formative forces. Rigidification has a calming effect right into the depths of the soul. Wherever a loosening or separation of the soul-spiritual from the body occurs, which often leads to confusion and psychiatric manifestations, modeling is a necessary adjunct therapy. Wherever control over the physical body is threatened, when appearances of dizziness, fearfulness, certain disorientation, or all kinds of blurred confusion, excessive nervousness, irritability and inattentiveness occur, modeling can always exert a healthy effect.

In general, it can be said that the widespread paralysis of the innate creative forces brought about through radio, movies, and television, as well as other dangerous factors in our culture, create the necessity for artistic therapies to be developed in medical thinking as a counterbalance. The artistic therapy meant here is fundamentally different from the use of artistic products as diagnostic tools. One always works with the patient in such a way that the therapeutic guidance remains in the artistic realm; as a result, the personality can unfold in an unviolated fashion and is not disturbed in its almost childlike, naive activity.

Thus, soul and spirit are addressed and made active through the various levels of the arts. This is a building up of new soul forces, not an analysis. The therapist must be carefully educated to be able to lead the ill person or, in a wider sense, the person damaged by the times through insight into this area. Occupational therapy was the first step in activating dormant forces toward a satisfying fulfillment of illness and recovery. Artistic therapy embraces these viewpoints fully, but when it is seriously practiced, it goes far beyond them in its effects.

Curative Eurythmy

Speech Curative Eurythmy

Curative eurythmy is a therapy of movement. Its underlying principles were created by Rudolf Steiner in 1921,[1] and developed as a special extension of eurythmy, a newly inaugurated art of movement.

In eurythmy one experiences visible speech. Its medium of expression is the moving human body. Hence, it encompasses the human being as he manifests in space and time, in form and movement.

The human form of the supersensibly comprehended human being becomes manifest as it originated from the creative formative forces of the cosmos. Genesis expresses it as follows:

man was created as an image of God from the power of the Word, the Logos.

All possibilities of movement and also of speech, which is a shadow of the cosmic Word, originate from the inner nature of man in his encounter with his environment in his first years of life. Speech and limb movement are closely connected, a fact best observed in the gestures accompanying speech.

In eurythmic movement the separate elements of speech—sounds, words, sentences, etc.—find their essential expression. In artistic presentations speech thus becomes outwardly visible, and in streaming into space it becomes a language in itself that is separated from the body.

In curative eurythmy these movements are modified according to the illness. The sound is brought to expression in such a way that it works back on the organism of the performer. Every sound has its characteristic gesture and its particular physiological point of attack. One can thus affect definite organ systems and heal their damaged forms and functions by stimulating the original cosmic formative forces.

Curative eurythmy is indicated especially in illnesses of the inner organs, the apparatus of movement, and the nerve-sensory system. A special area of application is found in developmentally disturbed or retarded children.

Curative eurythmy forms a supplement and support to medical therapy. It is prescribed by a physician and is carried out by a curative eurythmist who is trained in the therapy and has a qualifying diploma. From the multitude of eurythmic possibilities of movement, a definite selection is made for curative eurythmy that includes rod exercises, three part walking and form walking, which mediate the person's orientation in space. Observation has shown that the sick adult has in most cases lost his awareness of the space behind him. This must be regained even if with great difficulty, so that the sound movements can be properly performed.

The time element comes to expression in an enhancement or retardation of movements; the feeling for this can be trained through the practice of various rhythms.

The sounds of the vowels and consonants encompass and

shape the relationship of space and time to the inner aspect of man. They can be done while standing, walking, running, with or without jumps, while sitting by those handicapped in their walking and, if necessary, by those reclining in bed. Acute inflammations are contraindications. Single vowels and consonants are used, and also sequences of vowels, of consonants and of mixed vowels and consonants. The exercises must be performed regularly for weeks to unfold their effectiveness.

The sequences of movement cannot be explained theoretically; therefore, a detailed description of them will not be given here. Only the principle will be indicated. One must do the exercises oneself to experience the specific quality of this therapy and the way it interacts with the organism. In what follows, a few fundamental aspects of the various sound exercises will be mentioned.

1. The Vowels

In German, vowels are characteristically called "self sounds" (*Selbstlaute*). When we speak a vowel, something is expressed that lives in man in feelings, sensations, etc. Soul reactions toward what enters from outside are expressed in interjections of astonishment, wonder, pain, fear and disgust. Thus, the vowel is the expression of the inner activity of the soul. The self expresses itself and gives an individual sound-color to language. Whenever a man has too little "self," he can be strengthened through curative eurythmy vowel exercises, and those who are not able to awaken properly can also be strengthened psychologically and organically. Formative forces are stimulated right down to enhancing the mineralizing processes—in osteoporosis and fractures, for example.

The formative forces in the organism emanate from the nerve-sensory system, the head pole. The working of the vowels, however, is also closely connected with the breathing process in which the forming forces stimulate expiration. Hence, the vowel exercises can be applied in all disturbances of the inner and outer exhalation.

The planetary spheres are the cosmic home of the vowels.

The creative forces of the Word resound through planets and fixed stars. In keeping with their inner possibilities of movement—in how many ways one can speak a vowel—they are connected to the moving stars, whereas the consonants belong to the fixed stars of the zodiac. From the nature of the vowels and planets the following arrangement is evident: *A*—Venus, *E*—Mars, *I*—Mercury, *O*—Jupiter, *U*—Saturn.

In the curative eurythmy course Rudolf Steiner characterized the five vowels—A, E, I, O, U—with leading thoughts:

A works against the animal nature in man;
E fixes the ego in the ether body;
I reveals man as person;
O reveals man as soul;
U reveals man as man.

1.1 The Sound A

A (as in *alms, art, calm*) is the sound of the beginning; it opens the *Alpha*-bet. Adam, the name with which man was called to consciousness, is like the epitome of *A*. It is often the first sound a child makes when, in amazement, it perceives the world.

In the eurythmic *A* gesture both arms are opened at an angle; one reaches into the world in two directions. An *A* gesture can be seen when a baby reaches out its arms while lying horizontally—a position the animal retains but which man must overcome as he gains his upright posture. In the healthy child *A* works physiologically in the first phase of life. In the ill child, one will be able to support the attainment of the upright position and a proper grasping the world with the senses through the *A* exercise. This also means that in cases in which a child wants everything or when the joy of eating becomes a craving for eating, *A* can be therapeutically applied. Pathologically, such phenomena are based on an excessively deep connection of the higher members of man to the body; therein we must look for the "animal nature" in man.

In this, the indications for *A* are given. It regulates the transition from astral to ether body and vice versa, for here higher and lower members work into one another; the specific organ of this process is the kidney system, as is described in the chapter on the kidney. Therefore, the *A* as sound has a special connection to this organ, and it unfolds its effect in the two directions of the kidney's activity. The proper astralization, the breathing through, and the light permeation of the stream of substance—a task of the kidney system—is stimulated by *A*. This connection to the kidney makes it comprehensible why the *A*, this single vowel, can also activate inhalation.

Besides this effect of *A* connected to the kidney radiation, it has, like the other vowels, formative forces that are connected with exhalation and excretion. We apply it in disturbances in this area and in deformations within the kidney area.

It is a characteristic of the vowels that they work regulatively depending upon the various organic situations in which they occur.

1.2 The Sound *E*

E (as in *aid, cape, way*) is formed by crossing the limbs. The contact thus developed leads to a focal perception of one's body that is characteristic of *E*. In volume I it was explained that the ego experience is always directed to a point. This is valid in relation to the environment; in defense against external assaults as well as in psychological experience, the arms are instinctively crossed in front of the face. This self contact in *E*, which always elicits a brief shock to the experience of the ego, is a consequence of a brief stopping of the streaming movement. Thereby, it is possible for the *E* gesture to impregnate the ether body strongly with the ego-organization.

We have two areas in the human organism in which the interaction of the ether body and ego-organization are especially characteristic. All disturbances that are connected with an excess or insufficiency of bile formation and secretion, including depression and mania, and which also correspond to vitalization, breakdown, etc., can be treated with *E*.

In the nervous system, the interactions of ether body and ego are completely different. The ego-organization works much stronger on the formation of the nervous system, making it possible for it later to live freely in the soul activities of thinking and perceiving. In all areas of the nervous system we find as a formative principle the exemplary crossing demonstrated by the optic chiasma (also in the pyramidal tract crossing in the medulla). The crossing of the optic axis is necessary for every visual process. An organically fixed *E* is thus present in the nervous system.

When this predominates constitutionally, we have the asthenic type in whom the ether body tends continually to stretch and become a line. Here, the second area of indications for *E* is given, that is, against "organic thinness," as this constitution has been described in the curative eurythmy course. Generally, the ego-organization always works via the astral body into the ether body, and by way of the *E* one can from the ego order the relationship of the astral body to the ether body. In a "thin person," however, there is too little astral activity in the metabolism, whereas in spastic phenomena there is an excessively deep interaction of the astral body. Through an *E* exercise, the astral body can be loosened in spasms and the *E* is thus active as a cramp-loosening remedy. It is understandable from this that in epilepsy it is possible to prevent an immanent attack by forcefully performing *E* movements. This, however, is not valid for every organic attack.

1.3 The Sound *I*

The *I* (pronounced as in *seat, bee*) gesture makes the human being manifest as an individual personality and is performed by stretching the body and arms. The upright posture itself is an *I*. The personality reveals itself in the upright bodily and psychological posture. Still more clearly, it is shown in a person's gait. His inner being can be detected in the way he walks, whether heavily, firmly, lightly, floatingly, sloppily, etc. The ego-organization participates intensively in walking; its activity is characterized by bringing imbalance into balance and constantly striving to lead over from the dynamic to the static. This ego activity is directly visible in the way one walks; it is a measure of the person's incarnation. Here, through the curative eurythmy *I* exercise, the ego-organization can be addressed in all those who "cannot walk properly."[2] Rarely is a person encountered today who walks with a beautiful, elastic, upright gait comparable to that we see in Greek sculptures.

The *I* exercise is also indicated when a person is prevented from manifesting himself as a complete individuality and suffers from various inhibitions, fears and compulsions. In the chapter on psychiatry it is described how the compulsive illnesses are connected with the lung. The sound *I* is connected to the planet Mercury, which is connected with the formation of the lung, thus the special connection of the lung with the *I*.

Because the free unfolding of the personality is enhanced and made possible with the *I* gesture, this exercise should be done with joy. This is especially important for children. To do the exercise without joy and under duress would be harmful. If it is impossible to do it joyously, then the goal must be striven for in other exercises.

From what has been said so far, the therapeutic application of the *I* exercise in various illnesses of the spinal column, whose healthy function is a precondition of upright posture, is also obvious. Often surprising changes can be brought about by the *I* exercise in all rigidities and deformations.

How the *I* gesture is made is always important. Balance in the spinal column is held between the various directions as they come to expression in the three planes in which the vertebrae articulate. Disturbances in right-left balance, propulsion, symmetries, etc., can be treated with the *I* exercises.

In strabysmus, an asymmetry of the eyes, the *I* gesture must be made primarily with the fingers and toes. In children much can be achieved with such an exercise.

When attention is directed to the striving of the ego-organization to establish balance, one is concerned with an activity in the metabolic-limb man; in terms of substance this is closely connected with phosphorus. It can be imagined that the ego-organization can work through phosphorus as it does through the sound *I*, that is, deeper into the metabolism when it is too weak, as in diabetes for which *I* is one of the main sounds and also in all states in which the formation of warmth is to be stimulated, as in circulatory disturbances.

1.4 The Sound *O*

The *O* (pronounced as in *boat, over, no*) makes man manifest as soul. This sentence characterizes the *O* sound. Poets always let the soul speak through the interjection, *O*! and it can express the entire gamut of feelings from highest bliss to deepest pain. In making the *O* sound, the lips are rounded and pulled together. In making the *O* gesture, both arms form a rounding that can be felt by all their muscles. It is a loving, embracing of something.

In the sequence of vowels in the alphabet, one is faced with the development of the human being. He incarnates in the *A* and *E*; in the *I* he is entirely internalized; in the *O* and *U* he again turns out into the world in excarnation. Schiller, in his letters on the aesthetic education, answers the question as to how the soul of man becomes manifest. He places the impulse for play between the form impulse and the material impulse. In the impulse for play the soul of man experiences itself. Thus, one can point to the realm indicated by *O*. It is always indicated where the free space for play has been lost. This is valid for disturbances on a bodily as well as on a soul-spiritual plane. Therefore, in chronic inflammatory and degenerative illnesses of the joints, the *O* exercises can be used.

As described above, the vowels stimulate the development of form. Where deformations of the joints already exist, the *O* exercises must be practiced in conjunction with consonants whose effects will be discussed later.

The formative property of *O* is therapeutic in obesity and in the tendency to become obese, which may happen when the formative forces from the nerve-sensory system penetrate the organism inadequately. The balance between the formative forces emanating from the head pole and the upbuilding metabolic forces is shifted to favor the latter; then the soul-spiritual becomes too active in the metabolic area. The *O* exercises lift the soul out of the metabolic system, freeing the formative forces of the soul so that they can work formatively upon the body with the dynamics of the nerve-sensory system. The tendency to become "round" is consciously projected outward by this curative eurythmy exercise. The procedure can consciously be enhanced when the patient's attention is directed to his obesity as he does the *O* forms. It is apparent that the *O* exercises will not be effective in all cases but only when the underlying cause of the described imbalance can be found.

Thus, *O* stands in contrast to *E*, which can heal the excessively strong formative forces of the nervous system. *O* and *E* can therefore be used for a general stimulation of the functions of the liver-gall system in which the *O* influences particularly the liver activity and the *E* the gall process.

1.5 The Sound *U*

The *U* (pronounced as in *too, through*) gesture is formed by holding the arms parallel. In curative eurythmy the hands and legs are pressed together, and the feet brought close to each other with the weight carried equally on the balls and heels. This gives the body a strong, enclosed appearance. The upright posture is emphasized, which reminds one of the *I* sound that rules all three directions of space. The *U*, however, is active in the vertical between up and down.

Man becomes manifest as an individuality through *I*; through *U* he manifests as a man, as species in the supra-personal sense. The upright body standing on earth differentiates him from all other beings of the world. While the *I* emphasizes the upright, *U* brings about firmness. In fact, one speaks here of a "steadfast" person, of one who "stands fast."

Through the curative eurythmy *U* exercise, the patient can learn "to stand properly." To do that there must be a harmonious relationship between levity and gravity, between lightness and heaviness. If a person is unable to do this adequately, he sinks too much into heaviness, and manifestations of fatigue rapidly occur. In many deformations of the feet, such as splay, flat, and weak feet, etc., the burden of heaviness is a visible manifestation. Such changes often lead secondarily to postural anomalies which in children, just as the changes in the feet, ought to be immediately treated with these *U* exercises before they develop further. Sinking and ptosis of the inner organs, varices, etc., are primarily indications of the predominance of heaviness for which the curative eurythmy *U* can be used. The *U* is always indicated when the form loses its physiological parallelism. This is the case, for example, in knock knees and bowed legs.

The cohesiveness of the bodily form is lost in the various tics. *U* exercises can be used successfully here. Holding oneself together is made more difficult when the ether-organization is influenced excessively by the astral body. This is also the case when diarrhea is caused by anxiety. Here, the astral body works too strongly into the intestinal organization. *U* forms lift out the astral body by the ego-organization and bring it under control.

The two words, "fear" and "courage," (*Furcht* and *Mut*) though psychologically opposites, can be encompassed with the *U*. Bone is the system in which this activity is found. In language, the *U* sound is used to describe the frightful and cold; in poems and fairy tales, for example, we find such phrases as "Oo, how cold I am!" In humans, the *U* works by rigidifying, pulling together, making cold. This process is necessary in the formation of bones, and wherever the process of mineralization is disturbed, as in osteoporosis, badly healing fractures, and rickets, the *U* must be applied. Wherever deformations are already present, however, it must be used with the consonant exercises.

The hardening principle in bone is localized in the cortex, whereas the spongy bone of the marrow is the carrier of continuously renewed life. The warmth-blood process emanating from the breakdown processes, gives us the other side of the *U*, the force with which man wrestles free from the earth heaviness to devote himself to the spirit. In this sense, *U* works against being unable to stand properly bodily as well as soul-spiritually. Man should stand firmly on the earth as man, enthusiastically striving to the spirit.

2. The Consonants

The consonants form the covering, the supporting structure for what resounds in the vowel as soul-spiritual life. Vowels are formed primarily on the stream of the breath, but the accompanying movements of the organism are much more evident when consonants are spoken. In curative eurythmy the sound gestures for consonants also bring the body much more strongly into movement than the vowel forms.

The creative forces of the zodiac are active in the consonants. Here, the formative forces give external form to man. These work also in nature and can be perceived in the gestures of a blossoming bud, for example. In the elemental environment, the blowing wind, and the rustling water, we are confronted by consonantal elements, too.

When the inner soul life is expressed in poetry, the lyrical element of the vowels dominates, but in the epic description of an event the plastic force of the consonants is used predominately.

While man finds himself in the vowel, he integrates himself into the being of the world through the consonants. The consonants regulate the relationship of man to world, of world to man. Nothing of the environment may enter the organism untransformed. This applies especially to the metabolic system; an important example is nutrition. Here, the consonants unfold their therapeutic power; the overcoming of nature in digestion is supported by them.

But the loosening, activating force of consonantal curative eurythmy can also be helpful when a patient cannot enter into a proper relationship with the world, that is, cannot get outside himself and thus suffers various inhibitions and phobias. An organic situation that corresponds to these soul phenomena is present when an organ can no longer integrate itself harmoniously into the organismic whole as, for example, an arthritic joint. These vitalizing, constructive forces are connected with inspiration. With the exception of *M*, all consonants work by enhancing the breathing in.

When the movements for the consonants are done in curative eurythmy, the person doing them must also form an inner picture of the sequence of movements and the bodily postures he assumes. Through this objective consciousness, the working of the formative forces is enhanced.

The consonants are distinguished on the basis of their place of origin—lip, teeth or palate. This division is related to the threefold human being—the lip sounds have a closer relationship to the upper organization; teeth sounds bring upper and lower organization into balance; palatal sounds are connected with the metabolic-limb system. These connections can be experienced directly in the movements of eurythmy in the contrast between the active movement of the palate sounds and the quiet lip sounds; the tooth sounds have a middle position.

Another division of the consonants is that of push, blow, flutter, and wave sounds; these are based on the movements of speech.

Push sounds:	B, P, D, T, G, K, M, N
Blow sounds:	H, V, F, S, Sh, Ch
Flutter sound:	R (rolled)
Wave sound:	L

Push and blow sounds behave in a way opposite to each other. In speaking the blow sounds, one wants to leave oneself too much, wants to devote oneself to something outside, to influence what is outside; in the push sounds it is difficult to move outward, and one wants to remain within. The colloquialism, "to give oneself a push" to do something, expresses this. Eurythmically, blow and push sounds are differently formed. In the push sounds the attempt is made to present clearly the plasticity of the sounds, and at their termination the movement is held for a moment. The blow sounds, however, stream out; the movements for the sounds are followed with the entire body. Wave and flutter sounds are intermediate.

The division of the consonants points to their relationship to the elements. The solidifying activity of the push sounds is connected with the earthly, the solid. The wave sound *L* works formatively in the realm of the fluid. In the airy, the flutter sound *R* is active. Warmth lives in the streaming out of the blow sounds.

As examples, only the consonants *L, R, S, T, M* will be discussed in more detail. A complete exposition would lead too far. (See note 1 for available literature.)

2.1 The Sound *L*

L is the only wave sound. When one speaks *L* and holds the sound, something of the character of the sound can be experienced as gliding, supple, soft, rhythmically swelling up and down. Rhythmic repetition is part of the being of a wave and also of *L*. Its position in words is indicative of its manifold activity and the extent of its application.[3] In the eurythmic gesture, one confronts a most complex movement. While the entire body moves elastically backward and forward, rocking on feet and toes, the movement of the arms strives upward. Rudolf Steiner characterized *L* as "what is creative and formative in all things and beings; it is the formative force that overcomes matter."[4]

We have an image of this *L* before us in plant forms. The roots of a plant develop downward and take hold of matter. Then the plant sends living, streaming substance upward into lightness, opens in the unfolding of the blossoms in the light, and in the formation of seed bends again toward the earth. This flowing movement of the living is the property of the *L* gesture. It dives into the realm of gravity and darkness and lifts substance upward into light and levity, forming it so that it does not spray out but rather remains in the realm of the flowing. The arms must become supple, since this movement is determined by the ether body. The *L* works in the fluid man where the physical goes over into the etheric. The formative principles work in the etheric in which the physical substance is taken up. The formative force of water can be expressed in the concept "streaming creation of forms"; this also characterizes the application of *L*. In practicing the *L* forms, special attention must be paid to the fact that the separate elements—the diving in, lifting up and unfolding—are harmoniously experienced even when isolated components in a special illness are to be emphasized.

Thus, the *L* exercises can be used wherever the activity of the etheric is to be stimulated. In all processes in which there is a drying, hardening and rigidifying that should be brought back into movement, where gravity is too strong and matter is inadequately grasped, the *L* movement works by directly activating in-breathing that is connected with the living stream of substance.

Next to *L*, the *M* is the consonant most often used. Because of its connection to the ether body this is quite understandable. It is always applied in conjunction with other sounds, and this topic will be discussed in greater detail in the section on sound sequences.

2.2 The Sound *R*

R is a tremulant, airy sound. When *R* is spoken, a rhythmic tremor in the expired breath develops. It has its rhythmic nature in common with *L*, but it is the much more active sound. The spirit of language expresses this in right and left; that is, the right side, which is related to grasping the outer world, is the more active.

It is the sound of rhythmic movement in itself; that is, the movement does not cease but returns into itself in a rotating way. Rudolf Steiner calls *R* "that which turns, rolls, rounds itself."[5] This rolling movement is brought to expression in the eurythmic gesture, and the body follows it in generalized movement.

Every rhythmic process is connected with the astral body, which lives in polarities. In the rotating movement of *R*, the poles inside–outside, center–periphery, are brought together in a harmonious connection. Thus, with the eurythmic application of *R* we can support all rhythmical activities of the astral body. In general, the active participation of the legs in the *R* exercise stimulates excretion. Rudolf Steiner indicated the *R* exercise to regulate the rhythm of elimination.[6]

The *R* exercise, performed primarily with the arms, works by regulating the metabolism, including the circulatory and respiratory rhythms. A special form of the *R* exercise, the so-called rhythmic *R*, is indicated in irregularities in the breathing and circulatory rhythms.

The cabala related *R*, *Resch*, to the sixth day of creation, the day when man is created as a being who can understand the world. *Resch* is the head of man gifted with senses. Perception of the world through the senses, the capacity to become conscious of the world, is made possible by the astral body. This activity can also be stimulated by the application of the curative eurythmy *R*.

If the life of the soul is too strongly affected by the astral body and the person is given over excessively to his sympathies and antipathies, then *R* can work in a harmonizing manner. This is so because of the participation of the ego in the *R* gesture. In the active, rolling movement of *R*, it is the ego that always retains control and guidance, and every gesture and movement returning into itself is addressed to the ego-organization. A turning wheel, whose axle traverses a goal-directed straight line despite a complex movement of its periphery, offers an image of this.

2.3 The Sound *S*

S is closely connected with the fiery element. It has a special place among the consonants. When it is formed in speech or eurythmy, the region of the will must be activated. S-s-s-s used as an interjection can immediately bring about quiet; will control arises. Next to S, *M* is the only consonant that has this independence of being and can be used apart from words.

To form *S* as a eurythmic gesture requires the fire of the will and strong formative forces in the person doing it. It is far-reaching, encompassing the catabolic as well as the formative activity of the nerve-sensory system in the metabolism and the metabolic activity proper; it brings both into a definite relationship.

The manner in which the digestive activity proceeds recoils upon the entire organism. Inadequate nourishment or digestion can cause states of tiredness and fatigue, or disturbances of the circulation that can bring about sensations of anxiety, headaches, and the inability to do anything. The organism is overcome by the unmanageable metabolic processes that result as a consequence of inadequate breakdown. The circulation of the bile juices, with separation and enteric resorption, plays an important role. The latter is especially important in unfolding the activity of the will. Here we have the field of activity of the S. The gall impulse—not so much the substantial formation and secretion, but the activity—can be considered to be representative of the S. The connections apply equally to the pancreas.

Disturbances that are expressed in these states and also in meteorism, excessively sluggish peristalsis and a tendency to stone formation, can be treated with the S exercise. Depending upon how the exercises are performed, one can work with S to activate or to calm.

The staff of Mercury is the image of S. Here, the force of the ego organization works to rule the lower astral nature, which is symbolized by the two snakes. Whatever is touched by the staff of Mercury is transformed; the old declines and the birth of the new occurs. The disappearance of the physical becomes the foundation for the development of soul-spiritual qualities, whereas the soul-spiritual, through the formation and densification of substance, can become physical.

2.4 The Sound *T*

T is a push sound that eurythmically demands a more strongly formed gesture. The body movement retreats behind the body posture. In the *T* movement the vertical is emphasized. It is a dignified gesture expressing a spiritual influence radiating inward from above, from the heavens to the earth. In language, too, the character of *T* can be seen in words such as *Tod* and *Tat* (death and deed in German). The connection to the vertical comes to expression in words such as *Turm* and *Tür* (tower and door), and with the densifying, tautening force of the push sound as in "halt!," or "hold tight!" The Hebrew *Taw* is an expression of the eternal nature of the infinite; the Chinese *Tao* means The Way and the divine ground of the world. In the ancient mysteries, *Tao* or *Taw* were experienced as sacred sounds.

In the human organism the spiritual influence that comes to expression in *T* is always related to the activity of the ego organization, which works from above downward. The intensive activity of the legs in the curative eurythmy *T* exercise is directed right into the metabolic area. The digestion of food, from the organic to the limits of the minerally dead, occurs primarily in the small intestine and is a function of the ego-organization. The alkalinity of the small intestine indicates that this activity proceeds in the realm of the etheric. This processing of food can be enhanced by the *T* exercise and it should be repeated until the patient becomes fatigued.

Thus, with the *T* exercise, the ego-organization is stimulated in the etheric realm. It is therefore used in illnesses of the gall bladder/pancreas and also in the heart and circulatory system. At every beat of the heart that is impressed on the blood stream coursing in time as a spiritual ego impression, we must think of the activity brought about by the force of *T*. With the curative eurythmy *T* it is thereby possible to strengthen the force of the heartbeat.

2.5 The Sound *M*

The sound gesture of *M* in speech and eurythmy is gentle, supple and warm. It is often the first consonant used by the child when it moves tenuously out into the world. In many languages the word for "mother" begins with *M*. Out of matter, which we must think of as being in the living stream of time, objects make themselves felt in space. Here, one has the two poles of "M": the infinite—*m*atter and *m*ass—confronted by the finite—roo*m*, ho*m*e, ger*m*. In between in the *m*iddle, *m*oderation, *m*an. *M* is thus a most comprehensive sound.

The active balancing of opposing poles is always a problem of rhythm. In man the forces that create balance are anchored in the rhythmic system, and it is with these forces that the curative eurythmy *M* sound is connected. That expiration is related to the predominance of the nerve-sensory system and the vowel element and inspiration to the metabolic-limb system and the consonants has already been discussed. *M*, however, is an exception; it works as a consonant on expiration. When the *M* exercise is performed, expiration is brought about by the movement and position of the body, and one finds oneself in the final phase of the transformation of substance in which carbon dioxide is exhaled as the end product of metabolism. Here, the *M* creates balance by being able to elevate the metabolic processes to the influence of the nerve-sensory system, where they can then be excreted.

Not only carbon dioxide is exhaled with every breath, but also warmth. The blood streaming from the heart into the lungs warms the respiratory air. The warmth of the blood arising from the will-warmth of the metabolic region is transformed into heart warmth and connects man with the world. *M* lives and works in this interplay of carbon transformation and warmth. It is the physiological precondition for the comprehension of world phenomena. That *M* regulates all the processes of the metabolic-limb organism that stream upward can be explained by these activities. Thus, the *M* exercise contains a certain complicated movement of the legs, the so-called Kiebitz step.

At puberty the metabolic system gains predominance over the rhythmic and nerve-sensory systems. Physiologically, this is expressed in the change of voice in boys, in clumsy movement and in psychological behavior. Pathological changes can be seen in juvenile acne for example. The curative eurythmy *M* exercise can be harmonizing in all these disturbances.

As a push sound, *M* has a connection with the earthly element. It is therefore applied in hardening processes of all kinds to permeate with warmth whatever is being solidified, thus bringing it into solution. Today, degenerative illnesses are generally predominant not only among older persons, so the possibilities of this method make the *M* sound one that is used most frequently in curative eurythmy.

3. Sound Sequences

Rarely will a single sound be applied; in most cases various sounds or sound sequences will be prescribed. It is possible that general vowelizing or consonantizing with corresponding indications, or definite sequences, can be practiced in curative eurythmy. There are consonantal, vowel, or mixed sequences. Rudolf Steiner gave particular sequences for certain patients, and thus, just as one can work on remedies for typical illnesses to discover the principle and direction of treatment, so also with these sequences the principle and direction for treatment with curative eurythmy can be developed. Since this presentation can only be aphoristic, only a few examples will be given to elucidate the significance of sound sequences.

3.1 The Sound Sequence *I A O*

The sequence *I A O* is the most important vowel exercise other than that of the complete vowel sequence *A E I O U*. The three sounds are formed one after another. The upper body is stretched with the inner experiencing of *I*. The legs jump into *A*; *O* is formed with the arms at the level of the heart, and all three gestures are held for a moment. Thus, a threefoldness is brought into unity. This experience corresponds to the building up of the human organism from its three members. The exercise is applied when the three members work inharmoniously together; for example, in "school illness." Rudolf Steiner called the *I A O* exercise a hygienic and therapeutic exercise, and it can be done together by children from different grades.

Among adult patients there are many disturbances, particularly of a vegetative nature, that are related to an improper interaction of the human members. This is applicable to the threefoldness of body, soul, and spirit as well as that of the metabolic-limb, rhythmic, and nerve-sensory systems. Both are encompassed by the *I A O* exercise. In *I* the individuality as spirit being comes to manifestation; in *A* it takes hold of the corporeality; in *O* it creates a soul space for itself.

Through stretching into the vertical, the head sphere, the region of thought force, is strongly experienced. The connection to the earth through the metabolic-limb man comes to expression in the *A* jump; the will area is grasped. The jump can be avoided, however, by simply moving the legs into the *A* position. One can often observe how one-sided these impulses can be today. This becomes perceptible in the heaviness of the middle, the region of feeling that lives in the rhythmic system, and it can be experienced in how difficult it is to form a beautiful

O, to lovingly embrace something. The sequence of sounds also becomes comprehensible. Thinking is most readily accessible, but the middle, the courage to feel, must first develop from the harmonizing of the poles.

3.2 The Sound Sequence *T L R S*

The sequence *T L R S* was given for a patient with multiple sclerosis. This illness stands between the inflammatory and the purely degenerative diseases of the nervous system. One can get the impression that the degenerative components predominate in a chronically progressive course of the illness, while the inflammatory aspect is predominantly important in the acute exacerbations. Later, however, the degenerative aspect also prevails. The proteinaceous substance itself degenerates.

The consonant sequence *T L R S* can be used to stimulate and properly shape the structure. There is something like a "formative phantom" in it. The *T* lets the ego-organization penetrate more deeply and guides the cosmic forces from which a patient with multiple sclerosis is too far removed back into the organism. It is particularly difficult for such patients to do *T*. The exercise addresses itself to the actual disturbance, the prevailing breakdown in the nervous system, and guides this into the metabolic system to build the proper digestion of food. Through the force of *L*, the etheric vitalization of the stream of substances is brought about, in *R*, the astralization, and *S* leads it into the field of activity of the ego-organization, which structures the anabolic process in an appropriate manner. How this sound sequence exercise is to be applied must be determined by the individual case.

3.3 The Sound Sequence *L M*

The *L M* sequence is the simplest and most frequently used of the consonants. It could be considered as a curative eurythmic breathing exercise in which the *L* intensifies inspiration and *M* expiration. It can be observed that patients today frequently breathe poorly, superficially, or arhythmically. At the beginning of a curative eurythmy treatment it can even happen that the patient will at first hold his breath; this can also occur during intensive listening. The inspirational pole predominates, either because inspiration is forced or because expiration is too weak, or both. This is connected with the tendency of our time that makes releasing psychological out-breathing, mirrored in physical respiration, difficult because of the continuous haste of an increasingly hectic life style. Contemporary events cause us to hold our breath, and it is interesting to observe that patients suffering from cancer, which leads into out-breathing, often have great difficulty doing *M*.

In this sequence it is important that the exercise is begun with *L*, which deepens inspiration, so that one begins with a superabundance of breath; only then is the movement led over into the *M*. This principle of starting with what is already there and then leading over to what is to come is frequently applied in curative eurythmy as well as in other artistic therapies such as painting. The action of the lungs demonstrates the primary image of a rhythmic movement. This is harmonized by the *L M* exercise. Beyond breathing air, this exercise can be applied in the various breathing processes of the organism whenever something that has rigidified or hardened is to be rejoined to the life process.

3.4 The Sound Sequence *L A O U M*

In this sequence consisting of consonants and vowels, the effect of *L M* is further enhanced. Whereas the *L M* exercise harmonizes the breathing processes, the *L A O U M* works more strongly on expiration. This is indicated in the treatment of asthma and glaucoma, for example. It has been shown that asthma is not an organic kidney illness but nevertheless presents a problem of the kidney system. *O* appeals to the forces of the soul, the middle, and the asthmatic, who threatens to lose himself, finds inner soul peace. Thereby *U* can become effective; his spirit being can unite with the environment. The fear connected with respiratory insufficiency in asthma can be dissolved with *A*, with *O* fear is overcome, with *U* courage for life can be developed. Thus, this exercise can be experienced in many different ways, just as it can also be performed in many forms of eurythmic activity.

3.5 The Sound Sequence *T S R M A*

This sequence was prescribed for patients suffering from hay fever. It is also used in the general therapy of allergies, which are connected with the astral body. In confronting a patient with hay fever, one can directly experience the disturbed activity of the astral and ether bodies. The reaction of the astral body is over-sensitive. There is, for example, an excessive reactivity to pollen, showing that its perception has been displaced far outside the organism. It is like an excessive but erroneous sense perception. The actual sensory region in which the astral body should be active can no longer serve its function; seeing, smelling, and tasting are inhibited and overcome by a watery, billowing ether body.

Through the strict *T* gesture one reaches into the environment and brings the fluttering astral body back into the body and under the control of the ego. The uncontrolled foreign proteinaceous process is grasped and shaped by the *S* gesture. Through *R* the watery is aerated and the normal sensory function reconstituted. The excessive warmth is exhaled with the force of *M*, which also frequently liberates the disturbed respiration. The *A* does not work in this sequence by activating inspiration as in the asthma sequence, but rather from the direction of the pole of nerves. The formative, shaping forces of *A* direct the activity of the astral body deeper into the kidney organization, fixing them and bringing about increased excretion.

This exercise can bring about an improvement of hay fever in a short time. How the sounds are performed, however, is of utmost importance, and the curative eurythmist must note in the manner in which the patient moves in which region of his body and with what degree of intensity the sounds must be practiced.

4. *Soul Exercises*

In the practice of curative eurythmy the heading "soul exercises" is given to a group of twelve exercises whose effects unfold through the soul. All manifestations of the human soul—thoughts, feelings, and will impulses—originate from the totality of one's being, and these various soul activities can be expressed with certain eurythmic gestures. To transform an inner soul experience into movement causes it to reach much deeper into the organic than it normally would. The ether body is especially influenced, becoming inwardly more supple and mobile. Rudolf Steiner, therefore, ascribed a didactic pedagogical value as well as a therapeutical hygienic value to this group of exercises. They ought to be done regularly by adults and children; patients should do them energetically.

When people doing eurythmy for the first time are observed, one can see from their movements that most ether bodies are quite rigid today and need to become more supple. Similarly, this tendency can be observed in the ever increasing illnesses of deposition and in sclerotic illnesses in which substances drop out of their living context. The reasons for this rigidity can be found in the soul, that is, in an inactive soul life, inadequate interest in the environment and the organic, sedentary living, inadequate nutrition, a disturbed warmth organism, etc.

Generally, only one or two of these exercises are practiced at one time. Since it works through the ether body, it is especially important that the exercise is done regularly and continuously. Other curative eurythmy exercises can certainly be combined with the soul exercises. Two examples of such "soul exercises" will be described in more detail.

4.1 Love—*E*

In the gesture of love, one attempts to express a feeling of love for something. A gesture encompassing a wide periphery is made approximately at the level of the heart. This gesture is then led into a forceful *E* gesture in which the arms are crossed in front of the chest. The exercise thus consists of two parts—the love and the *E* gestures. Two completely polar components are brought to a unity by alternating the gestures several times. In the love gesture a streaming out into the environments can be experienced, and the one doing the exercise ought to feel himself extended right out to the horizon. The point-like grasping oneself in the *E* creates the contrast.

In this exercise we have a primary image of the harmonious relationship of center to circumference. A point-like ego experience in the center alternates with a spherical ego experience in the periphery. The sphere then draws together again to a point. One takes hold of oneself in the inner space and experiences oneself in the stream of time. It is an experience of a rhythmical alternation of time and space.

Within the organism we have the polarities of center and periphery united in one system in the circulation. Here the love-*E* exercise works by harmonizing, vitalizing, and warming the system. The phases of the exercise are also directly connected to the activity of the heart, the center and representative of the rhythmic system. The gradual distension of the diastole corresponds to the gesture of love, and the rapid contraction of the systole corresponds to *E*. Then there is a brief pause, corresponding to the rest after the systole before the next movement is initiated. So we actually have a threefold exercise corresponding to the functioning of the heart. The polarity in the circulatory system brings with it the possible danger of illness through a one-sided predominance of one principle over the other; that is, one may either lose oneself in the environment, or solidify in the center. Hardening encompasses all heart circulatory diseases—from poor peripheral circulation to angina pectoris and infarct—that develop because of a predominance of the nerve-sensory system. The other group of illnesses include "restless heart" syndrome, serious rhythmic disturbances, and cardiovascular collapse. The love-*E* exercise in the curative eurythmy therapy of cardiovascular illnesses can be applied in both cases; in myocardial infarct, however, it is naturally used only during aftercare. In each case, the aspect that must be particularly strengthened can be emphasized, for example, the periphery in angina pectoris. It is important to do the exercise calmly, breathing calmly and observing the pause.

4.2 Dexterity-*E*

One must have learned as a child to take hold of one's body in order to develop agility and nimbleness. It does not come naturally, which is quite evident in the clumsy, cramplike, inhibited, limping and other characteristic poor movements. With the so-called dexterity-*E* this clumsiness is addressed therapeutically and is practiced particularly with children. In this exercise, the child must alternately hit his knee with the lateral maleolus of his other foot while doing the *E* gesture with his arms. A twofold experience of self-consciousness is brought about by this exercise; it must be performed exactly and with concentration. The focussed, firm touching of the limbs, which may hurt, brings consciousness into the arms and legs. The deeper retraction of the astral body can also be expressed in the brief pains in the joints and limbs. The child gradually awakens his soul-spiritual aspect in his body and learns to use it properly as an instrument.

Tone Curative Eurythmy

Besides eurythmy as visible speech-sound, there is also tone eurythmy as visible song, in which the gestures for tones and intervals, pitch, volume, rhythm, and beat are expressed through regulated movements of the arms and legs.

Like speech eurythmy, tone eurythmy has a cosmic origin. The reality behind the concepts "harmony of the spheres" and "spheric tones" was still experienced until recent times. *Harmonices Mundi* was the title of Johannes Kepler's five volume magnum opus, and Goethe begins his "Prologue in Heaven" in *Faust* with the words, "The sun resounds as in days of old."

Speech eurythmy thus attempts to bring man gradually into connection with the spirit working in the cosmos, whereas in tone eurythmy it is more a matter of the world soul speaking to the human soul. Tone eurythmy appeals particularly to the soul forces of the patient. The major and minor modes, for example, bring man into a soul-breathing. In the major mode the movement flows from its point of initiation at the clavicles through the lower arms into the environment: Man wants to open himself joyfully. In the minor mode he encloses and separates himself off in the gesture of bringing his lower arms toward his heart: His soul experiences darkness and loneliness.

From the multitude of tone eurythmy elements, Margarete Kirchner-Bockholt and L. van der Pals have developed a number of tone eurythmy exercises for asthma, arthrosis, eczema, circulatory disturbances, etc. Certainly this area can be developed further in future.

The light ether is more strongly connected with the thinking of man, whereas the chemical or tone ether interacts deeply with his rhythmic and metabolic regions. Cosmic harmonies work in the formation of protein.[7] The chemical "laws" have as their basis the same supra-ordered harmonies of music.[8] Since much that hardens today enters the organism through life styles, eating, and medication, a wide field is open for tone eurythmy to work dissolvingly. As in sound eurythmy, the definite tone eurythmy exercises must be repeated daily for a number of weeks.

Preventive Eurythmy

From everything that has now been said about the effects of curative eurythmy, it should be clear that it might also serve as a preventive therapy. Thus, preventive eurythmy has developed, lying between artistic and curative eurythmy.

Today the human form is burdened with one-sided bodily and soul-spiritual activity from school-age on, and it thus tends to various deformations; to offset this tendency, this branch of eurythmy must become increasingly significant. The large group of disturbances that are brought about by the sedentary life style are open to such prophylactic treatment. Preventive eurythmy can be done in groups, thus improving the social, community building attitude of people. "Industry eurythmy," for example, is already practiced in various industrial settings.

The Difference Between Curative Eurythmy and Other Movement Therapies

The various kinds of curative gymnastics are the most important group of therapies apart from curative eurythmy. Certainly it will be necessary in many cases to perform gymnastic exercises. They are fully justified wherever it is important to develop the physical body in its static and dynamic aspects. The movement system, with the participation of the circulatory system, can be brought into a state of balance in space through gymnastics.

In the autogenic training that is frequently practiced today, thinking, feeling, and willing are activated. The soul activity is directed to influencing certain bodily functions, the realm of the physical and ether bodies. No consideration is given, however, to the connection of man with his cosmic origin. Whereas in curative eurythmy an attempt is made to stimulate the objectively comprehensible formative forces in the organism, the autogenic training remains completely imprisoned in the subjective, carrying with it the danger of a tendency to egotism. This one-sidedness does not permit the full participation of the person's body, soul, and spirit that is possible in eurythmy and curative eurythmy.

The Rhythmical Massage of Ita Wegman

The extensive field of massage must be revised to include the spiritual scientific knowledge of man. Such an endeavor was started in the late twenties by Dr. Ita Wegman, founder of the Clinical-Therapeutic Institute in Arlesheim, Switzerland, now the Ita Wegman Clinic. She began with Swedish massage; with its five simple, fundamental movements it proved to be most appropriate for a modification by new guiding thoughts.

The new points of view are based on the knowledge of man's different members and of the various interactions of the three large, functional areas of the nerve-sensory, the rhythmic, and the metabolic systems. The theoretical foundations are to be found in my book.[9]

The rhythmic system provides a healthy balance between the catabolic nerve-sensory system and anabolic processes in the metabolism and is thus the basis of health throughout the organism. Breathing and pulsating circulation are the result of a rhythmic interaction of the higher members of man with the lower ones. This is a binding and loosening, a deeper penetration of the astral body, anchored in the air organism, into the ether body, which permeates and vitalizes the fluids. Rhythmical massage works first by strengthening the rhythmic system in which the self-healing forces are hidden. When successful, it brings irregularities into harmony again. Binding and loosening in massage have been spoken of ever since the time of Hippocrates, but the meaning of this becomes apparent only when it is realized that it is the astral body that is bound or loosened. It is at least a contributory cause of illness when it is too deeply or too loosely connected with the organism. It can readily be seen, therefore, that an effective treatment can significantly contribute to healing through this binding and loosening. To accomplish this, however, the organism must be fully understood. Every member of man's being works through the element akin to it. The superordinate spiritual principle works through warmth and can re-establish harmony, whereas the astral-soul principle works through air and the etheric life principle through water. In rhythmical massage the hand is able to imitate the forms of movements of these elements by working in warm, fluid, or airy ways, and the quality of the touch must be such that the activity of the therapist brings about a response of inner activity in the different members. Mechanical movements must be avoided because they estrange bodily activities from life and draw them into the purely physical, mineral, lifeless realm. Massage is the epitome of *hand* treatment. Furthermore, the hand is an image of man. It is flat and pointed—palm and fingertips correspond in their polarity to the point-like differentiations of the nervous system and to the metabolic system active on an etheric surface. Depending upon what one wants to stimulate, it is thus possible to differentiate in a living way to help re-establish the balance of both poles.

A further characteristic of this massage is that when one wants to affect the life processes that occur in fluids, the quality of the movement is directed more to the effect of suction rather than to that of pressure. In all living fluids there is a tendency to levity that is stimulated by the suction movements. Our living feeling immediately confirms this effect after such a treatment. Pressure, however, brings about enhanced consciousness and catabolism, an effect that is required when the metabolic processes predominate and breakdown must be stimulated. Special attention must be directed to the warmth organism, since in all healing processes the individual spiritual principle, the ego, must participate in warmth.

The separate parts of the human organism are connected in

many different ways. These connections are decisive in the localization of treatment as well as in determining the location of the illness. An unjustifiably excessive astral activity that brings about a cramp, pain or even inflammation in one location can be diverted by treating its polar body area. These polarities must be studied especially. Massage is always a holistic treatment that attempts to bring into balance a displaced interaction of forces. In accordance with the law of polarity, the astral body is integrated into the physical and ether bodies. We take it in with our first breath. On one side, it is bound to the metabolic system; on the other, the astral body is partially separated so far from the nerve-sensory system that it envelops the latter. In rhythmical events the members of man's being alternately merge with one another only to separate again. Illness develops when the peculiarity of one pole is displaced into another system.

Rubbing the various organs has a special place in the rhythmic massage. This consists of rhythmically rubbing the area above an organ, thus stimulating consciousness in the area and causing a slight awakening to better functioning. These rubbings especially must be done with warmth; they may last approximately two minutes and must be performed with concentrated rhythm. One could think of the sound to which the organ reacts, resounding or co-sounding in the depths, as it were. Since each organ is related to a planet, metal ointments are frequently prescribed here. The choice, however, must be left to the physician. The organ rubbings are indicated widely because some participation of an organ can be established in almost all illnesses.

It is evident from this brief description of rhythmical massage that it is not just another new technique. Rather, it presents a basic understanding of what one would fundamentally like to do with therapy in this area. Here we are attempting merely to describe the archetypal phenomena of the activity of massage; this can then provide the basis for individual treatment. The massage of the future, the seed of which exists in rhythmical massage, will have a significant task.

Today it is especially important to bring the entire field to a level on which the new insights into the interactions between the body, soul, and spirit can lead to concrete means of treatment. Hippocrates said there is no better way to make the soul feel well in the body than through active and passive movement. Curative eurythmy is an entirely new active movement that is based on the same foundations, whereas a new passive movement has developed from the principles of rhythmical massage. It is necessary today to perform movements on the body that will bring the sick person into a newly oriented, active interaction of his higher members with his organism and to facilitate this interaction so he can be given, as far as possible, the mastery over it.

Here, massage is an effective means of reactivating soul and bodily energies. It is a help in achieving either the necessary degree of incarnation of the higher members so that they awaken completely in the body, or the loosening of the higher members when they cling too firmly to the physical body or to one another. In the above-mentioned book, the anatomic bases for this new way of treatment can be found. The basic forms of this massage are brought into a system for the different body areas, and indications are given for specific applications, including massage of the organs with their special forms of movement. The book provides the basis for judgments concerning the free applications of these new massage movements that are derived from the body itself—from the living, ensouled, and enspirited body of man. Thus the possibility is given to lift massage out of the sphere of technique into the sphere of an art of healing.

The Therapeuticum: The Social, Preventive, and Therapeutic Task of Anthroposophical Medicine

A therapeuticum as meant here is designed to satisfy the longing that developed from the changed conditions brought about by living in cities. This estrangement from natural realms of experience depletes the constructive forces gained from traditional sources and increases the loneliness, isolation, and anonymity of large groups of people. The disposition to so-called psychosomatic illnesses that have been brought about by civilization is enhanced by one-sided occupational activities, excessive sensory stimulation of eyes and ears, and habits that contradict a healthy life rhythm with its corresponding nutrition of body, soul, and spirit.

Expanded by anthroposophical spiritual science, the art of healing can counter these newly developing social and hygienic conditions of deficiency with meaningful and healing activities.

The tasks are three: cognitive work and the communication of knowledge, balance, and healing. Correspondingly, the tasks of a therapeuticum are also threefold and consist of lecturing, artistic preventive courses, and artistic and physical therapeutic measures.

Let us consider the three areas separately. The spiritual activity of lecturing is in its character preventive or prophylactic. It is a guided conversation that can help the patient master crises and make possible a comprehension of illness through insight into greater relationships. The question of destiny and meaning in illness can be addressed here. This is hardly possible in the regular course of medical practice; yet this question is experienced by the patient as a most urgent need. The basis for this work lies in the anthroposophical image of man. Here, as in medical practice, appropriate waiting room literature can be of help in preventive therapy.

A patient's specific soul-spiritual states of deficiency can also be addressed by having him work with others in cultural events. These should be guided activities to meet the needs of specific cases.

The character of the artistic hygienic field is partially prophylactic and partially therapeutic–balancing. Its instruments are the arts of painting, modelling, music, eurythmy, and speech formation. The possibilities for activity depend entirely on the skills of the various therapists. These hygienic courses are aimed at human beings who in active artistic practice work together to avoid their deficiencies or illnesses as well as to balance any one-sidedness that develops from technology and occupational situations. Based on their own special artistic responsibilities, the leaders of the courses can be active quite independently in the realm of prevention. It is their task to establish a balance between artistic creation and special harmonizing exercises.

In the actual therapeutic realm disturbances of a pathological nature ranging from functional to organic illnesses are treated. Here, the activities of the curative eurythmists, the masseurs, the bath and artistic therapists are supplemented by the medical therapy of the physician. The indicated measures are prescribed exclusively by a physician in accordance with the individual situation of each patient. This forms the precondition for the activity of the therapist. Here lies the therapeuticum's actual field of activity. The patient himself is partially active in curative eurythmy, or in painting or modelling specific individual themes, or in physiotherapy; he is partially passive in rhythmical massage or in a bath. Besides the three described areas, there are various transitions. For the second and third realms, the essential factor is the weekly conference of the therapists, whose function is similar to that of the weekly meetings of the teachers in the Waldorf schools. If possible, the referring physicians, or at least one of them, ought to participate in this meeting. Ideally, there ought to be a regular exchange of experiences between all special therapists active in a therapeuticum. The reports of the masseurs or the curative eurythmists can often be of greater value to the physician than a laboratory finding. On the other hand, the therapists may be more conceretely active as a result of the image the physician has of the patient. Thus, there can be a fruitful collaboration between physician and therapists regarding questions of human destiny.

In this brief section the tasks and boundaries of a therapeuticum have been described. Such an institution will gain full significance only in the future but represents a demand of the times even now. The forms of therapy mentioned here supplement the medical and artistic measures that were described earlier.

Remedies

Mineral Remedies

To use mineral remedies properly, an understanding of the essential nature of mineral substances is required. This understanding is acquired through studying the physical, chemical, and biological properties of the substances. These properties are essential, but one must also go further, and out of these properties we must allow a picture of the substance to arise that reveals its true nature. In this chapter a few brief examples of this method will be demonstrated. Here the approach is to be found in the experience an observed phenomenon brings about. As these experiences are deepened, it becomes possible to arrive at a picture of the essence of a substance.

We usually evaluate substances by their physical appearance. In mineral remedies, however, it is necessary to pay more attention to their function in the total organism. The amount of a substance found in an organ, for example, says nothing in itself about its significance. Such information must be joined with insight into the function and the essential nature of the substance. We have mentioned in earlier chapters that iron occurs in the body in various forms—in hemoglobin, serum iron, cytochrome, etc. The same applies to calcium. When compared to the large amount of calcium found in the bones, the small amount found in the blood is insignificant. Considered functionally, however, it is of the greatest importance. Depending upon the state in which they exist, substances in different parts of the body have different functions. This is the case with phosphorus, for example, which occurs as ATP (adenosine triphosphate), etc.

Basically, the substances we plan to discuss here occur in two forms: either in a living, liquid state, or in a dead, mineral form. Every living liquid contains salts or minerals, but they are not dead. Like the water in which they are dissolved, they are carriers of life and other impulses. As we will show, the higher members of man's being rule these substances which are ordinarily considered to be merely lifeless ions to be interpreted by physico-chemical means, but which belong in reality to the sphere of life. They are not merely dead salts and minerals but rather part of a high living state.

Many of these substances can pass from the active, living, liquid state to that of the solid mineral. For some of them—calcium, for example—uric acid provides the transition, indicating that they belong to the ego-organization since "whatever comes into the realm of the ego-organization dies away."[1] In the transition to the mineral state, living forces are released and liberated that now become accessible for other purposes, especially those of consciousness.

Silica (Quartz)

The connection between the mineral state and the ego-organization is most clearly evident in silica. The entire human organism is permeated by a fine network of this substance, which can be found in all organs, particularly in connective tissue and the sense organs. Its presence in relatively small amounts, averaging only a few thousandths of a percent, long led people to underestimate its significance. Only recently has its biological importance come to be recognized.[2] The different concentrations of silica in various tissues are quite revealing of the dynamics prevailing in those tissues. This is seen, for example, in the different concentrations in the lungs, adrenal glands, and pancreas.

The alchemists' division of substances into the three categories of saline, mercurial, and sulphurous can be helpful in understanding silica and its opposite, the sulphur. The concept "sal," the saline, includes all that is salt-like. The concept "sulphur" includes all substance that has taken something immeasurable and imponderable, such as warmth, light, or life, into itself. These two archetypically opposed tendencies are mediated by the archetype of mercury.

Silica is a typically mineral, crystalline substance; that is, it has all the qualities of the saline as opposed to the sulphurous substances. The nerve-sensory system in man corresponds to the salt pole with its ruling, form-giving, and catabolic tendencies. These polarities become comprehensible through the threefold nature of the human organism. (See also the chapter on the heart.) Silica is thus the mediator of the formative forces, which through it permeate the organism. Understandably, the presence of silica is needed particularly when the human form is being created from the undifferentiated embryonic tissue. The formative forces do not work from within the embryo but from outside via the membranes, where the concentration of silica is exceptionally high. It is thus possible for the cosmic formative forces to be led into the living substance.

The amnion contains a large amount of silicic acid (22.2 percent SiO_2 in the ash),[3] and the skin of embryos and newborns is also rich in it. When one notes also that in adults the skin is much richer in silica than the internal organs, and that the hair and nails also have a high silica content, then one can infer that silica is especially related to the periphery. Familiarity with the nature of silica helps one to understand this. Silica in its purest form, quartz, is used in therapy and is permeable to light, but this is only an external expression; in addition to light, it is also permeable to other "imponderable" forces. Similarly, the sense organs are permeable to "imponderable" forces —the eye to light, the ear to tone, the brain to thought—and it is silica that enables these forces to stream in. These "forces" are sense impressions as well as the shaping and forming forces that stream into man from the environment. It is quite evident that the formative forces are especially necessary for the development of the embryo. Silica rich organs such as the hair and skin are, as it were, feelers, antennae, which allow the structural and formative forces to stream into the body, guiding them on further once they are there.

This assimilation of forces lies at the foundation of all sense perception, no matter how conscious this perception may be. The most conscious sense organ, the eye, demonstrates clearly that light, which can be understood here as a force, enters it or permeates its substance because the eye has been created by the forces of silica so as to be transparent. Every sense organ is unique, but the silica process is common to all of them. This is true even for the substance and functions of the nerves, which are involved in perceiving and then transmitting percepts.

Silica makes possible not only conscious but also unconscious perception. It is, for example, a perceiving function of the liver "to taste" the stream of substances passing through it, to recognize unsuitable substances as such and to eliminate them. Something similar is also the case in the absorption of foods by the intestines. In order to function in a harmonious and organic way, the organs must all be able to perceive each other. These functions assume or require the activity of silica; thus it is possible to approach them therapeutically with silica, or with plants that contain it in crystalline or dynamic form. The form-giving effect is essentially one of delimitation. Pure life forces alone would produce only growth but never form and only proliferations of disordered and undifferentiated cells or cell groups, as in bacterial colonies, would result. If there is insufficient silica, higher organisms are not adequately receptive to formative forces, and particularly in the young organism a retardation of growth and formation of the body results.

It is quite revealing that the silica content of malignant tumors is significantly higher than that of healthy tissue. In the blood as well the silica content is increased, though its excretion in the urine is lowered in cancer patients. In the sense organs, silica forms the basis necessary for their activity (see above). Thus the concentration in the tumor shows a tendency here that is physiological in the sense organs. In the tumor, one can recognize a "tending towards becoming a sense organ" (R. Steiner); there is a kind of sense organ formation at the wrong place in the metabolic region. On the other hand, "silica forms the foundation of the ego-organization" and mediates the formative forces.[4] From false distribution, a disturbance in the domain of the ego-organization can be recognized.

Tumor formation is a "failure to control the silica process on the part of the ego-organization." The latter, in a healthy person, works formatively on the life processes—the ether body, that is—by way of the silica forces. If, because of illness, the ego-organization does not have sufficient formative forces at its disposal, then its instrument, the silica, cannot be utilized and builds up, without being able to fulfill its actual function. The organism suffuses the tumor with silica, since this formative principle is absent here. Yet the essence of the disease is that guidance (the ego-organization) is lacking for the instrument (silica). Alone, it is impotent or is put to other service, namely for the "selfish" life of the cell, i.e. a foreign formation. The unitary structural principle of the organism, the ether body, is thus incapable of taking effect in the area of the tumor; the tumor becomes a living foreign body.

In this we see a situation corresponding to diabetes: here it is sugar—like silica, a carrier of the ego-organization—that cannot be grasped by the latter and accumulates. The fact that diabetes and carcinoma are close in other respects is known today (increasing common occurrence, "cold" diseases). For both the superordinate principle is the ego-organization, or a disturbance of it. From these findings one can recognize the partially deficient formative forces vis-à-vis the cell principle. (See chap. Cancer). Hence in carcinoma, suitable silica therapy is also indicated.

A low silica content in the connective tissue is also observed in arteriosclerosis. In the course of life there is a normal decrease in the intima of the vessels, but in arteriosclerosis this far exceeds the normal decrease. Simultaneously, the elasticity of the vessels decreases; this is viewed as a premature aging process. Accompanying these changes, there is an increase in the permeability of the vessel walls which allows lipids to be deposited in them. The role of silica in sclerosis has been experimentally verified but it is rarely used therapeutically today. One sees here the forces for reconstitution and maintenance of function of the human form, forces which are connected with silica. But it, in turn, is overcome in the course of time by its opponent, calcium. Related to this process is the overcoming of merely biological life—a necessity in old age; otherwise, one succumbs to sclerosis.

This delimiting function of silica extends to and orders other life processes. It indicates an inhibition of life, enclosing it with and metamorphosing it into forces of consciousness. Thus, silica represents the forces active in the nerve-sense system. On the inside as well, however, the organism requires a termination. This is given in the bone, which naturally is closer to calcium in its substantial make-up. Nevertheless, in the human being, the elongation of the bone and its finer structuring in regard to uprightness, show that a superordinate, straight, radial principle is imposed upon calcium with its essentially rounding tendency, as manifested in shell and snail formation. This superordinate principle is the ego-organization, which is served in this process by the forces of silica. Thus, the outward and inward growth tendencies are limited by the forming power of silica.

In the final analysis, this delimiting function of silica also brings about a separation from the "pure" natural forces. As was said above, the independent, mineral qualities of all substances entering the human organism must be overcome. This is the case in nutrition, in the course of which substances must be broken down and not be allowed to pass unchanged into the sphere of the person's own life processes. This is true also of perceptions in that light reaches the retina but cannot penetrate deep into the organism, etc. This overcoming of external influences is a process involving the activity of silica.

Forming, delimiting and overcoming occur in outer and inner life processes, weakening the life forces and thus providing structure. Silica thus proves to be an element of the ego-organization, for "what comes into the realm of the ego-organization dies away."[5] Higher spiritual life is possible only by virtue of the fact that lower, biological life, especially life other than one's own, has been overcome and transformed. Since silica is a bearer of the ego forces, one can understand that in diseases of the ego-organization, such as rickets and diabetes, the amount of silica in the blood is significantly decreased. The relationship of silica to the ego-organization also illuminates its aforementioned relationship to the pancreas, an organ of the ego-organization.

A further bearer of the ego-organization is warmth, so it is reasonable to say that silica also is connected to it. An inadequate or insufficient silica process can express itself, for example, as a tendency to feel cold or to have colds. Here, the warmth organism flows too strongly out to the periphery; the forces that form and delimit the warmth organism are inadequate, and silica in a high potency can often be most helpful (Quartz D60 injections once a month). A further sign of an inadequate silica process can be sweaty feet, which occur when the protein processes are not properly controlled and delimited so that breakdown products appear. Cold sweats can also occur. They do not serve to dissipate warmth as do warm sweats but instead represent a pressing out activity of the astral body, which does not work in a properly, orderly manner and thus stimulates the contractile forces of the nervous system in the wrong place.

In its purest form, quartz, silica manifests its essential relationship to light, being formed in such a way by light that it is permeable to it. This relationship is shown by the fact that radiating forms are found wherever silica is present. One need only think of the snow crystal-like structure of Radiolaria whose skeletons consist of finely organized silica. (In contrast, many Foraminifera with their calcium skeletons have the typical round, hollow form so characteristic of calcium.) The grasses, especially barley, also demonstrate this radiating form. In the human organism it finds expression in hair, whose thickness and constitution perfectly express the forces of silica. The nails are another manifestation of the silica process, a deficiency of which causes thin and brittle nails. Silica gives the necessary elasticity to connective tissue. They, along with the nails and hair, are influenced by calcium, fluoride and iron processes. Therefore, disturbances can also lie in these areas.

Generalized hypersensitivity of the sense organs and skin is a characteristic of a weak silica process. This must be understood as compensatory; that is, perception is based physiologically on silica, which also leads percepts deep into the organism. If the silica forces are too weak, then the ego-organization is not sufficiently able to act and instead the astral body mediates, causing a different kind of wakefulness and irritability that express themselves as hypersensitivity. Thus, one notices, particularly in children, a fearfulness or a defensive or subconscious protective stubbornness. Rudolf Steiner indicated that silica is especially suited to bring about the proper relationship between the ego and astral body.

In summary, one can say that a fine scaffolding of silica permeates the whole human organism. Its presence in such small quantities contrasts sharply with its great importance. It is actually a cosmic substance that mediates perceptive processes of the most varied kind as they lie at the foundation of the sense organs. In this network of silica one may well see the genetically oldest structure of the human organism; it is an expression of the image of man, which underlies creation and interacts with the earth. In the embryonic period, in particular, but also in the whole course of life, these relationships are mirrored in the opposition of silica to calcium. Silica predominates in the early stages of development and slowly decreases, while the calcium content gradually increases, expressing a later process.

Indications for silica therapy can be derived from what has been discussed thus far. The main indications are for problems of the nerve-sensory system and the skin, especially in inflammations. The higher potencies are most useful here (Silica D20 to D30).

Although the amount of silica in Arnica is quite small, Arnica is nevertheless a typical silica plant by virtue of its growth and habitat. It contains silica in a form almost specific for the nervous system. What is important here is the way silica is active in this plant. The total plant (Arnica planta tota) acts in a vitalizing, healing manner upon the nervous system, while the root has more regenerative effects and is indicated more in later treatment. Arnica is for that reason indicated not only for neuritis but also for concussions and other traumas.

Silica is basic to all sensory functions and thus can normalize the sense perceptions and support the formative impulses of the sense organs. Here specific compounds containing silica must be used for different problems, namely chrysolith or chrysolite (silica in combination with iron and magnesium) for the visual process, onyx (a special form of agate and thus a finely structured silicic acid) for the auditory process, jasper (chalcedony, a fine, thready silica tinged red by iron) for the olfactory process, among others. In all cases it is necessary to direct silica to the sense organs, but it must be in the form that corresponds to the specific organ.

The use of quartz in chronic diseases of the liver, such as cirrhosis, appeals to the dully perceiving and selecting capacities of that organ and helps to structure it. To treat the metabolism, lower potencies are used (Silica D3 to 50 percent, preferably with magnesite). The formative force of quartz is used to structure an overshooting or unruly metabolism—in chronic suppuration, for example, or migraine. Silica is indicated for migraine and for that reason is an essential constituent of Bidor.

Sulphur

Sulphur is a dynamic antagonist to silica. It is representative of the "sulphurous" substances. These contain the imponderable qualities of life, light, warmth, etc. Every living substance thus has a "sulphurous" character and is combustible. Sulphur itself is filled with inner, stored warmth that is liberated during "combustion." In contrast, the "saline" substances characterized above are structured in such a way that the imponderables cannot be found in the substances themselves but rather are able to stream through them freely (as light streams through a quartz crystal, for example). One can see that sulphur must have an inner connection to life. As prototype of the forces that can serve as a physical bearer of life, warmth, etc., sulphur can be found commonly in protein, and in almost every living substance. By virtue of its strong tendency to take up warmth and to store it in its substance, sulphur is turned more toward the supersensible than the physical; at least, it mediates between them. As Rudolf Steiner has said, "The world spirit works through sulphur." An expression of this quality of binding supersensible life to substance is the fact that sulphur is so loosely bound in protein. As soon as life ceases, sulphur separates from its organic connection; this can be recognized in the odor of decay and suggests that sulphur has the task of holding protein intact, keeping it alive and organizing it. Through its connection to life, sulphur is most active in the realm of the metabolism in the lower man. Here, also, it is seen as being opposite to silica.

The function of sulphur in detoxifying particularly metal and mineral poisons is based on the stimulation of the metabolism. Detoxification is a well-known function of the liver, which combines poisons with organic substances in a metabolic process so they can be excreted. The metabolic dynamic is thus related to the process of excretion, and therefore sulphur and compounds containing it can be used therapeutically to stimulate the excretory processes.

These facts help explain some known properties of sulphur, for example, its keratolytic quality of dissolving hardened protein. This process can be seen as an inflammatory, vitalizing tendency of the lower organism, as opposed to the hardening, catabolic tendency of the upper organism. Sulphur makes the physical body more accessible to penetration by the ether body.[6] The therapeutic use of sulphur is based on this idea. With sulphur the metabolism can be led so far that consciousness is diminished and vertigo or headache occur. On the other hand, with sulphur one can also facilitate falling asleep or deepen sleep. Because it stimulates the metabolism, sulphur is useful in all illnesses that result from a sluggish metabolism, such as arteriosclerosis, and in various diseases of deposition where premature or local aging processes arise chiefly in the realm of protein.

Finally, it has long been known that chronic illnesses that are in a state refractory to therapy can be reactivated with sulphur to become again accessible to therapy (Sulphur D6 to D30). The encompassing action of sulphur on the metabolic process, which proceeds chiefly in the venous areas, also explains its use in congestions in the venous system (varices). Here, one sees the tendency of metabolism to proceed from below upward.

Silica and sulphur, as dynamic antagonists, work hand in hand; the form created by silica is filled with substance by sulphur. Substance vitalized or enlivened by sulphur, however, is delimited, shaped and led to a higher and purified form by the "saline" silica.

Sulphur does not only occur physically in organic compounds in the biological realm. The so-called double bonds have internalized imponderables just as sulphur has. Substances of this kind have a sulphurous character that frequently explains their properties, use, and character. The degree of sulphurousness varies; sulphur-rich, highly active compounds can be found in plants such as onions, yarrow and horseradish. Their vitalizing, dissolving activity is represented in the characterized structure.

Phosphorus

Phosphorus is essentially similar to sulphur. While sulphur primarily internalizes warmth, phosphorus, as the name indicates, is a bearer of light. The luminosity of white phosphorus is well-known; it even ignites when in contact with air. By virtue of its low level of energy of activation, it is exceedingly reactive and so can easily unite with other elements. Through this property it is most suited to establishing the connection of the ego to the substances of the body. It is the bearer not only of light but also of the ego. Light is of a spiritual nature and thus related to the spiritual core of man, the ego.

The workings of the higher members of man's being are quite varied. The astral body lives in opposites that can best be seen in the concepts of sympathy and antipathy. In the organic realm these opposites exist in a correspondingly transformed way as in the contrast between hypotony and hypertony, hyper and hypo-thyroidism, etc. The ego, however, has the task of standing between them, governing them but not succumbing to either. Phosphorus supports the ego in this function. "In working from imbalanced states toward the development of those that are balanced, the ego requires phosphorus."[7]

That phosphorus is easily combustible also indicates properties that can be useful in therapy. In inflammations, especially with fever, phosphorus is frequently indicated. This may appear paradoxical since the inflamed body is thus heated up even more, and to a certain extent this is so. The fever, however, is not a pathological process but rather a symptom that is exceedingly meaningful for the organism. By stimulating inflammatory processes in a more fundamental way, phosphorus makes fever as such unnecessary. By using phosphorus in fever, one undercuts the process of illness. The effect of phosphorus is thus in no way suppressive of symptoms but is actually therapeutic.

Phosphorus is found in the human organism in various compounds that represent everything from a highly living dynamic state right down to the most mineral:

1. Its most labile form, which continuously breaks down and reforms and in which the imponderables are bound or released, is adenosine triphosphate (ATP). This is particularly important in the carbohydrate metabolism.
2. Phosphorus is active in the protein metabolism even though it exists there in small quantity. The phosphoproteins show, for example, by their presence in milk and egg yolk the importance of phosphorus in the incarnation process.
3. In lipid metabolism, phosphorus occurs in the form of phosphatides—for example, in lecithin in the brain.
4. A tendency toward the mineral state of phosphorus begins with the phosphates in the blood. These are, as it were, an intermediate state on the way to becoming a mineral state in bone. In bone the active quality of phosphorus comes to an end; there it lies firmly bound to calcium, resembling insoluble apatite in its form.

The combination of phosphorus with calcium is mediated by sugar. Sugar is thus a necessary mediator on the path from the soluble to the insoluble state of phosphorus.

Phosphorus thus leads the ego step by step into the body, and we can follow the sequence from a highly dynamic state with physical substance present in small quantities, to a relatively inactive state when it is deposited in large quantities in bone. Here we reach the end of the activity of phosphorus in the formation of solid and insoluble salts in which it has lost its active quality by becoming bound to calcium. It has become earth. The ego thus participates in the total metabolism by guiding, maintaining, and binding the necessary heaviness to the bone system as mineral earth substance. Therapeutic use of phosphorus can ease the ego's way into the body, thus stimulating the incarnation process.

The phosphorus in phosphoric acid is to a certain extent in an intermediary state between elemental phosphorus and salt. The combustion of phosphorus takes place, however, in the formation of the acid after oxidation. It has combined only with water. The actual earth formation then takes place in the formation of salt. As the acid thus is a stage above the salts, like non-material warmth it goes a step beyond air, water, and earth. We will be correct in classifying phosphoric acid with the warmth ether. It has been mentioned that it is also phosphoric acid, even though bound in adenosine triphosphate, that represents by far the most labile form of the processes of phosphorus in the organism. Here, the activity of phosphorus is at the border between the non-material and the material. Finally, the acid quality clearly points to a relationship with the astral body.

Ego	Phosphorus	
	↓	
	Phosphoric acid (Hydrogen)	Warmth ether
Astral body	↓	
	Sodium phosphate	
	↓	
	Magnesium phosphate	Light ether
Ether body	↓	
	Potassium phosphate	Chemical ether
	↓	
Physical body	Calcium phosphate (Apatite)	Life ether

The activity of phosphorus can be directed therapeutically to the various regions through use of the diverse compounds of phosphorus. In the sequence diagrammed above, which represents a stepwise descent of phosphorus into the physical, the greatest tension is to be found between phosphorus and calcium. These two neutralize each other to a certain extent.

The largest amounts of phosphorus and calcium (99 percent) are to be found in the skeletal system, said by Rudolf Steiner to be "the physical image of the ego-organization."

Phosphorus and calcium attain their "end" in bone, in which calcium as such is guided by phosphorus; under the guidance of phosphorus and with the help of sugar, calcium is integrated into the ego-organization.

Calcium

Calcium has many tasks in the organism. It deposits living substances and in mineral form gives us the completely physical structure of the skeleton. As living calcium in the blood, it participates in the metabolism of substance to counterbalance the catabolic activity that emanates from the nervous system, which needs this massiveness and heaviness. It also acts as a polarity to silica and its forces. While silica mediates forces that are brought in from outside, the forces of calcium work from within outward. Silica is active on the periphery; calcium as well as all carbohydrates are active within.

Calcium, which is characteristically found in the animal realm, has a clearly recognizable connection with the astral body, whereas the closely related substance magnesium belongs to the plant realm.

In reference to the nourishing, anabolic activity, Rudolf Steiner suggested the use of Calcon. This is not to be taken as a material application of calcium but rather for the stimulation of calcium metabolism in times of malnutrition. (This was first introduced after World War I for the students of the Waldorf School in Stuttgart.) By malnutrition we refer not only to that caused by a shortage of food but to a chiefly qualitatively one—the faulty nutrition that occurs so frequently today. Excessive nervous irritability as well as inadequate growth can be treated with Calcon though it is not indicated in the prophylaxis and treatment of rickets.

Calcon I consists of apatite—natural Calcium phosphate D6

with pumpkin blossoms. It is taken in the morning. In homeopathy, Calcium phosphoricum is the remedy for the headaches of school children, which occur when the nervous system is over-burdened and catabolism becomes stronger than anabolism. The application of Calcium phosphoricum diverts the activity of the ego to the metabolism, thereby unburdening the head.

Calcon II consists of Conchae verae (oyster shells, hence organic calcium carbonate) 5 percent with the addition of oak bark. As a shell fish, the oyster forms two shells. The outward excretion of calcium is polar to an exceedingly active living protein within. Such an extreme development of life processes —protein formation and the excretion of everything mineral— is found only in the lower shell-forming animals. The shells are formed by continuous deposition of calcium, which remains permanent after excretion, unlike the bone formation and calcium deposition in higher animals in which a continuous restructuring of the growing bone occurs.

The formation of the oyster shell, therefore, is polar to the life process. On this level life and death are cleanly separated, whereas in higher animals, and most extremely in man, the death and mineralization process is taken into the organism. It is no longer separated out. This is a precondition for a higher consciousness.

From such considerations one can arrive at the therapeutic application of calcium preparations, particularly when the life processes in the lower organism predominate. In instances such as a watery constitution, exudative diathesis, or lymphoid hypertrophy, when the soul-spiritual being is submerged in the watery life, one can administer Calcium carbonicum or phosphoricum to lead the etheric life back to the physical in a healthy way. Thus, the soul-spiritual activity is liberated to function in the upper organism. Also the vessel-sealing, dampening, antiallergenic effect of the intravenous administration of Calcium gluconicum can be understood from these relationships. In general, the application should be in potentized form as Conchae D6 to D10, but cranial entabes responds to D30.

Antimony (Stibium)

Although antimony is a metal, it is included in this chapter on mineral remedies because of its effects. In earlier times antimony was used almost universally as a remedy. Evidently the art of using it properly was lost, and it was banned in the sixteenth century. Rudolf Steiner repeatedly referred to antimony, and through modern spiritual science it is again possible to make use of its hidden, irreplaceable healing forces.

In nature, antimony is most frequently found in the form of stibnite (antimony sulfide), which consists of innumerable radiating spines grouped in bundles. This structure is an indication that it is subject to effects radiating into the earth from the circumference. In stibnite, antimony shows its inner relationship to sulfur, which is "to mediate between the spiritual and its formative force and the physical." In this forming process for which the ether body is responsible in the organism, antimony intervenes in a structuring way, primarily through protein. Rudolf Steiner indicated how the proteinaceous substance, especially protein forming processes, are confronted by the polar forces of antimony that work in a plastic formative activity; they give the necessary inner structure to living substance—protein, in particular. Antimony is able to do this because it meets "the activity of the ether body halfway."[8] In other words, it brings the formative forces of the higher members of man to activity within the ether body.

An image of this relationship of the proteinaceous to the antimonizing forces is the dividing cell, whose round form originates from the proteinaceous force, and the "centrosomes are called forth by the antimonizing processes."[9]

Here the therapeutic indications for stibium, that is, stibnite, are given. A deficient inner formative force in the blood can be at the basis of problems of coagulation. In these cases Stibium D6 may be quite effective, particularly when several millilitres are injected intravenously. One also finds an uncontrolled unformed protein process in typhus, which works itself out on another plane, however. In gastric and duodenal ulcers, and in ulcerative colitis, the same conditions apply, namely a disturbed formative activity that clearly comes to expression in ulcerative diseases; the astral body then works destructively on the mucous membrane. The ether body and the activity of the organism is "directed" by stibium, that is, by Antimonite D6 or Kalium aceticum mustibium. This is also the basis for stibium's effect in "calling forth a strengthening of memory, an elevation of the creative forces of the soul, and an inner cohesiveness of the soul constitution. The organism is regenerated from the strengthened soul."[10] This effect is also important for the "ulcer personality."

The formative force of antimony in its capacity to harmonize the astral and ether bodies is basic to its use in dermatological diseases. The balancing and inner form-giving activity of stibium preparations can be applied in bronchitis and pneumonia —for example, as Tartarus stibiatus, which is contained in Peumodoron II. In asthma, Stibium arsenicosum D10 to D15 given as injections can be quite helpful. In chronic bronchitis, Stibium sulfuratum aurantiacum, in which the sulfur component predominates, comes into consideration.

In higher potencies (D20, D30) stibium can also stimulate the regeneration of the disintegrating nerves in multiple sclerosis. Under certain circumstances the mineral berthierite is more effective, as is dyscrasite, the compound of antimony and silver.

Antimony thus takes a middle position and is the mediator par excellence between body and soul. It works in "what is active in an organizing way under the influence of the unconscious thought forces."[11] Furthermore, it is related inwardly to the human will. In this tendency it is active in a centrifugal, dissolving way. According to Rudolf Steiner, external application is preferred in weak-willed individuals, while it should be applied inwardly in those of strong will.[12]

By virtue of these encompassing effects, antimony forms "a strong phantom in man." This antimonic phantom was still perceived by medieval physicians and alchemists when they attempted to produce the homunculus in their laboratories. In the experiments they performed with antimony to activate its forces, the battle between the proteinaceous and the antimonizing forces projected out from their own being. The homunculus appeared before their spiritual vision as the image of this battle that is fought in the lower man where the will forces unfold. The alchemist's experiment was a process that led to concrete self-knowledge. This image-like experiencing of one's own (lower) being resulted directly in the moral impulse toward self-transformation. Thus, one can understand why Goethe, who was well-acquainted with alchemy, introduced the homunculus into his *Faust*. As Rudolf Steiner has pointed out, "He did it because he strove to represent in Faust the human being wrestling for self-knowledge."

Silica, antimony, and calcium can be represented in their relation to the members of man in the following way.

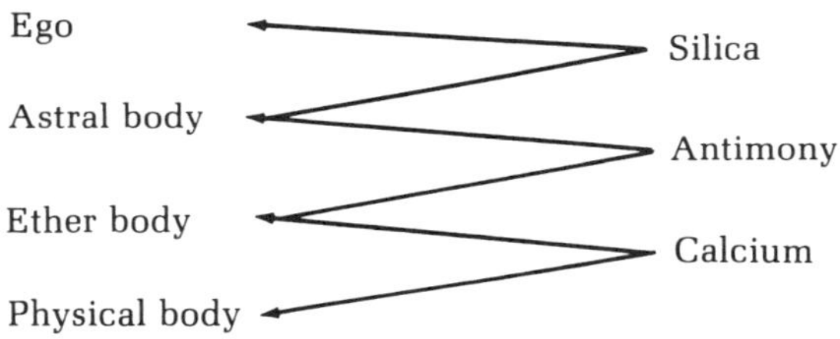

The activity of the three substances, silica, antimony, and calcium consists, among others, in establishing the proper relationship between the members of the human being.

A further understanding of the polarity of silica and calcium can come from Rudolf Steiner's comment that quartz encompasses the activity of the three metals lead, tin and iron, while calcium embraces the effect of silver, mercury and copper. One could also say that quartz attracts the three metals beyond the sun, and calcium pulls in the effects of the three below the sun.

Arsenic

Arsenic is chemically similar to antimony but has lost even more of the metallic character. The fact that arsenic immediately passes over into vapor without passing through the liquid stage when heated, points to its strong connection with the airy and thus also to the astral. In the organism, arsenic works similarly to the astral body. Rudolf Steiner used the word arsenizing as an equivalent of astralizing. Especially at the moment of waking, a slight physiological arsenizing takes place that is equivalent to the astral body's penetrating into the physical and ether bodies.

From this, the effects of chronic arsenic poisoning are quite comprehensible. Here, one finds weight loss as well as a pale, chalky facial color; even while still alive, the person is mummified by the excessively strong arsenizing process, and the astral body works to desiccate, harden, and preserve.

The indications for arsenic follow quite naturally. If the astral body does not tend to penetrate and permeate the inner organs, it then becomes difficult for the organism to break down food and assimilate it. Its vitality thus persists, causing irritation of the intestinal mucosa and the formation of a suitable soil for the development of pathological bacteria. Consequently, the most varied forms of diarrhea and enteritis can develop. Arsenicum album D4, D6 (better Stibium arsenicosum D4, D6) is indicated. In acute situations one would prefer charcoal or plant preparations—for example, Veratrum, the "plant arsenic." In general, arsenic ought to be used as the last remedy after the intestine has been cleansed and pretreated with these other remedies. Arsenic is then suitable to strengthen the condition that has been achieved through this therapy.

Generally, when the astral body has incarnated inadequately, the patient experiences it as fatigue, apathy, or depression. Often there is hypotonia. Waking is difficult, and such patients are often really awake only in the afternoon or toward evening. From the constitutional side, such disturbances can be successfully treated with arsenic but, from another side, phosphorus could also be indicated in disturbances involving the ego. This is the case chiefly when the astral body is too active, though not adequately incarnated, so that the patient tends to have insomnia (phosphorus D5, D6 mornings and at about two o'clock). Arsenic is indicated, too, when there are flighty thoughts, confusion, poor memory, and nightly states of fear (Arsenicum album D30).

Often in these situations of inadequate incarnation, iron is indicated. Here, the combination of iron and arsenic must be emphasized (Skorodit D6 to D10, which also counters fear). The effect of Skorodit D30 on infantile polio must be mentioned.

An especially fortunate and useful way to apply arsenic is possible with Levico water, which comes from a spring in northern Italy. In this water arsenic is favorably related to iron and copper. It is not only indicated in dull apathetic children, but in various hematological problems as well, and is used generally to stimulate the process of incarnation. The practical application of the Levico cure was mentioned earlier.

By virtue of being specially related to stibium, arsenic is strongly connected to the middle man; it unfolds its effect not only on digestion but also on respiration. The application of Stibium arsenicosum in asthma has already been mentioned.

Potassium

In the chemical sense today, potassium, sodium, and magnesium are counted among metals. One must clearly understand, however, that their metallic character is quite ephemeral. They are exceedingly "unrefined" in that they do not occur in nature as metals but as salts. Potassium undoubtedly belongs to the plant realm and to the ether body. As a matter of fact, there is not a single plant juice nor any living fluid that is completely free of potassium. Chemically pure water is more or less an abstraction; it is dead and cannot become the carrier of life. This can occur only when other elements upon which life depends are dissolved in it. Potassium is an essential element here.

The ether body takes hold of water and works into it through calcium. It is thereby connected to the plant realm and to carbohydrate and the general metabolism. In the human organism it can be found in all cells and is particularly significant for the liver and heart, which is understandable considering their connections to the ether body.

From this brief description the indications for potassium can be understood. Kalium carbonicum D6 makes it possible for the ether body to permeate water that remains excessively physical. If the organism is too watery, which is experienced most unpleasantly in the morning, and if this can be clearly differentiated from kidney or cardiac edema, then Kalium carbonicum D6 can actively reduce the water. The "cold" water can be revitalized, which means that the ether body can be taken up in it, thus making it accessible to the astral body for excretion.

Kalium phosphoricum D6 leads the ego into the stream of the watery metabolism. Especially when the astral body is activated too strongly by the nerve-sensory system (so-called nervous exhaustion, neurasthenia), the use of Kalium phosphoricum can bring relief; the ego is switched to the metabolic side and the nervous system can again be nourished properly.

A special pharmaceutical preparation that goes back to Rudolf Steiner is Kalium aceticum with stibium. Here the rhythmically forming activity of stibium is guided into the realm of potassium and hence into the watery activities. It is indicated in poor circulation, in all kinds of peripheral blockages that manifest in eczemas or ulcus cruris, and in psychological disturbances that can even manifest in cramp states.

Sodium

Sodium, which is chemically so similar to potassium, has a kind of adversary relationship with the latter in the biological realm. It can be found everywhere in the animal realm, but for plants it is almost poisonous. In contast to potassium, which is primarily found intracellularly, sodium is found in extracellular fluid. In the circulation of man and animal, however, both follow completely different laws than those governing the streaming sap of plants. The large vessels are where the astral body takes hold (blood pressure). By way of sodium, the astral body enters into and takes hold of the water organism. Potassium and sodium both have an intense relation to water. As the foundation for their interaction, however, potassium serves the ether body and sodium the astral. This explains the presence of sodium in plasma, urine, the cerebrospinal fluid, and in the liquid in the anterior chamber of the eye, that is, in all liquids that are not permeated by the stream of life. Beyond that it is extraordinarily related to the nervous system. These are all findings showing that the astral body utilizes sodium and how this is accomplished.

The homeopathic use of Sodium phosphoricum in all acid disturbances resulting from over-indulging in sugar and fats can be understood from these presentations. The formation of acids occurs because of an excessive activity of the astral body; through the combination of sodium with phosphorus, the ego is able to intervene in the realm of sodium—the water acid region—in an ordering way, whereby the acid formation is reduced and the cramping is relieved.

Natrium carbonicum (soda) was suggested by Rudolf Steiner for external application in poliomyelitis and other illnesses of the nerves, especially as follow-up treatment of encephalitis (20–30 gms. of soda per bath). Through the sodium, the astral body is diverted to the skin and is there released from imprisonment in the illness. Such a diverting effect is also prophylactically effective and is also a prophylaxis against flu.

Magnesium

A polarity similar to that between potassium and sodium also exists between magnesium and calcium. Chemically, they are quite similar, but there is a certain antagonism in their activity although they work together.

Through its occurrence in chlorophyll, magnesium shows its relatedness to the plant realm, while calcium, in bone formation, shows its connection to that of the animal.

Magnesium forms the basis for the working of calcium. Like potassium, it is the carrier of the effect of the ether body, whereas calcium mediates the astral activities just as sodium does. Thus, one also finds magnesium primarily intracellularly and calcium primarily extracellularly. These relationships, however, are not so clear as they are with potassium and sodium. Both are involved much more with the cell wall, and they touch the water organism indirectly rather than in a highly organized way.

Access to the nature of magnesium is gained from the well-known fact that through chlorophyll it makes photosynthesis possible. Here, a deep relationship between magnesium, light, and the forces of the sun is revealed; this comes to expression in the production of radiating light when it is burned. Magnesium is related to the sun and thus is able in a most specific way to take up sunlight, transforming it into life through chlorophyll in the plant. Magnesium is related to the light organism as potassium is related to that of the water. Both are, however, instruments of the ether body.

Half of the magnesium to be found in man is in the bones. This is to be understood to indicate that magnesium as a light mineral makes possible an inner light structure for the bones that is adequate for the ego organization. It is well-known that bone formation depends on the activity of light because of its dependence on the function of vitamin D, which is provided by light. In rickets, the bones contain more magnesium than normal; here the structure remains living too long and cannot be led over into the solid mineral state by calcium.

Apart from the bones, the other half of magnesium has an active, living significance, partly bound to protein, in the liver, striated muscles, kidneys, and brain. Although these are astral organs, the presence of magnesium in them is understandable from the previously mentioned interaction with calcium. Magnesium activates the intracellular enzymes, especially in the intermediary phosphorylization of carbohydrates. Here, too, the etheric behavior of the plant becomes evident particularly in its connection with the light ether.

The antagonism to calcium and the astral body is evident because their activity is switched off when magnesium blocks the liberation of acetyl-choline; that is, it works similarly to curare, and one can thus even achieve narcotic-like effects with magnesium. It is also applied therapeutically against pains and cramps that are brought about by the excessive penetration of the astral into nerves and muscles.

In a certain sense, the effects of magnesium and calcium touch or overlap one another, particularly when applied in substantial amounts. The guiding thought for magnesium is that it is indicated for an exhausted, overstressed ether body, that is, in excessively nervous, thin people. In contrast, calcium is indicated if an astral body does not take hold adequately, in which case the ether body can overflow, coming to expression in an allergic reaction or in a strong, seemingly healthy constitution. Other findings, such as decreased magnesium values in cirrhosis of the liver or hyperthyroidism, can be understood as expressions of a weakened ether body or an excessively active astral body. In all these illnesses, magnesium is also indicated. For its effect, the form in which magnesium is administered is essential. Magnesium sulfate (Epsom salts) is a constituent in many healing springs for liver and gall-bladder ailments; it has a purgative and choleretic action, but not in the above-mentioned sense on the intermediate metabolism. For this, organic magnesium compounds are needed (with ascorbic acid, orotic acid, sugar, et al.), or else potentization in order to achieve an "unlocking."

The combination of two light elements in Magnesium phosphoricum is frequently and meaningfully applied. Through it the ego is directed into the light ether. It speaks to the human light-form. Its effect is relaxing, and by way of the ether body it builds up and gives direction.

An inner lack of light can be found in depressions. There, magnesium is indicated, particularly in the form of Hepar-magnesium, which has been developed especially for this purpose (see chap. Psychiatry, vol. III). A further polarity is that between magnesium and iron, which manifests itself in nature as chlorophyll and hemoglobin, green and red, vegetative and animal life. Hence magnesium therapy can be necessary when the iron impulse cannot be properly assimilated.

Rudolf Steiner saw in magnesium a substance that has to fulfill important tasks in the organism. This is true particularly in the first seven years of life, when it must actively bring about the structuring and formative processes that stream from within to the periphery. This activity of magnesium can be externally visible in the sunlight radiating from the faces of children.

Fluorine

The magnesium process would, if it were one-sidedly active, bring about an essentially watery structure that would inadequately support earthly existence. Thus, an opponent to its activity is required; this is fluorine. Its forces act in the human organism as a "plastic artist," restraining the radiating magnesium forces and delimiting them. This "turning off and integration of the firm structure" is brought to a conclusion in the formation of the second teeth. Rudolf Steiner put the greatest emphasis upon a harmonious relationship of the two polar processes, especially in the first seven years. According to him, the proper balance between magnesium and fluorine is exceedingly important for this first stage of life. The first teeth can give an indication of the nature of the balance, based on whether the teeth are relatively too small, whether they erupt too late, or what the condition of the enamel is. All these facts are important for diagnosis and therapy. It should be mentioned here that the radiating form of dentine is an expression of the forces of magnesium, whereas the forming of enamel is subject to the fluorine process. Silica and calcium as a substrate also play roles in the formation and structuring of teeth.

The change of teeth is significant for the organism in that through it the ether body is partially liberated from being so firmly bound to the physical body; it can now be accessible for learning and other mental activity. The tooth is not only a tool for chewing, but also an indicator of the spiritual capacities of the human being. Thus, the proper orientation of the antagonists magnesium and fluorine is important for the total constitution in later life. In 1920, Rudolf Steiner pointed comprehensively to the relationship between magnesium and fluorine, as well as to the spiritually productive capacity in connection with the formation of the teeth.[13] These results of spiritual scientific research can be verified in every detail statistically as well as experimentally.

It has been discovered, for example, that mentally deficient and weaker students show a lower percentage of dental caries than normally developed children. On the other hand, many studies have shown that an inadequate supply of fluorine encourages the disposition to caries. It has also been shown that fluorine alone does not control caries but that magnesium contributes essentially to this process, which is dependent much more upon the relationship of fluorine to magnesium.[14] So, quite independently of one another, these studies of fluorine and magnesium, and of the intellectual-spiritual capacities, have produced results showing that all of these factors contribute to the formation of teeth.

It follows that such connections are not only valuable for medical therapy, but they must also be used in pedagogy such as that of the Waldorf schools. Here the child is educated, not in a merely intellectual way, but in a way that encompasses the whole human being. If one wants to stimulate tooth formation medically, that is, to stimulate the eruption of teeth, one will reach for magnesium, preferably in the form of Kieserit D6 (naturally occurring magnesium sulfate). For caries prophylaxis, Rudolf Steiner suggested chlorophyll applied as an ointment to the lower abdomen.

In the form of Calcium fluoride D4 to D6, fluorine can be considered for the treatment of enamel defects and caries and also quite generally to firm up the connective tissue. Here one can think of the ligaments of the joints as well as of varices and osteoporosis. In the human organism, fluorine accumulates in the enamel and also in the bones (as apatite: calcium fluorophosphate). Further, there are significant quantities in the skin, and in the nails and hair, wherever the organism closes itself off and hardens.

The occurrence of fluorine seems to parallel the occurrence of silica. As a matter of fact, they possess similarities even in therapy, but there are still crass and significant differences between them. The essence of fluorine becomes clearly apparent when one considers its physical and chemical properties. Of all the elements except oxygen, it is the one that has the strongest tendency to combine readily with other elements. It combines with hydrogen in the dark, forming a flame even at a temperature of –210° C. Similarly violent reactions, even explosions, occur in combinations with other elements. As an element, fluorine has the greatest chemical activity and is known as the strongest oxidant. It is therefore an element that strives with almost cosmic archetypal force to combine with all earthly substances, and it is also exceedingly difficult to separate it from these combinations. In nature, it is found primarily as fluorite, which appears in the form of little cubes, a form that is similar to that of sodium chloride crystals. Thus, it has a strong connection with the earth because the number four, which lies at the foundation of the cube, speaks of earthly forces.[15] In contrast, silica is and remains cosmic, which is expressed in the number six. This can be recognized in the shape of the quartz crystal, which is the expression of cosmic light forces. Silica represents and keeps these forces even if it becomes substantially earthly in its combinations. For his life on earth, however, man not only needs a connection to the cosmos but also to the earth, and one element that makes this possible is fluorine, the function of which delimits life. This is most clearly expressed in the enamel of the teeth, but it is also active in the whole organism. Rudolf Steiner called fluorine a "man-structuring process." An essential aspect of the being of man is an activity that delimits life and the connection with the earth. Thus, in its first seven years, the body of the child is formed in the balance between the two forces magnesium and fluorine. This balance impresses the primitive human form that originates in the cosmos into earthly etheric events. This happens in the field of tension between magnesium, which radiates from within outward, and fluorine, which delimits and mineralizes from without.

Carbon

As an essential remedy we must still mention Carbo, that is, carbon. Chemically, carbon is close to silica. What silica is to the inorganic world, carbon represents in the organic world, where it is the carrier of form and structure.

The name carbohydrates is fully justified. The water part of them, the hydrate, designates in a higher sense the vitalization of carbon. In the dry distillation, that is, in the forming of coal or the charring of wood, the whole plant structure remains recognizable. In the charring process, the separation of the being of the plant from its physical manifestation is initiated. (It is not until ash formation that this process is brought to its end.) The combustibility of carbon, however, shows that light

—"concentrated" light, in fact—and also warmth are still present in it. The intense presence of light in carbon can be seen in combustion: The bright portion of each flame is glowing carbon. This is even more clearly recognizable in the arc lamp.

Through its relation to light, carbon is also connected with the human ego. For this reason, Carbo helps in mastering the astral body. As a medication, Carbo enables the human being to "defend himself against the process of animalization that has entered in." This inner light-forming process is essentially connected with carbon, and in evolution is also bound up with the fact that the animal realm was expelled from the development of humankind. Compared to other substances capable of assimilating light, in carbon the phenomenon of light appears in conjunction with a structuring which in turn shows the kinship of carbon with silicon. The actual structural formation of plant, animal, and human being takes place through the carbon portion of the living substance. In carbon, the structuring force of light, taken up by Mg-Chlorophyll, comes to an end.

Coal needs strongly to unite with everything airy, which is shown in its combustibility and also in its capacity to absorb large quantities of gasses (activated charcoal). These properties can be utilized therapeutically by using coal in potentized form to enhance quite generally the permeation of the organism with air. Carbo is thus always indicated when there are signs of a disturbance in the air organism, which can, for example, be expressed in respiratory difficulties, including dyspnea. Since the kidney is the organ to which the air organism is subject, the application of Carbo in kidney therapy is understandable. Circulatory disturbances, however, especially acute circulatory collapse, are also an indication that the astral body is not taking hold. In these cases, Carbo D20 or D30 is applicable. It is also used in life-threatening situations to bring about a turn for the better.

In principle, meteorism and the corresponding intestinal metabolic disturbances are the same ailments but on a lower level. Here Carbo in lower potency but in substantial doses can bring about healing or improvement.

In general, the use of Carbobetula, birch charcoal, is quite adequate for Carbo therapy. The Carbo activity can be directed by selecting a plant specific for a particular organ; for example, Carbo equiseti for kidney therapy.

The Seven Metals[16]

Man is a sevenfold metal
—Rudolf Steiner

In contrast to other earth substances, the metals have a special position. They have properties that make them particularly useful in art and technology, almost forcing the thought upon us of a special relation to man. This inner relationship will be pointed out in what follows as it bears upon therapy. In this connection we expressly recommend W. Pelikan's book in which the phenomenology of metals and their essential nature is presented in detail.[17] In what follows, his point of view will be extended to medicine.

To begin with, it may appear curious that only seven metals are mentioned in Pelikan's book—lead, tin, iron, gold, copper, mercury and silver—especially since other metals occur in greater quantities in the human organism. The amount of the material, however, does not indicate the importance of the substance in the processes of the organism. The following table will make this clear.

The Seven Metals

Earth's Crust (elements in %, according to Clarke)				*Plant* (dry substance in %, according to Boysen-Jensen)	*Man* (elements in %, according to Hackh)			
O	47,3	Ti	0,33	C 40–50	O	64,43	Mg	0,027
Si	27,2	C	0,22	O 30–45	C	21,15	J	0,014
Al	7,8	H	0,21	H 5–6	H	9,86	F	0,009
Fe	4,7	P	0,10	N 0,3–4,5	N	3,10	Fe	0,005
Ca	3,8	Mn	0,08	The remaining substances comprise about 1–2% (at times, though, up to 20%). They are: S, P, K, Ca, Mg, Zn, B, Fe, Mn, Cu, Si, Al, Cl	Ca	1,90	Br	0,002
Mg	2,7	S	0,03		P	0,95	Zn	0,002
K	2,4	Ba	0,03		K	0,23	Al	0,001
Na	2,4	Cl	0,01		S	0,16	Si	0,001
					Cl	0,08	Cu	0,0004
					Na	0,08	Mn	0,00005

A relationship between metals and man is evident in the cosmic and planetary origins of metals and organ processes. Memories of an earlier knowledge of these connections can still be found in names such as mercury, which is identical for the planet and the metal related to it. The terms *saturnism* for lead poisoning and *aqua saturni* for lead water are evidence that in earlier times the effects of the stars were connected with definite metals, and these in turn were experienced as identical with definite effects in the human organism.

On the basis of his spiritual scientific research, Rudolf Steiner has presented the connections of planets, metals, organs, and processes in the human organism in a way that is appropriate to contemporary consciousness. From his studies, insight can be gained inot the seven different processes that constitute the functions and organs of the human organism. From this knowledge an understanding arises of the interaction of life, soul and spirit with related physical processes and organs.

Before the different metals will be discussed, procedures will be indicated that can enhance and direct their effectiveness. In general, these procedures apply to all metals.

At the beginning of a metal therapy, it is advisable to start with the vegetabilized metals and only later change over to the metals or minerals.

There is a special form of preparing metals that goes back to Rudolf Steiner. Here, the metals are subjected to a mirror-form before they are potentized. The metal is liquefied from its solid earthly state, volatilized and thereby reconnected to its cosmic formative processes. Not only is an exceedingly fine distribution and separation attained through the mirror-forming process, but the metals are removed from the earthly crystal forming forces and brought into proximity with the cosmic forces in the earth's circumference. This preparation of the metals is used when the formation of an organ or the re-formation of the soul-spiritual life in general is to be stimulated by the ego.

There are processes in the human organism that proceed in a polar way, but such that precisely through their continuous working together they create an organism in which man can live with soul and spirit. We are concerned here with seven obvious processes in the human organism, each of which corresponds to a metal, a planetary process, in nature. The therapeutic application of the metals follows this arrangement. Since, in the final analysis, one is dealing with the effects of metal therapy on life processes of the organism, one must consider that an appeal is hereby made in a special way to the activity of the ether body.

When the human being is observed without prejudice—and to some extent this also applies to animals—one can detect processes through which new living substance originates, particularly in growth. Here, the ether body is active, creating and maintaining substance. But an opposing process also exists in which substances continually fall away from the interrelationships of life and pass over to the dead mineral state. This can be seen, for example, in bone and tooth formation. The first process leads into life; it creates living substance. The second leads away from life to death; it creates mineral substances. These two contrasting, truly polar processes continually function in man. The first certainly predominates in youth, while the other, in aging, leads to death. They are expressions of the opposing activities of silver and lead.

Silver

As the moon is the celestial body closest to the earth, so the dynamic of silver takes hold of those processes that are first to go beyond earthly laws. These are life processes that have a cosmic origin. That they have a field of activity at all and are able to work into substance is due to the nature and dynamics of silver. Thus, the processes of vitalization, regeneration and reproduction—in general, all constructive processes that create living substance—are placed under silver. This refers to the function of the reproductive organs, whose connection to the moon is still clearly seen in the menstrual cycle, and also to the formation of new tissue generally.

In the course of evolution, the female organism, through the development of freedom, has become separated from its rigid relation to the moon rhythm. This cosmic connection has never been as strong in the male organism, in which the moon's effect is more functional. It is expressed in an enhancement of creative fantasy and general artistic activity. Herein lies the reason why men—at least, until today—were essentially more productive in the artistic and thought realms; their organisms enabled them to give more etheric forces to conscious processes. In women, these etheric forces remained bound physiologically. This does not mean, however, that this situation will remain the same for all time.

According to an indication given by Rudolf Steiner, the waxing moon primarily affects the vegetative processes and is directed more to the metabolic pole of the lower man. The waning moon exercises its influences more on the nervous function of the upper man.

Life can develop only in the watery realm, never in the solid and crystalline. Therefore, the point of contact of the effects of silver is essentially identical with the capacity of the organism to control the watery processes properly. The connection of the moon with the watery sphere of the earth is well-known.

The formation and growth of living substance are bound to light since the etheric organism is a light body. It is a silver process that takes up light and leads it over into life. The light sensitivity of silver salts is a final expression of the physical lawfulness of this fact. Organically, the brain is subject to silver and thus to the moon. Its form is completed earliest, and it is actually the oldest organ. Because the formative forces withdraw quite early and almost completely, it is almost dead, exercising its mirroring function by virtue of that fact; this is also typical of the silver process. In this mirroring function perception is made possible.

In summary, silver works primarily by enhancing the connection of the ether body with the metabolism. The nutritional process is thereby consolidated and the metabolism, which is concerned not only with resorption but also with building up living body substance, is strengthened. Ingested food is broken down and destroyed in the gastrointestinal tract—a precondition for resorption. The dead products of catabolism must, however, be taken up and revitalized by the ether body. That a living substance is thus newly created is a function of the silver process. It utilizes various substances, such as vitamin A, in its activity; they are its carriers and subsidiary organs. The disturbances of intestinal resorption that arise in vitamin A deficiency, particularly the occurrence of dry skin and the alterations in the mucous membranes, indicating inadequate life processes especially in the watery realm and bordering areas, point to the fact that vitamin A is a carrier of the silver process. This is explained in greater detail elsewhere.[18]

With silver, a connection is re-established between the earthly rigidification and the cosmic formation. The organism is loosened and re-opened for cosmic effects, and the preconditions are created for a partial rebirth from the bosom of the cosmos.

The symptoms of silver poisoning can be quite revealing to the relative medical picture of the homeopathic proof. Liquids are not resorbed properly and a tendency to watery diarrhea occurs, as well as tympanites, meteorism, burping, and various gastric disturbances. There are inflammations in the mouth, on the tongue, etc. These symptoms occur most commonly with dry mucous membranes of the mouth, neck and larynx; there is a consequent hoarseness. In animal experiments, dyspnea is observed with final paralysis of the diaphragm and respiratory arrest. Psychologically, dullness of thought, confusion, inconsideracy, fatigue, weakness and loss of memory are evident. Interestingly, time seems to pass slowly to these individuals. Time, however, is connected with the ether or time body. The damage and disturbance of the nervous system can go so far that temporary blindness results.

Headaches, primarily on the left side, which is connected especially with the ether body, can occur. The right side is more related to the earthly physical. These headaches can be improved by pressure on the head or by firmly binding it with a cloth; this stimulates skin sensation. The pressure causes consciousness to arise, thereby incarnating man's members more adequately.

This silver symptomatology becomes comprehensible from the way the members of man's being work. Relatively speaking, the ether body is separated from the totality of organic processes. It does not interact adequately with the substances so that a hardening, mineralizing process occurs, as seen in the drying of the mucous membranes in the upper body and neck and in the nervous system. Liquids cannot be resorbed, which means that they cannot be taken up into the ether body, and they thus pass through the gastrointestinal tract causing watery diarrhea. If, however, water is absorbed well but is not taken up into the ether body and instead accumulates as a result, then that is symptomatic of a disturbance of the potassium process.

Argentum is indicated for these conditions. Since silver enhances the binding of the ether body to the physical, it is indicated when this connection is weak. Naturally, this is true more of children than of adults. Children who unite weakly with their physical bodies and, in a larger sense, with their earthly existences in general, have build-up processes that are too weak. They will be pale, dreamy, often underweight and will look old.

At times, the ether body does not join the physical body as adequately as might be appropriate for a particular age. Here, the moon has an excessively strong influence on that part of the ether body that extends beyond the physical. This can lead to sleep-walking but it may also be connected with a pavor nocturnus and bedwetting. Whenever the symptoms depend thus on the moon, silver is indicated. It is best to begin with Argentum per bryophyllum during the waxing moon, and Phosphorus D6 when it is waning.

When this condition is carried over from childhood into the adult years, it can lead to constitutional malnutrition of the asthenic type or to a tendency to states of fatigue. Silver therapy is also indicated in atrophic processes in the cerebral area, and for stimulation of regeneration after injuries of the nervous system. The potency used must be high, for example, Argentum prep. or Nitricum D20.

Constitutionally, silver is always indicated when the necessary constructive processes are excessively damaged or limited by an overly strong catabolic process. Said briefly, if Saturn has harmed, Luna will help. On that basis, the application of high potencies of silver in febrile illnesses can be understood. When dealing with a consuming fever in which the ether body is unable to call up constructive forces, silver in D30 can be indicated, preferably as injection and if possible together with Echinacea. If the breakdown by the astral body or ego is too strong, then silver can "drive the astral and ego-organization out of the metabolic and limb system."[19]

This situation can also arise after a shock, so that the ether body cannot be rejoined properly to the physical organism, especially in the metabolic region. It can be caused by a psychological shock, an accident, or even birth, causing the labile connection of the astral body to the regenerative organs particularly to be disturbed.[20] The shocked astral body is then cramped into another region—the neighboring digestive tract, for example. Such cramps are frequently loosened by the application of Oxalis alone. Argentum (either as Argentum per bryophyllum, Argentum D6, or Argentit D6) is combined with compresses of Oxalis, 20 percent externally; one teaspoon to ¼ liter of warm water, applied to the body (solar plexus). One thus works directly into the center of the vegetative nervous system, the "brain of the abdomen." This Argentum-Oxalis therapy (so-called "shock therapy") has proven its effectiveness in applications to intestinal neuroses, shocks in the region of the metabolic system, particularly the genitals, and also in disturbances in the vegetative nervous system.

Since silver supports build-up and regeneration, its use in promoting conception is also understandable. The younger the organism the more its effect is indicated and intensified. If the silver process works on the most delicate substance of the body, the germ cell, then it is the basis for the origin and maintenance of the human form.

Vegetabilized silver, Argentum per bryophyllum as injections and liquid, is used to begin silver therapy. In these preparations, silver is potentized by the vitally succulent leaves of bryophytes. It is suggested particularly when as a consequence of the excessively active astral body the patient needs rest because of disturbed sleep. A hysterical component also indicates this preparation since Bryophyllum alone is an important remedy for hysteria. It retards overshooting soul forces and leads them over into the ether body.

The indications for silver can be characterized by the two words, build-up and excretion. Silver as a remedy helps to attain a balance between both poles, insofar as excessive build-up with inefficient excretion and a stunted build-up with excessive excretion can be treated with it. The accent lies in a healthy life gained from fluid, plastic up-building. Silver leads from below into a formation that is offered to the forming forces of the upper pole, thereby making a proper excretion possible.

In the soul, this polarity can be characterized by the two words somnambulism and psychological desiccation. In somnambulic and similar states the etheric catabolic forces of the lower person, whose excretions are often blocked, act one-sidedly into soul life, causing various visionary, fantastic experiences that arise from this lower region. In the unconscious manner of this region, however, he is also united with the world from which he gets extra-sensory perceptions. This "abdominal clairvoyance," as Rudolf Steiner called it, is inappropriate for contemporary man. Thus, it is pathological and requires treatment.

The predominance of the other pole, a certain desiccation, is more frequent. As a consequence of inadequate anabolism that is at times connected with an excessive excretion, the person begins to dry up physically as well as psychologically. The death processes of the head, the passive, soulless perception and the abstract, imageless thinking predominate in the soul, which thus gradually loses its life. The ennui emanating from the psychological deprivations of modern man is the first result of this condition, and the epitome is found in the cessation of all creative forces. The balance between these two extremes is to be found in a healthy fantasy, the actual soul silver process. It leads to new images and formations in the soul life just as the physically active silver process does in the physical body. In fantasy, too, the emphasis is on build-up, which here is united with the formative force of the upper pole. Thus during a proper silver therapy, one notices, besides the generally vitalizing effects, a stimulation of the life of fantasy. This allows the thinking to become replete with images again.

The combination of silver and sulphur, natural argentite, brings the metabolism into movement through the sulphur components, causes the blocked excretory processes to flow again, and stimulates the build-up of protein. It finds its application where there is a constitutionally weak build-up, cachexia and genital hypoplasia, in constitutionally excessively intelligent, usually small-headed children and also as an intermediate treatment in arteriosclerosis, in stone-forming illnesses, rheumatoid arthritis, etc. It stimulates excretion in the kidneys and in the digestive area. Because of the sulphur component it is less indicated in blond, sulphuric constitutional types than is silver.

The development of form that is connected with silver is addressed particularly by antimony's connection with silver; that is, dyscrasite. It is always indicated when a person overflows physically or psychologically, hence, in somnambulic or similar states. It helps to structure the blurring memory. In all these indications, it is the higher potencies that are required.

Silver, sulphur, and antimony are combined in pyrargerite. Through the silver, the vitalizing sulphur component, along with that of the structuring antimony, is especially active in the genital region and is indicated in chronic inflammations of that area.

Lead

It is obvious that processes occur in the human organism through which substances are led from the living to the dead state. One can think primarily of bone and tooth formation in which substances actually pass over into the crystalline, mineral state. Without doubt, these substances, such as mineral apatite that can be found in bones, did not always exist. Apatite was not introduced into the bones as such but rather originated from an organic substance. This transformation of living substance into the minerally dead can be designated a death process. In contrast to the lower animals, it is active in man and the higher animals. As is quite evident, however, the shells of snails are formed by a corresponding process that acts outside the actual living organism. But the bone and tooth formation occur within the organism, so that man takes part in this death process.

Just as life has the tendency to expand and grow, so an essential aspect of the death process is delimiting. Here the physiological foundation is given for man's feeling himself separate from the world, and recognizing himself as an *I* or ego. It is connected with the possibility of thinking. This thought process of separation, which reaches from physiological mineralization into the spiritual, was designated by Rudolf Steiner as the Saturn or lead process. As Saturn in the solar system, so does the lead process in man provide a border. Lead on the earth is the last material remnant of once spiritual living connections between earth and Saturn. Through it, the oldest and most widely comprehensive region is delimited. Two seemingly contradictory physiological functions of the lead process—formation and consciousness—are connected here. The strongest and most active growth is found in embryonic life, but this demands a similarly strong forming process to prevent disordered growth. This forming impulse acts via the nervous system, which develops first and is predominant in the embryo. To a certain extent, forming means the same as delimitation of growth, which, especially during this time, is as necessary as growth itself.

In the final analysis, the forming process works right down into the mineral structure, into bone and tooth formation. After birth and throughout life, the lead process is displaced into the processes of consciousness by the forming impulses, thereby making the entrance of the spirit into the organism possible. "We would not be human beings with spirits, but rather beings with body and soul, if these Saturn forces were not there," said Rudolf Steiner.

As long as the processes of consciousness predominate, as is the case during the day, aging and the death processes ensue. They increase with age and culminate in death. The polarity of death and life is preformed in the human organism. The sensory nervous system contains the oldest organs and life plays a small part in them. The youngest organs that are most removed from consciousness and full of life belong to the blood. The life of a human being springs from the tension of this polarity of the transformation of life into death.

The necessary transformation is a problem of the proper point in time. It can happen too early or too late. Thus, a growing child can develop well physically and blossom, but the soul's spiritual state will be dull; that is, the process of consciousness will be unable to penetrate and transform a predominating ether body. Here is an indication of a lead process that is too weak or insufficient, and the processes of consciousness can be enhanced by administering small quantities of lead. In younger children this condition can appear as rickets in which the forming and mineralizing is inadequate. How vitamin D can be recognized as a lead process has been described in another place.[21] Plumbum in a carefully administered form is also indicated in rickets and especially in cranial tabes.

It is obvious, considering the toxicity of lead, that only homeopathic amounts can be utilized. Then it unfolds effects that can be achieved by no other remedy. Especially in this therapeutic application, it can be observed repeatedly that it is not the quantity of lead contained in the potentized remedy that makes the difference, but rather the process, the dynamic effectiveness, that is freed by potentization. Particularly with lead medications, one can achieve practically the same results with quite a variety of potencies, even with the highest potencies in which lead as a substance is no longer present, as in Plumbum D60.

For the symptoms mentioned previously, in which the life processes are too strong and consciousness is inadequately asserted, Plumbum D6–10 is indicated. This can occur in children in which there is a deficient bone formation as in rickets, but it can also appear at a later age when the imbalance of the vitality and dullness with inadequate consciousness is present, or when there is inadequate delimitation against the environment, as frequently happens in most cases of allergies, including hay fever.

Lead is also to be considered in low potencies when the

organism requires calcium, as in eczemas that indicate a calcium deficiency. Then, occasionally Plumbum given with Concavera will activate the calcium by depositing it out of solution. Here, the profound relationship between lead and calcium, so well-known in geology and chemistry, becomes apparent. In general, lead rules and orders the salt processes. Because of the exceptionally deep penetrating effect of lead on the constitution, it should be administered only under the supervision of a physician and be dispensed only by prescription. The lower potencies especially ought to be given only for a few weeks, preferably a pinch in the morning and at noon, and then stopped. During this rest period, particularly in children, the positive effect of lead is stabilized with copper. If the treatment turns out to be negative, which will be expressed in loss of appetite and/or enhanced processes of consciousness such as irritability, poor sleep, etc., one can obviate the bad effects by giving Argentum or Argentite D6.

Although this lead medication, when given for the proper indications, can yield one of the most impressive therapeutic experiences, it is rarely indicated today. Because children today frequently suffer more from inadequate vitality, and the constitution is more marked by an excessively strong lead process, silver is indicated more than lead.

When lead is administered in such excessive quantities that poisoning occurs and the lead process works too actively, a destructive process results that takes hold of the whole organism and finally leads to its destruction. Even in this destructive process, lead demonstrates its relationship to the ego-organization and to the deadening processes, leading into mineralization.

Lead poisoning occurs most commonly when it is consumed in such large quantities that the organism is unable to excrete it. Then it becomes apparent that it is one of the most terrible poisons. It presses directly into the region of life. One of the first symptoms of chronic lead poisoning is basophillic stippling of the red blood cells, a sign of the profound damage to their life that finally leads to hemolysis. Further, hematoporphyrin can be found in the urine as a symptom of liver damage and disturbance of the light metabolism. The delimiting character of lead extends also to the iron process, so that iron can no longer combine with porphyrin. Lead penetrates all of the vitally important organs, damages and destroys their epithelia, takes hold of the smooth and striated musculature and destroys the joints. In the muscles, the extensors of the hands are involved, and their shaking tremor is a frequent symptom. Another point of attack lies in the vascular system. The blood pressure is increased; this is based on vascular spasms and is at first probably more of a functional nature. Finally, it severely damages the intima, causing endoarteriitis and sclerosis. Along with the general increased tendency to spasms, colicky abdominal pains, relatively frequent constipation and dysmenorrhea occur.

It is understandable that a patient suffering from lead poisoning feels quite ill; he will be anorexic, anemic and finally cachectic. Asthmatic episodes are an expression of the excessively active nervous system, the dynamics of which are no longer transformed by the renal system. The lung, however, is hardly touched by all this.

Toxic effects generally appear somewhat later in the nervous system. First, transient disturbances in sensitivity, which are easily overlooked and may be erroneously interpreted, can be observed. These disturbances manifest as anesthenias, parasthesias (the skin often becomes sensitive to pressure and cold air), neuralgias in various places, cramps including the legs, and visual disturbances caused by neuritis of the optic nerve. There can be transient blindness that ultimately becomes complete. Although all nerves are included in a disturbance that permeates the entire organism, it is nevertheless certain that the cerebral cortex is most strongly involved and the spinal ganglia somewhat less. Of the cranial nerves, the preference is for those of the larynx, the tongue, the eyes and the optic nerves. Thus, one is dealing with an exceptional involvement of those nerves that serve the conscious interaction of the ego in the organism; that is, thinking and speaking. In general, the ego-organization is invaded by the damaged blood and system of movement. The involvement of the cerebral cortex is shown in a decline of memory and comprehension; states of fear, melancholic and manic mood disturbances, and finally delirium and dementia are terminal conditions. Here, the ego can no longer interact sufficiently and thus predominates over the astral body, initiating spastic states. Lead dehumanizes the human being.

Women with lead poisoning have a tendency to abort; this is said also of the wives of men with lead poisoning. Lead passes even into the embryo, causing an illness analogous to that of the mother. It is clearly apparent that lead destroys its opponent, the silver process, which controls the processes of regeneration, the genitals and their functions.

Our time is characterized more by an excessive consciousness and lead process. It is expressed in a vitality that is deficient when compared to the man of five hundred years ago, and also all living and thinking is determined by it. The refusal to accept a living perception rather than that of the shadow-like images of our mental life, and the sharp outline of abstract concepts are effects based on the lead process. When they go beyond what is healthy, the death process becomes established in thinking. As a result, one-sided, analytic, atomistic thinking prevails through which the world disintegrates into multiple details without living interconnections. Then thinking is used only to register and establish the various details that are passively perceived through the senses. Finally, the sense impressions can only be grouped into superficial concepts. The "intellectual thinking" to which modern man tends—as represented by materialistic thinking" to which modern man tends—as represented by materialistic electrical theories of thought and as characterized by the end state of degenerative brain processes—when carried to its extreme, becomes primitive reflexive thinking. Thinking has been narrowed down to a fast-moving automatism in which the rigidifying component of the lead process is psychologically expressed. The ego becomes unable to remain in such a sphere so that one is finally dealing with the reflex reactions of the astral body, a condition that is common to animals: "Automatism unites with animalism." Thus, one can frequently observe exaggerated emotional reactions or the drive of an animalistic nature, all of which indicate astral reactions that are joined to the dullness and limited consciousness of reflexive thinking. This syndrome can also be found in various degenerative brain diseases, in brain damaged children and whenever the brain has lost part of its formative tendencies too early.

This way of thinking described here has become such general property today that its one-sidedness is hardly seen, if at all. Intelligence (measured as IQ!), counted as a gauge of spiritual capacities, encompasses only a fraction of the true capacities of thinking. Actually, thinking has potentiality and is extraordinarily multi-sided; it ranges from primitive, cunning common sense right up to wisdom, which is all-encompassing. The separation that is connected with the Saturn lead process brings with it, not only the possibility of ego consciousness but also the danger that the separation may be excessively strong, causing the narrowing of a spiritual area that will lead to the exclusion of other more encompassing spiritual capacities. Finally, only the one-sided intelligence that has been described remains. Insofar as one is concerned with an excessively strong lead process, it can be met with silver therapy. It is also a problem of education, however, in which man and his development must be placed on a broader basis that furthers not only his isolated intellectuality.

Alcoholism is another instance in which lead therapy is indicated. Alcohol specifically paralyzes the ego functions in the human organism. This is expressed in the disturbed upright gait, speaking and thinking in those under its influence. It also releases inhibitions, drives, and cravings that are no longer controlled by the ego, and the astral body becomes manifest in its animal nature. In addicted individuals, there is a relative soul-spiritual weakness of the ego, which, under certain circumstances, may have developed secondarily through the addict's failure to face a particular task in life.

Through lead, especially as lead oxide (minium D3, trit. D6 injection), the predominance of the astral body is delimited, and the ego has again a framework in which to work effectively. Naturally, the remedy alone cannot cure the addiction; it provides only the possibility to do so. It is the task of the physician to clarify the situation for the patient and to activate his personality so that he can use the offered help, practicing the control over his astral body by his ego.

Lead therapy is also indicated for sclerosis. Rudolf Steiner suggested a pharmaceutical modification of lead for this; that is, Plumbum mellitum. To produce this, lead is processed in a special way with honey, sugar, and warmth. The connection with the ego-organization is established through the sugar; the activity of the lead is harmonized thereby and its one-sidedness is expanded. In arteriosclerosis in particular, one is dealing with an inadequate breakdown of vital substances that are subjected to a hardening and deposition process rather than being broken down and excreted. Therapeutically, it is much more meaningful than the overvalued control of the consumption of cholesterol to stimulate the organism to process this necessary physiological product in the right way.

Frequently the entire physical organization becomes too dense, resulting in disordered salt processes and the most varied depositions. These can be approached naturally in many ways, for example, with formica, through which a re-membering, a re-integration of the rigidified life back into the life cycle can result. Belladonna also works against this tendency to woodenness. It is essential, however, that these substances are subjected to a breakdown process and that maturation occurs properly so that it is connected with the aging process. Then they are led further (for example, cholesterol broken down into bile acids and excreted) and do not enter the region of the deposition processes. The inadequate breakdown process that underlies arteriosclerosis is specifically approached by Plumbum mellitum. As Sclerone (Plumbum mell. D12), it is used above all for prophylaxis. For the actual therapy, the higher potencies are more favorable (Plumbum Mell. D20) and may be supported by Arnica, Belladonna, Formica, and Betula folium.

At times, silicic acid combined with lead, Plumbum silicium, may work better than Plumbum mellitum, or also naturally occurring barysilite, as trituration or injection in higher potencies. This can be used especially when consciousness is flooded by an excessively strong metabolism and one wants to appeal to the forming and enlightening activity emanating from above. Furthermore, Plumbum silicium can also be used in morbus Scheuerman to affect bone formation and structure with silica.

Once again, it must be pointed out that lead ought not to be used continuously. The prophylactic use of Sclerone should also proceed for 4–6 weeks and be followed by pauses of 2–4 weeks. Such "cures" should not be continued uninterruptedly. Sclerone is actually a "geriatricum" that is unique in its conception and activity. The principles of most geriatrica are based on the stimulation of declining vitality or the substitution of hormones, vitamins, trace minerals, etc. Development is not turned back by Sclerone, but rather a step forward is encouraged. The organism is assisted through the physiological metamorphoses of the formative forces that normally occur in aging, and that helped to unfold a free spiritual life instead of remaining in the biological realm. Thus, an active, encompassing, comprehensive spiritual life is the best prophylaxis against sclerosis.

The mildest application of lead is in the form of an ointment (Plumbum 0.1% unguentum) and it is primarily considered for local application in the treatment of cranial tabes. Furthermore, according to the principle of the vegetabilized metals, lead therapy can also be guided by the appropriate plant. Here can be named Plumbum per chicorium, through which the lead process is introduced into catabolism. It is indicated at the beginning of a lead therapy as well as in problems of fermentation and breakdown in the gastrointestinal tract as it is occasionally found in children as an expression of inadequate metabolic penetration.

If only silver and lead processes were active in man, his organism could unfold only between life and death. There would be no foundation for a conscious soul or spiritual activity. Other processes are necessary for that, and they act in such a way that a soul-spiritual activity extending right into the living substance is possible. This happens above all through the copper and iron processes to be discussed further on. In keeping with their nature, these are completely different from purely biological life. In nature, one can find a process whose specific task is to mediate, to combine opposites and bring them together.

Mercury

The substances that are only biologically vitalized by the silver process must be put in the service of the entire organism and led over into the higher members of man's being. They must not be allowed to unfold their own lives, which would be unformed and undifferentiated, because they would be free of the organism's control.

The process that brings this about is identical with mercury. It has been seen to contain mediating and combining forces since ancient times. Mercury, the messenger of the gods, mediates between heaven and earth, between the higher spiritual beings and man, and generally between the different spheres. In ages past, this world force that is active in the cosmos and man and experienced as actively emanating from the higher worlds was seen as the god Mercury. Mercury was the god of the merchants because it was their task to make adjustments between areas of abundance and deficiencies. In a higher sense this is actually a healing activity, which explains why Mercury was also the god of physicians. The original principle of healing lies in the adjustment of illnesses. Often, only a deficient or elevated blood value, etc., can be determined, but in many instances a correspondence can be found in another area. A deficiency of calcium in the blood, for instance, corresponds to an excessive irritability of the nervous system; in cirrhosis of the liver, which is a drying out and hardening of an essentially watery organ, too much "water" is found in the "wrong" place, as in ascites. The vitality that the diabetic lacks in his nervous system can be found in the "wrong" place and underlies furunculosis. The excessive growth of a tumor brings about a decreased vitality of the organism.

True healing will strive to remove what is excessive and also to put it in its rightful place. An important principle of healing is contained in the mercury process because of the inadequate mediation that underlies many illnesses. There is substantially too much of something in one place that is deficient in another, causing congestions. The mercury process dissolves these and brings movement into stagnation.

The metal mercury is the representative of this process and, in its purest form, shows it. It is understandable that not all disturbances can be treated with mercury, but this metal and its dynamics express the essence of the process. (Occasionally the disturbing congestion is caused by a deficiency that cannot be mediated by the mercury process and may, therefore, lie in the realm of the silver or copper processes.)

The essence of mediation consists in the mediator having access to and relationships with the contrasts. It must have the properties of both extremes and must partake in them.

If the mercury process is to carry life further, then it must be related to life and to its carrier, water. Through its liquid state and its striving to form drops, mercury shows its relationship to water; it also shows a direct tendency toward the living. Mercury easily forms a soluble combination with protein in the presence of salt. It strives to life, taking hold of the life process and guiding it into a higher level. Its well-known disinfective properties, for example, as a sublimate used to kill lower life forms such as bacteria, is based on that activity. In man, the area of the mercury process is there "where separating processes are formed in the organism that must again be taken into relationships with the total organism."[22]

Life processes that have become separated from the overall function of the organism are found in malignancies. Here, cells as living formed entities come to lead their own lives outside the borders and laws of the organism. True healing of such conditions consists not only in removing or destroying the exuberant growth but also in guiding it back into the totality of the organism. This is a truly mercurial therapy, and this goal is striven for through treatment with mistletoe.

Catarrhs are also examples of separations from the ruling forces of the organism. An organ that has been affected by cold is not permeated properly and so a catarrh becomes manifest. Through mercury the excretions can again be integrated and reabsorbed. The sulphur combination, cinnabar, is particularly effective in these cases.

The intensive connection of mercury with life and its tendency to take hold of it and carry it further are also the bases for its great toxicity. As a substance it is able to permeate the whole organism, passing from the mother to the embryo and to the suckling infant, destroying life broadly, especially where there are physiological transitions to dead mineral substances (periodontal disease, dental decay, and falling teeth). The nervous system with its decreased life is particularly endangered in chronic mercury poisoning. Tremor mercurialis develops, and later, polyneuritis, pseudotabes and its symptomatology of paralysis adjutans. Here we point to the polar metal stannum; in the potency of D6 to D10 it can arrest the effects of mercury.

It is a task of the glandular system, which is subordinated to the mercury process, to extend and permeate the living liquid substances with structure. Thus, all glandular organs can be affected with mercury, especially insofar as they are connected with the watery, mucoid processes, and this partly includes the nutritional. The absorbed, newly vitalized stream of nutrition enters the lymphatic system, the "region below the blood," by way of the portal vein to the liver, where the actual formation of human substance takes place. This process of mediation, this taking from the intestine into the blood—in which the venous circulation is dominant—is subordinated to the mercury process.

Thus, all disturbances of the glands as well as the lymphatic system and a part of the venous storage are indications for mercury therapy. Mercury rules the watery swellings, congestions, inflammations, and catarrhs in the gastrointestinal tract, and also the tonsils and mucous membranes of the eyes, nose and ears. The sulphur combination, cinnabar, is particularly indicated in chronically recurrent catarrhal states in the neck and sinus areas (pharyngitis, tonsillitis, Eustachian tube catarrh, etc., D6; sinusitis and bronchitis, preferably Pyrite D3/Cinnabar D20 tablets).

Mercury cyanide goes back to a recommendation of V. Villars for diphtheria—a stroke of genius! With this therapy the toxic components found in diphtheria are specifically attacked. It has proved to be of excellent help in diphtheria as well as in lacunar tonsillitis, etc., in which there is a similar, if weaker, toxic situation.

The lung as an organ is formed by the forces of mercury. It mediates in inspiration and expiration and in the vitalizing and destructive forces. The foundation for a heterotrophic life is given man and animal by this breathing process. It makes possible a higher soul life that goes beyond the biological vegetative life. Thus, one can appeal to the formative forces in the lung with mercury (in middle potencies) and, since the regenerative processes are quite minimal in the upper regions, at least inhibit the destruction that occurs in bronchiectases.

A constitutional mercury therapy is suitably begun with Mercury per-bryophyllum. This has proved itself in various compulsive phenomena that are based on the lung. Through the mediation of mercury, the therapy affords man the possibility of finding a mean. Mercury brings movement into a situation and as Mercurious auratus D15 is thus especially indicated in psychological imbalance and enhanced sensitivity as well as in rigidified depressive states.

Tin[23]

Of the seven metals, tin is closest to lead in its physical and chemical properties. It has the same relationship to lead as mercury has to silver, and as in these, the difference is profound, corresponding almost to another being.

While the lead process rules the mineral border between life and death, tin, like mercury, is a step above the polarity of lead and silver; that is, above life and death. The realm of activity of the tin process is not the firm mineral state, but rather the half-solid states that are typical of organic substances. It is well-known that salts crystallize from solutions, immediately passing from a liquid to a solid state. The same holds true for crystallized sugar; water similarly passes to solid ice. There are no intermediate stages or transitions. In the organic realm, however, there are all kinds of semi-solid inbetween stages, such as gel, mucous, jelly, oil, cartilage, etc., which are neither completely liquid nor truly solid. Here, the transitional states are especially characteristic.

A salt crystal manifests the result of death forces and also shows the corresponding forces that become manifest in the crystalline form. The form of the crystal system is thus determined by the substance. The radiating shape of radiolaria unmistakably reveals silica, while the round snail-like forms of the foraminifera are typical of the forms produced by calcium. Thus, in these protozoa and also in the siliceous, calcareous and horny sponges, in snails and bivalves, the forms are expressions of deposited substances that have been modified by the particular species. In higher organisms, particularly man, this is no longer the case. The bones, for example, are not formed by the inherent formative forces of calcium, but are pure expressions of the human or animal organisms that are better able to shape these forces. In the mineral realm, the inherent forces of a substance produce the form of a crystal. In the realm of the living, it is the building plan produced by the ether body of an organism that establishes the form. Utilizing the appropriate substances, it delimits their formative tendencies, overcomes them, and subordinates them to the higher etheric directives.

The semi-liquid state is particularly open to this organizing formative impulse. This forming and plasticizing of organic material comes about through the forces of tin. Wherever this semi-liquid stage occurs, the action of the tin process is to be found.

"Pure" water, H_2O, is dead, but a living liquid always contains salts, proteins and other organic substances and goes more or less beyond the liquid. This relationship between organic substances and the tin process is most evident in cartilage or the gel state. It is a task of the tin process to regulate and plastically form them. It is understandable that this means a processing of water, but it is completely different from the mercury process. It brings water into movement, decongests it and leads it further, whereas the tin process rules water, organizes and forms it, and as organic substance integrates it with the structure of the organism. This form-giving is naturally necessary, particularly so in the living watery substances. The establishment of the properly organized water metabolism is the function of the tin process. The forming and proper amount of water is necessary for the delimiting mucous membranes—the pleura, pericardium, joint surfaces, etc.—to function. The extremes of too dry, as in pleuritis sicca, or too moist as in pleuritis exudativa or pleural effusion, point to a disturbed tin process. In both cases the indicated remedy is Stannum D10, D8, as injection or by mouth.

In glaucoma the proper amount of water is also lacking in the vitreum, which shows the typical stannum consistency, and a special preparation, Corpus vitreum/stannum, has been put together to make stannum active in that part of the body.

In principle, the same conditions apply to hydrocephaly: Uncontrolled water is not integrated into the total function of the organism. Here, too, therapeutic experience shows it to be possible to control this illness by using Stannum D8 injections, D10 trit., and 0.4% ointment or gel on the forehead.

Arthrosis deformans points in a twofold way to a disturbed tin process and Stannum is primarily indicated. The substance, consistency, and formation of cartilage are typically affected by the activity of tin. When this is inadequate, it leads to a loss of cartilage as well as of form. Besides other therapeutic possibilities, Stannum is one of the principal remedies in this disease.

Connective tissue as well as cartilage also belong essentially to the form-giving living tissue. Its high silicic acid content indicates its formative forces. The many different disturbances resulting from prevalent and widespread connective tissue weakness, such as spinal and tendon problems, etc., are best approached with Stannum salicicum, that is Arandacite, along with silica-rich plant foods like barley and millet.

The liver is the organ that is formed by tin forces. Its consistency is typical of the half-solid state, and it is governed by water. This insight leads to a differentiated Stannum therapy with which the formative impulse of the liver and also the healing forces can be addressed. It should be noted that the impulse of the will is based on a healthy liver, and that all finer liver disturbances may appear to be psychological or psychiatrical, especially inhibitions, depressions and manic choleric outbursts. These, too, are accessible to Stannum therapy.

Copper

Substances come to be related to life and death through the polarity of silver and lead, the greatest of opposites among the seven metal processes. The "merely" living substances must be carried so far that they can take up soul-spiritual impulses; this uniting element was described as the mercury process. The transformation of these substances renders them capable of sensation, and it is brought about by the copper process. In man, it most closely resembles ripening outer nature; the same force is active in both. Here, a living substance is subjected to a new kind of transformation that does not entail continuous growth and new formation of living substance. Rather, its transformation and reshaping is necessary for new qualities—color, fragrance, taste, etc.—that can arise as an expression of ripeness. These are signs of an astral impulse and for it to be active, substances must be prepared and made receptive, and this is the task of the copper process.

This is a matter of the opening, yielding, and receptive component, which in ancient times was seen as a world force and given the name Venus. Opposing Venus is Mars, representing the active side, the iron process. The interaction between these two polar processes is much closer than that of the polarity of silver and lead (life and death), and they differ less.

One of the manifold activities of copper is the translation of living substance into blood, in which the ego lives in a special way. Here, copper works especially on the Venus side in being more subjected to the vegetative life. Relative to the stream of life, the transition from the lymph-glandular realm into the blood takes place here, and the stream of nutrition must also pass through this transformation. The organ in which this occurs is the liver. It takes up the venous portal blood and is the organ most rich in copper. Its copper content makes it possible to transform living substances in such a way that they can take up soul-spiritual impulses. Considered physiologically, this is the transition of the liver function into the gall process, that is, the working together of copper and iron. (That the formative impulse of the liver corresponds to the Jupiter tin process is not related to the liver process described here.) This is the basis for the constructive effect of copper therapy which is indicated because of its characteristic effect of furthering the blood formation and ensouling it, in contrast to silver therapy that vitalizes "only" in the vegetative sense.

In lymphatic children the vitality is congested and improperly permeated by the soul-spiritual. This can be an indication of a disturbance in the mercury process. Insofar as there is also relative malnutrition and inadequate astralization, copper is indicated. After puberty, which is a physiological astralization, this condition often improves. With the help of the corresponding constitutional therapy the situation can be transformed before puberty. Copper occurs earlier in organic evolution than iron. Although the mollusks and other lower animals utilize hemocyanin, which contains copper, in respiration, the higher animals and man have replaced copper with iron. Nevertheless, copper prepares the place in which iron can be active in them. Copper hands over the metabolism to the forces of iron, making room for them, so that an astralization is made possible. Thus, copper is also therapeutically effective in the formation of blood. Certainly it cannot replace an iron deficiency, but it may well improve conditions so that iron can find its "place." Thus, all hypochromic anemias are an expression of a disturbance in the copper process. Experimental and clinical evidence have confirmed the significance of copper therapy that was earlier recognized by homeopathy in these forms of anemia.

Copper also stimulates hydrochloric acid production in the stomach to produce conditions better suited to iron absorption. These forms of a possibly genuine iron deficiency are, however, disturbances of the copper process and therefore can be approached therapeutically with copper. Copper is not always specific enough, however. What is needed is copper that has been changed in the direction of iron, that is, cobalt, whose organic compound, vitamin B_{12}, is more specific in pernicious anemia than copper.

In nature, cobalt often occurs in the company of arsenic as a mineral—smaltite and cobaltite. The astral body is addressed by arsenic and is led into the blood-forming realm by cobalt. Here there are certainly still many untried possibilities for therapy.

The genetic priority of copper is also shown in embryonic development. The continuous increase of serum copper during pregnancy corresponds to the rise of the blood copper level in the embryo up to the fifth or sixth fetal month. Then the iron forces, whose place of activity has been prepared by copper in the build-up of blood cells, begin to predominate.[24] From what has been said, it will be understood that copper predominates in the constitution of women as compared to that of men.

Special mention should be made of the relationship of copper to warmth and life. As can be directly experienced, the element of warmth is connected with expansion, a greater capacity to absorb, etc. Thus, the copper process affords a foundation that stimulates warmth formation and distribution. Cuprum per melissum or Melissum cuprum culta especially work in this way by distributing and forming warmth. The activity of light in the organism, which is connected with the formation of color and the metabolism of pigments, is also a copper process. Here, however, the co-working of iron can hardly be separated. Firstly, through their working together, the human color, the *Inkarnat*, develops. The production and distribution of melanin, particularly in its pre-formed stages, and disturbances such as vitaligo, are subject to the copper process (melanin develops with the participation of copper and iron as catalysts). Thus, brunettes are more amenable to copper therapy and iron is more frequently indicated in blonds; this, however, is only a general rule. In brunettes, an astral impulse often cannot be taken up properly, which results in secondary disturbances.

It has been described how the copper process makes possible the correct interaction of the astral body by creating the basis for its action and opening substances and organs to it. This provides the indication for the use of copper in all kinds of cramping states. A cramp is based on the intervention of the astral body with the wrong dynamics, in a manner inappropriate to the organ or function. Because the astral body is unable to work into the metabolism and the substances, it secondarily attacks in the wrong way, that is, with the dynamics of the nerve-sensory system, which in the metabolic region leads to a contraction, a cramp. Copper therapy extends particularly to transformations and changes of chronic states, less so to acute states, and it is for this reason that it is indicated in stomach and pyloric spasms, leg cramps, pertussis, asthma, spastic constipation, epilepsy, etc. It can be applied locally as an ointment, but above all Melissum cuprum cultum is purposeful at first; this can be followed by Cuprum prep.

Chamomillam cuprum cultum particularly enhances the anti-spasmodic effect of chamomile; that is, the dampening of the excessively strong kidney radiations. Nicotianum cuprum cultum is especially interesting. Nicotiana is a plant in which a strong astral activity becomes substantial in the formation of nicotine. Through this preparation, the anti-spasmodic effect of copper is brought to activity, especially in the metabolism.

Because of its connection with the venous system, and also in its anti-spasmodic effect, copper is indicated in edematous swellings, venous thromboses, crural ulcers, flat feet, hemorrhoids and in peripheral vascular problems or circulatory disturbances. It maintains blood in a living flow.

It is possible to guide the copper process with various compounds. Copper sulfate enhances the constructive processes and is also active in the intestinal region in spastic constipation, for example. Cuprum aceticum is especially indicated in pertussis and asthma. In order to work inward, the carbonates are indicated such as Malachite D6 trit., which is naturally occurring copper carbonate, and as injection to treat ventricular and duodenal ulcers. Silica compounds such as dioptase, which is natural copper silicate, work on the periphery, the skin, sense organs and nervous system and are therefore helpful in nervous ailments which entail spasms, such as myoclonias (D30). The combination of arsenic and copper, olivenite, works particularly on the astral body and leads it into the copper region, hence into the venous circulation and the kidney system. Therefore, it is especially indicated in leg cramps, status varicosus, hypogenitalism, and cryptorchidism. A natural copper mineral also containing mercury and antimony is tetrahedrite (fahlore), which has an ordering (Hg, Sb) and anabolic (Cu) action on glandular metabolism (as salve 0.4% and trit. D3).

An untransformed astral impulse that has not been taken up properly is also present when there is an excessive sensitivity to the world of the dead, that is, if a connection with a person who has died does not continue properly. This can result in cramp-like abdominal pains and in ulcerative colitis, but such pains can also have other causes. Copper ointment applied to the region of the stomach, and also Cuprum D6, can bring about a healing effect.

An expression of an astral body that is working excessively strongly and cannot be received and transformed properly by the organism is the basis of hyperthyroidism or Grave's disease. With the rise in basal metabolism and the increased warmth, there is also a rise in serum copper. This rise is not an expression of the illness, but is an attempt of the organism to help itself in dealing with the fundamental disturbance. Copper is able to detoxify thyroxin, that is, to limit the breakdown of thyroxin. In addition, along with hyperthyroidism there is an excessive sympathetic tonus. The ergotropic, destructive forces are predominant. Copper, however, works parasympathetically, so that there is an antagonism between thyroid activity and the copper process.

In thyrotoxemia and Grave's disease the copper process is best stimulated by Cuprite D3, which is copper oxide. This is indicated more in light-skinned and blond individuals, while the sulphur combinations, Chalkosin D3–D6, are indicated more for dark-skinned brunettes. Cuprum sulphuricum D6 can also enhance copper build-up. Thereby, the breakdown activity of the thyroid is counterbalanced and the excessively strong shooting of the astral forces into the organism is diminished. Furthermore, in by far most cases, an elevation of the copper serum level is not a pathological symptom, but an attempt at self-healing by the organism. So, for example, an abnormal elevation of the copper level can be found in schizophrenia, manic depression, multiple sclerosis, carcinoma, etc. Characteristically, in carcinoma the iron values frequently behave reciprocally. The elevated copper values point to the organism's attempt to permit a more proper working of the astral body and iron. A therapeutic complement to copper is magnesium (magnes. phosph. or magnesite). Both substances show a polar relation to iron and have a spasmolytic action, stimulating or protecting the ether body.

The kidney system is formed from the forces of the Venus copper process. Its task is to switch the breakdown impulses of the nervous system into a guided constructive stream that is equivalent to an astralization and ensoulment of the living substance. This is then actually the task of the copper process and is the reason why copper is of central importance for kidney therapy. These conditions are presented in detail in the chapter on the kidney.

Finally, vitamin B_1 can be considered a carrier or mediator of the copper process, as has been presented in detail by O. Wolff.[25]

In the fullest meaning of the word, the copper process mediates constructively the taking over of the astral body into the ether body. This is exactly the function of the kidney, and it is therefore formed by and built from these forces. Since the air element is the carrier of the astral body, and the water element is that of the ether body, it can be said that bringing air and water together and thus producing foam occurs through the activity of the copper process.

In times past, these relationships were represented in picture form. The copper forces were experienced as a reality of the world and the names Venus or Aphrodite were given them. Their realm of activity was in the interaction of air and water, and they were seen as having been born from foam. They were most strongly experienced on the island of Cyprus. The name Cuprum or copper reminds one of that, and the metal can also be found there.

Iron

Iron has already been described in detail in the chapter on the third epoch of life and was characterized there with the essential physiological data as the metal of incarnation. The following discussion, therefore, will be limited to the place of iron in therapy.

The presence of iron in all the central parts of the organism makes it possible for man to work with his soul and spirit right into the body substance and to grasp and shape it actively.

The possibility of a substance being transformed by the spirit is bound to an element that allows such an impulse to penetrate right into the earthly material. To that end, this element must reach into both the region of the spirit and that of matter, encompassing them. Organically, this activity is connected to the iron process.

This role, which allows the ego to be active in organic substances and to permeate them, combining body and spirit, results from the special position of iron. It is the only one of the seven metals that is active in a dynamic way and that appears as substance in relatively significant amounts. This occurrence as substance takes many differentiated forms. Iron is found in hemoglobin, serum, cytochromes, and the nervous system, and in each it has a different task. More than with the other metals, it is therefore necessary to guide it therapeutically to the place where a desired effect needs to be achieved.

A strong iron impulse in the soul-spiritual realm can actually accompany an inadequate iron process in the gall bladder region or elsewhere. Then an undifferentiated iron therapy because it is wrongly used can even enhance the deficient symptomatology. So an excessively strong activity can continually demand too much of the relatively weak gall bladder, causing recurrent colics. The administration of iron in potentized form can aggravate the condition. In this case, the iron impulse in the area of the gall bladder must be specifically treated, for example, with Ferrum per chelidonium, and must occasionally be supported by the corresponding gall bladder therapy.

The functional multiplicity of iron is also expressed in the large number of elements related to it, such as cobalt, nickel, manganese, chromium, vanadium, etc., all of which belong to the iron group. Their use in medicine has hardly been touched, and they still present extraordinary possibilities.

The iron curve clearly shows that it plays a relatively unimportant role in earliest childhood, when it is of prime importance for the incarnation process to be constructively stimulated. This is best done with Ferrum per urticam, which has proven itself in pediatrics especially after the use of silver.

A clear iron crisis is present just before and during puberty. Here one is dealing with the albuminizing forces as they are ruled by iron, which means that the balance between iron and protein is achieved. A typical expression of an unruly protein process that occurs at this time, acne, has already been described. But around the tenth to twelfth years, frequent symptoms of fatigue, circulatory disturbances, weaknesses, and many other diffuse symptoms are observed that are an initial expression of an inadequacy of the iron process. They respond well to Ferrum prep. comp., occasionally with Cardiodoron. To interpret and approach these disturbances properly is important in the guidance of constitutional prophylaxis and often continues for decades.

A further expression of the disturbed iron-protein interaction is the orthostatic albuminuria that occurs from puberty to the twenty-first year. This requires Ferrum sidereum/pancreas, levico, and possibly Scorodit, because the inadequate protein breakdown can be approached therapeutically via the pancreas. At a later age, an excessive albuminization process can be the basis for the development of a polyglobulism or polycythemia. This can be taken as the stagnation of inadequately transformed blood. It can be treated with Cobaltum D20 to D30.[26]

The position of cobalt between iron and copper has already been discussed. Migraine is a completely different disturbance of the transition of metabolic forces into processes of consciousness, and it is related to protein metabolism. Here, iron can work into the excessive vitality, delimiting and guiding it when it is rightfully made active through the conception of

Cephalodoron. Then iron works counter to the impulses of the nervous system that create illness, and also against the excessive metabolic forces. Here, iron presents itself as the true mercury—as Rudolf Steiner once designated it—with the truly mediating function that is the primary healing impulse.

By selecting the proper combination, the iron impulse can be guided therapeutically. This has already been described as a principle of copper and is especially important of iron. Siderite, natural iron carbonate, works in the potency of D2 to D6, and is indicated in the metabolic region for problems of fermentation, pancreatopathies, etc. Ferrum muriaticum and Ferrum sesquichloratum work in the region of the lungs, and the pure metal works on the head system. Pyrite, the combination with sulphur, is particularly related to the upper respiratory tract and indicated in bronchitis, tracheitis, pharyngitis, and laryngitis and occasionally is given together with cinnabar.

The phosphor compound of iron, Ferrum phosphoricum, is directed to light and the ego. The ego and light character of iron is emphasized by the phosphorus. It is indicated in acute infections and pneumonia and is generally indicated as a fever remedy. Its effect does not depend on a suppression of fever but rather on stimulating the ego in the metabolism, making fever unnecessary.

Iron has a significant function in the brain. The iron-rich nuclei of the extra-pyramidal system (nucleus ruber and substantia nigra) are not simply depositories. They are the "old brain," the stem brain, that subserves the functions occurring in the subconscious. Parkinsonism is a typical disturbance here; occasionally it develops after encephalitis, flu, or as an expression of sclerosis. It afflicts mainly men over fifty. The pathological anatomical picture is that of a degeneration, particularly of the substantia nigra that becomes poor in iron. From this site iron rules the movements of involuntary coordination. In Parkinsonism, this iron process is blocked. Ego and astral body do not get through; the astral impulses become congested and thus are not freely available for the ego to use. This is expressed in the loss of a free, uninhibited gait, the poverty of movement, the rigidity and cramped posture. The form of movement emanating from the ego can no longer assert itself in the face of the cramped muscles caused by the astral impulses, since the instrument iron lacks its innate decisive place. (Experimentally, the iron can be replaced in this function by manganese, which is similar to it and results in a symptomatology resembling Parkinsonism. The therapeutic application of manganese in potentized form in Parkinsonism is, however, disappointing.)

In suitable form, iron works quite generally in a balancing, vitalizing and healing way on the nerve-sensory system. Skorodit D30 must also be mentioned as one of the main remedies in the treatment of poliomyelitis and Ferrum sidereum D20 for states of nervous fatigue that demand a strengthening of the cosmic life forces in the blood. (These substances are directed into the nerve-sensory region by the higher potencies.)

The connection of inner light with iron and its effect in light metabolism was discussed earlier. The more intensive working of light on iron therapy is based on that. The light component of iron is specifically represented by cerium, an element of the rare earths all of which have a characteristic relationship to light. The natural mineral cerite can be used as D4 and D6 to strengthen the light in the realm of iron activity—for example, in constitutional anemia (especially in those with auburn hair, hypoxia, and generally as an internal light therapy in carcinoma, depressive moods, psoriasis, etc. Vitamin C, in which the iron process can be recognized, is also an expression of the relationship between iron and light.[27]

The formation of gall arises from the Mars-iron impulse. We do not mean the gall bladder but rather the process of bile formation as it stands in its dynamics in relation to the activity of the liver, leading it further. This whole process from its physiological to its psychological aspects can be met with iron, and it is indicated when the gall function is sluggish. This can be treated externally with an ointment, but Ferrum per chelidonium is more specific. Through it iron is directed to the gall region, which is specifically affected by the healing plant celandine.

Ferrum per chelidonium is therefore therapeutically significant in gall diseases and in guiding the process of incarnation into catabolic metabolism.

Activity is stimulated by the iron-gall process. It extends from the physiological formation of the gall in digestion to bodily activity and right into consciousness. There, thinking, which is vitalized by silver, copper, and mercury, spiritualized by gold, formed by tin, and sharply contoured by lead, is activated by iron. In the region of feeling, the heart, the energy of iron is metamorphosed into courage, through which man can work actively and with self-control in the world.

Also connected with the gall-iron process are psychological peculiarities and disturbances that are indicated by the old designations of choleric and melancholic; they are explained in greater detail later. Iron stimulates the flow of bile and also activates and permeates the soul life with light. It is for this reason indicated in the treatment of depression. It also works against fear, particularly when used in the form of meteoric iron and Skorodite in medium potencies. It makes individuals active, awake, and conscious. It is the metal of the consciousness soul.

One of the most threatening and basic feelings of our epoch is that of a lack of time. This lies at the bottom of a complex phenomenon of the physical and psychical overburdening of modern man; it appears, for example, in the "manager sickness." The central cause of this "angina temporis" lies in anxiety, in a lack of consciousness, and in a latent weakness of the will. The absence of real significance in life is covered up by a zeal for work, by a work neurosis, by ambition and striving for external success. The feeling of the emptiness of existence can then lead to a reaction depression. The "time sufferer" no longer desires or enjoys anything, but he allows himself to be driven into a state of chronic overburdening. For this threatening situation of an erroneous attitude toward life, remedies such as iron as Ferrum sidereum, meteoric iron, possibly together with Aurum, can be taken into consideration because of their inner activating effect.

A certain exhaustion, anergy, also lies at the bsais of inadequate resistance to infections. If a sudden infection suddenly occurs in a healthy person, the otherwise constant plasma iron level decrases sharply and remains low until the infection has been overcome. This same regulation is found in chronic infections, particularly tuberculosis, rheumatism and malignant tumors. The iron enters the reticular endothelial system, which is an organ of defense.

Iron thus has a most essential role in the defense against infection and any foreign life as it is found in carcinoma or allergy. It maintains the self against foreign invasion. Here, too, the healing impulse of iron in the defensive processes of the reticular endothelial system touch on a spiritual impulse that is its special mark.

Gold

In the preceding sections, three polarities of each pair of metals were described. They are related to one another so that one prepares the way for the other, making it possible for a substance to arise in the human organism that is not only living but also ensouled and open to the indwelling spirit. Every one of these six metal processes is, relatively speaking, independent, but must be in balance with its antagonist. Beyond that, there must be a harmonious interrelationship of the three polarities to one another. To that end there must be a supradynamic that rules them and encompasses the totality; this is accomplished by the gold process. In relation to the other metals, gold takes the same position as the sun in the planetary system. It is the point of origin of light, life, and order that are received by the planets. Gold is the representative of the sun forces on the earth; it is sunlight congealed to a metallic substance.

It has been emphasized that it is possible to gain access to a problem only when one participates in it. In this sense gold has access to all the other metals, while they, on their part, each represent one aspect of the being of gold. (It is understood that these discussions are not meant to be taken in the sense of atomic physics, but that they are concerned with the spiritual being that recognizably permeates and is active in a substance.)

In a certain way, the inherent properties of particular metals can be found combined in gold. As an example, mention may be made of the fact that silver is malleable but cannot be cast, whereas the polar lead can be cast but is not malleable. Gold, however, is malleable and can be cast. To experience their total being, however, requires a detailed study of the phenomena.

The all-encompassing character of gold is an expression of its magnitude and truly kingly being; this was experienced everywhere in all ages. By virtue of pairing its noble character with strength, it may mediate without losing its properties, that is, without succumbing to either extreme.

Correspondingly, its ruling the other properties of metals is not compulsive but rather harmonizing and guiding. Thus, the effects of gold will rarely be experienced as occurring more rapidly than those of the other metals. Instead, true healings will occur that are less immediately obvious than the effects of the other metals.

Gold strives to harmonize and balance the polarities and this is indicated after the application of other metal therapies to regulate and stabilize them, leading them to a higher level. It encompasses the greatest contrasts—earth and cosmos, incarnation and excarnation, gravity and levity—without conforming to their laws. Its high specific gravity (it is the heaviest of the seven metals) as well as its exceedingly fine dispersion over the earth show its penetration into and permeation of the earth. Nevertheless, earthly forces cannot attack it; it resists oxidation and chemical transformation by virtue of its noble character, in which its cosmic origin and representation is expressed more than in any other metal.

These polarities can be approached with gold therapy. A disturbed relationship of gravity and levity as found in an excess of earthly material or of one-sided spiritual forces in a person's life is expressed as an excessively strong tendency toward the body, on the one side, or to spiritualization on the other. A person penetrates either too strongly into the organism with his soul-spiritual being and is then too much permeated and influenced by these physical forces, or the person may free himself prematurely from these earthly forces so that physical reality eludes him. The first case offers the basis for the psychological appearance of *fear of death* or *depression*. (One deals here with the psychological experiential components; an endogenous depression is based organically on a disturbed liver process. [See also the chapters on psychiatry in vol. III.] Theoretically and therapeutically, these two matters do not exclude each other.) In the second possibility, mania can develop. Through gold the balance can again be made possible. Here the choice of the proper potency is decisive. In lower potencies gold mediates the necessary heaviness, the unrelenting weight (Aurum prep. D6 in mania and tendency to rages; D6–10 in corresponding tachycardia). In higher potencies it gives the soul buoyancy from earthly surroundings. Thus Aurum D12–30, possibly even D200, is indicated in depressions, particularly when connected with self-reproach, and also in fear of death and stenocardiac disturbances (in combination with other therapies described in the chapters on the heart and psychiatry).

The therapy for inadequate incarnation and excarnation is similarly strongly dependent on the potency. When an abortion is imminent or threatens, lower potencies are indicated to firm up the connection with the body. In menopause, there can be a premature tendency to excarnate; this points to a disturbance of the gold process. When older persons hold on to their bodies too long and cannot find access to the spirit, however, the path can be eased with Aurum D30. In higher potencies Aurum works right into the thinking where it is combined with the light-filled iron process, which in turn is connected with the activity of thinking, whereas the gold process determines its quality and direction.

The gold process accompanies the incarnation process in all its phases right into the formation of the bones, which is subject to the lead process, while the fluoride process participates in the solidification. This is, however, directed by gold. Its light force can be followed through vitamin D into the lead process and bone formation. If there are disturbances in the building of the bones, especially in youth, Aurum in lower potency is indicated, while for example in bone metastases which, like carcinoma in general, are based on an excessively strong connection with earthly forces higher potencies are indicated (D20–30, especially favorable as a mixed ampule with Equisetum D20).

The vitalizing component of gold is connected with guiding the process of incarnation: "Man is strengthened by the sun." This aspect can be addressed by higher potencies (D15, 20, 30), or it can be guided into the metabolic sulphur region with Aurum Sulphuratum D10.

In general, the creative soul forces are called up and strengthened by gold. From this realm, the organism is regenerated through a forceful inner cohesiveness in the human being. Gold gives him a firm hold, overcomes flight from the earth as well as an excessively strong bondage to it, and places him properly on it. Gold gives direction; it leads. It does not overcome but preserves freedom.

The heart is the organ that arises from the sun-gold force in man. As his central organ, it binds spirit and body most intensively and harmoniously. Its position and function corresponds to that of the sun in the cosmos. Therefore, Aurum can be applied directly, and one can work directly on the heart muscles with it. This is explained in greater detail in the chapter on the heart.

In conclusion, the interactions of the seven metals and their characteristic functions can be sketched in the following way:

Aurum

Cuprum ———— Ferrum
Mercury ————— Stannum
Argentum —————— Plumbum

Harmony

Devotion ———— Activity
Mediation ————— Mastery
Life —————————— Death

Animal Remedies

A rationale for the use of animals, their organs and products, can be developed from the nature of animals. Unlike plants, animals have astral bodies that are active within their organisms and that create specific organs. From insight into the nature of an animal, access to the formative impulses leading to its form and substantiality can be obtained. The fundamental literature on this subject is listed below.[28]

One of the basic results of Rudolf Steiner's research—a key thought that can also be found in Goethe, Oken, and Carus, among others—is that man is the summation of the realm of animals. Expressed in a different way, this means that the animals were expelled from human development in the course of evolution, and details of the human form achieve a special development in them. Because of this specialization, this development of one detail, other formative impulses atrophy. For example, the extreme development of the middle toe of the horse occurs at the expense of the other toes. Specialization brings one-sidedness with it and a loss of the total harmony. From this the following indication of Rudolf Steiner can be understood. "Every animal is actually an illness." Only when the animal realm with all its contrasts is taken *in toto* does it result in a harmonious whole. Illness was characterized as an extreme, one-sided development of a process that is necessary to physiology. Therefore, it will be profitable to look in the animal realm for correspondences to certain processes of illness.

The anatomical and physiological peculiarities an animal manifests as a developmental impulse or within a family can be the theme here. Examples are mentioned in the chapters on the kidney and heart. The fundamental impulses expressed in poison or other specific substances can replace or stimulate forces that are lacking in man. Basically, it is astral impulses that therapy with animal substances makes use of, but it is important that they be differentiated since the working of the astral body is multi-layered.

A borderline remedy is the application of leeches that was discussed above. By applying them locally, the coagulation of blood can be inhibited, the lymphatic stream can be accelerated, vascular cramps lessened and inflammations suppressed. Especially the stagnating metabolic processes of the blood can be brought into activity. Thus, the application of leeches is indicated in local inflammations, vascular and lymphatic congestions, spasms, angina pectoris, migraine, pre-apoplectic states, hypertension and venous congestions. Wantschura also introduced this therapy to treat multiple sclerosis by applying the leeches in the region of the spinal column.

The effects of leeches cannot be based simply on a decongestion and removal of blood, but they are also based on the introduction of an animal product, that is, an astral substance and activity that helps to transform the vitality of the blood. It is from this that these indications result. Hirudo can be used as a dilution, an injection, or a salve. The effect, however, is stronger and faster when living animals are used.

Organ preparations play a special role in therapy. They are used primarily in potentized form. It can be understood that in this application hormones and active substances no longer play a role; it is not a substitution therapy. There are transitions, however. The administration of an organ extract usually contains even in concentrated form only such a small quantity of "active substances"—to which the effects are generally attribubted—that they cannot really be related to that substance.

Because of the inability to comprehend an action other than by a "definable substance," a therapy that uses organ extracts is, on the whole, excluded. Instead, a therapy that substitutes isolated hormones is given preference. Despite many theoretical objections, there is nevertheless no doubt about the effectiveness of organ therapy when the many decades of experience of thousands of practical physicians are considered.

In this organ therapy, it is not a question of using a substitution but rather of stimulating a specific organ. In the final analysis it is the ether body that is addressed by the preparation, bringing it to "interest itself" more in the organism. For this reason also, in contrast to hormonal therapy, the concentration is secondary but naturally not unessential. In general, this stimulation of the ether body will be achieved with lower potencies (or higher concentrations); these are indicated in degenerative and atrophic processes to stimulate regeneration. The organs thus treated, which generally have fallen away from the influence of the ether body, are through this therapy again integrated into the totality of the organism.

If one is treating an inflammation of an organ, however, higher potencies of the specific organ are indicated (D20–D30) and in cases of excessive function occasionally even higher potencies (D60 in hyperthyroidism, for example). Higher potencies work quicker on the nerve-sensory system, the astral body, which enters the metabolism catabolically by this route.

Further, organ preparations can be used as a "vehicle" to direct a metal or plant remedy. We have already indicated an expanded therapeutic principle by which a metal is combined directly with an organ to increase its effectiveness. These preparations are produced by Weleda.

Besides the diseases of various organs, the indications for using these preparations directly in therapy can also be arrived at from the natures of the various organs. Here we need point only to the polarity of the pituitary and pineal glands.

The pituitary or hypophysis is the uppermost of all the metabolic organs; it has a central position mediating towards the brain, and it coordinates the relationship of the ether to the astral body. Thus, Hypophysis D6 acts formatively on the formative forces and is indicated in rickets, but also basically in all growth disturbances, for example, stunted growth and adiposity. The treatment for enuresis is based more on the neural hypophysis, which regulates the fluid metabolism; here, again, the proper mutual working of astral and ether bodies is expressed.

The proper interaction of hypophysis and pineal gland is the basis for memory and recollection. The medication consisting of hypophysis with plumbum and copper is based on this fact (Hypophysis/Lac papaveris, to which Plumbum D15 or Cuprum D6 is added).

Whereas the hypophysis is directed downward to the body, the epiphysis is oriented upward in the reverse direction. In earlier times it was designated as the eye of God; it is the "first eye."[29] Among other cases, epiphysis is indicated when the soul-spiritual being "sinks" too rapidly into the physical, for example, in pubertas praecox, hypersexuality, leukemia, and others.

The insects play a predominant role in animal remedies. This is true especially of the social insects, the bees and ants, which have been used since ancient times and is understandable from their nature. Bee and ant colonies are not collections of individuals, as the name could imply, so that this designation is not quite appropriate. Rather, the whole hive is the animal, and the individual bee is comparable to a blood corpuscle in man's organism.

On the insect level, the bees (Apis) take on something like a homeothermic way of life. They can regulate temperature to a fine degree and, unlike the related wasps, by holding it constant can thus survive winters. Clearly, they have a disposition for a warmth organism that otherwise is only found in far more advanced higher animals. They also show a close connection to light. Their total orientation is bound to the sun, and the wax they produce, as seen in its capacity to illuminate, is densified light. The hexagonal structure of the honeycomb points to light forces, since the number six always signifies the working of the light forces of the sun; these are active in quartz also. In the beehive there is an anticipation of the ego impulse, which, in its activity, is bound to the forces of warmth and light. It is not by nature influenced by astrality as it occurs in the higher animal realm, and for that reason is close to man. The clearest expression of the connection of the beehive to the ego-organization is given by honey or sugar.

The ego, warmth, and light forces are stimulated by the therapeutic use of Apis. Thus, it is primarily applied on local inflammations. Apis D3–6 is indicated in tonsillitis, conjunctivitis, lymph angitis, adnexitis, etc. The stimulation of the warmth process, however, does not enhance the inflammation, but rather renders it superfluous through the light permeation and formation effected by Apis. (An ideal supplement is belladonna; added to the Apis therapy it calms down the astral body that maintains the inflammation.) According to Rudolf Steiner, it is also possible to support the activity of Apis with Levisticum; it is best mixed and processed with Apis. Especially in lumbago, sciatica, and other muscular-skeletal problems, Apis/Levisticum (also with arnica) has proved itself most useful.

The warmth and light permeating effect is indicated in the nervous system and degenerative processes, for example, multiple sclerosis, neuritis, etc. Depending upon the location, however, it is used in higher potencies (D20 up to D30). Finally, it ought to be mentioned that bee poison has a relatively high magnesium content (0.5%). Magnesium is almost identical with light. Apis is obtained by processing bees, whereas Apisan is the potentized isolated bee poison. It is used in the same way as Apis but appears to be more active than the preparation made from the whole animal. Problems of this nature, however, require further studies and elucidation.

The living space of the bee is actually the region above the earth. It takes nothing for itself but nectar, water, and pollen and for that reason can keep the light forces in a pure state.

Wasps represent a connection with the earth that is a stage lower than that of the bees. They make their nests from earthly wood chewed up to produce paper, or they make them in the earth. They feed their broods with insects. The fig wasp or hornet, Vespa crabro, is used for therapeutic applications. The effect is similar to that of Apis but more massive and intensive, though possibly less light permeating. Vespa brings formative forces into the tissues of the skin, the connective tissue in particular, and is indicated in all diseases of the tendons, fascia, connective tissue in the formation of keloids, scars, burn scars, vascular nevi, etc. It is applied generally as an ointment 1%, or as injection, D3 or 4. Thus, post-operative scars, which can lead to contractions and corresponding effects, can be favorably treated with Vespa crabro D3 or 4 together with Argentum D6 and/or Nicotania D6 as a local injection.

The ants are a step further down in the earthly connection. They live completely in the earth. The direct light and warmth relationship is lost to a large extent but still is present as a necessary requirement. Only their extreme craving for sugar reminds us of the ego connection.

Their task and significance in the realm of nature is again different; life that is dying off can enter various paths. On the one side, living substance succumbs to breakdown forces that end in ammonia, carbon dioxide, and water. These are truly dead substances and have left the life stream of the earth. On the other side, the living substance that has died rots but avoids the path to the inorganic. It continues to be organic substance and can, for example as compost, support the life of the soil, stimulating the growth of plants and thus maintaining the cycle of living substance. It is the task of the ants to maintain this cycle in nature and to support and enhance it. They do this by processing dead substances so that they do not enter the inorganic realm, but are held back for life, opening them up for the working of the etheric forces. To fulfill this function they use a special secretion that consists mainly of formic acid.

This natural process that is performed by the ants is also necessary to the human organism. Living substance is always potentially in danger of passing over prematurely, or in the wrong place, to inorganic mineral form; it may, for example, be deposited as uric acid or similar metabolic products. In order to complete this process in a proper physiological manner, man has within him a certain quantity of formic acid. This need not occur in a chemically definable form, but in a substantiality that corresponds to the activity of ants in nature. Since it is not necessarily the formic acid as a substance that is important, it is more correct to speak of the formic acid process. Thus, in biochemistry today one speaks of activated formic acid that corresponds more to the organism's lability than a rigid concept of substance. Finally, the ant's secretion is the result of an astral activity; formic acid is merely the main carrier of this process. It is for this reason that the poison of ants cannot be synthesized or replaced with "purified formic acid" and especially not with synthetic HCOOH.

Formic acid in nature and in man is intimately related to oxalic acid, a product that is found in many plants. Oxalis acetosella, from which this acid has been given the name clover or oxalic acid, is a typical representative of this formative process. Oxalis prefers lightly shaded, woody, acid soils, and in principle has the same task in nature as the ants, that is, to permeate metabolism with light so that it can be led over into the anabolic stream.

Rudolf Steiner frequently pointed to the relationship and transition of oxalic into formic acid.[30] The process begun in the plant with oxalic acid is carried further in the animal realm. Chemically expressed, this is decarboxylation.

COOH | COOH	H / COOH
Oxalic acid	*Formic acid*

An interaction of both of these processes occurs in the organism as is detailed later on. Oxalis can be quite helpful when Formica doesn't work, and vice versa. In both, it is a question of balancing the disturbed relation of astral to etheric activity. Oxalis is indicated in "inhibitory effects in the etheric" that cannot be managed properly by the astral organization. This is above all concerned with organ blockages that may proceed to stone formation and a deposition of organic substances. As an animal product, formic acid is more "the basis for soul and spirit," according to Steiner. It works on mineral hardening processes to stimulate the astral breathing function, and is indicated in rheumatic, gouty diseases, in the formation of tumors, and also in premature aging, arteriosclerosis, and nervous diseases.

The development of the movement of cosmic light forces down to the earth from the bee to the wasp to the ant is continued in the termites. They live completely in darkness, leaving the earth only to mate. Except for this fertilization period, the complete exclusion of the forces of light is connected with their nature, which consists in the destruction of organic substance. In contrast to the ants, there is no re-integration of organic substance into living relationships, and the formation of formic acid is necessarily absent. It is understandable that termites are a counter-image of healing impulses and cannot be considered for therapy.

Of the spiders, only Aranea diadema will be mentioned. According to Rudolf Steiner, it holds a special place in nature by being integrated into extra-terrestrial cosmic relationships. It has "much planetary life in it."[31]

To a certain extent, the spiders did not go through the regular earth evolution.[32] By using Aranea diadema, the astral forces, particularly as they manifest in movement, can be stimulated. Hence, Rudolf Steiner suggested using it in muscle diseases and in corresponding nervous disturbances connected with movement.[33]

Of the insects, Coccus cacti (now Dactylapius coccus), the red cochineal louse that lives in Mexico on cacti, still needs to be mentioned. This insect removes the strong, unruly vitality from cacti, which have a heavy outer covering but are still etheric-watery within. Through this remedy, the astrality of the insect is given over to the patient; he thus receives the force to permeate with form the vitality of mucous that is produced in bronchitis, whooping cough, and asthma. This brings about a proper astralization. In addition to these remedies, Coccus cacti is also a constituent of Pertudoron.

The sponges belong to the coelenterates. Their roasted skeletons are used in therapy. Ever since the thirteenth century their use has been verified for disturbances of the thyroid gland, but the indications then were much more comprehensive than later. Evidently, this remedy originated in ancient knowledge and not from an analytical method. Today its effect is attributed to iodine that is present in an organic form, but this effect is in no way explained or identical with it. The method of roasting shows a deep insight into the significance of this process. Roasting signifies taking an organic substance through an astral process, through which astral forces are led into the substance. Through this astralization the ripening process one wants to stimulate in the organism comes about through the therapeutic use of the substance. Roasting, a true pharmaceutical process, enhances its effectiveness.

Thus, the therapeutic indication for Spongia tosta is also sketched out. It helps to encourage the proper astralization. Spongia can, therefore, be used in diseases of the thyroid, in goiter, and in hypofunction of the thyroid as well. In homeopathy this remedy is indicated for croup in children, which is clearly exhibited in the barking cough and the sensation of burning and tightening in the trachea. It is considered in all evidences of a cramp-like activity of the astral body in the neck region. The astral body is addressed specifically and redirected into the metabolism with this remedy.

In the plant realm, Fucus vesiculosus corresponds to the sponges. Here, the relation is similar to that between formica and oxalis. Through the formation of large air vesicles in the "leaves," this plant demonstrates its uptake of astral impulses that naturally work differently than when they are compressed for iodine. The astralization by Fucus vesiculosus extends more to the breakdown activity of the astral body, and it is thus indicated in hypothyroidism and several forms of obesity.

The snakes verify the statement that every animal is an illness. They represent the end of an exceedingly one-sided development. Zoologically, the reptiles and birds are included in the class Sauropsida. The snakes show their one-sidedness among the reptiles in the absence of limbs, pelvis, and shoulder girdle. Notwithstanding their presence in vertebrates generally, these structures are lost in the evolution of the snakes. Related to this is the one-sided development of their lungs. This was mentioned in the phylogenetic discussion of the development of the heart. Because of the absence of limbs, a hypertrophy of the vertebral and spinal cord formation is brought about (up to 400 vertebrae). This animal has fallen completely onto the earth and actually represents the counter-image of the birds, who have freed themselves, again with the necessary organic structural changes. The extraordinary production of poison is related to this clinging to the earth, although in the birds such poisons are not to be found.

From ancient times on, the dangers apparent in such one-sided development were experienced by human beings. This union with the earth brings about a premature ego impulse that diverts man from his actual goal and development. Thus, universal effects, extending destructively into the blood and nervous system, are found in snake poisons, which contain hemotoxins, hemolysins, cardiotoxins, hemorrhagics, hyaluronidase, coagulases, neurotoxins, proteases, etc. That the formation of the poison proceeds from the salivary glands is most revealing, because the ego-organization is more active in them than in other digestive glands. This impulse is specifically transformed by an overly active astral body. It is not ruled by the ego, however, but lives organically without inhibition.

It is interesting that most of the snake poisons have a relatively high zinc content. This works in such a way in the organism that it paralyzes the intervention of the iron forces in the metabolism or, as was described previously, actually prevents them from intervening at all. Iron is the ego's metal of incarnation, and in the organization of the snake it cannot find a proper place of action.

Sulphur plays an important role in snake poisons. It can also be found in human saliva, but here, however, it is "detoxified" in the form of rhodanin. Regardless of the form it takes in snake poisons, sulphur works in the metabolism toward dissolution.

Appropriately applied, the forces present in these poisons can be therapeutically utilized, a procedure that has been thoroughly studied by the homeopaths. The study of these poisons by the natural scientists has led to the development of various preparations that can be used to alleviate severe pain and epilepsy and to staunch bleedings.

The nature of the snake can make therapeutic applications understandable. Let us mention two examples. The unique union of the snakes with the earth leads to the fact that there are forces in them signifying a strong impulse of consciousness. They have symbolized this ever since ancient times. If, for example, the constructive forces active at night persist too long and become misguided, leading not to a regeneration of the nervous system but rather through excess to headaches, then a person will wake up in the morning with a headache. This is a classical symptom for the application of Lachesis (D12, D20–30).

The homeopathic indications come from the remedy picture that is arrived at through proving. They can be understood by considering them in the way described above. Blue-red, poorly delimited wounds, sores or inflammations with foul smelling secretions and strong sensitivity to touch show the destructive breakdown tendency of the astral body that is not followed by a healing reaction. It is exactly the same as the results of snake bite. If this poison is then administered as Lachesis in a potentized form (D12, D20), an appeal is made precisely to the disturbed forces. The organism then "recognizes" the disturbance and can introduce the healing phase.

The poison of the rattlesnake, Crotalus, has a strong neurotropic effect. Although in many ways similar to other snake poisons, nevertheless attention must be directed to a little known but frequently beneficial indication—a D30 potency as injection. Women especially suffer more frequently from brachyalgia paresthetica nocturna. Here, too, one is concerned with a disturbed waking process. Since the ether body does not bring about a "pure" build-up of the organism, the astral body attempts to intervene in an ordering way that leads to a faulty and painful awakening. The disturbed relationship between the astral and ether bodies will again be harmonized by this therapy.

To understand snake poisons it is significant to know that they have properties similar to those of the plant saponins and can be called "animal saponins" (W. Pelikan). The saponins, however, have a combining effect in the formation of foam with air and water; that is, they combine the astral body with the ether body so that it can again be active in the organism in a constructive manner. In man, this is fundamentally a task of the kidney system, and this leads to recognition of snake poisons, especially Lachesis, as being indicated in kidney diseases. There is a relationship between the formative impulses that in nature have led to the snake and those in man that form the basis for the formation of the urogenital system.

Snake poisons, including Lachesis, are therefore indicated constitutionally and in chronic kidney diseases, particularly in hemorrhagic, chronic, and acute cystopyelitis.[34] Lachesis is also indicated in climacteric disturbances. This can be understood from what has already been said in that with age a transformation of the reproductive forces should come about. If this transformation does not occur, there can then be hot flashes and other well-known manifestations. The metamorphosis of formative forces is stimulated by snake poisons, and to a certain extent their destruction is necessary; herein lies the effect of snake poison. At the same time, however, consciousness is stimulated and "awakening," which was presented as an expression of the therapeutic effectiveness of snake poisons, occurs.

With respect to therapeutic applications, the social insects and the snakes are particularly notable. An ego impulse is recognizable in the social insects that corresponds to the created image of man, but on the level of the insects cannot become manifest in any other way. Thus, Apis and Formica are the primary animal remedies. They appeal to ego forces that are still capable of development. In contrast, with the snakes one is concerned with a premature ego impulse that is strongly exposed to earthly forces. Only higher potencies of these poisons are considered because they appeal to the ego to overcome and control the snake forces. In earlier times this was directly experienced as a healing impulse and goal of the physician. The vertical snake wound about the staff of the Aesculapius expresses the triumph over these forces.

SPECIFIC PATHOLOGY AND THERAPY

The Fourfold Organ System

Among human organs, liver, kidney, heart and lung have special positions. They are not only essential for life but stand in a solid relationship to one another and to the four elements that can be recognized when one studies the general nature of an organ.

It has already been pointed out that the members of man's being require fields and locations for their specific activities in and through which they can work. In this activity the organs are formed. In them, the members of man's being are active in various ways. In order to work into the organism, the ether and astral bodies and ego utilize various substances and processes that are related to their natures. Correspondingly, they form and use the organs that then serve them as instruments. The organs are thus the physical regions of receptivity for specific effects of the members of man's being, which work into the organs structuring them, forming substances and directing the elements. Therefore, in these events one can recognize the working of the members of man's being.

There lies in every organ a more or less unconscious soul-spiritual relationship, which in olden times was directly experienced as a reality. This is echoed in many expressions and words today. We find indications of them, but without insight into their relevance, in religious writings and mythology. Phrases in the Old Testament that refer to the testing of heart and kidneys, others such as "a louse ran across your liver," wishes that come from "the heart," etc., indicate a deep knowledge of a connection of soul processes with certain organs. This is also shown in the teaching of the temperaments in which the mental mood is expressed by the physical equivalent. The true knowledge of the essential nature of organs can provide the justification for these relationships. This will become evident in the subsequent chapters.

The special nature of an organ becomes more apparent when

examined before the background of the others. For didactic purposes, therefore, we will introduce the discussion of individual organs by first looking at all four together.

In ancient times the four elements, earth, water, air, and fire or warmth were differentiated. This provided the basis of macro- and microcosmic man. These elements were not considered to be the aggregated states of solid, liquid, airy, and warmth, but rather as the forces and beings at the basis of these manifestations. They were experienced as real by man in ancient times. Ultimately, these beings also correspond to the members of man's being that were already described in more detail in volume one. Every member is founded primarily on one of the four elements: ego/warmth, astral body/air, ether body/water, physical body/earth. Just as these relationships of being exist, each member structures an organ in which it is active through these elements, ruling it. The relationships are not readily apparent but only become evident as the organs are studied. The connections we will be dealing with are: heart/warmth organism; kidney/air organism; liver/water organism; lung/physical organism.

In the same sense, it is not by chance that protein, the basic substance of life, unites four chemical elements, namely hydrogen, nitrogen, oxygen and carbon. There, too, one can recognize the interpenetrating interaction of the four members and relating them to organ systems is possible, examples and areas of application of which have been given (vol. I). It must be evident, however, that this is a mere schema that, like every such arrangement, does not do complete justice to reality. It is important to note that, depending on the point of view, other relationships are also permissible.

The relationship of the members of man's being to the elements and substances is deeply connected with the whole evolution of earth and man.[1] They are an expression of stages of development that cannot be discussed in detail here. In order to come to know the true nature of an organ it is necessary to work out its uniqueness. The separate details can then be used to fill in a picture from which the significance and function of an organ becomes evident in a more comprehensive sense.

The Liver-Gall System and Its Diseases

The Anatomy and Physiology of the Liver-Gall System

The liver, the largest gland of the human organism, lies clearly on the right side of the body. This finding can be most instructive when one sees it in connection with the organism's structural plan.

The problem of symmetry has already been indicated. In the nervous system, symmetry predominates; in the metabolic region asymmetry predominates and is, as it were, a precondition for the unfolding of life. The position and form of the liver are asymmetric. They thus express a connection with the realm of life.

Undoubtedly, this fact would still stand even if the liver were on the left side. Its position in the right half of the body is, however, certainly not a chance occurrence. The right-left problem has also been discussed in detail in volume I. On the right side, the effects of the physical body predominate; on the left, those of the ether body. Especially the ego is united more strongly with the right side of the organism and thus indirectly with the earth. This is also reflected in the right-handedness that is so predominant today. Man takes hold more strongly of the earth by way of the right side. This is the side preferred for the process of incarnation. Thus, the liver shows a structural connection to the realm of life that, through the emphasis on the right side, makes possible a stronger connection with the ego and the physical body. In other words, from these findings one can see that the liver mediates man's physical life. It allows him to incarnate on earth, that is, to immerse himself with his ego into living substance. It will still be necessary to illuminate this basic function from various sides. This function contributes to an understanding of the extensive anatomical, embryological, and physical findings.

In the embryological life the liver holds a central position. In the third week the first primordia of the liver are developed. It originates from mesoderm and endoderm. The significance of the liver in the structure of the embryonal organism can be recognized in its size relationships: Its volume in a 31 cm embryo is approximately 10 percent, in the newborn, 5 percent, and in an adult, 2 percent of the total body volume. Expressed in a different way, the liver in the newborn weighs approximately 1/18th of the body, whereas in the adult, it is only 1/32nd to 1/36th. This means that relative to the total weight of the body the liver of the newborn is approximately twice as large as that of an adult.

The relative size of the liver in the embryo is an expression of its significance. Its functions are exceptionally extensive in the adult and even more so in the embryo. Beginning in the second embryonal month, the liver is the most important organ of blood formation. This activity continues right up to the seventh month when it is taken over by the bone marrow. The liver's relationship to the blood is also maintained later in that it regulates the composition and quantity of circulating blood. Then it also functions as a blood storage organ since the capillary net of the liver in the adult can store up to 20 percent of the entire blood volume. The maximum liver circulation consists of 2–2.4 liters/minute. These connections with the blood are related to the fluid component and will be discussed in greater detail.

The liver is the most encompassing organ of embryonic life, the *central organ of general* anabolic metabolism. It is fully active in the embryo even when other organs such as the nervous system, lung, kidneys, and intestines, and their functions are still more or less in a state of rest. The liver exercises its activities while these other organs are still in their formative states; their functions begin later, practically not until birth. Though it exercises its activities throughout life, its maximum activity occurs in the embryonic state, thus appropriately meeting the demands of the metabolic processes during that time. This is the time of strong impulses for organ formation since world forces shape the microcosmic man and prepare him for incarnation. "Those forces that attain their final completion in the liver have built up the human being. He will be liberated from these forces that bind him to the earth, as it were, by the forces he receives like fire from the air and that are expressed in his breathing."[1]

It can be said that as the archetypal organ of life the liver lives entirely in anabolism. How much anabolic processes are concentrated in it can also be seen in the unusual power of regeneration that it retains throughout its life. Experiments on animals show that after extirpation of 80 percent of the liver, it can regain its original size in approximately six weeks.[2]

The essential similarity of liver and life is also expressed through the genius of language. In the Germanic languages the connection is evident without any further ado. This is true also of the Romance languages. In French, *foie* has the same stem as the Italian word *fegato* and Spanish *hidalgo*. Underlying them is the stem "veg," which is again found in vegetation, etc., and in vegetative life (in contrast to the animalistic, something that was felt appropriately and correctly). Other peoples experienced another aspect of this phenomenon. Thus, the Hebrew word, *kawèd*, means both liver and heaviness. Expressed therein is the stream of incarnation indicated above which passes through the liver, filling the organism with living substance.

Although the liver retains its metabolic functions throughout life and in the aging process can be seen to decrease its weight by one-half; nevertheless, with birth there is a decisive change in the human being. The environment approaches the infant once it has left the protective enveloping sheath of the mother and with the first breath a fundamental change in metabolism begins. This will be discussed in the following chapters on heart and lungs. The life of the child undergoes a decisive change. With the first breath, oxidative processes begin, along with catabolism and warmth formation. This form of metabolic activity is bound to the animal, heterotrophic way of life. Only in this way is a higher life that goes beyond the purely vegetative life of the plant realm possible. The latter is always bound to processes of reduction. Before the child's birth these upbuilding processes practically predominate. The process that is connected with fire and air that tears man loose from those forces binding him to the earth begins only at birth. This catabolic process connected with oxygen and oxidation in the production of warmth is in principle opposed to the formation of the liver. It is almost hostile to it. It does actually touch on the anabolic stream in the liver, but by its nature does not belong to the liver.

In the past these connections were experienced, according to the consciousness of the time, as images. We have in the grandiose picture of the myth of Prometheus an imaginative description of these connections. Prometheus, who brought fire from the heavens to the earth and man, is chained by the gods to a mountain in the Caucasus. There an eagle comes every day to gnaw at his liver; in the night, however, it regenerates. The incarnation of the spirit and soul and their conscious life in an organism is possible only with the help of catabolic processes, that is, the destruction of life. In the final analysis, this involves the ego, which lives in warmth and has been given to man with the fire. In all mythologies the bird is the image of the nerve-sensory system that is active in the course of the day and from which the catabolic processes emanate. During the night, regeneration, the vegetative build up, takes place. The etheric body is regenerated so that in the course of the day the formative forces can again be metamorphosed in consciousness.

Thus, at birth a new element enters the human organism. What predominates before birth exclusively as anabolic functions is now supplemented by the catabolic processes that are needed by an ensouled organism. The interaction of these opposite processes was discussed in volume I. Connected with it, however, is differentiation. What was earlier united in the liver is now taken further by the beginning of a different activity of the astral body. The lungs, nervous system, and kidneys are organs of the astral body that now begin their actual function.

The sequential relationship of anabolism and catabolism as a characteristic of the metabolism of an ensouled organism is closely united with iron metabolism, with oxygen uptake, and with the formation of warmth. Icterus neonatorum gives clear expression to this transition. The vegetative constructive growth forces that led to the formation of the human form are limited by functions that are connected with processes of consciousness. The breakdown process also extends to iron—in hemoglobin. This is especially plentiful in the newborn, making the entry into earthly existence possible. After birth, the iron no longer is as "necessary" and a relatively low level follows during childhood. Thus, the relationships of incarnation with formative forces can be clearly studied in the liver. It is to be emphasized that pure anabolism is characteristic for the liver. The breakdown processes that begin at birth, which do indeed work into the liver and bring about a differentiation of its extensive activity, emanate from other regions that are directly opposed to the being of the liver. This will be discussed in detail later.

The Liver as the Central Organ of the Fluid Organism

In no organ can such highly differentiated fluid movements be found as in the liver. Besides the arterial and venous blood and the lymph that streams through all organs, the liver receives the blood from the portal vein. Further, bile flows from it. These five fluids become ordered into a highly differentiated organism of separate and lawful streams.

The liver is a somewhat amorphous, soft, sponge-like structure. Its consistency is characteristically plastic. It appears to be organized water, and closer examination confirms this observation since it contains hardly more solid substance than the blood itself. The blood is 78 percent water, the liver 71 percent. The liver can thus be considered to be a minimally solidified organ of liquids, that is, blood. As is well-known, the water content of all tissues decreases throughout life and is an expression of the process of aging. Even the adult liver, however, is 71 percent water, retaining throughout life the relatively high water content of the newborn. Thus, it can support the vitalizing anabolic processes of the organism that are connected with water throughout life.

The knowledge concerning the relationship of liver function and fluid metabolism is not new. As early as 1861, Frerichs, in his *Klinik der Leberkrankheiten*, reported a decreased diuresis in liver diseases. These findings were subsequently supplemented, and in 1923 the study of water excretion was suggested as a test of liver function (Wollheim's test).[3] After consuming six times 150 m. of tea in the morning at hourly intervals, a healthy person responds with an excessive diuresis, whereas a person with a liver disease stores the fluid. The connections between liver function and fluid metabolism are so varied that only isolated examples can be cited. In the liver, diuretic and anti-diuretic substances can be found. The inactivation of the anti-diuretic posterior hypophyseal hormone as well as of aldosterone and glucocorticoids is a function of the liver. This points to a connection of the liver with the kidney system.

Mineral metabolism, especially that of potassium and sodium, is primarily subject to the adrenal cortex but the triggering organ is the liver. In this connection, the hepato-renal syndrome, a functional concept, must be mentioned in which as a consequence of hepatitis or toxic liver damage renal insufficiency may develop. Kidney damage can also be found in Weil's icterus. Clinical studies show that, subsequent to a decline of acute manifestations of a serious hepatitis, there are clear disturbances in fluid metabolism. The development of edema frequently accompanies hepato-cellular diseases, but not mechanical jaundice.

The essential relationship between the liver and fluid metabolism can be truly comprehended only when the fluid with the dissolved salts, protein, etc., is not considered to be a passive substance but rather an organized, living totality, that is, as the completely living fluid organism that was described earlier in volume I as carrier of the life processes. This fluid organism is the carrier of the activity of the ether body upon which all anabolic processes are based. "The outer physical liver is, as it were, the exudate of the ether body and is structured like it."[4]

The liver is thus central to the fluid organism because it is the primary organ of the ether body. This naturally permeates all organs and the entire organism; in the liver, however, it is least "disturbed" by the activity of the other members of man's being. The influence of the liver on the fluid organism extends to the absorption, excretion, and distribution of water in the organism. As already mentioned, the liver is in the position to regulate the water content of the blood and to serve as an essential blood storage organ. The liver cell is, as it were, a sense organ that perceives the water relationships of osmosis, electrolysis, etc. in the organism. For that reason, the sensation of thirst is also connected with the liver. This was explicitly pointed out by Rudolf Steiner.[5] The existence of a center for fluid balance in the interbrain does not contradict what we have said, since its significance lies in bringing perception to consciousness. Both are necessary for the undisturbed function, and they are related to one another as the retina of the eye is to the visual centers.

The kidneys, heart, and lungs play into this activity of the liver. In these organs the disturbances of the fluid organisms or the liver, are often first evident. Frequently, the diuretic effect of a liver therapy has been successful in treating illnesses such as exudative pleuritis and heart and kidney diseases.

The control of the fluid organism by the ether body, that is, the liver, is achieved with the help of potassium. The ether body needs a substance through which it can work into the water, and thus potassium plays a large role in liver metabolism and wherever anabolic processes take place. This is also true in the growth of plants.

The Liver as Chemist

In addition to the water and mineral regulation mentioned above, there is hardly a metabolic activity in which the liver does not participate. It is the place of general substance formation and of the origin of human substance. In terms of substance, the process of becoming man occurs in the liver.

The liver's predominant activity in the carbohydrate metabolism consists in the synthesis of glycogen. Glycogen is "animal starch," that is, a substance that in man and animal is principally a somewhat transformed plant substance. As a matter of fact, the liver is the plant in us, unmistakably the place of an undisturbed, plant-like etheric working. The above-mentioned significance of potassium in the function of the liver is connected with this. Potassium is the element the ether body utilizes in order to be active in water in an organizing manner. Thus, it also plays a decisive role in the realm of the plants as well as in the entire liver function, particularly in carbohydrate metabolism. Glycogen formation is therefore a function of the ether body; the glycogen content of the liver is a direct expression of the working of the ether body in its main organ. It is well-known that the functional capacity of the liver is united with glycogen storage. When needed, the glycogen is transformed to glucose and given off into the blood. That is not yet an actual breakdown, which begins first e.g. in the muscles when sugar is broken down to lactic acid. Muscles are unable to resynthesize sugar. This can take place only in the liver through its undisturbed synthetic function, a process that is described by the Cory cycle:

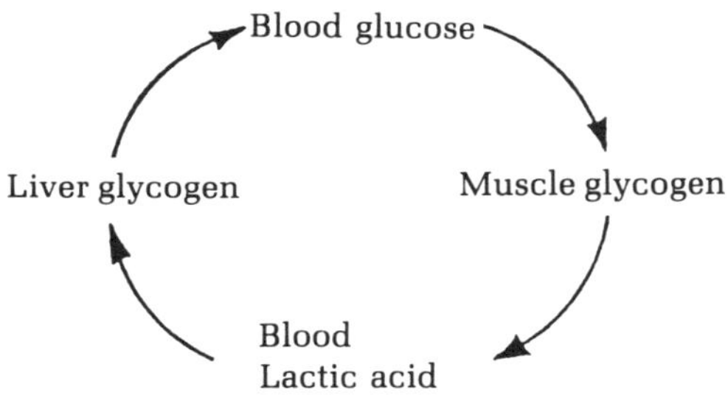

The transformation of carbohydrates from glycogen to lactic acid (Embden-Meyerhof-way) proceeds by way of phosphorylation. This is under the guidance of phosphorus, which as a light carrier is also the carrier of the ego. In this way it is possible for the ego to participate actively in the events of the carbohydrate metabolism and, by way of phosphorus, to intervene in a directing way in the intermediary metabolism. Since sugar is the physical basis for the activity of the ego-organization and since the ego works as described right into the last phases of metabolism, it is possible to permeate the body's substance with ego impulses and to form individual human substance.

"Because the liver exists and secretes gall that is added to the chyme in the intestine, thus permeating it all with liver products, it is then driven into the ego organism."[6]

The liver also plays a special role in the protein metabolism. In the formation of human protein the heart, kidneys, and lungs also participate, as was explained earlier. Their impulses work into the liver in such a way that it performs the function of forming body substance. The elements carbon, oxygen, hydrogen, and nitrogen are an expression of the mutual working of the four organs. Through nitrogen in particular, protein passes beyond the carbohydrates. The integration of the process through which the nitrogen fraction is eliminated is an essential function of the liver. Connected with this is not only protein metabolism but also the entire detoxification, the problem of deamination and transamination that was pointed out earlier.

That the liver plays a significant role in the establishment of an allergy is evident, not only from its central role in protein metabolism, but also from experimental research on animals that showed that anaphylaxis does not occur when the liver is excluded. The organism no longer reacts defensively toward foreign substances. The liver thus has an active function in allergies, a function primarily connected with its role in the formation and detoxification of substances in the protein metabolism.

The connection of the composition of serum protein with liver functions is studied chemically by electrophoresis and other laboratory methods. Albumin especially is quite undifferentiated and comes from the activity of the ether body. Hypoalbuminemia indicates a weakness of the ether body in the liver. The activity of the liver in deamination and transamination—its working with nitrogen within the protein metabolism—must also be mentioned here.

Several dermatological problems are also connected with the proper protein formation by the liver. They can occur together or vicariously with liver disorders. The connection is well-known today, but is hardly given the necessary therapeutic considerations. One can, for example, be dealing with inadequate protein formation that points to a disturbed stibium process or to an inadequate detoxification, so that the skin has to serve as an organ of excretion and is overburdened.

This essential detoxification function of the liver is mostly a function of synthesis, which means it is connected with an anabolic process. The glucuronization, that is, the bonding of substances in activated glucuronic acid is, like acetylation, ester formation with sulfates, etc., a synthetic function, and thus an anabolic process through which insoluble substances are made soluble. This allows the excretion of foreign substances. In the final analysis, there are problems with assimilation and the activity of making a substance part of the organism, that is, leading a dead substance over into the ether body so that the organism can work with the substance and then excrete it. This path provides the possibility of relieving the organism of foreign substance in the realm of metabolism. Another possibility in relation to foreign substances, insofar as these are not inert, consists of encapsulation and thus isolation within the body—in a granuloma, for example, or secondary elimination through an abscess. That this path can also be used in the intermediary metabolism or in an organ like the liver—for example, when physiological excretion fails—is indicated by the formation of necrotic foci in the aggressive form of hepatitis.

It is thus evident that every substance in the dead, mineral state is a burden for the liver, that is, every primary inorganic substance such as chemotherapeutic agents and also other substances that are completely lifeless, such as pure crystalline sugar. The capacity of the liver to detoxify and eliminate is tested by substances whose paths can be easily followed; these include dyes, bromsulphalein, indigocyanin green, etc.

The activity of the liver in the fat metabolism is evident in the fact that the fat of the liver shows the highest content of unsaturated fatty acids, which are the active form of fatty acids. The multiple unsaturated fatty acids have a higher kinetic but lower caloric value. They stimulate growth and are of great significance during growth. They have the characteristics of vitamins, etc. The saturation of fatty acids and their attendant elevated melting points constitute a hardening and rigidification process. This shows that they are a considerably heavier burden for the liver than the unsaturated fatty acids. Here, the metabolic activities of the liver can be seen especially in the synthesis of phospholipids. It is calculated that approximately two percent of the entire cholesterol is renewed daily in the liver. Finally, the bile acids play a significant role here; this, however, will be discussed later.

Along with the liver's capacity to sense fluid conditions, it is also one of its significant physiological functions "to taste the stream of nourishment." Rudolf Steiner designated the liver as a kind of inner eye that, like a sense organ, "perceives everything that enters the body as nutriment." Thus, "if it is healthy, it spreads useful substances throughout the body and excludes those that are detrimental."[7] In order to be detoxified the poison must first be recognized. That both capacities, detoxification and recognition, can be disturbed separately has been shown through modern immunology. This perceiving and judging of substances is to a large extent the function of the liver. The significance of a specific disturbance of this function will be discussed later.

The Formation of Gall Fluid

It is evident from the preceding discussion that the actual liver function extends to pure anabolic processes. This corresponds to the metabolism of the plant, which is representative of the human liver. The plant lives entirely in the formation of new living substance through assimilation, which is based chemically on a reduction maintained by light (photosynthesis). The transformation of starch into glucose during sprouting as well as anaerobic glycolysis are not actual catabolic processes but rather transformations.

The most apparent form of catabolism is evident in oxidation, which is typical for animal and human metabolism and upon which their way of living is based. Man and animal can unfold their beings only on the basis of catabolic activity. For that, however, a foundation must be provided; this stems from the plants (heterotrophic way of living). It applies to nutrition as well as to their own metabolism. Every day new body substance must be formed. As has been shown, this occurs in the liver and may well proceed undisturbed by catabolic processes. In its formation, however, it must be oriented toward the future tasks and kinds of catabolism. The "pure" anabolic metabolism corresponds mainly to plant metabolism, that is, chemically it is a reduction.

With the interaction of reduction and oxidation which as a kind of metabolism—expressed schematically—lies at the basis of plant and animal (liver and gall) are connected with warmth transformations. Fundamentally, reduction proceeds endothermically, requiring warmth, whereas oxidation is an exothermic process and yields warmth. It must be realized, however, that the gall impulse does not lead to oxidation but brings about transformations as described; they are only slight catabolic processes that provide the foundation for subsequent combustion. (One need only think of the breakdown of glycogen to glucose and the anaerobic metabolic events whose energy yield, compared to oxidative processes, is minimal.)

Despite the interaction of liver and gall functions, one can nevertheless see in the liver "pure" anabolism that is connected with reductive processes and proceeds endothermically. In other words, the liver requires warmth for its function, and the gall forms warmth. This alternating sequence of build up and breakdown has been touched on in various ways. It is connected with the nature of animal metabolism in an ensouled organism.

The finding that the temperature of the liver is from 0.2° to 0.6° C lower than the body temperature is connected with this. These findings were also confirmed under different conditions —Grayson in Nigeria, for example. The older studies, which give in part extremely high temperatures, were not done under physiological conditions. In healthy human beings the curve of the liver temperature runs parallel to that of the body temperature but is clearly about 0.5° C below it. When one considers the plant-like function of the liver, however, then it is understandable that the processes proceed endothermically because warmth is needed for actual anabolic activity just as it is in the case of a plant. It is only through oxidation that warmth is produced by the warmth organisms of men and animals. It is true that following build up in the plant, various transformations occur, especially when the forming process is completed and ripening begins. A transformation of substances occurs that can be seen in blossom formation as well as in the reddening of green fruits, and the presence of sugar and aroma is an expression of ripening.

A different kind of activity begins there. The formation of substances and growth do not simply continue but rather experience a qualitative change, a metamorphosis that is connected with a slight but incomplete breakdown. It is world astrality that calls a halt to vegetative growth and initiates the reversal of this process.

An exact image of this world process can be found in the liver-gall system. In the liver, the *formation* of substance takes place, the becoming and growing that in accordance with the substance makes possible only a vegetative life. The "merely" living substance must be taken further so that it can become a carrier of soul-spiritual impulses. This requires a ripening process, an initially slight breakdown. This impulse has its operative site in the activity of the gall. It proceeds from the gall bladder into the liver, extending into the individual liver cells. Although there is an intensive connection of the contrasting processes, it is yet of greater importance for a knowledge of their nature and therapy to realize that in liver and gall activity we have a true polarity. Despite their perfect interaction, the direction of their activity is of an opposing nature.

We considered pure build up to be typical of the liver, and we can see the impulses of the gall in the liver's breakdown processes. That they take place there says nothing of their origin. The breakdown character of the gall activity can be seen typically in all regions, particularly in the transformation of hemoglobin into the bile constituents, bilirubin, biliverdin, and urobilinogen. The breakdown occurs in the liver and also in the bone marrow and spleen. Yet it is a bile process that brings this about. The activity of an organ is not limited to its anatomical boundaries only. When one recognizes the unique nature of the function, it can then also be discovered to be active in other places. The enzymes of hemoglobin breakdown exist practically everywhere in the organism.

That one is dealing with a catabolic process, in a certain sense with a destruction, can be seen in the opening of the heme ring; this is an oxidative splitting of the methane bond with elimination of CO_2. As a matter of fact, this physiological breakdown requires the presence of iron. Porphyrin, which is free of iron, is not accessible to this breakdown. Here is an indication of the basic connection of gall and iron. Iron is made available for new tasks and will subsequently be bound as ferritin and stored, while the breakdown products of the porphyrin portion are excreted as bile substances. Thus, in the breakdown of the heme portion there is a destruction of porphyrin with the separation and liberation of iron.

The nature of bile is typically expressed in its bitter taste. Rudolf Steiner characterized the nature of bitter substances when he pointed out that they predispose the ether body to receive the astral body. From another point of view, however, this has been described as the gall function. The purely vegetative living substance resulting from the activity of the liver must be processed further so that the astral and ego impulses can be received. This is the task of the gall activity.

The bile acids are the primary substances that carry the gall impulses. They result from transformations of cholesterol and originate in a slight breakdown process. These steroids, to which bile acids as well as cholesterol belong, combine astral and etheric activities in a characteristic way.

The characteristic functions of the gall can also be rediscovered in its "external activities." The emulsifying function of the gall opens up the food substances, making them accessible to the intervention of the astral body, through which they are broken down. The emulsification of fat and water can also be understood to be a unification of astral activity with the ether body.

These examples may suffice to characterize the essential nature of gall activity, which, though by nature opposed to it, continues the liver function further. Finally, the polarity of liver and gall corresponds to the polarity of the metabolic and nerve-sensory systems.

Liver-Gall Rhythm

The rhythmic system's function is to mediate between the metabolic and nerve-sensory systems, which makes their healthy function possible. Likewise, the healthy working together of liver and gall is rhythmical; this rhythm allows their activities to be effective. The improper working of one into the other brings about illness, which is described below.

Liver and gall show a rhythmic activity that is to a large extent entirely independent of meals. The assimilatory phase of the liver begins at 3:00 P.M. and reaches its maximum at 3:00 A.M. During this time glycogen is stored. This assimilation leads to a significant increase in the weight of the liver. The secretion phase, which corresponds to the beginning of gall activity, begins at about 3:00 A.M. reaches its maximum about 3:00 P.M. During this phase glycogen is decreased and is transformed into blood glucose.

These phases correspond to the general in- and out-breathing of the earth. They point to a man's connection even in functional aspects to the life of the earth organism.[8] What is evident in the nature of the organs can also be recognized from these findings; the gall is a day organ and the liver one of night. The gall is united more closely with processes of consciousness, whereas the liver is related more to the anabolic processes during sleep.

Naturally, it is the harmonious rhythmic cooperation of both organs that produces the functional unity of the liver-gall system with which still higher tasks are connected. The stream of substance formation proceeds with regard to the subsequent function and is normally oriented to it. This formation of substance must be directed so that it will be able to receive spiritual impulses. It is one of the fundamental insights of spiritual science that volition is based on the metabolic system, just as thinking is based on the nervous system and feeling on the rhythmic. In this respect, the liver-gall system has the task of realizing the mental intention. "The liver always mediates the transformation of intended ideas into deeds performed by the limbs."[9]

If this organic basis is incompletely developed, which can be especially detrimental in a child, it is possible that the person will remain inactive despite his best intentions. He will be unable to will, because the organic basis, the liver, does not provide the "material." Hence, a will-defect develops that appears as an inhibition of the will. This must be exactly distinguished from weakness of will. The latter is primarily a psychological, while inhibition of the will is an organic defect: a weak-willed person could, but does not have the will, i.e. does not want to; the will-inhibited person has the will, but cannot come to the deed. If, despite proper initial development, the liver "is not properly formed, then a will-defect develops that is expressed in the child's wanting to do something that does not pass over into the carrying out of the will impulse but remains stuck in thinking." This realization of the liver as an organ of the will is of the greatest significance for education, psychiatry and therapy.

In conclusion, here is a schematic summary of some of the polarities manifested in the hepatobiliary system:

Liver	*Gall*
Build up	Breakdown
Substance formation	Activity
Plant	Animal-human
Leaf	Blossom, Ripening
Reduction	Oxidation
Night organ	Day organ
Sleep	Consciousness
Anabolic phase	Catabolic phase
Magnesium	Iron
Potassium	Sodium

The Liver-Gall System and Temperament

The teaching of the human temperaments as basic attitudes of the human being goes back to Greek times. It certainly originated in old mystery wisdom. Underlying it are the four elements as well as the four supersensible members of man's being.

Although the expression "temperament" characterizes a soul mood, the different names for the temperaments designate physical organs or body fluids. From what has been said, it is evident that the preparation of bodily substances occurs with their later functions in view, that is, their service as instruments of the ego and astral body. This formative process takes place under the guidance of the ego, which creates its substance for itself. This means that the possibility of experiencing the ego and astral body also depends on the physical foundation. For this process, especially the qualitative formation of substance, the liver-gall system is of decisive significance.

The polarity of liver and gall can be displaced to one side or the other. If it is imbalanced and the liver predominates, the anabolic processes will prevail. The liver was described as the central organ of the fluid metabolism and the ether body and as active in vitalizing and organizing fluids. Life can never support itself on "chemically pure water," but only upon living fluids containing organic substances and salts. The perfect example of such a living fluid, which is however only "alive" and not permeated by the ego like the blood, is mucous. All living fluids are actually always of a muco-viscous nature, whereas fluids from other organs—for example, those connected with the nervous system and subject to its catabolic character—are free of protein, clear, and quite fluid like the cerebrospinal fluid and tears.

If this mucous building process predominates everywhere in the body, then the ego and astral body have difficulty penetrating it. Such a person is sluggish, dull, less conscious—in brief, phlegmatic. This is what the Greeks experienced and why they called such a person a "mucous" person. Mucous was only the expression for this kind of substance formation that remained entirely in the living vegetative, and thus within the way of life that is connected with the predominance of the liver activity over the gall process. Here the water element and the liver rule. The phlegmatic individual could also be termed, "the hepatic." His life is too much and for too long like that of a plant. His soul-spiritual being incarnates inadequately and is thus hardly recognizable.

If the equilibrium of the liver-gall system is displaced in favor of the gall (ή χολή), the opposite occurs; the living substance is grasped too strongly and metamorphosed catabolically by the ego and astral body. Not the vegetative, but rather the transformed, sparkling spirit-soul life becomes apparent; the spiritual vigor that conquers the physical is the insignia of this gall man, the choleric. In his excessive activity, he breaks down his bodily substance more intensely than other humans, and not only his own substance, but if necessary also that of his fellow men and environment. The catabolic character of the gall impulse can proceed even to destruction if, for example, a resistance is "overcome" in an outburst of anger. Such catabolic processes are accompanied by combustion processes, oxidation, and warmth formation in the organism. This was felt by the genius of language when such people are called "hotheaded." It is the fire element through which the spark of the spirit comes to be active.

This entire activity is deeply connected with iron. The essential relationship between iron and gall has a common origin; what is cosmically Mars is iron in nature and gall in the organism. Iron has already been described as *the* incarnation metal; it brings the spirit to earthly activity. This integration is at first, however, a moving away, a dissolving or destruction of what already exists. This physiological process finds an exceedingly strong expression in the choleric as he brings his spiritual impulses prematurely to activity. Finally, however, all courage, vigor, initiative, grasping and transforming of the world is united with this iron process for which gall forms the physical foundation. If the gall impulse is too strong in the choleric, it does not mean that there is simply too much gall fluid or bile in the blood. On the contrary! Such an excess of gall fluid in the blood would indicate a blockage as in jaundice and thus an illness process. The blocked bile in the blood in no way stimulates deeds or enthusiasm, but leads to paralysis, as is described below.

Part and parcel of a healthy gall function is the separation of the unity of heme or hemoglobin, that is, the differentiation and excretion of the two substrates iron and bile fluid. Only this separation and excretion makes possible the formation of a new polarity and new functions; in this process the bile pigments and the bile acids in the bile fluid have very different functions. These will be discussed in the chapter on gall pathology.

On one level, the equilibrium of liver and gall can be considered quantitatively. But such an equilibrium can also be qualitatively altered. When the phlegmatic is united too weakly and the choleric too strongly with his body, the manner of working into them can differ. As described, the gall process brings about a separation in the living blood: The iron portion is separated but remains within the organism, while the porphyrin is broken down and excreted with the gall fluid as bile pigment. Thus, two simultaneous streams develop: (1) an "incretion" of iron and (2) an excretion of bile pigments. Both processes are also polar and have different functions in the organism. The iron bound in hemoglobin is freed and thus receives another function. By becoming free, it is in the *status nascendi* like a luminous spark that permeates the blood with light. The light process is a characteristic aspect of the nature of iron that comes to expression here. An image of the relationship between cosmos and earth is that of light and darkness, into which man is placed too. Both permeate him and thus address the gall forming process. The physiological separation of iron and bile pigment is a separation into light and darkness.

Naturally, we are not talking here of optically perceptible light, but rather of what lies as activity at the basis of the light metabolism. Similarly, this differentiation can be understood as polarity and intensification in the sense of Goethe. Just as colors develop in the interaction of light and darkness, so the human being is permeated by the forces of light and darkness, giving color to his bodily substance and being and uniquely stamping him in a light-permeated or darkly muted sense.

When the forces of light, which are connected with the iron impulse that extends into the blood in this polarity, predominate, there is a stronger buoyancy, an uplifting above the heaviness of the earth; we then have the sanguine individual before us. His element is the air, and the genius of speech characterizes him as "the flighty or airy personality." He is much more strongly affected by the qualities of soul, which are connected with the air element.

When the forces of darkness predominate in this polarity, the basis for the melancholic temperament is given. Then the organism is more permeated by darkness and the stream of gall becomes darker (μελάς = black). The bile pigments are the organic counterparts of the iron-light process. The gall fluid contains practically no iron—this remains in the blood—but rather iron's opposite, the bile pigments. The mineral substances of the bile have approximately the same relative relationships as they have in serum, excepting magnesium, which is found in a much lower proportion. It, however, is a significant carrier of the light impulse.

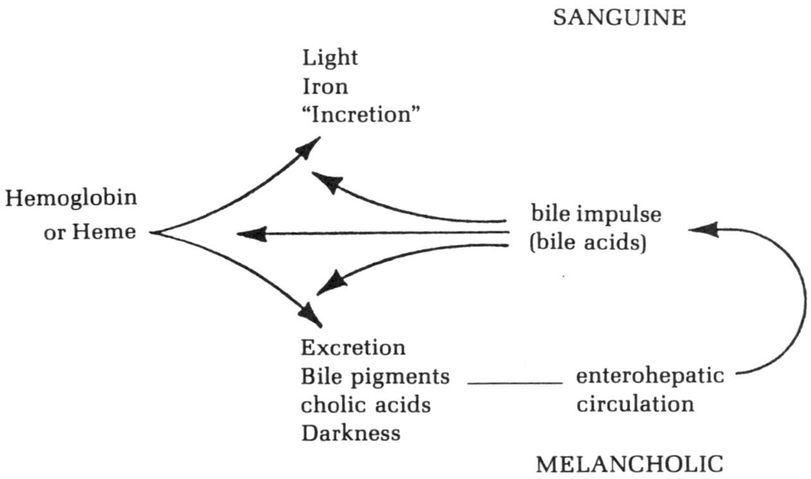

The working of the forces of darkness can be followed right into the substances. Just as the light originates from the cosmos, so darkness is connected with the being of the earth. The latter predominates as an element in the melancholic, giving him the thoroughness and depth, but also the depressed nature of his being. On the other hand, the hopelessness that is often a predominant aspect of his way of life, is an expression of inadequate light processes.

From this brief discussion of the relationships between the organs and the temperaments, it can be seen to what extent the liver-gall system provides the organic foundation for an individual's inherent mood and for the way his spirit and his position in relation to the earth and cosmos manifest.

When it was said in earlier times that the liver produces mucous or phlegm, the yellow and black gall fluids and the blood, it was certainly not meant in an anatomical, physiological way. Rather, it is to be understood imaginatively. It thus corresponds absolutely to reality.

Concerning the connections of exceptional psychological qualities with a rigidity of the liver metabolism, Rudolf Steiner pointed out in various places that "it is important to observe people in whom a sense of self-importance, stubbornness and a tendency to always want to be right occur, all of which represent a certain immobility of the conceptual system, to see what the state of the liver process is in such persons. For in these people it is always the inner organic chemistry that does not work properly. Those who suffer from a discontinuity of thoughts always bear within themselves connections to an improperly functioning liver process."[10]

It must be added that anabolic processes do indeed take place in the liver-gall system, but the interconnections with other organs play into them. This will be discussed in detail later. Again, the four organs—liver, kidneys, lungs, and heart—have definite connections with the elements and the members of man. Thus, the liver processes come to unfold in these other organs and they in turn work into the function of the liver. As will be shown, the kidneys have a special connection with the air organism. Their interaction especially makes possible the development of the sanguinic temperament. The same goes for the lungs and the melancholic, the heart and the choleric temperament. If the liver is "undisturbed," that is, largely uninfluenced by other organs, then the foundation is laid for the phlegmatic temperament. Thus, the following sketch can be presented:

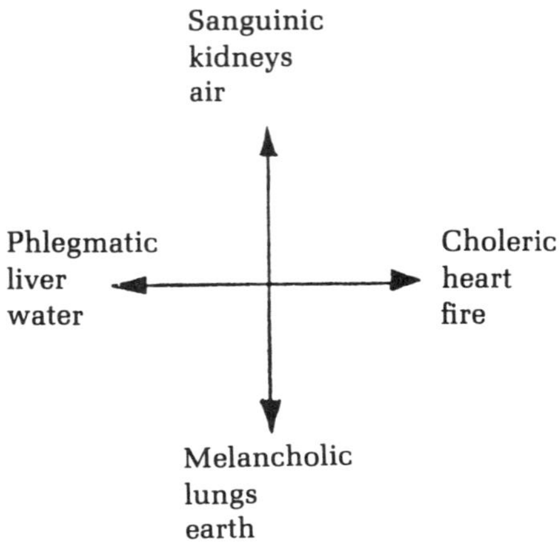

This interplay of the four organs is of decisive significance, especially for psychiatry, and it is described in the appropriate chapter. The temperamental state, however, always remains in the constitutional realm. Only extreme intensification leads to pathological manifestations.

Before discussing the actual pathology, a few other factors that play a significant role in the healthy or diseased function of liver and gall need to be mentioned—for example, the geographical influence. If one compares people from the north with those from the south, it is apparent that the liver function is emphasized in northerners and the gall function in southerners. It can be said that the south predominately activates the gall so that the "southern temperament" physiologically has a stronger gall impulse. The outer warmth favors the gall constitution and vice versa. This explains why northern people in tropical areas are susceptible not only to gastrointestinal disorders but also to liver diseases and why the latter progress differently in hot regions than in cold. The curious finding that the polar bear and polar fox have stored such large quantities of vitamin A in their livers that to eat them is toxic is related to the fact that these animals must continuously defend themselves against an excessively strong cold and hardening process; thus, the anabolic function of the liver must be stronger.

In vitamin A one can see this anabolic tendency as an expression of the silver process.[11] Therefore, in assessing the liver-gall function one will need to consider how the constitution and geographical conditions relate to each other.

The Pathology of the Liver-Gall Process

Liver Pathology

The polarity of inflammation and sclerosis, whose significance was explained in detail earlier, is a decisive key for comprehending the general processes of illness. At first glance, such a clear division in the liver does not seem to be possible since mixed forms seem to predominate. In other words, there is a simultaneous occurrence of inflammation and degenerative forms such as cirrhosis. Considered more accurately, however, the fruitfulness of this fundamental distinction is also apparent here.

The most frequent liver disease is acute hepatitis. It is subdivided today into epidemic hepatitis or hepatitis virus A and serum hepatitis (hepatitis virus B), which has a worse prognosis. Processes of swelling, enlarging, and inflammation take hold of the organ. They can be only very slight or in the most serious forms, especially tropical hepatitis, they can lead to obvious and evident inflammations. However, high fever as an expression of the acute inflammation that involves the entire organism is absent. At the beginning of the illness, exogenous influences from spoiled food or rancid fats are commonly present. Depending on a preexisting constitutional or acquired weakness of the liver, they create the conditions in which the virus thrives. The conditions are certainly somewhat different when viruses are transmitted by transfusion or inoculation. Then one is dealing with an infectious illness. Depending on the state of the organism, this foreign influence is balanced by the liver with weaker or stronger inflammatory reactions.

Acute hepatitis usually heals completely since the regenerative force and healing tendency of the liver is exceptionally great. Before the course of the illness is described, it must still be remembered in case a complete healing is not achieved that, despite obvious inflammation, acute hepatitis is accompanied only by sub-febrile temperatures. There is, however, a liver disease that proceeds dramatically with high fever and the extreme inflammatory nature of it can be recognized. Against this background, then, the polar sclerotic illnesses will become more evident.

The symptomatology of acute yellow liver atrophy hardly plays a role today, but it may be mentioned here because one can study the extreme reaction capacity of the organism in this illness. In a febrile, brief course the organ is almost entirely dissolved, corresponding to the localized highly febrile process. The fact that this illness hardly occurs today may be connected with the fact that in general the capacity of human beings to have highly febrile diseases has declined markedly; this can also be shown in other diseases. In this connection, it is interesting that in tropical areas—for example in Africa—acute yellow liver atrophy can still be found. This is connected with the different living conditions there and also with the geographical location.

The liver was described above as an organ of the ether body with an anabolic character. Astral body and ego intervene only slightly in a catabolic fashion. If they work too far into the physical structure, serious destructions result that appear to cause the liver's dissolution or self-digestion. This then leads to a most rapid course of the illness. The fact that acute yellow atrophy of the liver is caused by toxins or poisons, especially phosphorus and arsenic, is most informative concerning the substance functions of this organ. These substances are revealed in the spiritual scientific study of substances as carriers of definite activities: Phosphorus is an ego carrier and arsenic a carrier of the astral body. When they are administered in larger quantities, then the ego through phosphorus and the astral body through arsenic intervene directly and excessively strongly in the ether body and thus in the liver. The result is the destruction of the entire organ.

That mushroom poisons are as dangerous for the liver as phosphorus and arsenic is well-known. This is comprehensible from the above considerations since mushrooms through their heterotrophic nutrition reveal the catabolic character of astral impulses—something that is exceedingly enhanced by the formation of poisons. Groman designates the metabolism of mushrooms as a destructively catabolic one, which leads back into the dead mineral.[12] Also, the effects of the other liver toxins—for example, the chlorinated hydrocarbons—are based on the fact that chlorine evokes catabolic astral impulses.[13]

Acute hepatitis can be completely healed, or the liver can remain "weak" for a long time, which can manifest as a so-called post-hepatitic syndrome or post-hepatitic hyperbilirubinemia. But also without clinical findings and often as the only symptom, there can be a continuing loss or decrease of vitality. Frequently, a disturbed sleep-waking rhythm, fatigue, tiredness, and poor appetite are connected with inadequate energy. The symptomatology is typical for a lack of the anabolic processes of the ether body that cannot properly take hold in this organ. Often delicate disturbances remain as long-lasting weaknesses of drive and will, thereby supporting the significance of the discussion of the liver as an organ of the will. This non-specific symptomatology is nevertheless typical, on the whole, for the inadequate grasp of the ether body and therefore for disorders of the liver function. Organic symptoms such as weak digestion, intolerance of certain foods, etc., may indicate how to interpret seemingly psychopathological symptoms correctly and how to approach them therapeutically.

There can also be a transition from acute hepatitis to chronic hepatitis. When the illness is prolonged, one speaks of a chronic persistent hepatitis; here, signs are found of inflammatory portal infiltrations, but the lobar structure is retained. Frequently, this can also heal after one or two years, depending on the individual's constitution and way of life.

The disease can progress to chronic, aggressive hepatitis with low or high activity. The immune system participates here, which is why this disorder can also be taken as an autoaggressive disease. Histologically one finds the so-called "motheaten necroses."

Finally, connective tissue strands and foci of regeneration

can develop with a scarified liver that is permeated by scars and presents a defective healing. If the illness process now comes to rest, the remaining liver can again fulfill its function adequately. If the process proceeds, then an aggressive increase of connective tissue takes place that displaces the liver parenchyma; this is the case in cirrhosis. In aggressive hepatitis and cirrhosis, strongly inflammatory and degenerative sclerotic processes are directly adjacent to each other. This signifies that the ego is no longer able to separate and to rule the two polar tendencies of illness through its activity in the metabolism. In a healthy person both poles, inflammation and sclerosis, are bound to their respective physiological foci and are mediated by the rhythmic system. A direct meeting of them makes the enhancement of their polarity impossible. Also, an equilibrium is not attained since the overriding order is lacking. Therefore, this state is the image of serious illness—an expression of deficient ego function. Considered from the point of view of process, the controlling and holding apart of these two polar forces is a stannum process, while the ego function is addressed by phosphorus.

According to the points of view presented here, the occurrence of other kinds of cirrhosis is also comprehensible. In all cholestases (cholangitis, chronic obstructive jaundice, chronic intra-hepatic cholestasis), the obstruction of bile flow brings about a paralysis of the polar liver process so that biliary cirrhosis results. The essential relationship of bile and iron is shown also in the occurrence of a pigment cirrhosis (in hemochromatoses, Brown's diabetes). Iron—here as hemosiderin—is just like bile; in excess it is a specific liver toxin.

Cirrhosis represents, in any case, the other form of the end of an illness process in which the hardening, as in sclerosis, finally so predominates that the parenchyma is displaced and is incapable of functioning. It is definitely conclusive that in a morphological, clinical sense there are transitions in all forms of illness, and in every situation the process can cease and healing, though partial, will still be largely possible.

The clinical course of an illness is exceedingly revealing regarding the working of the members of man's being and the consequences for therapy. An early clinical symptom in cirrhosis is meteorism. This reflects an excessive independence of the air organism. The astral body is inadequately active in the intestinal tract, resulting in an insufficient breakdown of food and an excessive formation of gas.

The next stage is the development of ascites. Here we are dealing with the excretion in the abdominal cavity of unorganized fluid that has lost its life and buoyancy. Because of the hardening process that takes place in the liver, the ether body is no longer able to vitalize the fluid.

The last stage in the course of cirrhosis is an insufficiency and imbalance of the liver's function. Its occurrence shows that the liver is no longer in a position to hold back the hardening processes. The physical body dominates the ether body, and if bleeding from esophageal varices does not end life prematurely, death in hepatic coma occurs.

The progressive independence and destruction of the harmony of the members of man's being can be followed step by step. In the beginning there are the inflammatory processes without fever. Chronic inflammation here is one of the frustrated attempts to bring a sclerotic process into balance. An adequate intervention of the ego-organization, which lives in warmth, is missing. Even necrosis can be considered an attempt by the organism to dissolve foreign processes or to encapsulate them. Clearly, particularly in aggressive hepatitis, there is an absence of the control the ego exerts over the opposing processes of inflammation-dissolution and hardening-fibroses or sclerosis. Next, the air organism becomes independent and partially separates. This manifests as meteorism. The same then happens with the ether body and the water organism. It succumbs to gravity, can no longer be organized and ascites results. With the further separation of the ether body, the physical organism comes to predominate, insufficiency, and imbalance result, leading finally to death.

It must be emphasized again that the inflammatory reactions are "cold," and thus proceed in a sub-febrile state so that the ego-organization, which lives in warmth, cannot adequately take hold.

On this basis, it is also understandable that alcohol is an obvious liver toxin. A large portion of cirrhotics have abused alcohol. The specific liver damage brought about by alcohol can be understood from the nature of this substance. It is the product of a bacterial breakdown of sugar through fermentation. Such a breakdown stands in contrast to the transformations of carbohydrates that take place in the organism. There lactic and oxalic acids are built up again, whereas alcohol cannot again enter an anabolic process but holds the dying process within itself. Its preservative effects are based on that. It is by nature hostile to life forces. Although it stems from life, what has been said concerning the effect of mineral dead substances on the liver is also applicable to it.

The occurrence of alcoholic cirrhosis, however, far exceeds its toxic effect. It is also a human problem. It is not experimentally possible to bring about cirrhosis in animals with alcohol. Despite that, there is no doubt that alcohol is a pathogenic factor in the development of cirrhosis of the liver in man. It may bring it about, but this is not necessarily so.

It is evident from the manifold confirmations of the connection of alcohol consumption and liver cirrhosis that there is a strong individual factor in that development. This becomes recognizable when the true significance of alcohol for the human being is considered. Just as sugar is a substance that is required by the ego-organization in order to work on the organism, and just as the ego continuously battles against fermentation in the organism—that is, it fights against alcohol formation in favor of other breakdown processes—so alcohol specifically inhibits the activity of the ego and paralyzes it. The "anti-ego" becomes active through alcohol, "the battler against the deeds of our spiritual ego."[14] Thus, in typical manifestations of alcoholic intoxication, the exemplary human forms of expression—walking, speaking and thinking—are affected; the drunk cannot walk, talk, or think. The release of inhibitions after alcohol consumption signifies an exclusion of the critical faculty and the capacity for judgment that are based on the ego; thus, the lower instincts of the astral body can be expressed without inhibition. It has already been mentioned that the formation of bodily substance in the liver occurs under the guidance of the ego, while in the battle between dissolution and hardening in the aggressive phase of chronic hepatitis or cirrhosis guidance by the ego in this metabolic region is missing. For this activity of the ego in the function of the liver, alcohol is specifically destructive.

In conclusion, the two polar disease tendencies for the liver, inflammation and cirrhosis, will be schematically presented; healing must be thought of as lying in the third dimension.

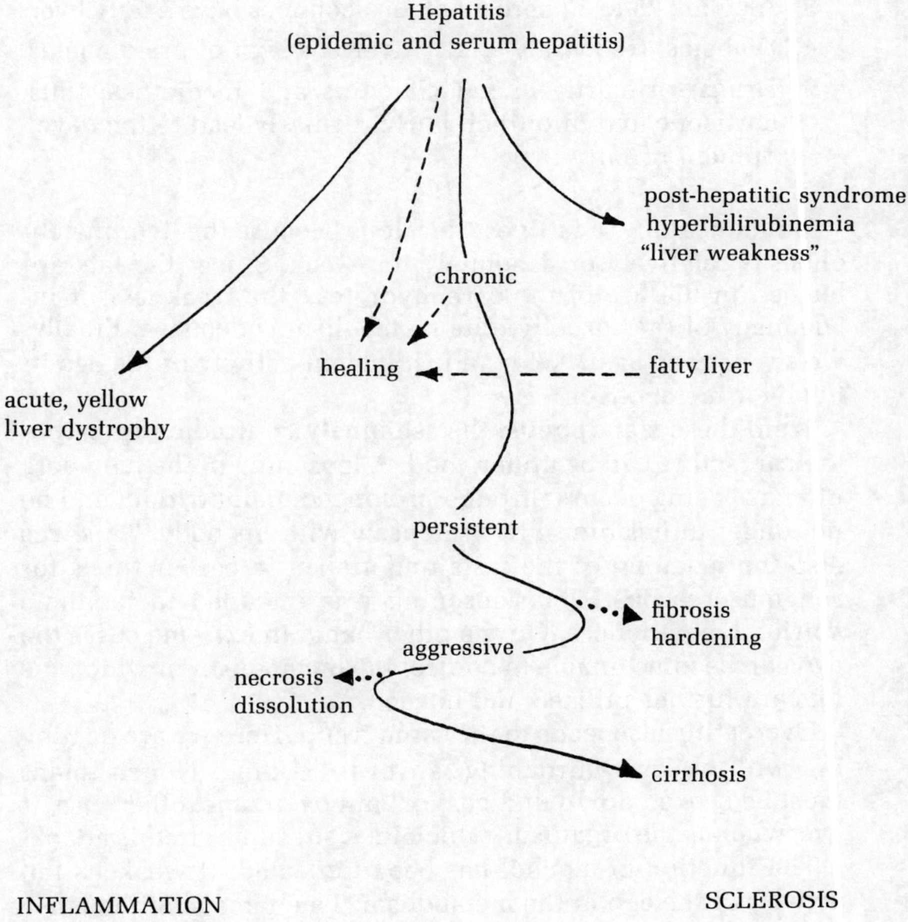

Special mention must be made of fatty liver. It is especially widespread, is relatively harmless and is reversible if the noxious agents are excluded. Fatty liver, however, is most revealing for an understanding of the organ's function and its connection with the members of man's being. The following factors lead to the development of a fatty liver:

1. Hunger, when it is primarily caused by protein deficiency.
2. Excessive food consumption; here the primary cause lies in overeating.
3. Alcohol; 75 to 80 percent of all alcoholics have a fatty liver.
4. Diabetes; frequently a fatty liver is a sign of pre-diabetes.
5. Drugs; primarily chemical toxins and medicines; thus, cortisone and thiouracil fairly regularly lead to the development of fatty liver.

Fundamentally, a fattiness develops because the liver metabolism is relatively or absolutely too weak. Since "the fats are burned in the fire of the carbohydrates," the weakness or inadequacy of the carbohydrate metabolism is decisive. Finally, we are dealing again with an insufficient activity of the ego in the liver metabolism.

From these standpoints, the seemingly contradictory pathological factors can be understood. A loosening of the members of man's being occurs through prolonged malnutrition, and he no longer unites himself so intensely with his body. This was also the meaning of the fasts undertaken in earlier times for religious reasons. This loosening was intended to facilitate spiritual experiences. On the other hand, in extreme cases the ego can become unable to control the metabolism in which the fats are further utilized and burned.

Overeating also leads to the same result. Here we are dealing ing with an over-burdening, an over-flooding. Nourishment must be broken down in digestion and overcome; otherwise, it overwhelms the organism, which then succumbs to this attack.

The function of alcohol has been indicated. It weakens the activity of the ego in the metabolism. The damage of the ether body in the liver through mineral substances was also touched on. Finally, through thiouracil and cortisone, specific combustion processes are inhibited. The important phase in the liver-gall system of continuing the ripening of substance formation, which goes hand-in-hand with the breakdown processes thus becomes impossible. In all these factors, as varied as they may appear, the interaction of the ego with the metabolism is made difficult, which is, in the last analysis, the cause for this disorder.

It needs still be mentioned that hepatic cirrhosis occurs three times more frequently in men than in women, which is certainly not only connected to external influences such as alcohol consumption. This difference has recently declined. A man is united more intensely with earthly corporeality and therefore is more subject to hardening influences. In him, the gall impulse is physiologically stronger and the balance of the liver-gall polarity is shifted in favor of gall. This, however, brings it about that from the first the liver function is often relatively weaker and is frequently continuously over-burdened.

Naturally, the opposite conditions exist in women. The frequent occurrence of gall stones in women, which is approximately double of that in men, has been noted ever since ancient times. Only in the last few years has there been a leveling off of this difference. Nevertheless, one can still say today that in principle men are more subject to liver illnesses and women more to those of the gall bladder, a difference that is connected with their different incarnation relationships.

Certainly exogenous factors such as poisons, alcohol, and nutrition play essential roles in the development of liver diseases. Nevertheless, it cannot be overlooked that an inner factor of a constitutional nature can determine decisively the reaction to outer influences. Why does one person have an organically inadequate liver and another not? According to an indication by Rudolf Steiner, this inner tendency of the liver to harden, which is in the last analysis the problem of chronic hepatitis and cirrhosis, at bottom lies in that the person was "nourished as an infant with the wrong milk." When a child is given the wrong milk, its liver is constantly aggravated.[15] The formation of substance by the liver can still take place, but the organ is prematurely exhausted. Then the increasing tendency to harden that occurs with age finally destroys it.

The perceptive function of the liver characterized above lies on the same level. In advancing age, this can prematurely decline, just as the sense organs lose their acuity in the aging process. In a weak liver, which can, for example, be caused by inadequate nourishment in infancy, the organism has become blind, as it were, to the perception of foreign substances and to its body. Cancerous illnesses, especially in the metabolic organs, can be connected with this. Particularly through modern immunological considerations of the cancer problem emphasis has been placed on the incapacity of the organism to recognize the carcinomatous tissue as "foreign." The role of the liver here is recognized, but there is no explanation for this functional disorder.[16]

Nutrition and the entire life-style play a significant part in the proper development of the organs. Naturally, in children education is also most important. Rudolf Steiner pointed out that, in the eighth or ninth years, the telling of stories and imitation by the children are of positive significance for this proper development, whereas merely visual instruction inhibits it. It is understandable that telling and repeating stories stimulate the child's innate fantasy; purely visual instruction is in principle rigid and has a paralyzing effect on the formative forces of the growing organism.

The Pathology of the Gall Bladder

The increased occurrence of gall bladder illnesses and gall stones in women has already been indicated.[17] The iron process working in the gall is less developed in them; their gall function is weaker and is frequently over-stressed.

From what has been said, it can be understood that the pyknic constitution also is more frequently subject to biliary diseases. In them, the anabolic processes predominate and the formative forces are relatively weak.

Biliary colic is a typical symptom of over-stress brought about by outer and inner demands. In the case of excessive fat consumption, the astral body attempts to produce as much bile as possible to emulsify and digest them. In colic, however, the interaction of the astral body does not occur in the metabolism of bile formation, but rather works by concentrating and excreting with the dynamic of the nerve-sensory system. This leads to cramping of the smooth muscles.

Attacks of gall bladder colic are characterized by the time when they occur—virtually always at night. From what has been said about the rhythmic aspects of the liver-gall system that is easily understood. Gall fluid is a diurnal substance. For it to be under stress in the evening is unphysiological, and thus the same stimulus causes it to react pathologically with the colic in the evening rather than in the morning.

As was described above, in the healthy process the effect of the astral body transforms cholesterol into bile acids. If this process is disturbed, cholesterol remains behind and is not changed into cholic acids. This is a matter of deficient breakdown, lack of "ripening," an insufficient bile-impulse, in other words. Instead of being transformed into cholic acids, cholesterol is excreted in greater concentrations, and can thus be deposited as gall stones. This deposition is a process that increases with age. Thus, in approximately 40 percent of those over sixty, and 50 percent of those over seventy, gall stones can be found even though these individuals have to a large extent been symptom-free throughout their earlier lives.[18] These findings, however, depend upon geographical location and are exceedingly varied. Thus, in Sweden cholelithiasis was discovered in 50 percent of women and 32 percent of men older than twenty.[19] Without doubt, however, there is presently an increase of gall stone diseases. This is not only an expression of an increase of sclerotic illnesses in general, but it is also connected in part with changed eating habits, that is, increase of fat consumption, of saturated fats and of sugar. The extent to which nutritional influences are important is shown by experiments in which feeding a sugar-rich diet to dogs, or a fat-free but sugar-rich diet to hamsters, can produce gall stones. Here it can be seen that the deposition of cholesterol is not primarily a result of consuming it, as it is always said to be in the development of sclerosis and atheromatosis. Rather, it comes from an impairment in the ability to utilize the cholesterol.

In the development of biliary illnesses, psychological influences play an essential role that has been known for ages. It was described above how gall generally represents the physical foundation for vigor and initiative and how in a choleric, and also in every outburst of anger, a copious production of bile occurs as a physical correlate. As long as this impulse can develop outwardly psychologically and physically, man feels himself to be unburdened and liberated; in fact, his own activity gives him a new impulse. If, however, an outward reaction is impossible, there is then a congestion with the psychological correlate of worry or trouble. Instead of ordering the outer world anew, or destroying it in a choleric burst of anger, his inner world, his own organism, more exactly his liver, is attacked. The result is self-poisoning caused by congestion rather than the excretion of bilirubin. This leads to embitterment—a most fitting expression—to self-accusations, even to a kind of self-destruction or auto-aggressive illness.

It is known that anxiety, excitement, and alcohol can cause increases of bilirubin. Frequently bad moods, depressions, and pessimism are connected with this heightened bilirubin level. These are often the only, or early, symptoms of a post-hepatic hyperbilirubinuria or juvenile jaundice (Meulengracht). As already mentioned, and as is quite evident from this discussion, the blocked bile does not make one active because it is toxic; normally it is detoxified and leaves the liver combined with a digluceronide to be transported to the intestine. The key is provided by the bile acids, which, like bilirubin, naturally belong to the bile; they have, however, another destiny and task. As is well-known, they are resorbed again and provide the impulse for the formation of gall. In general, bile acids are the strongest choleretics. Thus, they bring about a loosening of congestion. If, however, the forming of bile becomes too strong, the attendant activity is then intensified to outbursts of temper.

On the other hand, patients with a biliary fistula become lethargic since they lack the recirculated bile. This can also be the case in diarrheas of long duration. Forming bile alone is inadequate; it also requires the specific stimulus of the resorbed bile acids. To see in this intestinal resorption merely an economic measure—as, for example, the re-utilization of an emulsifier—is superficial. The meaning of these events lies in the fact that they make possible the soul-spiritual activity of man.

This also makes comprehensible the characteristic symptom pruritus of jaundice that is connected with the bile acids. The activity of the astral body which cannot be unloaded outwardly because of the congestion is directed to its own organism, thereby causing the predominance of a misguided process of consciousness. In accordance with their nature, the bile acids also have a toxic effect, and in their combinations with glycocoll and taurine they are detoxified and excreted by the liver as glycocholic and taurocholic acids. Bile is necessarily a slight poison that is needed for man's activity. Higher animal life is not possible without the formation of poison.

In this enterohepatic circulation of the bile acids we have the physiological basis for a process that has entered technology under the name of a feedback loop. This process is an astral phenomenon; it also occurs in the psychological realm when a reaction is favored, a reflex is initiated and a positive reaction takes place. This can easily be observed in the psychological realm in mood states. The continual enhancement of an impulse can, however, operate negatively, for example in allergic sensitization or any vicious circle. Whether positive or negative, the fundamental process is certainly the same. The physiological prototype of this astral phenomenon of the feedback loop or self-strengthening and self-help is the enterohepatic circulation of the bile acids. On this basis, the same process can also take place on the soul-spiritual plane; that is, the exercise of every activity favors its further exercise; it becomes easier through habit and is "solidified" in the ether body which we see in the process of learning.

Concerning Therapy

It is evident, or should be, from the description of the liver and gall polarity that a therapy must take into consideration the uniqueness of the organs and the rhythmic relationships.

In principle, it is also not sensible to mix typical liver and gall remedies.

In every organ therapy one can support those forces that have formed the organ and continue to maintain it in the adult. With the kind of knowledge that comprehends both nature and man, essential relationships can be discovered between natural substances and the processes in the human organism. By virtue of this inner affinity it is then possible to affect an organ and its formative forces with a plant or a mineral.

Liver Therapy

In this area there is almost a therapeutic nihilism today that stems from the customary way of thinking and judging. Clearly recognizable "effects," like those seen in the medicinal influence on blood pressure, are not to be expected here. Nevertheless, a rational, meaningful therapy in the field of liver therapy is possible and can be developed from pathological processes if one starts with the essential connections between nature and man.

Based on insight into the nature of disease and regenerative processes, bed rest is fully justified in all acute phases of illness. This is, however, only one part of the total transformation that is necessary to make possible the regeneration of the ether body. Just as bed rest and rest from unnecessary sense impressions are necessary, so a soul-spiritual hygiene is also needed. This applies not only to liver therapy, but actually to every illness, which should always be a new beginning.

The application of moist warmth to the liver is generally practiced and fully justified. It was described above how the liver requires warmth for its function; therefore warmth is indicated because of the great danger presented by the hardening processes that ultimately end in cirrhosis. These hardening processes are countered by the dissolving and vitalizing tendency of moist warmth. An addition of suitable teas, such as yarrow, to the moist compresses enhances their effect.

A remedy that is unique in therapeutic concept is the liver remedy made from plants, Hepatodoron. It is one of the so-called "typical remedies" the principle of which has already been presented. These go back to Rudolf Steiner. In principle, Hepatodoron does not address a single function of the liver, but rather its composition represents the image of liver activity. Thus, it is the primary remedy of the entire liver function, and is not only directed against a particular illness or symptom. The indications for its use can therefore not be understood by pathological and anatomical diagnoses.

Hepatodoron is prepared from the leaves of the vine, Vitus vinifera, and the wild strawberry, Fragaria vesca, whose leaves are not extracted but are used as they naturally are. Neither plant is common as a liver remedy; nevertheless, closer study shows that one can actually see an image of the liver's function in them that works by balancing all disturbances of it and by providing a basic remedy with a supra-ordered broad general effect in the liver region.

As is well-known, plant leaves are organs of assimilation; that is, processes that form substances occur in them. Both Vitus and Fragaria clearly are connected with sugar—more exactly, with sugar formation; yet both show contrasting natures that can only be indicated here. Whereas the vine demonstrates an enormous ability to form sugar from warmth and light (it grows only in areas where both are abundant), the wild strawberry, on the other hand, thrives in the cooler earth realm. It is a Rosaceae, as are most of our species of sweet fruit, but without their tendency to lignification; it remains embryonic, as it were.

The assimilative activity of the liver is addressed through both of these plants. This is seen in the leaf process, which corresponds to glycogen formation in the liver. Here, in this preparation, Vitus vinifera takes hold of the initial formation and the Fragaria vesca portion leads the substance further so that it can pass into the bloodstream to be prepared for its later function. In both plants, however, the effect is oriented toward the function of the ego through the special processing of sugar.

The stimulation of the activity of the liver should proceed in accordance with rhythmic events; since the liver activity reaches its maximum at night, Hepatodoron is most effectively given then in a dose of two to four tablets. Certainly the absorption of food can also be readied by prescribing one or two tablets to be taken prior to meals. The use of Hepatodoron in suitable cases is supplemented by Choleodoron, which represents an image of the gall process. In this way, through both the entire liver-gall system is addressed.

The formation of the liver is connected with the forces embodied in tin (stannum). This fundamental connection was described in the chapter on metals. Therefore, with stannum in a suitable form, one stimulates the *forming* rather than the function of the liver. Stannum, then, is always indicated when the liver passes over into a deforming or degenerative state, that is, in the constitutionally weak liver, post-hepatic states, and cirrhosis.

Certainly potentized Stannum in D8 to 12 is effective alone. A more intensive activity can be attained, however, if the broad effect of Stannum is directed right to the liver. This can be brought about in various ways by first treating a plant with Stannum and then using the plant. This pharmaceutical procedure of the "vegetabilized metals" goes back to Rudolf Steiner and has been described in volume I. To use Stannum in this way, one certainly selects plants that have an intense connection with the liver. These will be discussed next. It is remarkable that almost all remedial plants for the liver-gall system are bitter. We have already pointed to this fact. They prepare the etheric to take up the astral. In each case, this happens in a different way.

Taraxacum (dandelion) is a spring plant containing much milky juice that is a true rubber latex. The plant is watery and shows that it can vitally stimulate the metabolism. Its effect on the water organism and the liver has been known for a long time. Its sap is actually organized living water and therefore contains much potassium. The diuretic effect of Taraxacum to which the French term "pissenlit" points, is not determined by the potassium content alone; rather the remedy helps the liver to vitalize and organize water insofar as it addresses the vitalizing, anabolic function of the liver. One can use the young plant therapeutically in a salad or take the juice of the plant and also use Taraxacum in lower potencies. It is especially effective in the form of Stannum per taraxacum or Taraxacum stannum cultum, when stannum therapy is directed to the field of activity of Taraxacum. It is most effective when one begins with an injection—for example, with a mixed ampule of Stannum taraxacum 1%/heparbovis D4āā a day, up to twice a week subcutaneously over the liver area. In sensitive patients the 1 percent preparation can cause local infiltrations, and it is then advisable to use the 0.1% preparation. Later, Taraxacum stannum cult. 1% is given as a dilution, 10 drops 3 times a day. This remedy is indicated as an after-treatment of all chronic processes in every liver disorder at the beginning of Stannum therapy when regeneration is to be stimulated.

The plant Stannum therapy mentioned here can be continued for some time and then be intensified by applying another form of stannum. Especially for longer treatment in cases of chronic hepatitis or cirrhosis, Hepar/stannum (produced by Weleda) is indicated. For the principle underlying this preparation see volume I. Stannum in suitable form (stannum hydroxide) is here brought in contact with fresh liver, worked over and combined with it so that a unified combination is formed. Stannum can thus work directly on the liver. For a long treatment, as in cirrhosis or its threatened development, Hepar/stannum is indicated, given twice a week as a subcutaneous injection. Acute effects can also be observed, especially on the water metabolism as in ascites.

Phosphorus is absolutely necessary in liver therapy. It has already been indicated that the main processes in the transformation of substance take place in the carbohydrate metabolism and always proceed under the influence of phosphorus. Thus, by way of phosphorus it becomes possible for the ego to be active in an organizing manner right into the metabolism. A deficiency of phosphorus, however, was described as the basis of an actual liver disorder and thus of disease. When phosphorus is then given, the ego is stimulated to rule the metabolic processes; phosphorus leads the ego into the metabolism. In the morning and at noon, five drops of Phosphorus D5 can be given. Phosphorus given in the evening can cause disturbed sleep because it has an incarnating effect in lower potencies.

Thistles are especially connected to the liver, the most commonly used of them at this time is Carduus marianus. It is used as a tincture or in low potencies. In the pharmacological thinking of our time, the "active substance" has been isolated from the plant (Silymarin) and is available as Legalon. Carduus benedictus (Cnicus benedictus) is also used in liver therapy, especially to relieve ascites and edemas; it works better, however, when combined with Peonia.

The silica process is directly perceptible in thistles. All ray-like formations, here seen in the wealth of thorns, point to a silica process that is completely active in the metabolic region. Thistles, therefore, address especially the sensory function of the liver, that is, the perception and evaluation of metabolic processes. This has great significance for it. Silica, as representative of the formative forces, is also addressed to the connective tissue of the organs. This points particularly to the use of silica in cirrhotic processes, for example, as Magnesit D4/silica D5 aa trit.

The artichoke, Cynara scolymus, is also used increasingly today in liver therapy, either dietetically as a juice or in a 30% tincture. Achillea millefolium, yarrow, is connected with the anabolic sulphurous element, and in the loose leaves of this plant one can also see processes that work by permeating the liver with form. It can be used as a tea, a dilution and particularly in enemas, or it can be applied externally as hot compresses.

Disorders of the water organism connected with the liver are best addressed with Kalium carbonicum. The significance of Kalium for the liver has been frequently emphasized; most plants providing liver remedies are rich in potassium. When the capacity of the liver to vitalize and organize water is decreased, when it cannot reintegrate "dead water" that the organism cannot properly control back into life, then Kalium carbonicum is indicated. A guiding symptom is the generalized, almost intra-cellular, swelling; this is not the same as edema. Such patients describe swollen eyelids, for example, that occur especially in the morning and can easily be seen. Frequently, water is consumed excessively; there may be a profuse vaginal discharge and often a feeling of coldness. This is based on the fact that water with its high specific warmth also behaves like a foreign body because it is not properly integrated into life. This swelling can be clearly distinguished from kidney or cardiac edema. The homeopathic picture of Kalium carbonicum shows the described symptomatology, which is also noted in the picture of potassium and can thus be understood rationally. In the therapeutic process, potassium first organizes the water. Only then can it be excreted. It is best to give eight to ten drops of Kalium carbonicum D6 three times a day. This often leads to the desired diuresis in a few days. Certainly this remedy is not a diuretic as such, but works only in the situation described here. Once the effect declines, Kalium carbonicum D10 can be given; it then frequently improves the given constitutional components.

Occasionally mercury is indicated for liver therapy. Mercury, as well as tin, both work on the water organism. Stannum, however, organizes water right up to the well-known semi-solid consistency of liver, whereas mercury brings water into movement, leading it further and mediating. It works especially on the life of the cell so that it neither proliferates profusely nor stops. That gives us the indication for using it particularly in states of inflammatory watery disease such as acute hepatitis in which there is a kind of watery congestion. Mercurius vivus D6 is given five times a day as a tablet, and occasionally as an injection. Homeopathic therapy prefers Mercurius dulcis. Soon after the acute states of the illness subside, one will want to change to Stannum in one of the described forms, that is, at first preferably to Stannum per taraxacum or Taraxacum stannum cult.

Copper plays a role in liver therapy not only because the liver is the organ most rich in copper, but also because the ascending, nourishing stream of substance in blood formation is connected with the copper process. Generally, copper works in particular in the venous portions of the blood, which makes up a major portion of the blood in the liver because of the portal vein. This points to the application of copper in liver illnesses that are based on disturbances of nutrition and dysfunctions of the venous circulation. But also generalized disorders such as anorexia and protein formation can be addressed by way of the liver with copper. Here, there is a connection with the radiations of the kidneys, an interrelationship of the kidney system and liver.

Despite the polar activity of the liver and gall, there are naturally smooth transitions, just as substances are taken from one process to the other. In a corresponding sense, there are also therapeutic measures that work upon this process as it has been described for mercury or that are indicated for both organs. Above all, warmth belongs into this category. It is evident from previous discussions that warmth may well have different functions in these organ regions. As has been shown in different ways, however, in every case the significant fact is that the ego works in warmth, which is therapeutically required here. More specifically, warmth facilitates the assimilative activity of the liver, just as it also favors the incarnation stream through the bile. The well-known antispasmodic, decongestant effect of warmth is based on its fundamental connection with the metabolic system, whereas cold indicates a corresponding relationship to the nervous system from which all impulses to cramping emanate.

Clinically, the application of moist warmth, whose benefits and effectiveness the patient experiences directly, in liver as well as gall diseases is among the most ancient of the physician's remedies. Nevertheless, in recent times theoretical arguments have been raised against the external application of warmth because supposedly it does not reach the organs and therefore must be ineffective. Certainly, measured results should not be doubted. Insight and practical experience, however, speak for the application of warmth, and it does not matter whether the effect comes directly or by way of reflex zones. Every application of warmth or cold addresses the warmth organism of man which will of necessity react. Should we agree that the external application of warmth has no effect, then the crucial experiment of applying an ice pack in a biliary colic should be performed. It would similarly have to be without effect. This simple, practical experience can take these "experimental verified findings" to the point of absurdity.

There are two substances in nature in which the mutual working of liver and gall can be recognized as in a mirror image. These substances are oxalic and formic acids. Both are closely related, which is evident in their formulas:

Formic acid: HCOOH

Oxalic acid:
$$\begin{array}{c} COOH \\ | \\ COOH \end{array}$$

Oxalic acid comes from the plant kingdom, formic acid from the animal realm. In therapy the products of nature are used as they are.

Oxalic acid is widespread in the plant kingdom. It appears most obviously in the plant Oxalis acetosella. This small, unseemly plant grows in shadowy woods. Characteristically it is exceptionally sensitive to light and, according to Hegi, can survive in only one-seventieth of full daylight. In the biotope of the woods its function is similar to that of the ant. It works into the earth organism from the plant side, permeating it with life and light; thus, humus remains living and does not become inorganic. The same function is taken over on the animal side by the ant. Its effect in the totality of nature and also in the human organism is such that organic life is maintained and organic substances are reintegrated into living circulation.

Chemically, oxalic acid can easily be transformed into formic acid by decarboxylation. This is the process also used by the organism. It is a transformation through the astral body, a taking further of a substance that stems from the ether body. Both of these substances can be considered as prototypes of the substantial events in the transition of liver to gall.

Oxalis brings about "an energizing of the etheric system in the digestive tract." Again, "were man never to develop oxalic acid in his digestive tract, he would not be able to live at all, because his ether body would not have a foundation in his organism. Were man not to transform oxalic acid into formic acid, however, then his astral body would not have a foundation in his organism. Man requires oxalic acid for his ether body and formic acid for his astral body. He does not need these substances as such, but he needs the activity that occurs in the oxalic acid and formic acid processes."[20] Disorders in which the application of oxalis is indicated "show themselves in a sluggish activity of the lower body, in inhibitions or disorders of the liver and spleen activity, in crystalline or stone-like depositions in the gall bladder and similar problems. If in these cases oxalic acid is given, one supports in an appropriate manner the ether organism in its activity."[21] Thus, Oxalis is indicated "when there are effects of inhibition in the etheric." Oxalis establishes the basis for an undisturbed gall activity. Though it is not to be designated absolutely as a gall remedy, Oxalis nevertheless creates the basis for the undisturbed gall function. Thus, if there is a tendency to biliary colics, an injection of Oxalis D3 is given twice a week over a longer period of time. Occasionally one can give Oxalis comp. dil. 3 times a day, 15 drops at the same time. This will not stop a colic, especially not if it is already at its peak, but that is not what matters here. It is crucial that the illness be healed and the recurrence prevented. A beginning colic can occasionally be influenced with injections of Oxalis D2 or Oxalis comp., possibly several ampules.

Since formic acid boosts the formation of oxalic acid, we have in it a furthering of the oxalis processes in which interactions exist. Evidence for the fact that substance can also separate in the metabolism of the liver and be deposited is most evident in fatty liver. Here, the indication for Formica is given, namely, for all processes of deposition that tend to hardening and sclerosis. It is evident from this that Formica is not only indicated in fatty liver, but also in all sclerotic and hardening processes that extend from chronic hepatitis to cirrhosis. Application is most favorable in the potencies D4 to D6 three times a day, eight drops, over a long period of time, or twice a week as subcutaneous injection into the liver area.

Gall Therapy

The gall requires a suitable foundation to function healthily. Frequently, despite obvious biliary symptoms, one must begin with liver therapy. The example of Oxalis has already been described.

The situation with magnesium is similar. It is characteristically related to the plant world in being the metallic portion of chlorophyll. It is thus considered to be the receiving substance for light. In this property it is polar to iron, which has the same but reversed function in hemoglobin. These relationships were described in detail in volume I.

An image of this interaction can be found again in the liver-gall system. It has already been described how the iron impulse is active in the gall. In it lives the animal activity that reverses the vegetative process. The vegetative process, however, is here represented by magnesium, and in this respect forms the specific basis for the working of the iron impulse. Liver and gall are thus polar in exactly the same way as magnesium and iron, or as chlorophyll and hemoglobin.

Often the iron impulse cannot become active because it does not find a suitable foundation. A characteristic symptomatology can be discovered here. It has been described how the anabolic liver activity reverses to a dissimilating bile activity at 3:00 A.M. At this time, the main phase of regeneration is concluded and a new incarnation process begins. This is more or less completed by the time of awakening and is then accompanied by catabolic processes—consciousness, etc. If the ego cannot become properly united with the organism by way of the bile stream because the substance was not properly prepared in the night, it seeks to be active in another way in the organism. It bumps, so to speak, into its own organism, extending its activities into the nervous system rather than into that of the gall. As a result, one awakes. There are individuals who experience this impulse in the organism and regularly awake at 3:00 A.M. In these cases it is not the iron impulse or the gall process that are disturbed—although that is where the symptoms show up—but the liver or the magnesium underlying them. Thus, magnesium therapy is indicated in such patients. Experience has shown that the form of magnesium one uses is less important. One can use natural magnesium carbonate, namely Magnasit D4–6, which can generally be given in the evening as a pinch once an hour for three times. Now that the iron impulse can be taken up properly, success is achieved in a short time causing symptoms to disappear that have often persisted for years.

Accordingly, it can also be understood that in serious liver disorders, especially cirrhosis, there is a lowered magnesium level in the blood. In these cases magnesium is also indicated, either in the form of Magnasit or as Kieserit (natural Magnesium sulfate) D6. Justifiably the homeopathic school prefers Magnesium phosphoricum. Both components are related to light and thus supplement each other. The latter is particularly indicated to stimulate the intermediary liver metabolism, for example in the continuation of Phosphorus medication, but also in spastic or cramped states and, in this case, in bilious colics.

The effect of magnesium can also be directed to the liver with the preparation Hepar/magnesium. It is based on the same principle that was described for Hepar/stannum. This preparation can be used in the treatment of organic liver illnesses as well as in the treatment of the depressions for which it was developed. There the light-permeating, illuminating effect of magnesium becomes active.

While the interaction of liver and gall is stimulated with this medication, the catabolic side is clearly more emphasized with Cichorium intybus. Overall, this plant is quite similar to Taraxacum but is different in essential respects. The radiant yellow of the spring dandelion, which lives entirely in the watery, is contrasted here with the blue of this plant of late summer with its exceptionally hard and tough stem. Relatively little sodium is found in it, which points to the bile production, while Taraxacum is an out-and-out potassium plant, hence related to the liver function. Cichorium works in a formative way without being a definite gall plant, however. Its activity extends to the gastrointestinal tract, and since it removes congestion, it is therefore also indicated in dyspepsia as well as in cholangitis and jaundice. Cichorium intybus dec. in 10% or D3 can be used. If one wants to affect congestions in the liver area, then Cichorum stannum cult 1% is given as injection or as a dil., that is, whenever the "substance stream" must be brought to "maturation" i.e. the bile flow must be stimulated. Often the feeling of fullness can be relieved immediately.

Chelidonium majus or celandine is a definite gall plant. It is a member of the poppy family and a tough, resistant weed. Its connection with the gall process is mirrored in its production of a yellow, milky sap that permeates the whole plant; this is lighter in the upper parts and orange-red in the roots. The plant tastes sharp and bitter. Its simultaneous cholegogic and spasmolytic effect has been known since antiquity. Lipases and a multitude of alkaloids are active in this sap. The application of Chelidonium ferrum cult 1% as injection or dil. is especially effective. Through this typical gall plant, the iron impulse is made more specifically active than through the use of iron alone. It is therefore indicated in all dyskinesias as an interval treatment and, in general, to stimulate the process of incarnation.

Iron, too, is used in gall therapy. Iron in nature corresponds to the gall bladder in man. Therefore, one can address the gall forming impulse in man with iron. The same fundamental connections exist here as between the liver and tin. The gall organ, the gall bladder, however, plays a secondary role. The formation of bile is decisive, but certainly there are functional relationships between it and the gall bladder with its contractility. Iron comprises the entire process; it is most comprehensive. Therefore, it may well happen that iron, which is indicated, may bring about an activation but a wrong one. This will then encourage the development of colics. Such effects can be avoided by guiding the iron to the inner activity of the gall by means of Chelidonium Ferro cultum or, for example, by addition of Oxalis to the iron preparations.

A mild stimulation of gall activity can also be effected by application of iron salve to the liver region; this also leads to a decongestion. Iron is also indicated in cases of hepatocellular jaundice (Ferrum sidereum or met. praep. D10 inj.) in order to eliminate the bile congestion. A finer diagnostic question, however, is whether fluid congestion does not initially play the larger role, as is most often the case in the first phase of acute hepatitis. This requires mercury!

Choleodoron addresses the gall process in an almost classic way. Here what was said above about Hepatodoron in relation to the liver applies also to the gall. Like Hepatodoron, Choleodoron is a universal, basic remedy in gall therapy.

Choleodoron consists of Chelidonium majus, discussed above, and Curcuma xanthorrhiza, a tropical Javanese plant with almost no stem. The blossom sits almost on the root and goes right into the earth. The root, the part that is processed, has a strong yellow color from the blossom impulse, and a most sharp taste. (A relative, Curcuma longa, is the main constituent of curry powder.) The volatile oil in the root has a predominantly choleretic action, while the pigments known as curcumins act cholekinetically. Thus, this plant, like chelidonium, is also permeated by a blossom process that works into the sap of the plant. Despite all similarity, these two plants show a certain polarity. In gall we also have two possibilities of dysfunction: The gall bladder can either become congested, or it can show a "wrong" activity in the sense of a colic. In one sense, one requires stimulation, in another, a sedation or calming. The stimulating component is given through Curcuma, the calming through Chelidonium. They supplement each other to the healthy, harmonious gall function.

The physiological events must also be considered when applying any gall therapy. Since gall activity begins in the morning, it is especially advisable to "apply" the remedies then. This is fundamentally important for iron therapy and also for Choleodoron, which is given almost in opposition to Hepatodoron in the morning or, when more frequently indicated, after meals in order to address the digestive activity of the gall.

An attempt has been made with this therapeutic sketch to point the way to a rational therapy for the liver-gall system. In this area today an extensive therapeutic nihilism or pessimism exists. It is unjustified, however, when one comes to understand and use the forces underlying the forming processes and functions of these organs.

Diet

The concept of the protective bland diet was in vogue for decades. Today, however, a dietetic nihilism is acknowledged that allows one to eat what is tolerable. Even the experiences of the ancients are ignored though their rightness is easily proven. This is a dangerous and unfounded simplification of the problem. It corresponds to the contemporary thinking that will only take as valid what is "proved" under the present "valid" points of view—an expression of the ruling passivity in the field of knowledge. One can, however, make a factual statement based on the fundamental relationships of foods and organ functions, and this is what will be attempted in the following.

It ought to be self-evident that the primary metabolic organ that encounters all nutriments, the liver, is quite decisively influenced by their nature. In a proper therapy it is absolutely essential that a diet be followed that is restricted according to the state of the illness. Tolerance of a food is only the most minimal precondition for choosing it, but this is not at all an adequate measure of correct dietary choices. A so-called bland diet is certainly tolerated better than a normal one. It is not beneficial, however, to continue such a diet after improvement or healing, not only because of its one-sidedness but also because of the inadequate stimulus to and demand on the forces that overcome the nutriment. These forces are actually a precondition for a healthy organ function.

Choice of diet is easier in biliary diseases because errors are immediately discovered. That the gall bladder is sensitive to an excessive consumption of fats belongs generally to the oldest dietetic knowledge. In addition, all roasted products are more or less burdensome to it. In sensitive patients roasted malt coffee and toast can excessively burden the gall bladder even though they won't directly elicit a colic. A combination of fat and roasting—that is, fried and fat-fried food—is especially dangerous. Indirectly, these products also burden the liver since by stimulating the gall they work too strongly on it and shorten its regenerative phase. Furthermore, regarding fats, the burden on the gall bladder is more of a quantitative problem, and that on the liver a more qualitative one. The intolerance of fruits with pits by those suffering from gall bladder disease is also ancient clinical experience.

Although the liver-gall rhythm described above is well-known, it is hardly considered in therapy and dietetics. It becomes evident, however, when it is realized that the consumption of fat or fried and roasted products is tolerated somewhat better in the morning than in the evening. Practical experience also supports this. On the other hand, a rich carbohydrate meal containing sugar in the evening is more appropriate to the liver's ability to assimilate sugar. The English, Dutch and Scandinavians, in taking a hefty breakfast, consider the physiological relationships more than do Central or Southern Europeans. Their habits date from a time when the liver was healthier than it is today. For the person with a healthy liver, sweet food in the morning still gives a good foundation, since it is rapidly processed. Few people today still have healthy livers, however, so it is better to consider physiological facts. The positive effect of absolutely avoiding sugar and honey in the morning is soon experienced as beneficial.

Sugar holds a special place among the carbohydrates. Although it stems from life, it is so far removed from life by purification that only a crystallized mineral substance remains. As such, it represents exactly the opposite of life; sugar shows all the criteria of mineral dead substances. Its easy absorption and passage into the blood do not change this fact; on the contrary, this only shows that it is lifeless. Characteristically, sugar is a mineral to the liver, and thus it is in no way suitable to stimulate life processes. (The fact that one quickly feels better after the consumption of sugar is based not on the addition of vitality but rather of energy that aids breakdown rather than buildup.) Thus, sugar is a burden to the liver and that even moreso in the morning than in the evening.

The quality of fats is of essential significance for the function of the liver. The highly active unsaturated fatty acids, rich concentrations of which are found in linseed, thistle, and sunflower oils, are much more readily accessible to the metabolism than the unsaturated fats. A related fact is that they are more sensitive to spoiling, as they can easily become rancid and thus toxic, which is why they may not be heated. The saturated fats may well be easily digestible and have better qualities for use in the kitchen, but that ought not to deceive us about the fact that hardened fats, particularly the customary margarines despite their later enrichment with polyunsaturated fatty acids, profoundly inhibit the metabolism of the liver and encourage the premature development of degenerative and sclerotic processes. Butter, it is noteworthy, is nearly the only fat to display a universal and harmonious mean position, making it the ideal fat for the healthy human being. Cream contains milk fat in finest dispersion; this facilitates absorption since the emulsification, in contrast to oil, has already taken place. For those suffering from liver illnesses, it is probably the fat most easily digestible, insofar as the tolerated quantity (depending on the illness, up to 60 gms) is not exceeded. To be sure, individuals may show a better tolerance for oil. Its tolerance in gall bladder diseases is almost always a quantitative problem; in general, too much is consumed during a meal.

Today, animal protein is almost exclusively considered to be fully valid for nutrition. Great differences exist, however. Milk protein, for example, is quite different from meat protein because it is not differentiated and individualized so strongly; it is therefore more readily tolerated. As has been known since antiquity, this is heightened by preparations such as souring and processing for the various milk products. By such methods, especially by physiological souring, a slight modification occurs, a breakdown in the sense of a ripening, through which tolerance is increased. For that reason, sour milk, yoghurt, cottage cheese, and similar products excepting hard cheeses, if consumed within limits, represent the ideal sources of protein for persons with liver diseases.

The preparation of sour milk still needs to be especially mentioned. It has been known to humanity since antiquity and is used in the preparation and preservation particularly of cucumbers, cabbage, and other vegetables. This method of preparing food makes it easier to tolerate and absorb. Through lactic acid, in contrast to acetic acid, the anabolic process is strongly addressed. These products stimulate liver activity.

From what has been said thus far, it may be seen that the inner stimulation of the life processes in the liver can be brought about only by living substances. The practical significance of this is that, regarding the quality of foods, it is their content of formative forces that is essential, not the energy content; nor is the vitamin content a valid standard here. It is also necessary to establish a true view of quality here. It is evident that fresh food for the liver is of great significance. In every one of the customary methods of canning there is a decrease or loss of formative forces. The maintenance of formative forces is a problem of agricultural method, and the biodynamic method deals concretely with those forces. It can also be a problem of the method of preparation, which can either preserve or deplete the life forces in the food.

Fundamentally, dietetic prescriptions should not simply be prohibitions but rather should arise from insight. In this sense, illness can be an educator of man, a mandate for self-transformation.

The Renal System and Its Diseases

Today, the kidneys are considered almost exclusively to be excretory organs, the task of which is to rid the body of nitrogenous wastes, salt, and water. As important as these functions are, the kidneys also have related but opposing capacities. Certain synthetic or anabolic functions of the kidneys were already discussed in volume I. A comprehensive picture of kidney function is gained when one considers it in connection with the adrenal glands, and thus with the dynamics of the whole organism. It remains to be shown how the kidneys and adrenals form a functional unity that can be encompassed under the term, the *kidney or renal system.* This system is deeply connected with the polarity of buildup and breakdown that can be recognized in the formation and function of the entire organ.

Morphology and Embryology

When one compares the liver with the kidneys, completely different dynamics are evident. While the liver hardly has an individual form and the watery element predominates, the kidneys appear strongly formed. The typical kidney form shows both a rounding off and the beginning of invagination. One is reminded of the form of a gastrula. Invagination is the essential aspect of this formative principle, which means that something outer is internalized. Gastrulation is the typical animalizing process that internalizes the vegetatively unfolding growth. An inner space is created that is also a closing off of the outside. This is a precondition for the development of an animal; something of a soul nature enters the corporeality and becomes active within it. The plant is surface, environment; the animal is body and possesses an inner world. It is evident from this discussion that the astral body is active in this principle of internalization; as can be seen, it is also active in the formation of the kidneys.

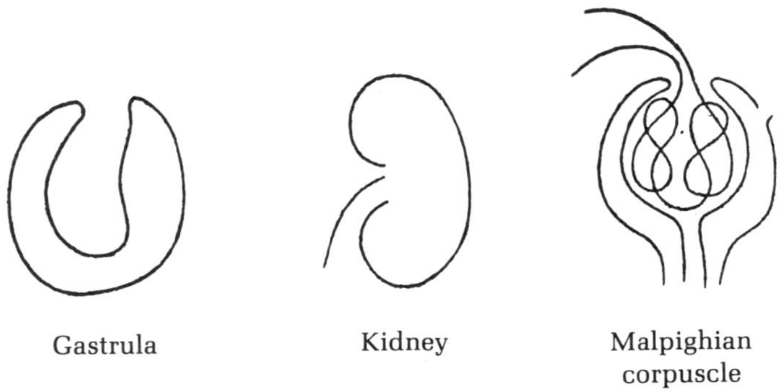

Fig. 1: Formative Processes of the Kidney

More than in any other organ, a direct expression of this strong enclosing can be seen in the formation of the kidney capsules that encompass and enclose the organ.

The same formative principle can also be found within the kidneys. Every Malpighian corpuscle shows a rounding and an internalization in the Bowman capsules, as well as the invagination and head formation in the rete mirabule of the glomerulus.

The origin of this formative principle can be found in its purest form in the formation of the head. The rounding off as an enclosing principle is found particularly in the upper organism but also in the bones where the dynamics of the upper organism come most strongly to expression. From these phenomena one can see that in the kidneys the astral body is active with the dynamics of the upper man; this will show itself again and again in the most varied manner.

A well-known morphological aspect that is hardly taken into consideration today becomes comprehensible from this point of view, that is, that renal and genital systems are placed symmetrically in the organism, something that is unique in the region below the diaphragm. It has already been shown how the total outer form of the human organism is symmetrically structured, and how internal symmetry can be found only in the nervous system. Asymmetry rules the metabolic system and is related essentially to the nature of life. The structures of the inner organs form many steps in the transition from the symmetry found in the nervous system to the asymmetry of the organs below the diaphragm. Here, however, the urogenital system is an exception. It is symmetrically structured, which shows that even though its organs are part of the metabolic system, they originate from another region than the neighboring organs.

The relative strictness of this symmetry, which is even more evident than that of the lungs, shows that the urogenital system really belongs more to the nervous system than do the lungs. A key to these curious relationships can be discovered in their embryology and physiology. The first kidney rudiment, the pronephros, is found in the cranium, close to the head-trunk border, directly behind the labyrinth. This portion of the kidney remains purely embryonic in all higher vertebrates and man. Nevertheless, this fundamental aspect of the kidney extends dorsally through the body cavity of the trunk. The final kidney as a metabolic organ is located in the region below the diaphragm, yet in its development one can see its connection to the nervous system, the dynamics of which are also still recognizable in the final kidney. In its caudal "descent," the primordial kidney actually takes a piece of nerve with it, namely the sympathetic nerve, which metamorphoses into the adrenal medulla. The kidney system is thus based on a connection of the nerve-sensory and metabolic systems.

The metanephros, from the caudal portion of which the final kidney arises, shows in its anterior portions a connection to the gonads. The differentiation of kidneys and gonadal area is thus a stage in development. Its one side is the morphological differentiation; the polar opposite is the structuring of the nervous system. This will be discussed later.

On the one hand, the kidneys are thus typical metabolic organs. On the other, they continue to show their dynamic connection to the nervous system. They are also located extraperitoneally and actually "belong" not in the region below the diaphragm, but above it.

In the formation of the kidneys, one gets the impression that the "idea" for them comes from the later nervous system, but that their "material" is formed by the later metabolic system. The connection to the nerve-sensory system as well as to the metabolic system cannot be missed in the kidneys. Two spatially and functionally opposing centers with their corresponding tendencies thus work together in the formation of the kidneys. The finished kidneys, however, have not only bridged over the spatial separation, but also the functional contrast between the two centers, which they have taken right into the structure. The kidneys, in accordance with their nature, are structured in a polar manner.

It has been mentioned several times that the dynamics of the nervous system have a catabolic, contracting character. The astral body works by way of the nervous system in a catabolic and therefore in a consciousness-creating, manner. This activity is confronted by the buildup activity of the ether body that works via the metabolic system. Both of these opposing activities would destroy each other if they were to meet without mediation. The rhythmic system is inserted as a mediator between the two. In the kidneys, however, a direct encounter does take place. Nevertheless, there is no mutual cancelling and extinguishing of dynamic activities; rather, a necessary interaction occurs. This will be discussed further below. A key to this understanding is given by the adrenal glands, which must be seen as being in functional unity with the kidney.

The Adrenal Glands

The adrenal glands are not generally considered in conjunction with the kidneys. Both organs, however, have related functions. In the following discussion we will consider the functional unity of both organs under the term kidney system.

The anatomic and functional structures of the adrenal glands show a clear separation into cortex and medulla. The hormones of the adrenal medulla, of which about 75 percent is adrenaline, are stored in its chromaffin tissue. This tissue originates from the neural crest and is closely connected with the sympathetic ganglia. In the course of development these chromaffin cells move into the initially compact cortex structure. Thus, in the adrenal medulla one is dealing with a nerve impulse that enters the metabolic region by way of the sympathetic nervous system. This impulse becomes hormonal substance, adrenaline or noradrenaline, that transmits the initial impulse as messengers. As explained earlier, one can see in adrenaline the dynamics of the astral body working by way of the nervous system. Therefore, the tendency of both of these amines has an awakening, breakdown character.

The adrenal cortex comprises approximately 80 percent of the organ. Its anabolic, life-sustaining effect is unmistakable. It is already well-developed in fetal life and forms a large retroperitoneal cell mass that increases until birth in keeping with the generalized growth process. After birth there is a partial involution and further development occurs around puberty. Steroid hormones can be found in the adrenal cortex. Five functional groups can be distinguished: The glucocorticoids, mineral corticoids, androgens, estrogens, and gestagens. Despite the difference in their effects, they have a common basic structure and generally work anabolically. Cortisol is the main cortex hormone (approximately 70 percent; corticosterone 15 percent). The significance of the steroids was discussed in volume I. The peculiarity of these substances consists in the fact that they are clearly connected to the astral body but are yet active anabolically. These substances do not develop arbitrarily but are yet active anabolically. These substances do not develop arbitrarily through blind chemical reactions, but result from the guidance of substances by the higher members of man's being.

Thus, in the adrenal gland the anabolism of the cortex and the catabolism of the medulla come in contact in the most intimate way and in the smallest space. The anatomical structure shows that the catabolic pole is encompassed by the anabolic, the substance of which also predominates. Thus, the adrenal gland is a predominately anabolic rather than catabolic organ. Nevertheless, when the catabolic effect of the astral body is led by way of the nervous system into the inner aspects of the organ, it can be understood in terms of its entire structure that the principally destructive impulse is to be overcome by anabolism and to come to an end.

It was already pointed out that the human form never comes about by "pure" catabolism or anabolism, but anabolism must always be preceded by catabolism. This is a distinguishing characteristic of the way of life of ensouled organisms. Catabolism and anabolism are closely correlated; one influences the other. The adrenal cortex offers a picture of how the life activity of catabolism directs anabolism. The ether body of an ensouled organism is distinguished from that of the plant in that it can form the basis for the intervention of an astral body. The human and animal substances thus are not only living but must be formed so that they can also be ensouled. That means, however, that the astral body directs the ether body and that the life processes must be ensouled. Finally, it is the task of the kidney system to take the vitalized substance prepared by the liver and modify it so that it can be ensouled by the active astral

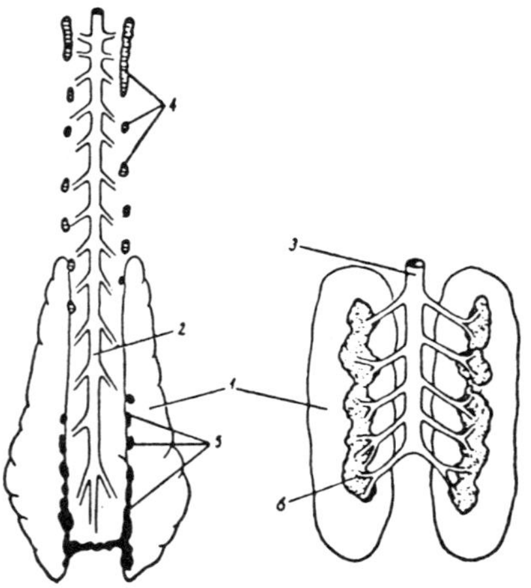

(1) Kidney
(2) Aorta
(3) Vena cava
(4) Supra-renal organs (chromaffin; medulla)
(5) Inter-renal organs (cortex tissue)
(6) Adrenal cortex

Fig. 2: Inter-renal and supra-renal organs. Left: separate (selachians); Right: connected to the adrenal cortex (amphibians). (From: A Portmann, *Einfuehrung in die vergleichende Morphologie der Wirbeltiere*. 4th edition, Basel/Stuttgart, 1969.)

body. In other words: Through its "plant-like" function, the liver forms primarily carbohydrates (glycogen). The impulse toward protein formation stems from the kidney system, which transmits this impulse to the liver via the adrenal cortex. It is the liver, however, which is the executing organ. (The anabolic action of the androgens, primarily aimed at the protein metabolism, is based upon this.)

It is an interesting fact that in the lower animals the cortex and medullary parts are still spatially separated. Thus in the selachians, the inter-renal tissue that corresponds to the cortex portion is found as accumulations of cells between the kidneys under the diaphragm, whereas the chromaffin medullary tissue can be found in the form of the so-called supra-renal bodies along the aorta. Only the quadrupeds possess adrenal glands. In the amphibians, reptiles, and birds, however, cortex and medullary portions are mixed together. Only in the mammals is the strict separation of cortex and medulla realized. This makes possible the enhanced development of their polarities and also their integration. Schematically, these polarities can be summarized as follows:

	↗ Medulla	Nervous system	Adrenalin	Catabolism
Adrenal gland		↕	↕	↕
	↘ Cortex	Metabolic system	Cortisol	Anabolism

The meaning of this intimate working together can be seen in a necessity based on the developmental history. The nervous system and its concomitant consciousness and catabolic processes are most strongly developed in man; his weak regenerative capacity is also connected with this. These breakdown processes would destroy him if they were not restrained by a specific inhibitor. The adrenal gland is the prototype of these relationships. In it, the deadly nerve-sensory impulse is surrounded and screened off by the anabolic function of the cortex.

The role of the separate factors becomes most clearly evident in pathological occurrences. Since the studies of Selye the significance of the hypophyseal-adrenal cortex systems in shock and stress is well-known. During shock the astral body is so strongly affected by a fearful experience, a positive or negative psychological involvement, fear, etc., that it can no longer be controlled by the ego. The results are excessively strong processes of consciousness, which work through the hypothalamus and the sympathetic system right into the adrenal medulla, causing an outpouring of adrenaline and noradrenaline. The enhanced wakefulness and the mobilization of the body reserves (increased blood pressure, increased glucose, etc.) are absolutely positive reactions. If this impulse is so powerful that it cannot be diminished, death can result. Examples are well-known.

It is the task of the renal system, through the adrenal cortex, to cushion this impulse and to delimit the catabolic activity of the astral body, switching it over to anabolism. If the organ is too weak or exhausted, the appropriate preparation (Cortisol) can be a substitute for this anabolism and thus work in a life-saving way.

The old expression that somebody's "kidneys are affected" [in the sense of "it gets me down."—Ed.] is still a correct experience of old knowledge. The genius of language still comprehends and grasps the interconnections of the organs and perpetuates such wisdom. Examples of this are also mentioned in other chapters.

If it is not a case of acute shock but rather one of continuing stress, the consequences do not arise immediately but nevertheless are just as far-reaching. Experimentally, animals were subjected to a long period of stress by exposing them continuously to a dangerous opponent without letting them hide or flee. If this frightful stress continued, the animal could die of a uremia in a few days. Thus, the pathological condition of these animal kidneys can be seen to be similar to that of human kidneys in shock. Definite damage to the kidney can be caused psychogenically. Here, the catabolic astral impulse does not penetrate merely to the adrenal medulla but right through to the kidney.

The Kidneys and the Adrenal Glands

As mentioned in the description of their developmental history, the medullary and cortex portions of the adrenal glands are initially completely separated, for example in the selachians. A further step is realized in the amphibians, reptiles, and birds; they have adrenal glands but without separation into cortex and medulla. Here, they are found to be a mixed tissue within the kidneys.

The term adrenal glands is thus applicable only to man and the other mammals in a strict sense. Nevertheless, the relationships in phylogeny and function show clearly that kidneys and adrenal glands belong together. A further step in development was necessary to separate the endocrine glands from the excretory kidneys. Finally, they find their place at the upper pole of the kidneys—something that certainly does not occur by chance but is rather the expression of a deep and essential relationship. This will be clarified when one considers the function of the kidneys more widely.

Just as the separation and arrangement of cortex and medulla in the adrenal glands were presented as a necessary stage in order to establish and integrate the polarity of anabolism and catabolism, so also does the separation of kidneys and adrenal glands make possible another polarity in the area of inner and outer secretions. The excretion by way of the kidneys corresponds to an "incretion" of the adrenals that works inward into the blood. In a certain sense, this polarity is a mirror image of that of catabolism and anabolism in which, as was shown, the adrenal glands are fundamentally connected with anabolic processes and the kidneys with catabolic ones, although it is only in their interaction that the function develops.

			Cortex —	Anabolism
	Adrenal glands	"Incretion"		
			Medulla >	Catabolism
Kidney System				
	Kidneys	Excretion	Cortex	
			Medulla —	Anabolism

The Kidneys and the Reproductive System

It has been mentioned that the material of the metanephros is closely connected with the gonads. In it, one distinguishes a cephalad sexual part and a caudal renal part. The separate kidney and gonadal regions result from a common origin. That the adrenal cortex not only forms its "action hormones," the glucocorticoids and mineral corticoids, but also male and female sex hormones, is an indication of this. An archetypal condition can be recognized here that still encompasses the male and female principles. The polarity of the sexes develops from a common intermediate stage. As in evolution, the development of polarities signifies an enhancement of tension and also possibilities of enhanced perfection.

	Male
	↗
Kidney system	
	↘
	Female

The separation of the gonadal system from that of the kidneys is now only one side of the matter. The other side of this polar development lies in the nerve-sensory region. Activities on one side have their effects on the other; this is the essence of polarity. In the sense of this polarity, the development of the nervous system must be considered with the formation of the gonadal system of the higher vertebrates.

In this case, one can look at the gonadal system as possibly the most obvious carrier of life in which the anabolic processes completely predominate and in which life forms new life. The opposite is the case with the nervous system. Here there is minimal living activity; regenerative capacity is almost completely absent, making possible the function of the nerves and of consciousness.

	Nervous System	Catabolism	Death
↗			
Kidney System			
↘			
	Genital System	Anabolism	Life

But also within the genital system a (secondary) polar occurrence can be found that develops out of a unity into the difference of male and female.

Just as the genital system is polar to the nervous system, this secondary male–female polarity also works back upon the nerve-sensory system. That the male is more strongly connected with body and earth has been discussed many times. He incarnates more intensively, while the female remains more cosmic. For that reason the two sexes work differently on the nervous system. Their brain formations and ways of thinking differ not so much quantitatively as qualitatively. The male nervous system experiences a more intensive and one-sided structure. The tension between the nervous system and the polar genital system is greater in the male. Based on this is the fact that in embryological development the male gonads differentiate earlier, whereas those of the female remain longer in an undifferentiated state. The corresponding correlate to this greater tension is the descent of the testes, which makes possible the strong emphasis on the nerve-sensory system. The meaning of these events does not lie in the genital area nor in sexual development, but rather in the polar events of the more differentiated structuring of the nervous system.

The descent of the testes has occupied zoologists as well as anthropologists. Frequently, it was designated as mysterious. It is often said that the higher body temperature would make the testes incapable of functioning, which is indeed the case in cryptochism. It is forgotten, however, that the testes of birds and elephants do not descend, yet are fully functional. Portmann clearly sees that developmentally the caudal displacement of the male gonads must be seen in conjunction with the development at the other pole:

> We observe in the caudal displacement of the gonads the removal of the highest foci of integration of the central nervous system toward the cephalad pole of the body—the forehead of mammals. The descent of the testes is a movement in the opposite direction and must be connected with the structural formation of the anal pole. It is a part of the self-portrayal of mammals.[1]

This polar connection is well-known, especially in the animal realm. The antlers of deer, the manes of lions and the more colorful feathers, etc., are male attributes. In antlers, also, many gonadal hormones have been found. Finally, the so-called *Perückenbock* deer clearly displays the connection of antler formation and testes. When the testes are destroyed by injuries, normal growth of the antlers ceases. Certainly in the animal realm, antlers, and mane, as well as the anal escutcheon and the emphasis put on the sexual area by the descent of the testes have an accentuating character, as Portmann points out. In man, however, there is no external correlate. It is in the nature of man to restrain what occurs organically in the animal. He does not permit it to develop so that the formative forces not used in the organic realm become free and accessible for the unfolding of the spirit. For this reason the development in the male leads to a more differentiated structuring of the nervous system and a much more acute, but narrower, object-oriented thinking.

Since contemporary thinking always proceeds linearly, and contemplation by polarities, as represented by Goethe, remains foreign to this thinking, the attempts to understand biological events almost always consider only bodily regions. Thus, there has been a plethora of explanations of ritual circumcision as hygienic prophylaxis. That may be one aspect, but ritual acts of earlier times were never restricted to biological aspects. One can see an enhancement of the "moving out" of the genital area in circumcision; this also intensifies the tension between it and the nervous system in terms of enhanced intellectualism. Thus, the union with the earth's forces becomes evermore enhanced and strengthened. Cryptochism, however, signifies a lessened tendency to incarnation, and a restraining, a remaining softer and more cosmic. Certainly this effect can also be overshadowed by other events.

The Physiology of the Kidneys

Many details of the process of the production of urine are known today. Here, it is our task to recognize the dynamics of the members of man's being in this activity, which will be relatively easy in the kidneys. One must not restrict oneself to the kidneys, however, nor to the nephrons, glomeruli, or isolated parts of the tubules in order to explain the mechanisms that are operating.

In contemporary thinking it is customary to attempt to derive processes of life from physico-chemical reactions. This creates the reductionist image of the world that lies at the basis of modern medicine. The uniqueness of life is not examined. Rather, the attempt is made to derive and explain life as emanating from physics and chemistry. As was explained in volume I, the realm of life, the etheric, lies beyond that of the dead; that is, it is superordinate to the laws of physics and chemistry but does not totally eliminate them. The physico-chemical events are used in a different way; they become instruments, not independent actors autonomously determining the processes.

The most apparent aspect of kidney function is the excretion of water. The color of urine clearly indicates its relation to the polarity of dilution and concentration—a polarity that also corresponds to the absorption and excretion. In another realm it is the interaction of inspiration and expiration, or systole and diastole. What occurs here on the physical plane has its correlate in the polarity of avariciousness and wastefulness, joy and sadness, excitement and dullness, etc. in the psychological realm. The entire life of the soul is structured in polarities that are the transformations of the archetypal polarity of sympathy and antipathy. As a member of man's being, it is the astral body that lives in these polarities. In the kidneys it is the polarity of excretion and absorption, dilution and concentration, in which the activity of the astral body is obvious and manifest.

In all living fluids, water is always united with salts. The connections of potassium to the plant world and sodium to the animal world are clearly distinct. It has been said earlier that potassium is the substance through which the ether body can become active in water, while sodium makes it possible for the astral body to rule over the water organism. The interaction of the astral body and the water organism thus takes place in the kidneys—more exactly, through the cortex of the adrenals by way of aldosterone and sodium.

The primary excretory function of the kidneys extends to

water, salts, and nitrogenous catabolic products of the body substance. The excretion of nitrogenous substances by the kidneys is evident from the fact that in renal failure a person dies from uremia, not from hydremia, since salts and water can also be excreted elsewhere. The excreted nitrogenous wastes are end products of the protein metabolism. Through them the organism is relieved of organically fixed nitrogen. An essential, primary function of the kidneys is thus the elimination of fixed nitrogen, which could virtually not be removed in any other way. What is the nature of these connections between the kidneys and nitrogen?

The element nitrogen makes up 80 percent of the air. As was described in volume I, air is the carrier of the astral element. Just as water is the carrier of life and the ether body, so the soul, that is to say, the astral body, lives in the air. Nitrogen is a representative of this astral working, not only in its elementary gaseous state but also in its fixed form in protein and its products. These relationships were described in detail in volume I.

The stimulation of diuresis by caffeine reveals much of the nature of the kidneys. Directly coupled with the diuretic effect is an enhancement of consciousness. This can also occur in other ways—through shock, for example. A diuretic effect always accompanies an enhancement of consciousness, a psychological involvement. There, too, the frequently mentioned influence of the nerve impulses into the kidney system is manifest. The impulse of consciousness passes into the kidneys. The dynamics that can be recognized in coffee (caffeine) were already mentioned. On the one hand, it is related to uric acid and to thinking, and on the other hand one can see it as the transformed end product of the protein—more exactly of the purine—metabolism, that is, a highly nitrogenous substance. Related on one side to the nervous system, and on the other to the kidney system, it is a substance shaped primarily by astral activity.

The anti-diuretic hormone (ADH) of the posterior lobe of the hypophysis inhibits diuresis. It brings about an increased concentration and is a typical astral substance. The coordination and contact of ether body (anterior lobe) with astral body (posterior lobe) takes place in the hypophysis. The dynamics of contracting and concentrating with which the astral body is active in the posterior lobe of the pituitary is generally the same as that in the head system. This activity is, however, specifically guided into the metabolic region. The effect of the oxytocin from the posterior lobe on the uterus is, in principle, just as concentrating as the actual concentration of urine in the kidneys. ADH is identical with vasopressin, which brings about an increase in blood pressure through an enhancement of the vascular musculature tonus.

These conditions in no way contradict the effect of caffeine described above. Hormones are mediators of astral activity in different regions and in each case their impulses have an appropriate character. Thus, the ways the astral body interacts with the kidneys can vary markedly. It must be possible for it to concentrate with ADH or dilute with caffeine. Both are activities of the astral body.

Nicotine, a typical astral substance derived from the tobacco plant, is also anti-diuretic and concentrating, quite in keeping with its effect on vascular system and psyche. On the other hand, alcohol enhances diuresis, which also corresponds to its activity of loosening inhibitions and dilating the vessels.

Our exposition so far has shown that the kidneys are organs decisively structured and formed by the forces of the astral body and then used by it. It is therefore understandable that the primary substrate they excrete—that is, residual nitrogen and other substances normally found in urine—also arises from astral effects.

Through the astral body, substances are taken out of life and into death. The product of this activity is excreted by way of the kidneys. Rudolf Steiner designated urine as "the mummy of the astral body." In earlier times certain people could look at urine and obtain a picture of the astral body. They thus gained understanding of an illness. The excretion of water by the kidneys should not hide the fact that the relationship of the kidneys to water is based on the function of excretion and is only superficial. Water is the carrier of life and is essentially connected with the liver and the ether body. The kidneys, however, are astral organs. The astral body is based on the air organism and respiratory function in which the "air" as nitrogen has become organic. This results in the connection of the kidneys with nitrogenous substances and also with the respiratory function. Air organism, nitrogenous substances, and kidneys are formations of the astral body and are ruled by it.

Just as the kidneys excrete nitrogen in the form of uric acid, urea, etc., so they also regulate the air organism. Here the situation corresponds to that in the liver, which regulates the water organism. The element related to the kidneys is thus air. That is why the regulation and control of the air organism occurs through the kidney system, not the lungs, which are only secondary.

The role of the kidney system in regulating the air organism is naturally not recognized today, since a merely organic way of looking at things does not permit this insight. The feeling for thorough breathing is also necessary for the regulation of the air organism. "Air hunger" is an expression of inadequate breathing. In a typical way it can occur, for example, in asthma, which is naturally expressed in the region of the lungs. To look for the deeper causes of asthma in the lungs, however, is misplaced because the regulation and control of respiratory events do not depend on the lungs but on the kidney system. For that reason the initially shocking formulation is justified that asthma is an illness of the kidney system that is only expressed in the lung region. This connection is made use of in therapy without really realizing it when one treats asthma by way of the kidney system; either adrenaline or its derivatives can be given. One thus draws the astral body into the kidney system so that it can become free in the lung region.

The same applies to theophylline and corresponding preparations. Or one gives cortisone preparations, that is, substrates of an already completed change over process. In any case, a therapy using adrenals or their derivatives works by way of the kidney system. Thus, unconsciously one makes use of the fact that asthma is a dysfunction of the kidney system.

The polar organization of the kidney system can also be found in the kidneys as cortex and medulla. This organization, which is anatomically and functionally especially strong in the adrenal glands, shows a clear transition in the kidneys to a functional interconnection. Schematically, it can be said that the glomeruli are located in the cortex and the tubules—Henle's loops—in the medulla. Their functions are clearly polar. In the glomeruli the ultrafiltrate is formed, while in the medullary region resorption takes place. The phenomena of dilution and concentration are, as it were, placed in two different areas.

A curious anatomical relationship should be mentioned here that can shed light on the activity of the members of man's being. It is well-known that the distal portion of the tubule returns after Henle's loop to make contact with the vascular

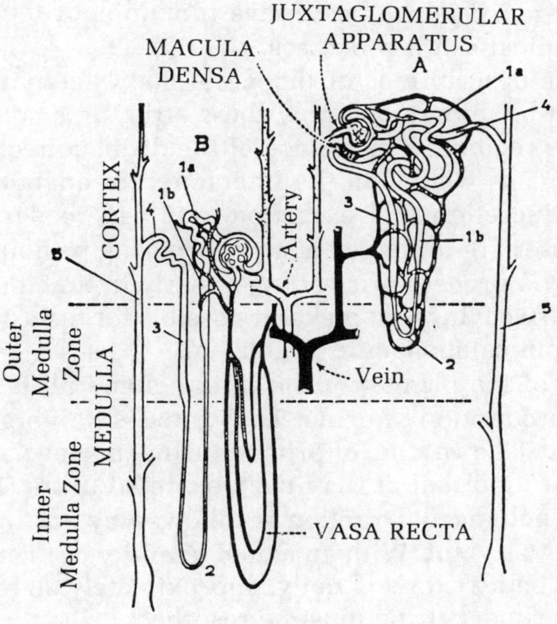

Fig. 3: Schematic Presentation of Two Nephrons: A) cortical; B) juxtamedullary. 1) The sections of nephron closely attached to Bowman's capsule are the proximal tubule, subdivided into a) the convolute portion and b) pars recta, 2) the thin part of Henle's loop, 3) the thicker, ascending portion of Henle's loop, 4) the distal convolutions and 5) the collecting tubules.

pole of its glomerulus. Here the macula densa is formed in the tubule; closely associated with it is the juxtaglomerular apparatus in the wall of the vas afferens. The macula densa can be considered to be a sense organ through which successful resorption is perceived. It effects the formation of renin, which takes place in the granules of the apparatus. Through angiotensinogen from the globulin fraction of plasma, renin influences the formation of two angiotensins, which in turn elevate the blood pressure. Here, anatomy and physiology are a clear expression of the working of the astral body. In the blood pressure we have a measure for the specific intervention of the astral body in the vascular system. However, in order to be physically effective, it requires definite receptive organs—the glands with their inner secretions and also cell complexes as described here. Also, the perceptive functions of the macula densa are typical astral processes.

From these descriptions of the astral body's activity in the cortex it can be understood how these structures come to be found in this region. In the return of the distal convolution to its glomerulus as well as in the interaction of anabolism and catabolism, incretion and excretion, one can recognize that these processes are united by a supra-ordering principle. This is not merely a process proceeding linearly in time but rather an inner interweaving that makes it possible for the astral body to switch from catabolism to anabolism.

Excretion of the primary urine in the glomeruli is the first step in the production of urine. Today, 150–180 liters per day are produced. The volume of primary urine, however, is many times greater than that of the finally excreted urine. Thus, an enormously enhanced excretion is followed by an "incretion" that is almost as great. With an actual quantity of urine of one to two liters being excreted daily, approximately 98 to 99 percent of the primary urine must be resorbed.

Considered naively, this mysterious rerouting of water is unnecessary, and it would appear to be much simpler to excrete only the substances normally found in urine with water. Actually, this process involves considerable activity. In 24 hours, 1,500 liters of blood course through the kidneys. The kidney circulation comprises 20 percent of the entire circulation volume per minute. At a weight comprising only 0.4 percent of the body weight, the kidneys are the organs with the amplest arterial blood circulation. In this respect they can be seen as a counterpart to the liver with its strong venous circulation. By its nature, one could call the kidney a primarily arterial, and the liver a primarily venous organ. Corresponding to its intake of oxygen, there is an excretion from the kidney of nitrogenous substances. The kidney system controls and regulates not only nitrogen, but also oxygen—in a broader sense the air: its intake through the lungs (respiration), intermediate nitrogen metabolism (protein formation), and elimination through the kidney as urinary excretion products.

oxygen—intake
↗
Kidney system
↘
nitrogenous substances—excretion

The resorption of water is seen to be a necessity today in that primary urine is formed by filtration; it "falls out" passively, while the subsequent concentration is an active achievement of the tubular cells. In this process, however, a deeper necessity can be recognized: the "kidney radiation."

The Kidney Radiation

The kidneys today are considered primarily from the point of view of their excretory function. This is, however, only one side of their reality. Even the final urine is the result of the interaction between excretion and "incretion." The reality lies in this polarity. Today, however, the resorption is not considered in its deeper significance because to see the necessary dependence requires the concept of polarities. Certainly no one will doubt that the resorbed fluid—in which not only the final urine is missing—differs from the ultrafiltrate. A qualitative process is connected with the quantitative process. To the same extent that plasma substances pass over into the realm of the dead mineral substances, finally entering the almost totally dead urine, the remnant of resorbed fluid experiences a revitalization. After separating from the "dead" material, it becomes more alive than it was in the plasma. Here it is a matter of the polarity of death and life. Out of an insight into such connections, Goethe said, "Death is an artistic device of nature designed to provide much life." When dead substance is removed from an undifferentiated state, the liberated life is enhanced. Thus, for the organism resorption signifies a means for the general urine concentration and it also represents a qualitative modification, *an enhancement of the life principle* within the organism, a stimulation of the ether body.

	↗ "Incretion"	Etherization	Life
Plasma			
	↘ Excretion	Substances normally found in urine	Death

It is significant that "incretion" occurs in the region of the tubules, which are in close connection to the vascular system. The meaning of this connection is seen today in the counterflow principle. This, however, can be understood only when one sees behind it the qualitative transformation that may occur in this way.

The processes can be followed further in detail. When one surveys the dynamics of the kidneys *in toto*, then it is the contracting–excreting activity of the astral body working through the nervous system that is clearly evident in the cortex, especially in the glomeruli. The tendency is forming, rounding off, shaping, which is tantamount to contraction, pressing out and excreting.

The metabolic system is polar to these dynamics. Its activity is receptive, filling out, growing, vitalizing. It extends primarily to the medullary portion of the kidneys, the tubules, and Henle's loops. That the substrate in both cases is water is understandable as it is the basis of life. The functions of resorption are an expression of the activity of the ether body, which works in these dynamics in the metabolic system. Here, an excretion is followed by an “incretion,” giving off by taking in.

↗	Cortex	Glomeruli	Ultrafiltration	Excretion	Astral Body	Nervous System
Kidneys						
↘	Medulla	Tubules	Resorption	“Incretion”	Ether Body	Metabolic System

It has been pointed out repeatedly that in ensouled organisms the precondition for anabolism is a preceding catabolism. This working together can be clearly followed throughout the kidney system. It is unmistakable here that one depends on the other. The first phase in resorption is also a result of the anabolic processes of the ether body under the guidance of the astral body. Expressed in a different way, the catabolic dynamics of the astral body experience *a turning back, a change over* in the kidney system. The astral body is now active within the ether body and guides anabolism. It is thus possible that a substance can be living not only in a vegetative sense but can also be ensouled; this, however, is not the case in a “pure” plant substance.

The filtering of the bodily substance through the kidneys is a problem of the integration of nitrogen, thus of the protein metabolism. Here, too, lies the deep difference between the bodily substances of plants and animals; that is, carbohydrates and protein. Only protein, through its nitrogen content, can provide the basis for soul activity.

Rudolf Steiner was the first to point to the anabolic function of the kidneys apart from their generally known excretory activity. He showed exactly how the human organism is active through the working together of the upper, plastically forming principle and the anabolism of the metabolic principle. He pointed out that “radiations emanate from the kidney-liver system that are met by the plastic formative activites of the head system. The kidney system radiates the forces of metabolism outward, and the nervous system gives the organism its inner and outer forms; it is a sculptor.”[2]

This "kidney radiation" is a dynamic, supersensible occurrence that works right into substance. The hormones are the mediators of this activity. From what has been said, it is evident that this radiating activity emanates from the kidney system. It can be recognized in absorption and particularly in the activity of the adrenal cortex, which is connected with resorption. Yet, as a supra-ordered principle it goes beyond that activity. In a wider sense, the entire activity of the liver as well as intestinal resorption are connected with it. Here we will only point to aldosterone, a product of the adrenal cortex that specifically affects water metabolism; it is broken down by the liver as the central organism of water metabolism. The processes of phosphorylation in the intestinal wall are also dependent upon the adrenals. In 1922, when Rudolf Steiner spoke about the kidney system, hardly anything was known of the central role played by the adrenal cortex in anabolic metabolism, but this has been increasingly elucidated in the last few decades. Its total effect is anabolic, vitalizing. It must be obvious that this must be coordinated with a purely etheric, living stream of substance from the liver that is active as a central organ of the water metabolism. The mediating role between the kidney and liver systems is taken on by aldosterone. One is not dealing in that situation with simple vitality, which is a liver problem, but rather with an astralized, living substance. This is evident in the entire phenomenon including the psychology of patients who have Cushing's syndrome.

This higher kidney function, the kidney radiation, is deeply connected with the formation of human substance. Its task is to so structure and shape the anabolic stream of life that living substance becomes permeated with soul, thus forming a substance correlate to the catabolic formative impulses that emanate from the head area. By virtue of this working together, in which the kidney radiation can be either too weak or too strong, the constitution of the human being is influenced more or less permanently.

If the kidney radiation is developed too weakly, then the astral body will be inadequately active anabolically from the lower man. Impulses of ensouling and movement of the astral body will be too weak and the circulation will become sluggish. Blood succumbs to gravity as an expression of inadequate buoyancy; the result is congestion, hemorrhoids, varices, meteorrhagia and especially hypotension. The excessively weak anabolic stream of substance leads to an adynamic state. Furthermore, occult febrile states can develop. These could be considered to be reactions of the organism to counter the excessively weak activity of the astral body and an attempt to improve its incarnation into the metabolism.

Among such disturbances there are without doubt also conditions that are called Addison's disease. The typical adynamic state, including asthenia, bradycardia and gastrointestinal disorders, becomes quite comprehensible when the insufficient anabolic stream of substance that works via the adrenal cortex is considered. Yet, the picture of an excessively weak kidney radiation is not identical with Addison's disease. This encompasses only one aspect of the problem.

From a psychological point of view, persons with an excessively weak kidney radiation also show a tendency to weariness, to a decreased tonus. The will may well be present, but it is more or less paralyzed. These conditions are primarily noticed in asthenics and neurasthenics since in these persons the nerve-sensory system predominates.

In a person with excessively strong kidney radiations the astral body is too intensively active in the lower person and cannot be restrained there. The astral activity bubbles over and rises upward, so to speak. As a first symptom in patients with excessively strong kidney radiations Rudolf Steiner mentions meteorism. Excessive flatulence can certainly be related to various processes, but in all cases we are essentially dealing with an excessive metabolism that is not completely controlled. An even more important symptom is cramps, which indicate that the strongly active astral body cannot properly stream into its organs. It remains without and takes hold of them from the outside, that is, with the contracting dynamics of the nervous system. Thus, the cramps are a secondary phenomenon. The strong activity of the astral body is primary, but it does not include the ether body; this is a kidney problem. The cramps develop when "the astral body influences the physical body directly without the mediation of the ether body." The ether body, living as it does in the watery or liquid, no longer works by receiving and balancing, and thus the astral body works in a different way, from outside or above.

Processes of this sort can take place everywhere in the organism—for example, as stomach cramps, dysmenorrhea and cramps in the vascular system. A lasting spasm of the vascular system leads to hypertension, which points to an extremely strong obtrusion of the astral body. There can also be spasms in the region of the medium or smaller vessels that can bring about sensations of knocking, beating, or vibrating. In the head area spasms of the cerebral vascular system can create regions of locally inadequate blood supply. Finally, the uncontrolled and excessive stream of substance can lead to an undue metabolic activity in the brain and present the picture of migraine.

Psychologically considered, persons with profuse kidney radiation are generally active, emotionally volatile people of more or less pyknic constitution. A certain similarity to this type of constitution exists in Cushing's syndrome. In no way are the two identical, however. The inordinate kidney radiation is a dynamic problem of the astral body, while in the overproduction of the adrenal cortex a finished substrate is already available. This presents only one aspect of the problem.

Since the excessively weak or strong kidney radiation does not represent an organic kidney illness and is therefore not accompanied by pathological urine findings, we will discuss its therapy here.

In the case of an unduly weak kidney radiation, it is our therapeutic task to bring the higher members of man's being more strongly into the anabolic metabolism. Here, we must first mention iron, which is particularly suitable as the metal of incarnation. It stimulates the soul-spiritual to a stronger intervention in the corporeality. Rudolf Steiner called it "an essential regulator of the circulation of the blood," the means through which the interrelationship between ether and astral organisms are achieved. The stimulating effect of iron leads to the permeation of the dull metabolic processes with light and also to a psychological activation toward healthy courage and impulsiveness. In the case of iron, however, the preparation and form in which it is administered are essential.

Sulphur is the typical representative of the metabolism. Through it an extremely weak metabolism can be intensified. Finally, through sodium and potassium salts an unburdening and stimulation of the water organism and the ether body can be achieved.

According to Rudolf Steiner, these effects are ideally united in the nettle, Urtica dioeca. Through this plant, which like every other plant represents a therapeutic organism, iron is specifically aimed in the desired direction. It is most favorably given internally in a potency of D3, and as injection into the right upper thigh. In the preparation Solutio ferri comp., the processes of the plant are imitated which can bring about an enhancement of the activity and effect longer duration. The mixed preparation, Glandula suprarenalis D3/Solutio ferri comp. D6āā, has proved to be especially valuable.

A rational therapy of an overly strong kidney radiation cannot, as happens when spasmolytics or analgesics are given, merely weaken the unduly active astral body or prevent it from taking hold, but rather will attempt to strengthen the upper man so that it will be able to handle the excess lower metabolic processes.

Silicic acid is the most important remedy here. It is representative of the anabolic and formative impulses emanating from the nerve-sensory system. Application of it strengthens the nerve-sensory organization. Sugar is of further significance here. It is the carrier of the ego-organization, which needs to be strengthened if a person is to handle metabolic processes that threaten to overwhelm his being. As a third remedy, the alkaline salts, which structure the fluid organism, need to be considered. They unburden the nervous system of the astral activity. According to Rudolf Steiner, here, too, proper substances are to be found in a plant—in the root of camomile. (Homeopathy uses the entire plant; the blossoms are used as a tea or external application.) This preparation as well has been produced in a form imitating plant processes (see volume I) and thus having enhanced efficacy, namely as Solutio sacchari comp. The action of Chamomilla is enhanced by Belladonna.

Chamomilla radix is most favorably applied in cramps, dysmenorrhea and flatulence if they developed in the manner described above. In localized spasms D3 to D6 have proved valuable, and in migraine higher potencies. In general, the constitution can be laid hold of better with higher potencies. D30 is also indicated if the spastic tendency extends over the entire organism with predominating unrest, fear, tachycardia, etc. Middle potencies work better on an increased blood pressure.

The Pathology of the Kidneys

In the preceding sections, it was described how the kidney system receives the catabolic processes of the nervous system and transforms them, and how through the kidney radiation a stream of substance originates that is poured anabolically into the entire organism. Healthy kidneys are a precondition for this function of building up this anabolic stream. The pathology of these organs will be comprehensible from an understanding of their dynamics. The fundamental polarity of inflammation and sclerosis can be rediscovered in kidney illnesses, but modified by the context of the specific organic situation.

Glomerular Nephritis

Acute diffuse glomerulonephritis justifiably has a special place among kidney diseases. It is a secondary illness and follows certain infections, involving β-hemalytic A-streptococci viruses. Despite the frequent relationship to streptococci, the participation of the kidneys in this illness fluctuates immensely; thus it is evident that the extent of involvement of the kidneys does not depend on the postulated nephritogenic groups of streptococci but rather on the extent of the kidneys' susceptibility to the effects of these bacteria. This applies to the entire problem of infection.

Acute diffused glomerulonephritis does not develop spontaneously in animals. It can be artificially created by heterologous kidney antibodies (Masughi nephritis). The pathological picture also corresponds to a large extent to a human acute nephritis, but it must be emphasized that it does not develop *spontaneously* in animals.

A cardinal symptom of acute nephritis—besides hematuria and proteinuria—is increased blood pressure. This need not always be present, especially not with interstitial and scarlet fever nephritis. A special hypertonic form occurs without kidney participation, a "nephritis without nephritis." The increased blood pressure is not a measure of the extent of the illness; it precedes the urine findings and is not a consequence of the kidney changes as in nephrosclerosis. In contrast to chronic nephritis, vasoconstriction in the acute form is nervous in origin. One speaks of a neurogenic increase in tone. The edema is also distinguished from that of "true" kidney illness because it frequently develops rapidly and is not determined primarily by sodium or water retention; it is of extra-renal origin.

Because of these symptoms, acute nephritis is today considered to be part of the phenomenon of a generalized capillaritis. Also, the blood supply to the kidney is not decreased in angiospasm, as Volhard thought, but is rather increased.

To understand nephritis as a secondary illness it needs to be pointed out that the primary illness frequently occurs in the tonsils or upper air passages. In all these illnesses one discovers an interaction of the astral body or the ego with the ether body. Especially in scarlet fever, in contrast to measles, the predominance of astral impulses is most evident. This explains the production of toxins, which stem from the activity of the astral body. In tonsilitis the organism with the help of the lymphatics, which are places of activity of the ether body, attempts to get hold of the astral impulses; in the process of healing a new balance is achieved.

The astral body, however, can also press through the protective wall and inflict its uncontrolled activity on another astral organ—primarily the vascular system. This can cause increased blood pressure or enhancement of capillary permeability. Another astral organ, the kidney, is taken hold of next if acute nephritis or the disturbance in the vascular system is not healed first.

It is well-known that acute nephritis is usually harmless provided it is discovered early. Rest and a relaxing diet are decidedly important here. These measures together with adequate warmth still verify Volhard's statement, "Every acute nephritis can be healed if the treatment begins early and proceeds in the right way." If the organism is not allowed to let the astral body quiet down, however, the illness cannot be overcome. It then proceeds, finally damaging the kidneys, often after a long latency period in which the persisting blood pressure elevation leads to an unfavorable prognosis. Volhard had already pointed this out.

In chronic glomerulonephritis the kidneys are specifically diseased, with the glomeruli being most involved. There is a proliferative inflammation of the capillary loops and proliferation of the tissue of the capsules. Finally, hyalinization develops with the complete obliteration of the glomeruli. The glomerulus was described earlier as the primary place of attack by the catabolic and excretory dynamics of the astral body. In this situation it obviously no longer acts properly within its organ, causing the primary excretion and resorption to decrease. Dilution and concentration capacities become reduced; the result is isothenuria. Here, too, the atonic state of the astral body can be clearly recognized in the kidneys.

There are certainly histological signs of the inflammation. Yet, one is dealing here with typically chronic processes—changes in the connective tissue—for which the word inflammation as polar to sclerosis is no longer applicable. The characteristic signs of inflammation—fever and the dissolving activity—are also missing. We are dealing here with a degenerative process that can be compensated for over a long period by the relatively great regenerative force of the kidney parenchyma.

The elevation of the blood pressure, in which the increased involvement of the astral body is expressed as has been described, is characteristic of chronic glomerulonephritis. On the one hand, this is an expression of the excessive working of the astral body from the head system; on the other, it may be a reaction brought about because the working and switching over of the astral body within the kidney system cannot occur.

In this connection, it is of interest that approximately two-thirds of all chronic nephritics are male and one-third female. It has been repeatedly pointed out that men are constitutionally more united with the nervous system than women. A man is therefore predestined to live out these dynamics in a stronger way, continuing them on into the pathological.

If the pathological situation proceeds, the disease picture becomes more serious; nephrosclerosis—shrunken kidney—and pale hypertension develop. This is the result of the persisting dynamics that lie at the basis of chronic glomerulonephritis. Nevertheless, it does not develop primarily by way of the kidneys but as a consequence of an essential hypertension. The pathogenetic process is nevertheless the same. The excessively active astral body, which is first supported by the vascular system, finally takes hold of the kidneys, thus working there in the same way instead of being switched over. The clinical picture of such a patient clearly shows the predominance of the nerve-sensory system and its impulses under inadequate anabolism. In principle, one is dealing with a sclerotic tendency.

The macroscopic morphology of a shrunken kidney shows us the disease processes. All such shrinking develops through the dynamics of the nervous system, while swelling and watery processes represent an anabolic function of the metabolic system. Thus, the nervous system, including every neuron, has a "shrunken" appearance. It is because of this tendency that the kidney is finally shrunken. An excessive formation and breakdown occur.

If apoplexy does not end the suffering, the final result is kidney insufficiency, kidney failure, and uremia. This is, however, not only caused by the increased urea nitrogen in the blood. Uremia cannot be explained only by the presence of these substances normally excreted in the urine; in fact, it cannot be created with these substances since uremic poison has not yet been found. It appears that freshly formed urine is exceedingly toxic. The death of an experimental animal occurs more rapidly if the ureter of a kidney is diverted into the vena cava than when both kidneys are removed. This finding cannot be explained as a mere phenomenon of excretion. As is well-known, one kidney can take over the excretory function of the organism. Such a finding, however, can be understood by the polarity previously described. By rediverting the flow of the newly secreted urine, the vitalizing incretion that is connected in polar activity with excretion is blocked.

Nephrosis (Nephrotic Syndrome)

In order to comprehend the nature of a disturbance, it is necessary to look for the prototype where it appears in its purest form. Only then will transitions and mixed forms become understandable.

In lipoid nephrosis (genuine nephrosis, "pure" nephrosis) we have a clear pathological picture. The most noticeable symptoms are edema and proteinuria, in which large amounts of protein are excreted. Because of this, it was often spoken of as diabetes albuminurinicus.

To understand this disorder, it is illuminating to note that it can also develop in children, even in infants. During this time, however, the anabolic processes almost completely predominate over the development of consciousness. Thus there are processes here that are opposite to those in nephritis. Obviously in nephrosis, anabolism is disturbed. The organism is permeated with water instead of with new substance, and that is expressed as edema. Thus, in principle there is a more inflammatory tendency that is characteristic of childhood and, in fact, necessary but without fever. That this is absent is significant even in therapy.

The clearest symptom of a disturbed anabolic process is dys- and hypoproteinemia. It was obvious to see hypoproteinemia as a consequence of proteinuria (Epstein). It is possible to develop a similar disease picture by removing protein experimentally, yet this is not identical with the nephrotic syndrome. The earlier assumption of a serious disturbance of blood protein in nephrosis is not verifiable today because there is to some extent even an enhanced protein synthesis.

There is, however, no doubt that in the nephrotic syndrome the constitution of protein in the blood is quantitatively and qualitatively inadequate. One can see this enormous excretion of protein (up to 40 grams a day) as a consequence of disturbed anabolic processes. The inadequate protein is excreted. The serious degenerative transformations of the kidney tubules are the most evident pathological anatomical finding. This condition, however, develops only in an advanced state of the illness.

One must be aware that protein formation is an extremely difficult process because, in addition to species and group specificity, every person produces individual proteins. The finest differences in the composition of protein, which cannot even be distinguished with electrophoresis, are enough for it to be excreted as inadequate, foreign, or defective. Secondarily, then, there can be allergic phenomena.

The findings support the idea that there is actually too much protein formed and that this is so constituted that it cannot be utilized by the organism but is excreted. This results in proteinuria, the consequence of which is hypoproteinemia.

Why is protein formation disturbed and what role does the kidney play in this? Rudolf Steiner pointed to the fundamental issue: Protein formation occurs through the cooperative activity of the four organs, liver, lung, kidney, and heart. This was discussed earlier. Through healthy kidney activity an ensouling and astralization of the living substance takes place. It is this, in particular, that seems to occur improperly, for protein is formed quite easily as living substance, but it cannot be taken hold of nor led further by the astral body, and that is why it has to be excreted. The organ through which the astral body intervenes in the ether body and the anabolic processes is the kidney. Its anabolic results are achieved, but they lack formation and structure. To this extent we actually have in nephrosis a tendency to an exact polar illness to nephritis. In the latter the catabolic component predominates via the nerve-sensory system. In the former, metabolism predominates with its anabolic activity. In addition, in both processes a qualitative element is present in that the catabolism of nephritis is not prevented from destroying the organ, whereas in nephrosis there is an excessively strong and pathological anabolism.

Proteinuria

It has been pointed out several times that every anabolism in an ensouled organism must be preceded by a catabolism. According to Rudolf Steiner's view, the disturbance in a pathological protein excretion must be traced to an inadequate protein breakdown. From the specific function of the ego-organization in protein breakdown, one can see that it participates in causing that process. The ether body requires protein that is completely broken down. If catabolism does not proceed completely, then this protein is not suitable for nor accessible to the ether body, and because it is "hungry for protein," it thus utilizes protein that still contains etheric effects foreign to it. As a result, the person "takes into his ether body effects that do not belong there. These must then be excreted in an abnormal way. Pathological excretions thus develop that manifest in albuminuria."

Protein that is improperly broken down virtually cannot penetrate a healthy intestinal wall. It was found, however, that in the nephrotic syndrome an increased penetration of plasma proteins through the intestinal wall occurs that leads to "protein diarrhea." In any case, in untreated nephroses there is an increased permeability of the intestinal wall. Up until now only the direction of plasma into the intestine has been studied, but it also seems possible that proteins of high molecular weights are resorbed.

Depending upon the illness in which proteinuria occurs, the nature of the excreted protein can change notably. Thus, in cases of empyema or furunculosis and severely damaged tissue (late stage of carcinoma), proteins can be excreted that can be differentiated from those excreted in nephrosis—all of which makes it obvious that the disorder lies in the realm of the protein metabolism.

That the excreted protein is foreign becomes evident from the Bence-Jones protein that can be found in cases of multiple myeloma, in the various leucocytoses and osteomalacia. This phenomenon deserves to be mentioned for another reason. In this disease one is dealing with the occurrence of malignant plasma cell tumors and it goes hand in hand with decalcification and destruction of bones. When one understands that the bony skeletal system is the physical image of the ego-organization, and that as a process counter to the deposition of the mineral the erythrocytes of the blood, in which the ego has its primary place, are formed within the bones, then it is obvious to think that here the fundamental disturbance must be sought for in a weakness of the ego-organization. That may certainly be connected with the well-known fact that there is no other malignant tumor other than multiple myeloma that is connected with such an enhanced protein excretion. Thus, proteinuria can develop because the ego-organization does not act adequately and protein breakdown is insufficient, which then secondarily disturbs anabolism. There can also be a disturbance in protein anabolism when the astral body does not sufficiently guide it via the kidney system. This takes place especially in the region of the tubules; therefore the disorder is expressed histologically in that area. "The damage of the kidney epithelia is symptomatic of the diversion of the astral body from its proper activity there."

Significant symptoms of nephroses are lipemia and hypercholesterolemia. Lipoid metabolism and the significance of increased blood values were discussed in detail in volume I.

Cholesterol must be looked at as an undifferentiated substance. It unites the nervous and kidney systems and arises from the excessive activity of the ether body. Elevation of the cholesterol level points to a failure of the astral body to differentiate it into pro-vitamin D, bile acids, adrenal cortex, and sex hormones. In this symptomatology, too, the inadequate activity of the astral body in the kidney system can be traced. A confirmation of this is provided by the finding that in the nephrotic syndrome there is even an inhibition of fat metabolism.

Another indication for the insufficient activity of the astral body in the nephrotic syndrome is the by approximately 60 percent decreased basal metabolic rate found in lipoid nephroses. Correspondingly, there is a remarkable tolerance for thyroid preparations. The thyroid, however, is a definite organ of the astral body. Here, too, an inadequate intervention is evident.

The genesis of the nephrotic syndrome can also be comprehended from these conditions. Thus, it occurs particularly as a consequence of or subsequent to chronic infectious diseases such as syphilis and tuberculosis. Indeed, chronic diseases indicate that the higher members of man's being are no longer "adequately interested in the disease processes." That in tuberculosis there is an inadequate striving to incarnate is further explained in the chapter on the lung.

In summary, one can see that in nephrotic diseases one is dealing with an excessively weak process of incarnation. Also, the astral body and ego remain too long in the anabolic dynamics of the metabolism, which is physiological and appropriate for embryological development and early childhood. If it does not change in the course of time, however, the same "correct" situation becomes pathological later.

The further displacement into the nervous system and the creation of further forming and processes of consciousness comes about too late; thus, the free unfolding of the personality is delayed. One could say, "The nephrotic takes hold of his body and the world inadequately. In a certain part of his being he remains retarded."

In contrast, the astral body takes hold of the organism too strongly in nephritis. It has become separated too far from the formation of substance and takes hold of it with the catabolic dynamics of the nervous system. These persons unite themselves too strongly with corporeality and with the earth; they age too rapidly. Thus, polar disease tendencies are at the basis of nephritis and nephroses. Since the nature of the kidney is to join polarities and to switch them over, however, it can be understood that especially here the two extremes can come into contact. Thus one can have in nephritis a nephrotic tendency (nephritis/nephrosis, pseudo-nephrosis). Here, too, one can see the organism's attempt at self-healing, albeit with inadequate means. A healing would lie not merely in a bringing together of opposing tendencies—i.e. nervous system and metabolic system or sclerosis and inflammation—but in controlling them and leading them back to their proper place and time of action.

Finally, we must briefly mention stone formation. All urine becomes cloudy if it is allowed to stand long enough. Frequently, however, salts precipitate out in the bladder as solids that must have still been dissolved in the kidneys. Thus, a certain aging process takes place here. After leaving the organism, the urine becomes increasingly subject to the laws of the outer world, whereas while still within the organism these changes are guided by the latter. When stones are formed within the organism, it means that a local, excessive mineralizing tendency exists that is unable to maintain the urine in the realm of life. Today one knows of protective colloids that maintain salts and poorly soluble constituents in solution in the urine. In the protective colloids one may see the working of the ether body. They cancel, as does the ether body, the effect of gravity on the substance by giving it a kind of levity. It is well-known that the composition of kidney stones can vary. This is not a question of the food that is eaten but also of how it is handled.

It is interesting to note that individuals with kidney stones have a lower vitamin A blood level. As described in detail elsewhere,[3] vitamin A is a carrier of the silver process, the function of which is to bring substances from the mineral into the living realm.

Chronic pyelitis has great practical significance. From it there are all kinds of transitions, to cystitis (cystopyelitis) and especially to nephritis (pyelonephritis). Chronic pyelonephritis is today the most frequent kidney disease. Serious pyelonephritic changes are discovered in approximately 10 percent of all autopsies. Pyelonephritis leads to death through uremia in about 33 percent of the cases, and in 40 percent because of cardiovascular complications.[4] The problem lies in the fact that the illness is too rarely and often too late recognized. Especially in childhood, next to afflictions in the respiratory passage, it is the most frequent disease that can lead to lasting debility. In children, 50 percent of all deaths through kidney diseases occur because of pyelonephritis that has been neglected. There is no doubt that the occurrence of the illness has increased immensely in the last years. Certainly there is a bacterial infection, but why do the bacteria thrive today in contrast to earlier decades? Evidently the "kidney situation" has become a different one. The urinary passages must have become more sensitive and must form a more favorable nourishing soil. This is not a problem caused by bacteria.

Certainly various factors are involved, one of which may well be the deficient warmth hygiene of our time. On the one hand, the organism is debilitated by overheated rooms and inadequate humidity. On the other, clothes are often such that many people have cold feet without knowing it. It was mentioned above how sensitive the kidneys are to cold. In a high febrile course one can see the organism's attempt to overcome these foci of coldness and to form itself better.

It has already been mentioned that children in particular frequently succumb to this illness. Among pediatric patients approximately 50 percent are infants less than one year old. This preference for the earliest period of life and also for the female sex can be understood when it is realized that children, and also the female constitution provide a better nutrient soil than older individuals or the male constitution. In the susceptibility to bacteria one can recognize the improperly organized etheric working which provides the nourishing soil. With age, the ether body becomes weaker. There is no longer a surplus of etheric forces. It is also characteristic that acute pyelitis goes hand in hand with high fever, which points to a reaction that is more frequently found in children than in adults.

These phenomena thus seem to point to an improper structuring capacity within the kidney region. To a certain extent the structural constitution is similar to that described in nephroses. The course of the illness, however, is completely different. One is dealing here with an improper integration of the astral body into the kidney area. Rudolf Steiner's remark[5] that the soul life of man in various epochs has a preferential relationship to the various organs is of significance here.

In this connection the kidneys have gained an enhanced significance approximately since the nineteenth century. The life of the soul and the modified reactions and behavior of the human being are related to that change. In order to enable a proper integration of the astral body in the kidney area, it is necessary not only to take up thoughts externally, but rather to penetrate them with intense inner activity. Unpenetrated thoughts become abstract, intellectual, and live only in the head. They are powerless and do not touch the rest of the organism. Thoughts permeated from within emanate from the activity of the human being. Within them live the heart forces of feeling and the creative force of the will. Here lie indications for a comprehensive soul hygiene.

Therapy of Kidney Diseases

A true comprehension of pathology must pass over directly into therapy. The kidneys were described as organs that actively undertake the switching over of the dynamics of the nervous system into those of the metabolism. The attendant polar tendencies to illness are manifest in opposing pictures. They were briefly designated as nephritis and nephrosis and require different methods of treatment.

According to Rudolf Steiner, a "plant image" of the kidney function can be seen in the horsetail, Equisetum arvense. To better understand this plant and its connection to the kidneys, a few points will be mentioned here. It has an exceedingly high content of silica, which gives it a radiating, stem-like, almost spine-like character. Furthermore, in Equisetum one can find many sulfates—substances in which the sulphur process is led over into the mineral or salt state. Silica, however, is representative of the forces active in the nerve-sensory system. Similarly, sulphur is representative of the metabolic system. In Equisetum arvense we thus have a most intimate connection of silica and sulphur processes. It is therefore an image of the working together of nerve-sensory and metabolic processes, as was described for the kidneys. It can be understood that for this intensive working together of two forces only an "old" plant can come into consideration. In the flowering plants the polarity of roots and blossom is worked out corresponding to the human form. Equisetum, however, belongs to the ferns. It represents a one-sided development of the stem principle, while the ferns have developed the leaf. Equisetum is thus truly an image of the interconnection of silica and sulphur processes: It represents a state in which the blossom and root are still combined in a unity. This intimate cooperation corresponds in man to that of the nerve-sensory and metabolic systems localized in the kidneys.

In comparison to other species of Equisetum, Equisetum arvense seems to have the greatest vitality. This may well be due to the separation of fertile and sterile sprout in it. By removing spore formation, which corresponds to a blossom impulse, from the plant, the devitalizing influence retreats and the sterile sprout is manifest in a "purer form."

By administering Equisetum in a suitable form, one gives the organism a picture by which to orient itself toward a more harmonious penetration of the two polar elements. With this "model" of a healthy function the organism can unfold its forces as if in accordance with a kind of leitmotif. Equisetum is the extra-human image of the forces that form the kidneys in the human organism. According to Rudolf Steiner, it corresponds "exactly to the anabolic forces that we have in the kidneys."[6] Through its application "we strengthen the anabolic forces of the kidneys that have become too weak." In the nephritic processes, which finally lead to the shrunken kidneys, one can see how the organ atrophies, how the anabolic forces are too weak. Equisetum arvense is therefore the specific remedy in nephritis and its consequences.

The sulphur component in this remedy can be enhanced by a preparation developed from an indication given by Rudolf Steiner: Equisetum cum sulf. tost. By virtue of the sulphur portion and the toasting, the warmth impulse is worked into the remedy. In the preparation, Solutio siliceae comp., the processes active in Equisetum are imitated and enhanced. Thus, through Equisetum an intensification of therapy toward continuous effect is made possible.

Nephritis was described as an illness in which the astral body, from the nervous system, takes hold of the metabolism too strongly and finally destroys the kidneys by letting them atrophy (atrophic kidney). A basic therapy will begin by attempting to block off these excessively strong processes and to transform them. Warmth must be mentioned as primary here. It is the essential carrier of the ego that is hereby called on to grasp the metabolism in an ordering way. The ego of man lives always in the balance of various processes. Furthermore, warmth is connected in a special way with the metabolism, while the nervous system is the "cold pole of the organism." Through warmth one thus enhances the dissolving, receptive tendency as opposed to the formative, catabolic tendency. Here, too, the profound therapeutic significance of warmth for the kidneys is shown.

The effect of cold is neglected as a pathogenetic factor in kidney diseases. It is well-known that cold stimulation of the skin can bring about disturbances in the vascular blood supply of the kidneys since cutaneous visceral reflexes directly determine an enhanced permeability of the glomeruli, and exposure to cold and moisture plays an essential role in interstitial or so-called trench nephritis. Even a proteinuria can be brought about by the influence of cold.

The organ building impulse of the kidney system corresponds to those forces in nature that are active in copper. The archetypal connection of metal to organs has been described in greater detail elsewhere in this volume. The nature of copper can be characterized by the forces of receptivity and devotion. It corresponds to the forces of the planet Venus, which also lie at the foundation of kidney formation. The task of copper in the organism is to receive the impulses that work through iron. Copper and iron represent wordly forces, the cosmic forces of the male and female principles, of Venus and Mars. The task of the kidneys—better said, the kidney system—has been presented as being active in receiving and transforming. This task and thus the formation of the entire system belong to the activity of copper. It is therefore indicated when the organism is to be made receptive for receiving the astral body, and transforming its dynamics. Thus, copper takes hold of the specific pathogenetic condition in nephritis. Its activity can best be described by imagining it as a vessel that receives the impulses working in from the astral body, and then gives them off transformed. It is not, however, a simple concave mirroring that does nothing, but it is rather an active process, a kind of turning around, a transformation.

The application is external by ointments over the kidney area or internally as Cuprum sulfuricum D4–D6 in which the sulphur components strengthen the anabolism. By uniting the two, it is possible to bring the effect of copper even closer to the kidneys. Copper has a specific affinity to nitrogen compounds and forms strongly colored complexes with them. Since nitrogen is the carrier of the astral processes, it can be seen in these reactions that copper is well-suited to receive these impulses. This, for therapy, therefore, naturally suggests combining a copper nitrogen complex with the kidneys. The corresponding preparation is Cuprum/ren (produced by Weleda). With it one strives therapeutically to stimulate the astral body to be more active in the kidney area. It is thus a basic remedy for treatment of chronic nephritis. Since proper respiration is also connected with the kidney system, as was described before, Cuprum/ren. is also indicated in asthma therapy and has proved to be of benefit.

Phosphoric acid copper is another copper combination. The mineral, phosphoro-calcite, was suggested by Rudolf Steiner for cases of nephrosclerosis (D6 two times weekly injections, and also birch leaf tea) but it is also indicated in other serious kidney disturbances. Here, too, the principle applies that mineral therapy, particularly using phosphorus compounds, appeals most to the ego. Mineral remedies reach deeper than those of plants or animals, and they are also indicated for the more advanced states of an illness rather than for the beginning.

As is well-known, chronic nephritis leads to anemia and hypoplasia of the bone marrow. This is connected with inadequate erythropoetin formation, which is produced in the kidneys and the liver, and which stimulates the formation and release of reticulocytes. This is not only an indication of the anabolic work of the kidneys but particularly of the copper process. Through it the activity of iron is made possible. (Erythropoetin is a mucoprotein containing cobalt. Cobalt, however, stands as a mediator between copper and iron, as can be seen in vitamin B_{12}.)

As was elaborated in the section on mineral remedies, carbon has a definite connection to light and air, i.e. to ego and astral body. For that reason, one can, with the help of the higher potencies of Carbo, enhance the whole kidney process. Thus, one can rule the astral body through Carbo and also stimulate the ether body. Generally, higher potencies come into consideration here—D15 or D20—of which injections have proved especially useful.

As a general treatment, absolute bedrest and relaxation apply in acute nephritis. It also requires a proper diet. Volhard, who introduced fasting and decreased fluid consumption that protects organ activity, was a pioneer in this area. More exactly expressed, the change is caused by decreasing the sodium supply; this prevents the astral body from intervening too strongly. The change also depends on limiting protein consumption, since the elimination of nitrogen is an activity of the kidneys. Dietary restrictions can gradually be relaxed as time goes by.

Today, a dietetic therapy of chronic nephritis is considered about as unnecessary as limiting salt intake, which is suggested only in cases of hypertension and cardiac insufficiency. From the reasons given, however, limiting salt consumption is advisable.

However, in chronic renal insufficiency, an extreme limitation of salt can even become dangerous; because of isothenuria, three to four times the amount of urine must be formed to remove the substances normally found in the urine. Thus, an insidious salt loss takes place that can even lead to a salt deficiency uremia. In such cases, gradual salt administrations are required. The daily control of weight is the simplest way to control salt and water metabolism.

The consumption of protein is considered only quantitatively today. Certainly it must be adequate, but quality is just as important. Meat is essentially more astralized than milk protein, so the consumption of lacto-vegetable food with an equivalent protein content is to be preferred.

A diet which can be of great value in kidney disorders is that devised by Hays.[7] This is based on the separation of carbohydrates and protein in a meal, while the fats may be combined with each of them. The principle is that the carbohydrates disturb the digestion or metabolism of protein and vice versa. As a disturbance of protein formation and digestion is characteristic precisely of kidney ailments, as described, such a relief appears to be well-founded. In any case, practical successes speak in favor of this diet.

Many renal teas contain, along with Equisetum, also Ononis spinosa or Genista tinct., for example. These are Leguminosae, a family possessing a particular relation to nitrogen. According to an indication of R. Steiner, "blossoms contain many healing forces in relation to the kidney system."[8] Blossoms not only correspond to the metabolic system, but bring astral activity into the etheric nature of the plant—just what was described as the task of the kidney.

Besides the described basic medical and dietary treatment, it is necessary in the later stages and for prophylaxis to change the life style. The underlying dynamics, which work too strongly from the nervous system, must be limited by changing the life style (preventing job stress, etc.) in favor of a more harmonious outer and inner life.

Nephrosis was described as the inadequate working of the members of man's being because of an excessively strong but one-sided anabolism within the kidneys. It is an incomplete, partially delayed process of incarnation. The goal of therapy will be to so strengthen the upper man that it will be able to penetrate the metabolic processes in a more formative way. On the one hand, this can be attempted by stimulating the organism in the sense described above, so that protein breakdown can be completed. This is concerned with the function of the ego-organization, which works by way of the pancreas. "It is the force of the ego-organization in the pancreas that is too weak. This must be strengthened." This can be done primarily through iron, which generally stimulates the incarnation process. The remedy Ferrum sidereum, alone or with pancreas, comes into consideration here. The working of iron can still be enhanced through arsenic, which in turn is addressed to the astral body.

Scorodit, which is natural iron arsenic, and Levico, a healing water in which iron, arsenic and copper appear in harmonious balance, can also be used.

The illness processes can be approached from another side, however. Just as in nephritis the anabolic forces in the kidneys are too weak, so in the nephrotic syndrome they are too strong. (No clinical diagnoses were given by Rudolf Steiner for this description. It is evident, however, that the cases described suffered from nephrotic syndrome.) The necessity then exists to enhance catabolism in the kidney area. "In this case, we must reach to the lower plants, perhaps to the ferns that enhance the catabolic forces." That the ferns have a catabolic tendency can be seen in the male fern; it can kill the lower astrality—worms in the intestinal region, for example. The use of several ferns as essential constituents of Digestodoron is based on this enhancement of the catabolic element in the region of the intestinal tract. As mentioned above, the ferns generally are typical representatives of the leaf element within their group. Hart's tongue is a fern that strongly permeates the watery and lives in the metabolic realm—Scolopendrium (D3 as dil. and inj.). Experience shows this treatment to be more effective for proteinuria than other ferns.

Measles is a "natural remedy" for lipoid nephroses. It has been shown in detail that most childhood illnesses, measles in particular, are health-giving processes through which a structural permeation of the organism, improving incarnation, takes place. This is especially required in diseases such as lipoid nephrosis, and thus attempts were made to bring about infections with measles. After the course of a measles infection, there is generally an improvement of proteinuria and dysproteinemia.

The customary application of corticosteroids in nephrosis today can easily be understood from the points of view presented here. The anabolic aspect of the kidney system is qualitatively deficient. The impulse is misguided. Giving the finished product that should result from the proper action of the members of man's being makes it possible to guide and replace the anabolic process through such a replacement therapy.

In the discussion of kidney stones, it was said that the stone-forming tendency goes beyond the pure precipitation of salts. In the organism, processes of solidification and dissolution take place constantly. This balance is displaced in stone formation in favor of solidification. The organism lacks dissolutive forces.

This interplay is most highly developed in nature in crabs. Besides chitin, they have a large quantity of calcium in their exoskeletons. Before molting, when the crabs shed their exoskeletons, the calcium is dissolved and then laid down in the gastric wall as little stones. Once a new exoskeleton is formed, they dissolve the calcium in the gastric wall and secrete it in the exoskeleton again, thus giving it its well-known hardness. This event is repeated with every new molting. Calcium finds itself repeatedly in the rhythmic alteration of solidification, dissolution and vitalization. One can appeal to these forces when using crab-stones therapeutically in potentized form.

The remedy Renodoron goes back to Rudolf Steiner. It has two polar constituents. On the mineral level it represents the same polarity as does Equisetum on that of the plant. The silica component is here represented by flint, which occurs in chalk. With it, and opposing it, is calcium in the form of these crab-stones. Calcium and silica are similarly polar. This polarity is not only enhanced in the mineral, in contrast to the plant Equisetum, but is also an extension of the indication—especially but not only—of stone formation. Fundamentally, the dynamics that lead to stone formation more closely approximate nephritis than the nephrotic processes.

Experience has shown that the exclusive application of Renodoron is not adequate to prevent new stone formation. The effect can be strengthened, however, when one adds to it a potentized kidney stone from the patient in a D15 strength as dilutio. The potentization is done by Weleda.

In this sense, the capacity to retain a mineral substance in the realm of light is lacking whenever there is stone formation. This, however, corresponds to the silver process to which we have already pointed. Thus, administration of silver (as ointment, 4 percent, as Argentum D6, or Argentit D6) is indicated for kidney stones.

One could also approach the tendency to stone formation even more specifically by either potentizing the removed or excreted stone, or by administering substance that lies at the basis of the stone—for example, Oxalis D3 to D6 in oxalate stones, etc.

To prevent kidney stones, the unmastered substances (food containing oxalates, urates, etc.) should be avoided and excretory dissolutive possibilities favored by increasing fluid intake. As urate stone formation generally takes place only at a pH under 6.5, an alkalization of the urine is necessary, e.g. by means of Fachinger water, lemon juice, potassium sodium citrate (commercial preparation: Uralyt®-U.). Phosphate stones, in contrast, require acidification of the urine (e.g. with Wernarzer water, vitamin C).

The therapy of chronic pyelonephritis demands intensive therapeutic efforts. As already mentioned, often children affected by it go unnoticed. The customary antibiotic therapy in acute pyelitis is almost always successful in removing the bacterial infection but this is generally only transient, which means that the fundamental situation is in no way addressed. Absence of bacteria is not identical with health. Thus, even after adequate antibiotic therapy, one finds new episodes of pyelonephritis in 80 percent of the fiive to nine-year olds and 56 percent of the ten to fourteen-year old girls.[9]

Lachesis D12 or D20 is especially indicated in acute pyelitis as a basic treatment. Furthermore, in all highly febrile illnesses, Argentum D30 (possibly together with Echinacea) as well as Carbo D30 are indicated.

From an evolutionary point of view, snakes have a marked connection to the urogenital system. Their peculiarity in the formation of the sense organs and lung formation is also connected with this. With the administration of snake poisons one addresses, besides the nerve-sensory activity, also the formative forces in the urogenital region.

There can exist a direct transition to this from cystitis. Here,

Cantharis in particular has shown its value. This is the so-called "Spanish fly," Lytta vesicatoria ("blister beetle"). Its organotropy is clear in the pharmaceutical test. The application goes back to the homeopathic principle of similars. In the proving test, administration of Cantharis results in cystitis, urethritis, and acute glomerulonephritis. Characteristic of its therapeutic action is a symptom of burning. The action is harsh but quick. D4, D6, or Cantharis comp. are used.

The decisive therapy of pyelonephritis, however, occurs in the symptom-free phase, the interval. It is known that a chemotherapy directed at the bacteria, even when conducted over years, does not appreciably improve the long-term prognosis. Apart from its undesirable side-effects, increased resistance and new infections can result. A rational treatment will be based upon the described pathogenetic situation. Following an acute phase, a long-term treatment must be carried out. This can only be outlined here, and requires individual variation.

Since the genital area and also the lower part of the urinary tract stand under the action of silver (see the section on the seven metals) silver is also indicated particularly in cystitis (e.g. as a salve). The silver effect can be specifically guided to the urinary passages by Thuja, e.g. in the preparation Thuja argento cult. Mercury embraces all proliferative processes, as in this case an unformed etheric element, helping it on into the copper domain. In the preparation Thuja comp., Thuja D6 is processed together with Argentum D3 and Mercury D3.

This is indicated particularly in recurrent pyelonephritis. In view of the quite powerful mercury effect, the preparation should always be given only a few weeks at a time. In recurrent bladder infections, Kalium/Teucrium comp. is indicated in the interval, in order to "bring the secretions into a regular incorporation under the effects of the astral body."[10]

Other medications may also be indicated in the interval, and can be combined. Resina laricis, larch resin, has a strong enlivening and also forming action. As in every local inflammation, Apis is better indicated together with Belladonna (e.g. Erysidoron 1 or Apis D3/Belladonna D3 aa mixed ampule). These medications can be "steered" by means of an 'organ preparation (Pelvis Renis D4, D6). The remedies in question can be mixed in accordance with the clinical picture, and should be given over a period of months, or in alternation with Argentum Thuja cultum or Kalium/Teucrium comp. (see above). Depending on the stage of the disease (pyelonephritis), treatment will also extend to the kidney itself, with Equisetum or copper, for example (see above).

An absolute precondition for efficacy of the therapy is attention to warmth. This means sufficient warmth protection not only of the kidney region, but also of the legs, as well as sitz-baths, in order to achieve a local hyperthermia, etc. As in most cases a population of E. coli bacteria is present, an effective treatment is an alternating diet that shifts the urine back and forth between alkaline and acid in intervals of several days.

In long-term therapy, which is unavoidable particularly with children, medications must be changed again and again. The aim of the therapeutic measures is to bring about the correct engagement of the higher members of being in this region.

These therapeutic possibilities, which could be described only in outline, have arisen out of the essence and nature of the pathological disorder. With them it is possible to come to a truly rational therapy of kidney ailments.

The Cardiovascular System and Its Diseases

> The heart is the key to the world and life.
> *Novalis*

That the heart holds a special position among the human organs has been felt since time immemorial. It is taken as the symbol of life and love, the seat of the soul, the place of courage, etc.—and all this consistently in all peoples and mythologies. This original feeling that is still retained in language when relationships with the heart are established, when a person wants to unite himself with his whole being or a cause, has gradually disappeared from our consciousness. Today, one only looks at its physiological functions, and the closely adjoined soul-spiritual side is more or less consciously denied in modern thinking. Even the physiological aspects are considered only from a mechanistic point of view.

By contemplating the heart through spiritual science, it is now possible to rediscover the deeper meaning of the old wisdom and to understand the heart's true function. It is certainly a necessity of our time to study this organ's form in relation to its physiological function, but an understanding of it can develop only when its form and function are placed in the context of their higher tasks. To ignore them, which methodically happens today, leads to erroneous interpretations and failure to fully understand the heart. The purely physiological results could be arrived at with other structures and functions. Sufficient examples are available in the animal realm to verify such a statement.

When the idea of the heart in man is realized in such a complicated manner, however, it comes about in view of the soul-spiritual functions that require these structural and functional principles as their correlates. It is necessary for a true understanding of the heart to look at and compare its development in man and animal, and to delineate the forces active in it. To that end a brief presentation of embryology, ontogeny, and phylogeny will be given.

Development of Blood, Heart, and Circulation

The Earliest Development

Though the heart and blood vessels are later highly differentiated structures, they go through their first stages together since they are of one origin. These first structures are called blood islands. They consist of angiogenetic tissue that contains blood stem cells, the hemocytoblasts. These cells originate from extra-embryonal mesenchyme and move first in a random and later in a directed stream into the heart region of the embryonal disk. (These observations were made on chick embryos.)

After the cells form strands, they gradually flatten out and differentiate into enclosed vessels and separate spherical cells that can move freely. Thus the vessel walls and first blood cells are developed.

We have here the prototype of the phenomenon of circulation and later heart function. There are two polar tendencies: The striving toward densification and dispersion. The densification goes hand in hand with concentration and decrease of surface area. It is the centripetal tendency that later works from the upper, formative pole of the organism. The last expression of these contracting dynamics is systole. The polar opposite of these forces is the centrifugal dispersal and flow of dissolving and increased surface area. Here, the metabolic pole from the lower human organism is active. This archetypal polarity of form and substance arises later in the heart as the systolic and diastolic principle, as contraction and expansion, as center and periphery. These forces are already recognizable in their first beginnings.

The Extra-Embryonal Primordial Heart

Toward the end of the third week, angiogenic tissue develops in three places:

1. At the periphery of the embryonic envelopes that characteristically for man are developed first, in the chorionic region that is later transformed into the placental circulation. The vessels of the embryo move into the placental villi, which contract rhythmically as has been shown by measurements of pressure. One could say that the placenta already represents a peripheral heart. All functions first begin in the embryonic membranes before they appear incorporated into the embryo. When this internalization is completed, thereby finishing this phase of the incarnation process, birth occurs.

2. Angiogenic material collects around the allantois in the body stalk region and forms the allantoic circulation, which has the function of connecting extra- and intra-embryonic vessels. This connection is established between the chorionic circulation and the intra-embryonic vascular structures. Only later do the arterial and venous umbilical vessels develop.

3. Angiogenic islands appear within the embryo, again in three primary places:

a) In the region of the yolk sac where later the great veins develop.

b) In the mesodermal region at both sides of the future spinal column, which will develop later into the arteries of the aortic arches.

c) In the actual cardiogenic zone (see Fig. 1) that is originally located in front of the future head. Around the twenty-second day, this zone is displaced into the chest region through the increased growth of the embryo.

Blood—Vessels—Heart

In these stages of development we clearly see the formative impulses gradually moving from the periphery into the center. It can be seen clearly how the blood in striving toward incarna-

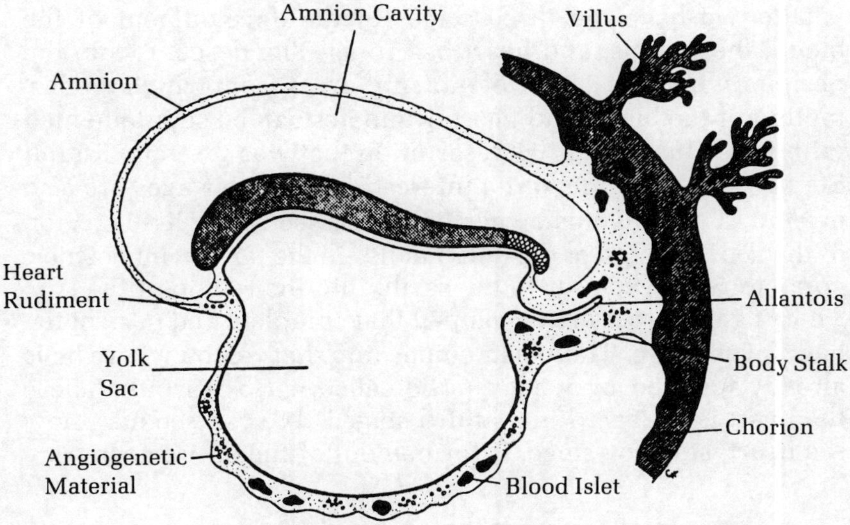

Fig. 1: The development of extra-embryonic blood vessels in the chorion, body stalk and wall of the yolk sac in the nineteen day old presomite embryo (from Langmann, *Medical Embryology*, Stuttgart, 1970).

tion forms the heart. The content creates an adequate vessel for itself not the other way around.

One could also consider the growth of the vessels towards the center from another interesting point of view, that is, that the forming of the heart as a functional suctioning center draws them in. They are attracted, at least, by the streams of force that emanate from the heart center.

From the development of the circulation it can be seen that the streaming of the blood exists prior to the functioning heart and for a relatively long period of time is independent of the heart's contractions. In the chick this can be clearly observed; the embryonic blood moves through the vascular system at first without specific direction. As soon as the heart begins to contract, the blood begins to flow in *one* direction, but since the heart valves are not yet developed, the direction cannot be determined by them. The primary event in the embryo is thus the movement of the blood to which the pulsating beat of the heart is added only later.

Thus we have the three stages of the development of the blood, the vessels, and heart before us. The descent from the periphery into the center of our sun forces from which the formation of the blood and heart originates can be supplemented with a spiritual-scientific description that was given by Rudolf Steiner and in which, quite interestingly, three stages are also evident: "For man must, when he has passed through this region of the zodiacal sign of the lion that lies in the far distant cosmos, come to regions closer to the earth, into the region of the sun. There again forces are developed that complete and perfect the heart even more. Then man comes into that region where he is already touched by what can be called earth warmth. There the heart is prepared in its third stage."[1] We can see here how the heart, stage by stage, is formed out of the entire cosmos.

Ontogeny and Phylogeny of the Heart

In the preceding discussions it was shown how the future material of the heart consists of the extra-embryonic mesenchyme. It is, as it were, the universal substance of the middle region, which in its plasticity is able to take up formative as well as life forces. Thus, bones and blood develop from it—bones when the intercellular substance hardens, walling in the cells so that the physical form is rigidified in space; blood when the intercellular substances liquify while the cells round off, so that living movement liberated in time develops.

We have the same polarity in the moving form of the vascular walls and the formless movement of the blood. In the following, the ontogeny of the heart against the background of phylogenetic structures in the various animals will be considered because only in looking at ontogeny and phylogeny together can the true significance of the heart in man be perceived.

The Ontogeny of the Heart

1. The first primordial heart structure is discovered to be in keeping with the bilateral symmetry of the head. It consists of two mesenchymal strands of cells that become hollow, and as they descend into what later becomes the chest cavity, they join to form an asymmetric organ in accordance with the asym-

metry of the lower man. In the form of the double heart primordia we have the phenomenon of polarization. Thus, the spatial principles of the upper and lower organisms are brought together in the heart. It is interesting that the duration of the ununited double heart is correlated with the capacity to develop separate circulatory systems. The earlier the union takes place, the sooner the chaotic mixed blood develops, such as in the anamniotes; the later it occurs, the sooner is the circulation separated depending upon increasing levels of development, as in the birds and mammals. We can see here how what works as idea in the beginning is realized at the end, so that beginning and end must be looked at together.

The descent of the primordial heart into the later chest cavity—of which the routes of the cardiac nerves are still witness—from the head where it originated as the center of the circulatory system, represents an incarnation process that also mirrors the internalization of the organs. In the newborn, the heart still lies somewhat higher, in approximately the fourth intercostal space, than in the adult in whom the apex is generally found as low as the fifth intercostal space. Thus, with the participation of the lungs the heart becomes increasingly the central organ.

The heart here is still on the level of the fishes, in the form of a sequentially arranged four-chambered organ (sinus venosus, atrium, ventricle, and bulbus) with simple peristaltic streaming movements (Fig. 2).

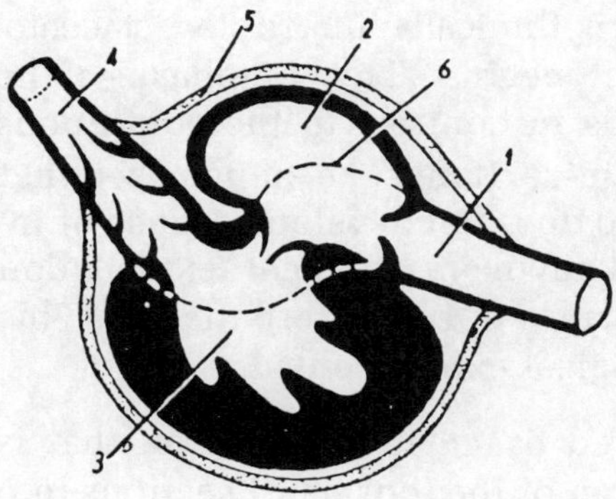

(1) Sinus venosus
(2) Atrium
(3) Ventricle
(4) Heart bulbus (here as conus arteriosis with several valves)
(5) Pericardium
(6) Rudiment of the heart utricle

(Fig. 2: From: A. Portman, *Einführung in die vergleichende Morphologie der Wirbeltiere*, 5th ed. Basel/Stuttgart, 1976)

At this stage, almost plant-like regularity holds sway. The ether body predominates and the formative astral influences have hardly become active. Thus, one can see neither a marked differentiation of form nor a clear forming of the blood stream. To a large extent, this corresponds to the primary "streaming" in the plants.

2. The second stage in the development of the heart is characterized by an increasing separation of the polar arterial and venous forces; this is equivalent to an increased arterialization or formative tendency. We see here again the clear tendencies of densification and dispersal or dissolution. There is in densification also the tendency to bind to the earth which is brought about by oxygen. This corresponds to the active nature of the arterial that is emphasized on the right side, whereas the dissolving tendency is connected with carbon dioxide, that corresponds to the spiritualizing activity of the receptive side of the venous system emphasized on the left.

The separation of these two forces leads the arterial pole to turn to the right and down, and in the heart it leads to a thickening of the ventricular wall, which confronts the bloodstream. The venous inflow pole, however, is lifted upward with a left turn that leads to a distension of the atrium, moving along horizontally with the blood. Thus the arterial pole begins to be shifted toward the left and the venous to the right, and the heart loop begins to form as a phenomenon of intensification in the Goethean sense. Also, the transition from a purely streaming, peristaltic movement to a rhythmically interrupted, staccato-like systo-diastolic movement begins. This emphasizes the astralizing process that stands in contrast to the continuous etheric streaming of the plant juice. It must be emphasized that the formation of the heart loop does not develop because of inadequate space, as a well-known mechanical explanation claims; rather, it develops because of self-differentiation. This has been verified in embryological experiments.[2]

3. The third stage is marked by an internalization that is characterized by the integration of the four heart sections into two, as well as the splitting of these two sections again into

four parts, now in the right–left tension of the arterial and venous systems of the great and small circulations. Comprising, integrating activities are, however, always an indication of the ego function. Thus, we get the actual human organ of the ego-organization. This integration consists of two aspects. On the one hand is the merging of the sinus venosus with the right atrium, whereby the sinus forms the new atrium and the old atrium becomes an auricle. The venous region is transferred to the *right*, as an expression of the balancing function of the heart. Thus, a reversal of the poles takes place. It is interesting here that the veins of the nerve-sense system are arranged in pairs, according to the principle of bilaterality (V. cava cran. dextra et sinistra) whereby the left vein regresses. The veins of the metabolic system, in contrast, do not appear in pairs.

On the other hand, the integration of the bulbus arteriosus into the *left* ventricle must be noticed. It later becomes the course of the smooth outflow, while the old chamber forms the course of the trabecular inflow. At the same time, the aorta turns to the right and attaches to the left ventricle, winding around the pulmonary artery. As a result, we have before us the finished human heart as a wonderful symbol. A cross has developed that includes the pulmonary vessels entering the left atrium, the horizontal pulmonary arteries, and the vertical body veins. We see again the reversing function of the heart in which the arterial vessels lie horizontally, the venous vertically. In a contrast laden with tension, the blood streams run into each other, held by the venous blood of the coronary vessels

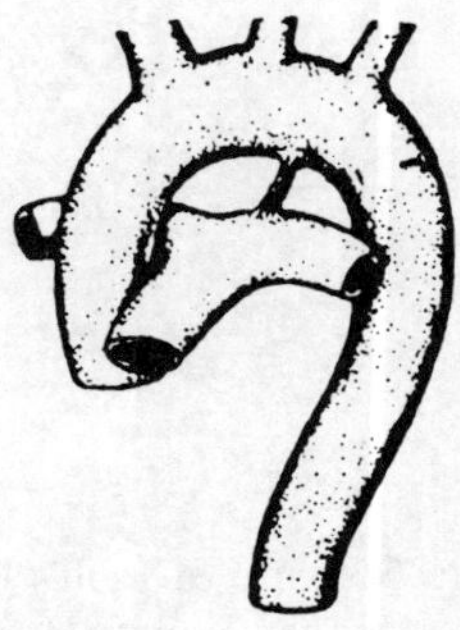

Fig. 3: Curvature of the Aorta.
(From: Langmann, *Medizinische Embryologie*, Stuttgart, 1970)

flowing into the coronary sinus to be balanced and newly vitalized in the lung, then leaving the heart again; this is expressed in the double looping of the aorta and pulmonary vessels (Fig. 3). Thus we find the synthesis of polarities as an integral part of the heart's structure.
From this, as a new creation, arise internalization and the development of a center of freedom.

The Phylogeny of the Heart

Among the invertebrates, pulsating channels perform the functions of circulation. They are capillaries, conducting vessels, and pulsating heart in one. This can be seen in the lancet. In the course of evolution, however, we see an increasing differentiation of functions.

Fishes (Ontogenetic Stage 1):

The fishes still have a purely extrinsic, venous circulation in which the simple fourfold heart tube beats in the periphery of the venous flow (Fig. 4). This "beating" is actually a peristaltic

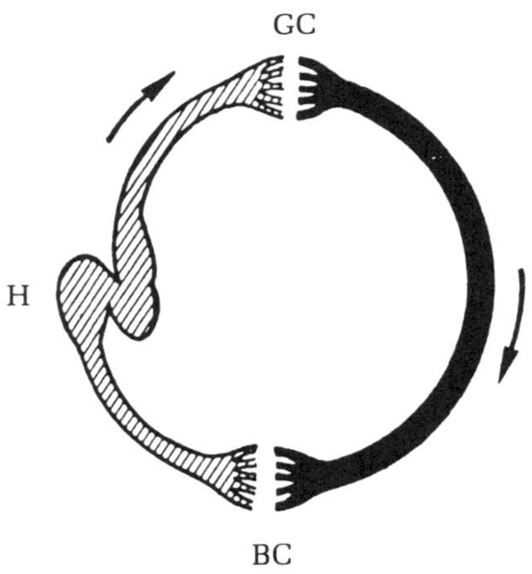

Fig. 4: Scheme of Fish's Circulatory System (GC: gill circulation, H: heart, BC: body circulation; black: arterial shaded: venous)

movement. From the tendency of the venous blood to come to rest, whirlpool flow patterns develop that give rise to repeated vascular valves. So the fish is formed in a rhythmic metamerism from the repeated beat of the waves. Its circulation shows its whole being: cold blooded, without an inner life, one with its environment as it loses itself in the waves of the ocean. Its heart still lies behind the gills in the neck in a peritoneal pocket. The frequency of heart beat and gill respiration rate have a relationship of one to one. Thus, nutrition, breathing, and heart beat are undifferentiated and closely united, thereby completely documenting the animal's unity with the environment. This is also shown in the circulation.

Lungfishes (Ontogenetic Stage 2):

The first step in the emancipation from the environment and toward the individualization of higher evolution is found in the lungfishes.[3] In them, the swim bladder is transformed into a respiratory organ; they are thus able to live on land, where they bury themselves in shoreline mud. Now the lungs are the organs needed to live on land. Through them oxygen is taken up, allowing catabolic oxidative processes that reverse the purely vegetative anabolic stream to take place. Only through this oxidative, catabolic process is the incarnation of the soul life made possible. Through the lungs, venous blood is oxygenated and brought back to the heart. They are thus placed in opposition to the originally extrovert, simple circulatory system, and through making the heart the central organ the lungs make possible the development of a new, internalized, lemniscatory circulatory system. This, however, splits the old unified circulation into two new circulations that cross in the heart, bringing about mixed blood conditions.

With the formation of the lungs and the introduction of oxygen, a new disharmony develops, a contrast that is connected with the transition to living on land which is experienced as the polarity of ego and world. This contrast must be balanced and overcome by the heart, something that comes about through the separation of the circulations and their unification in the heart. The lungfishes have only a functional, not an anatomic, separation of the two circulations.

The contrast of lungs and heart becomes clearer when we recognize that the lungs have their embryonic origin in the intestinal region of the lower body, whereas the heart has its in the head region of the upper body. The lungs develop as an outpouching of the frontal gastrointestinal tract and thus are derived from the endoderm. The veins of the swim bladder, which are analogous to the pulmonary veins, at this stage flow into the liver vein; the swim bladder artery, however, flows into an intestinal artery. These lung vessels become only later attached to the heart. Thus, developmentally the lung arises from the lower organism, whereas the heart descends. The middle organization has developed from the upper and lower organizations, not only through making contact, but also through reaching over one another so that the contrast can be united by mediation. Also, right and left sidedness is balanced by the fact that the heart is placed more to the left, the lung more to the right.

Amphibians (Ontogenetic Stage 2a):

In the amphibia the gills disappear, the heart is placed in the chest cavity and limbs develop—all as new evolutionary trends to make it possible to "tread the earth." Concomitantly, the head is set off from the rest of the body. However, even with the disappearance of the gills, the lungs do not yet dominate respiration; it is also developed through the skin. While the oxygenated blood from the lungs flows into the left atrium, enhancing the splitting of the heart, this effect is cancelled when the blood oxygenated through the skin flows into the right, the actual, atrium; this creates conditions of mixed blood in the heart (Fig. 5). Respiration through the skin thus inhibits the trend toward the development of an internalized respiration and thus the emancipation from the environment. Rather, it favors again a direct relation, a merging with environmental conditions by unifying the circulation as in the earlier fishes.

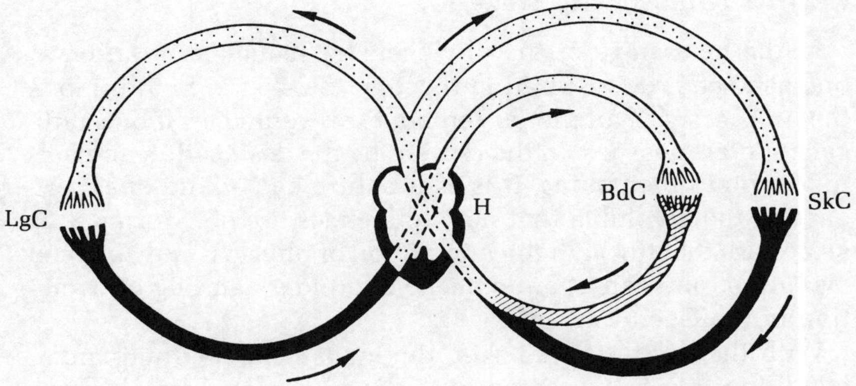

Fig. 5: Diagram of Amphibian Circulation. LgC = lung circulation; H = heart; BdC = body circulation; SkC = skin circulation; lined = venous blood; dotted = mixed blood; black = arterial blood.

Outer and inner breathing confront each other in an exclusive polarity. The pulmonary vessels do, in fact, establish an attachment to the heart. However, the sinus venosus and the bulbus arteriosus are not yet included in the heart, since the circulation is still too chaotic to enable a concentration of the heart. Actually, the septile formation in the heart is possible ontogenetically only after the integration of the four parts into two. Thus, in the frog only the atria are separated, and the separation of the blood streams in the chambers is attempted by a complicated septile formation that appears in many different forms in the various species of amphibia.

Thus, the amphibia have a double life, as their name indicates, vacillating between skin breathing that is directed toward the environment, and an internalized, individualized, lung breathing that will increasingly become the carrier of the soul. They can, as it were, still not decide between connection to the environment and emancipation, between water and life on land. Thus, there are salamander species with completely dominant skin respirations and mixed blood conditions and others, representing more advanced forms such as the frogs, with marked lung respiration.

Reptiles (Ontogenetic Stage 2b):

In the next stage of the phylogenetic sequence of animals, one can see how respiration through the skin, which inhibits the progressive evolutionary trend, is prevented, as if by a radical counter-measure, in the reptiles by the desiccation and cornification of their skins. It is as if nature had a kind of experience in the amphibia that now influences the new forms. It is clear here that through the interaction of physical and spiritual evolution, one can attain a deepened understanding of evolution in the Goethean sense.

With the drying of the skin, the lungs become dominant, a condition that is expressed in the fixed morphological lemniscatory circulation formed by the intersection of pulmonary veins and aorta that emanate from the polar heart region; the arterial aspect now begins to dominate the left side. The opposition of the lungs and the influx of the completely oxygenated blood lead the formative forces from the periphery into the heart's center. This leads to an integration of the bulbus and sinus venosus into the left chamber; it is an expression of a concentration that characteristically begins at the arterial pole.

There is also a reduction of the multiple valve formations to the semilunar valves and the hardening into tendonous threads of the muscle fibers that hold the valves. Through the chiseling by the in-rushing blood, the many septi of the chamber are hollowed out and pressed back into its wall. Thus, the chamber becomes larger and the outer wall compactly densified. Only the papillary muscles that resist the streaming blood and the septum in the middle of the chamber remain; growing out from the middle, it separates the blood streams.

We see here the initiation of a purifying and demixing process that is carried from the periphery to the heart through the formative forces of the newly vitalized blood in the lungs.

As amniotes, the reptiles show in the development of embryonic membranes their liberation from the environment, making respiration through the lungs possible. And thus, after the successful inclusion of the arterial formative forces of the blood we see the separation of the blood streams realized in the bulbus arteriosus through the septile formation in the heart. Yet, the complete splitting of the circulations must again be given up, since the periphery cannot tolerate this discrepancy because it carries along old remnants of development in the form of the paired aortic arches, which remain after the reduction of the gill arch arteries. This leads to the intestinal tract, by way of the left right-chambered aortic arch, only receiving purely venous blood, and that cannot be tolerated. Therefore the middle septum is secondarily broken through by the foramen pannizzae, and the dorsal aortic anastomosis develops, through which the overflowing of the arterial blood becomes possible (Fig. 6). Through the internalization and increasing independence brought about by the victory of the lung over skin respiration, it is interesting to follow up the psychological expressions of animal nature. On land, through increased lung respiration, an increased pressure develops in the left chamber that provides the nerve-sensory system with more arterialized blood via the right aorta; this makes the animals more awake,

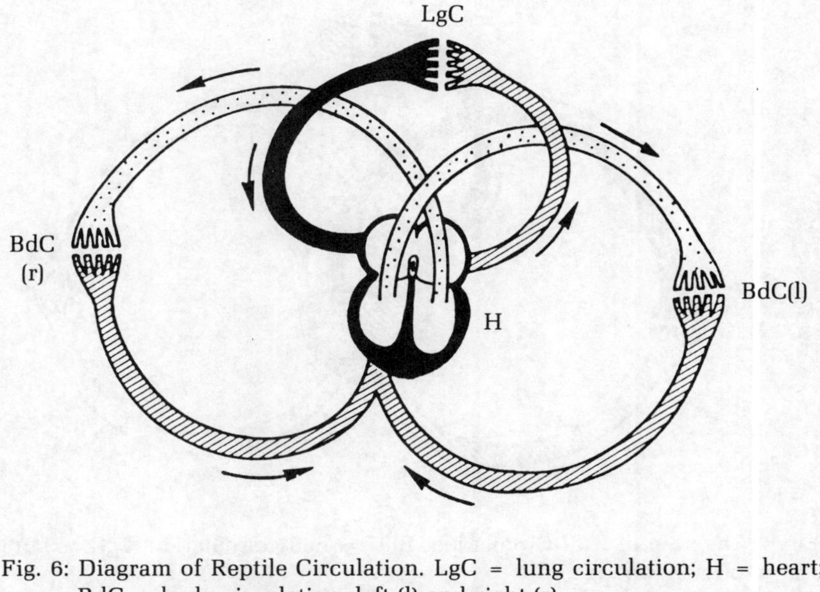

Fig. 6: Diagram of Reptile Circulation. LgC = lung circulation; H = heart; BdC = body circulation, left (l) and right (r).

alive, more "sanguine" and related to the airy element. In the water, however, because of the inadequate lung breathing, there is a decreased pressure that leads to an increased venous influx; this makes the animals duller, more sluggish, and more phlegmatic. We can see that with the dominance of the lung and the increasing arterialization an actual increased influx of the "soul" takes place that makes it possible for us to speak of an internalization.

Birds:

Now it is again as if nature gained by the experience, because the previously disturbing venous left right-chambered aortic arch of the reptiles does not develop. One can clearly see the goal and direction of evolution. The consequence is a complete septile formation in the heart with the separation of the venous and arterial blood, as well as an almost excessive dominance of the lung and the arterial circulation (Fig. 7).

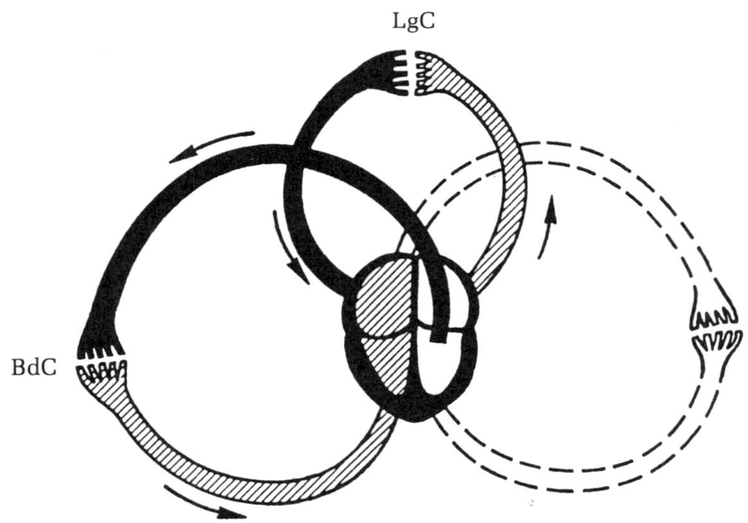

Fig. 7: Diagram of Bird Circulation. BdC = body circulation; LgC = Lung circulation.

This fact is quite evident in the nature of the bird; it is a typical representative of the nerve-sensory system. These forces dominate and impregnate the entire shape.[4] It is permeated by the forces of the astral body living in the nervous system. Here, air is not only the element of life, but it also permeates the organism, aerating even the bone marrow. This shows that the birds do not truly incarnate their being into substance but rather escape from the earth, which accounts for the fact that they have no inner life as other animals do, but rather express the moods and tenor of the environment. This again comes to expression in the formation of the heart, which is developed by the blood rushing into a smooth and drop-like pointed form. The high pulse rate and blood pressure similarly show the high metabolic rate. The birds "gulp down" their environment in a kind of feverish life of the senses, taking it up only fleetingly without establishing an intensive relationship with it.

The musculature along the newly developed heart skeleton is formed correspondingly through the astral formative forces and winds around the heart in lemniscatory spiral paths. At the same time, with the hardening of the heart skeleton, the leading stimulatory system develops from material that retains its plasticity and makes possible the functional unification of the separated chambers of the heart. Interestingly, it develops at the stage of the birds. We thus see the polarity held within a unity, yet still with a one-sided emphasis on the arterial formative forces and without achieving a complete inner harmony.

The function of the heart, seen in the image of a lemniscate balancing contrasts, is achieved by a reversal of directions at the center. This means that the right arterial flow must be turned toward the left, and the venous flow, directed toward the left, must move toward the right. Since in the birds the right aorta becomes the main artery of the body, they do not achieve this reversal and balancing; rather, they enhance the one-sidedness of the arterial aspect and thus of the astral. This also comes to expression in physiological tachycardia and hypertonia. These dynamics are expressed in the form of the heart, which is pointed, elongated and internally smooth.

Mammals (Ontogenetic Stage 3):

In the mammals the right aortic arch is no longer present and the left arch is directed through a final torsion into the left chamber (Fig. 8). The reptiles thus form a left venous, the birds a right arterial, and the mammals finally a left arterial aorta. Thus, the complete reversal of the contrast is achieved, and the unity that was lost in the fishes has been regained at a higher stage. A free middle as a new element can only appear as active achievement of the polarity of upper and lower forces.

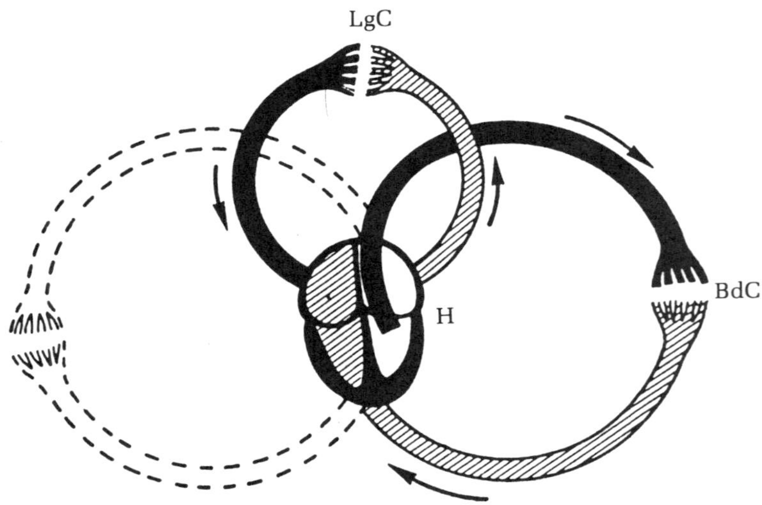

Fig. 8: Diagram of Mammal Circulation. LgC = lung circulation; H = heart; BdC = body circulation.

A final purification, a further differentiation, and a pronounced inner architecture of the chambers is achieved in the mammalian heart. The internalization is shown clearly in the inverse structure of the atria and ventricles, in that the atrium (the former sinus) is smooth, while the auricles (old atrium) are trabecular, whereas the ventricles are trabeculated but the outflow tracts (the former bulbus) are smooth. Here we see in the integrated part of the form of the heart the internalization of the outer world and the reunification of the arterial and venous forces. The internalization is appropriate to the nature of the mammals, since the early development takes place in the uterus through placentation.

The Human Being:

Of all the organs, the heart is the center of the human form. It is turned forty-five degrees in all directions whereby the spatial planes (above–below, right–left, front–back) are reversed, as we saw. Thus, it is related to the new spatial planes, yet remains independent of them by not being placed into them. Hence, it can redeem the forms of space into those of time. It actually belongs to an *in-between realm*, a new creation within the world. It is the realm of the middle, which is actively formed between the upper and lower organizations.

The heart is attached to the heart skeleton, and the venous cross is included in its plane. This venous cross is an image of the contrasting qualities of the upper experience-laden and the lower substance-laden blood. They flow against each other in the earth battle, dying out of space. In the diastole the heart is nailed to the cross, from which it is liberated in the systole. Thereby the blood offers itself to the outer world through the lungs in order to leave the heart newly vitalized by oxygen through the arteries, which embrace twice in love and harmony. This harmony now develops functionally through an exchange of polarities: The venous inflow occurs in the vertical although by its nature it ought to be horizontal; the arterial inflow is horizontal although it ought to be vertical. The outflow, however, occurs venous-horizontal and arterial-vertical, as it ought to be. Like a deep symbol this cross and the embracing lemniscate are contained as a mystery in the structure of the heart.

The complete harmonious balancing through inversion of the left and right forces, of the arterial and venous and the horizontal and vertical planes, we finally see realized in a wonderful way in the coronary vessels. The right coronary artery moves horizontally forward to the right, the left one moves vertically backward to the left, while the small heart vein on the right in front takes a vertical course, the large one on the left behind, a horizontal one. Altogether, the veins emanate from the left in accordance with their nature, and end in the coronary sinus. Finally, we see that the venous right heart is embraced by an arterial coronary vessel, the arterial left heart is embraced and held by a venous vessel. The venous vessel is horizontal on the left and vertical on the right. The arterial vessel is vertical on the left and horizontal on the right. Beginning and end are united in a balancing, harmonious way. Altogether the coronary vessels do flow more horizontally; the conducting system, however, flows vertically so that here too we see the substance or blood pole balanced by the formative or nerve pole.

In the embryonal circulation we see how the human circulation has developed in a wonderful way from the evolution it still mirrors; it is a true circulation as we saw it in the fishes, for the organ circulations are still dormant and bypassed through certain vessels of which the most important are the ductus (liver), the foramen ovale (heart), and the ductus arteriosus (lungs).

Body and lung circulations are still parallel to each other and the arterial and venous tracks are still placed sequentially; the heart has only a discharge path as in the fishes. These organ bypassses, however, lead to venous inflows—even though only to a slight extent—that mix with the arterial blood, corresponding to conditions in the amphibians. That the arterial blood from the umbilical vessels appears in the right atrium is also reminiscent of the amphibians. We saw in the skin respiration of the amphibians that arterial blood also still flowed into the right atrium.

We recognize the circulation of the reptiles in the passage between the atria created by the foramen ovale, which corresponds to the foramen pannizzae, as well as the aortic anastomosis of the ductus arteriosus. Similarly, we recall that the left right-chambered aorta still contains venous blood in the reptiles, which we can also see if we think the pulmonary vessels continued above the ductus arteriosus in the aorta, representing the venous vessel running on the left. We thus see that in keeping with their nature and without inversion in the embryonic circulation, the arterial vessels are still right-oriented and the venous vessels still left-oriented.

This foundation illumines the significance of the dramatic moment of the first breath and the incarnation of the soul-spiritual. At this point, the old forms of evolution are relinquished and the preformed paths of circulation are now utilized. The pressure of the pulmonary blood closes the foramen ovale, thus separating the right venous and left arterial heart. The center of the heart trembles from the discrepancy of the streams of blood coursing into one another. This is shown also in the size and weight of the heart, which from birth to the third month decreases in weight from seven to three grams per kg of body weight until it finds the middle of five grams per kg of body weight in the balance of upper and lower forces in later development. Thus, the heart becomes the image of the process of birth in the center of the human being. Correspondingly, the less incarnated woman has a lower heart weight than a man.

The opposition of the lung permits the internalized lemniscatory flow to be developed through the centering position of the heart. The oxygen streaming in through the lung creates completely different conditions. Breakdown processes begin that reverse the purely vegetative functions. Thus, the embryonic dream consciousness also ceases, and with the catabolic transformations of substance by combustion instead of the previous exchange of substance, the possibility is provided for waking consciousness and sense perception. By including the middle system in its function, the soul-spiritual of man now constitutes the threefold organism. The goal of evolution is thus realized in the appearance of the archetypal image (Fig. 9).

We saw how in ontogeny through three stages of enhancement in the Goethean sense—the polarity (tubal/heart), enhancement (the heart loop), and the synthesis and enhancement into something new (unified heart) by the interaction of the astral formative forces—first an astral animal organ and finally a human organ developed from an etheric plant-like organ. This

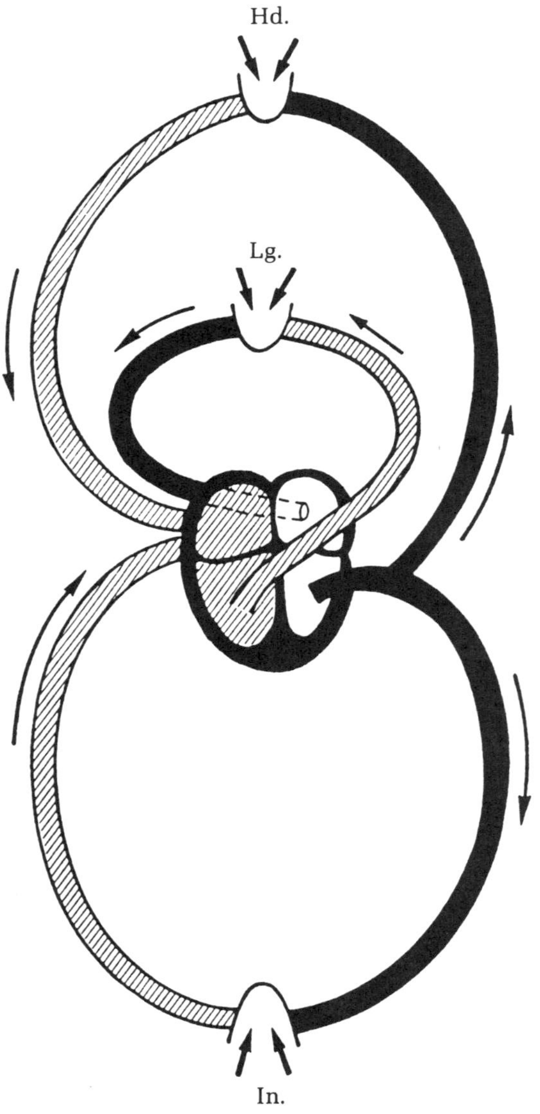

Fig. 9: Diagram of the Threefold Human Circulation. Hd ½ Head; Lg = Lung; In = Intestines.

human organ could then be the carrier of the ego function. Every being has *its* heart, the structure and function of which is developed in such a way that the uniqueness of the being comes to expression in it; this organ can then be used as an instrument.

In the human heart the earthly and the cosmic are intimately united; in it, the mechanical necessity of the bone rigidified in space and the spirit-forming, dissolving force of the blood, moving in time, is mediated, balanced and maintained. Between rest and movement, space and time, form and substance tendency, systole and diastole, the human ego experience can develop in freedom experienced within.

The Location and Position of the Heart

The special position of the heart as compared to the other essential organs is connected with its central location in the body—central in many respects—and this is an expression of its nature. Topographically, the heart lies not only approximately in the middle of the human body between above and below, left and right, front and back, but functionally it also forms the middle between the nerve-sensory and the metabolic systems. In the structure of its musculature it shows a unique intermediate position between the striated and smooth muscles. Striated muscles serve voluntary movements, whereas smooth muscles serve involuntary movements within the vegetative functions. The heart muscle stands between the two, as is appropriate for feeling as a half-conscious soul capacity; conscious thinking is based on the nerve-sensory system and the unconscious will on the metabolic system.

The heart is also placed between two contrasting streams, the body and lung circulations. These also have polar functions. The blood experiences in them not only the finest dispersion into the periphery but, in addition, a reversal of the arterial-venous state. Both streams meet in the heart, which thus encompasses both the arterial and the venous blood.

In the following discussion the briefly characterized central position of the heart will become even clearer. Only through this is its balancing function made possible, and characteristically for the heart, its central position extends to many other contrasts and polarities, as will still be shown.

The heart does not merely stand passively in the middle, but rather plays an active role as mediator in the most varied areas of life. In one of these active functions the heart separates the dynamics of the nerve-sensory and metabolic systems, yet in a unique manner allows them to interact with each other. This occurs through the rhythmic system. Only because of this is harmony created as an active process, as a positive force of the middle. An understanding of this role of the heart in the human organism becomes apparent when one contemplates it as representative of the rhythmic system.

The Rhythmic System

Only in the last decade has attention increasingly been directed to the study of rhythms, and they have been recognized as an independent factor that works deeply into almost all biological processes. Today there exists extensive literature on the subject.[5]

Rhythmical processes or events can be most clearly studied in astronomy. The nature of rhythm becomes immediately evident here. It consists of a persistent repetition of a process that never remains the same, however. No planetary revolution, for example, will be exactly like the preceding one. Conditions change continously, yet the whole proceeds harmoniously. These higher regulations were recognized by Kepler, and he thus called his magnum opus *Harmonices Mundi*. Never is the same event repeated in the cosmos; this would be an inharmonious beat, whereas rhythm is the repetition of the similar. "The beat repeats, rhythm renews" (L. Klages). The beat is the persistent repetition of the same event; rhythm is the continuous modification of a preceding similar element. Thus, there is a harmony in rhythmical events that leaves open new possibilities of development. Beat, however, through the repetition of the same, may well be more exact, but it is also more rigid and fixed. Here an event is led over into a state that remains the same and is held there. Beat leads to isolation from interconnection; it creates a separate independent life, whereas rhythm is an expression of an active harmony. Beat is dead rhythm. It is for this reason that beat is so tiring. True rhythm, however, is vitalizing. Thus, beat is suitable to mechanics and rhythm to living systems.

The typical representative of the principle of beat is the motor, which functions optimally when the number of revolutions remains the same. Embodiments of a rhythmical system exist only in the organic realm, and yet certain aspects of such wholes can also be found and studied in inorganic conditions. What is characteristic is the alternation of frequencies and their overlapping and capacity for modulation.

Life manifests in the continuous transformation of a process that repeats itself. For example, the succession of generations remains similar, yet it is continually over-ruled by supra-ordered impulses and transformed, so that no generation is exactly identical to its predecessor. This possibility of transformation is one of the basic principles of life. This is why the possibility of development is associated with irrational numbers: each year has 365.24 . . . days; the human body is built according to the golden section, etc. The rational comes to an end and goes no further; hence it can be exactly computed and reproduced. Its sole sphere of validity is the inorganic, dead world of the eternally unchanging.

In the realm of life, transformation and development reign. No day and no year is like the other; and this is in fact the very basis for the possibility of individualization. Nevertheless, a fixed order is also an integral element in harmony. It is the "framework"—in this case the rational relationship—that corrects the deviation from the order once again. Examples of this are found in the human organism.

harmony →	fixity	order	rational
harmony →	openness	development	irrational

Rhythm can go through two contrasting transformations. *Beat* is one side of the deviation of rhythm. It leads to an inability to accommodate physiological and soul-spiritual demands, thereby fixing life and preventing possibilities of development. It is a sclerotic process within life. The other side of the loss of rhythm is *arhythmia*. Life is also possible arhythmically, without rhythm, but only in the form of anarchy; this happens on a low level that never achieves the biological plane. It exists, for example, in the growth of bacteria under constant conditions. Here, there is no intervention of a supra-ordered principle, no organism. In contrast, higher plants show a rhythm of their own, which they maintain even without a "time keeper," that is, without the involvement of a yearly rhythm, as in the tropics.

Beat . . . . Compulsion
Rhythm . . . . Freedom
Arhythmia . . . . "Anarchy"

Rhythm thus represents a principle that stands in the middle between beat and arhythmia. It is by virtue of this fact that it makes possible the raising of life to a higher level, giving expression to and manifesting higher life in freedom. The loss of rhythm in rigidification into beat is, like arhythmia, a loss of the middle. Thus a path to illness is opened.

Through the rhythmic system the possibility is created for a supra-ordered spiritual principle to manifest physically. A mirroring of cosmic rhythm can be found in all life. Rhythm itself is, similar to warmth, half-spiritual; to be sure, it is physically perceptible, but by nature it is nonmaterial. Thus, it can become a carrier of the supersensible principle. "Neither in nature nor in man are rhythmic processes physical. One could call them half-spiritual. The physical as object disappears in the rhythmic process."[6]

"Rhythm has been implanted into matter through the spirit; man carries rhythm as an inheritance of his spiritual ancestry."[7]

The resonance of biological organisms with cosmic rhythms is today an extensive field of study, and though frequently ridiculed a few years ago, lunar influence on the reproductive rhythms of many lower animals is today a proven fact. Cosmic planetary influences on plant growth have also been shown to exist with equal certainty, but they are not as familiar.

For man, certain conditions apply by which the entire human, as well as the individual, development proceeds in rhythms. There are rhythms of long durations as well as short rhythms. The longest cosmic interval is the Platonic year, during which a complete revolution of the equinoxes is accomplished in approximately 25,920 years. Rudolf Steiner repeatedly pointed out that in the course of a human life this number is mirrored again: On the average, the resting adult takes eighteen breaths a minute, 1,080 an hour and in twenty-four hours, 25,920.

If one takes the average length of life as seventy-one years and a year as 365 days, then a human being lives approximately 365 × 71 or 25,915 days which is the number of times he experiences the sleep-wake rhythm.

This relationship is by no means external, but corresponds to the incarnation process. It has been described how in every inspiration we have an incarnation tendency and in every expiration an excarnation tendency. Similarly, awakening in the morning is an incarnation process while the astral body and ego exit in falling asleep. Between the breathing rhythm and the sleep-wake rhythm there is thus an inner connection. In them the incarnation process, man's relation to the earth, is expressed. Man is an image of cosmic happenings; he carries the laws of the macrocosm within himself as microcosm.

Human life proceeds in seven year rhythms. The first, marked by the turning points of the change of teeth (age 7), then puberty (14), and maturity (21), correspond to the "birth" of the ether body, the astral body and the ego that was described in detail in volume I. These rhythms continue throughout life but are only rarely so clearly recognizable as in the life of Goethe. The seven year periods correspond to the development of the soul (see the chapter on psychiatry) and are an image of the sevenfold planetary activity.

Fig. 10 gives an insight into the influence of the yearly rhythm on biological reactions. The results of eighty yearly averaged

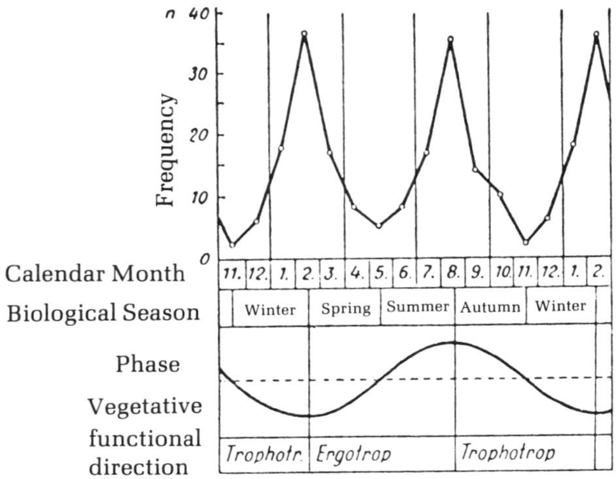

Fig. 10: Above: Monthly maximum and minimum frequencies in the course of the year of various functional quantities to determine the turning points in the biological year. Below: Phase, position and vegetative functional direction of the yearly rhythm in the biological seasons. (Hildebrandt, G., "Saisonphysiologische Gesichtspunkte zur Bäder- und Klimabehandlung." *Arch. f. physik. Therapie* 17 (1965), 41; Hildebrandt, G., "Biologische Rhythmen und ihre Bedeutung für die Bäder- und Klimaheilkunde." In W. Amelung u. A. Evers: *Handb. d. Bäder- und Klimaheilkunde*. Stuttgart, 1962).

measurements of various physiological data were consolidated and the monthly maximum and minimum frequencies were counted in the course of the year. Clearly, the turning points peak in February and August.

It must be mentioned, however, that the semi-annual ordering of the vegetative direction of function is not generally applicable. Various values are in opposition to these curves.

The shorter rhythms are easily recognizable. The menstrual cycle of twenty-eight days is clearly a moon rhythm that corresponds to the general connection of the genital system with the moon. The "reliable" coupling of the reproduction of lower animals with moon rhythms has already been shown. The menstrual rhythm is no longer synchronized with the moon cycle, however. An internalizing has occurred that separates it from the cosmic system. The event surely still shows its origin and character, but it has become independent. Here is an example of the "physiology of freedom."

In ancient times the weekly rhythm as an image of the sevenfold planetary events was created from archetypal wisdom. The cosmically oriented festivals of the year were similarly determined.[8]

Without doubt the rhythm that has been studied the most is the day–night, circadian, twenty-four hour rhythm. Under normal living conditions, daylight works as a "time giver" (Aschoff) so that there is a strict coordination of the endogenous rhythm with the day rhythm. Man, however, has his own rhythm of about 24 to 25 hours; this continues to exist despite continuous illumination or continuous darkness. Man, through his conditions of life, is thus bound to a large extent to the sun rhythm, but he has emancipated himself from the moon rhythm.

There is an essential difference between man and animal here, since the lower animals still show a clear dependency on the moon, while man has internalized his rhythm and made it into an independent function. Thereby he has become free from the cosmic archetypal image. This is a stage in development. If man were to remain continuously dependent on the cosmos and the spiritual forces working within it, he would never achieve spiritual freedom.

A certain connection must be maintained, however, for were man to isolate himself completely from the cosmos, he would also become separated from the forces of life. "The tree of life" must be maintained and to a large extent must be far removed from individual access; the tree of knowledge, however, is now accessible to man. For that reason, bodily processes must proceed in natural rhythms while the human being can live unrhythmically from his ego, voluntarily breaking through the harmony of the organism and disturbing it. Up to a certain point, this is necessary. "The more human conditions of life have been integrated into the body, the more has the old rhythm been maintained; the more these conditions have turned toward the spiritual, the more disorder has been brought into them."[9]

Man acts out of his ego and tries to master his astral body; he cannot voluntarily influence the ether body, however. Thus, the reactions of the ether body proceed "by themselves" in accordance with inherent wisdom and order, independent of consciousness.

All functions that support consciousness such as the sleep-wake rhythm, can easily be interrupted. A person can voluntarily bring about another sequence or course of events. The deeper biological rhythms such as that of the liver, however, cannot be manipulated; they cannot be reversed by various life styles, but rather continue in their natural phases. Old observations such as that healthier sleep occurs before midnight and also modern observations of shift work can thus be understood. Since regeneration always originates from the ether body and the human being has a regulatory system of the rhythmical processes, he is able to balance negative influences for years or even decades. It is only in the last few decades that attention has been directed to the influences of unrhythmical or even anti-rhythmical life as brought about by civilization, for example among night workers. In the future, certainly more attention will have to be directed to the significance of a disturbed rhythm, especially in the development of chronic illnesses. In this connection we must point to the encompassing significance of eurythmy as a primary healing force. Every aspect of life that is lived unrhythmically, including disordered thinking, feeling, and acting, works disturbingly upon inner rhythms and thereby upon health.

Man has thus freed himself from the inner order in which he was originally implanted. Thus he has injured this order but has gained freedom. "A special characteristic of our age is that it has lost the old outer rhythm and has not yet gained a new inner rhythm. Man has outgrown nature and has not yet grown into the spirit. He had to . . . get out of the original rhythm in order to achieve his freedom. But he must again find the laws within himself to regulate the "clock" of his astral body. Today, he has no inner thought lines, no inner thought rhythm. Humanity would end in complete decadence if it would not take up an inner rhythm."[9]

It is the task of our time to create in freedom an inner condition of order on a higher stage, but this is not possible without insight into the relationship of man to the cosmos and the spiritual world. Only when man has found a new connection to the divine spiritual origins in himself will the disharmony and illness connected with this separation be overcome and a new unity and harmony be created that is maintained in freedom. This process was described as lying at the basis of every healing.

This union happens unconsciously during sleep. Physical and etheric bodies are here not subject to the working of the astral body in the sense of the actions of day consciousness because during sleep the astral body and ego are immersed in the spiritual world. They interact with the cosmos, receiving forces that provide the physical and ether bodies with new regenerative impulses. Thus, during the night the reconstitution of order and healing takes place. During the day, however, this order is continuously disturbed by the ego.

To a certain extent this is necessary; it does not lead necessarily to destruction, however. The natural rhythms when used today to accomplish something can even lead to enhanced effectiveness and achievement. This is the secret of the proper point of time, for which the Greeks still had the concept *kairos*. Expressed in a modern way, one could say that the acts and deeds of human beings ought to take place in phase with biological and cosmic rhythms. This would lead to relief and to the preservation of an economic principle and a harmonious way of life.

Although the year, month, and day rhythms in man are exceptionally complex, and every organ has a more or less typical rhythm, even vibrating in fractions of a second which can be verified in an EGG, rhythmic events are experienced most obviously in respiratory and heart activity. It has already been pointed out that man has freed himself from his relationship to the moon rhythm and has individualized it. That has been possible because he possesses a functional organism, a rhythmic system, for this purpose just as he also possesses water, air, and warmth organisms. This rhythmic system has a certain individual lawfulness, so that the rhythms can proceed independently and are not necessarily dependent upon a "time giver." It is only for that reason that rhythms gain their individual activity. Through the rhythmic system the organism again succeeds in coordinating the de-synchronization brought about by an unrhythmical life. Thereby the precondition for a necessary harmony and healing is given.

Even though almost all life processes proceed rhythmically, there are organs that manifest their rhythms in very obvious ways; lungs and heart are the typical representatives of the rhythmic system. Although here, too, there can be dependence upon external events (sensitivity to weather; the asthmatic heart senses when the weather changes), these organ functions are more inwardly oriented and attuned to one another.

The rhythmic system holds a position between nerve-sensory and metabolic systems insofar as it is alternately open to their impulses. The contracting dynamics, which is the characteristic tendency of the nervous system, can be found in inspiration and in systole, the expanding tendency of metabolism in expiration and diastole. Lungs and heart are thus at one time given over entirely to the impulses of the nerve-sensory system and at another entirely to the impulses of the metabolic system. Nevertheless, this does not happen completely passively. With each perception of these impulses there is a reaction that is an active answer in the sense of a balancing of and adaptation to the demands. Tendencies that produce illness —sclerosis and inflammation—emanate from the nerve-sensory as well as the metabolic system. These are perceived by the rhythmic system and actively mastered, diminished, and healed in principle.

Here lies the deep significance of the sentence, "Rhythm carries life" (Rudolf Steiner). Thus, the rhythmic system is also considered the carrier of health. The actual forces of healing emanate from it. "The entire rhythmic system is a physician."[10]

To understand the true nature of rhythm it is necessary to see that the polarities have a common origin that still comprises them prior to their differentiation and which thus represents a germinal state to which the word "chaos" in its original meaning is applicable. It points to a germ-like state that encompasses all possibilities and is pluripotential. With the disappearance of the understanding for a thinking in polarities, the word "chaos," however, came to mean a condition of destruction, but that completely contradicts the original meaning.

According to its topography and action, the breathing rhythm stands closer to the nerve-sensory system, and the pulse beat closer to the metabolic system. So the relationship of pulse to breath is an exceedingly valuable indicator of conditions of health and tendencies toward illness in a person. Stated more exactly, this relationship expresses connections of two rhythms to one another. Rudolf Steiner repeatedly pointed to this relationship of pulse and breath as an essential indicator.

Hildebrandt, especially, took up these indications and undertook comprehensive studies.[11] Since the heart of a man at rest on the average beats 72 times to 18 breaths, the ratio of pulse to breath is 4:1. It became evident that this ideal quotient of 4 is hardly achieved during the day and instead the value varies widely. During sleep the values closely surround the ideal value of 4, an expression of the free establishment of the inner order (Fig. 11).

At night the organism is left to itself in its biological foundation; it is then no longer subject to the impulses of the ego as in the conscious actions during the day. During sleep, more wisdom-filled impulses and forces are at work rebuilding the organism. They regenerate it and attach it to the cosmos and its rhythms.

It also became evident that the reaction to stress is more favorable the closer the initial position lies to the ideal value of 4. If the initial position is considerably different (see right and left part of Figure 12), then there is either a delayed return of the pulse frequency to its initial value, or an overshooting return with a decrease from the initial position. Both types of reactions show an increased lability of regulation. The middle group in which the value of the quotients lies around the norm of 4 shows, in contrast, the most rapid and goal-directed return to the pulse frequency of the starting point. The group finds itself at the optimal, healthiest starting point.

Further, it has become evident that the pulse respiratory

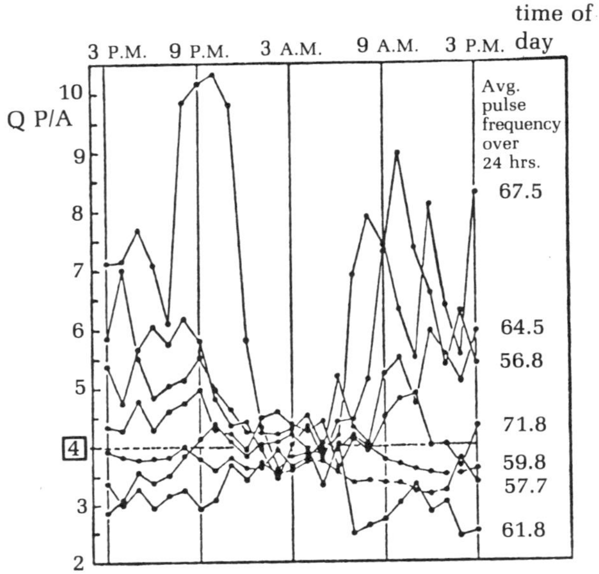

Fig. 11: Nightly Normalization of the Pulse-Respiratory Quotient with different Pulse Frequencies (average 24 hours). Hourly registration of pulse and respiration during at least 2 minutes. Healthy experimental subjects during bed rest and evenly spaced food intake. (Hildebrandt, *Med. Welt* 73 [1961] and *Zeitschr. f. angew. Bäder- und Klimakunde* 10 [1963], 402.)

quotient is also a measure for the improvement of the vegetative reactive capacity as seen in the increases during therapeutic baths. In the course of such treatments the various initial values during therapy strive toward the normal full number relationship of 4:1. Thus, it is also possible to verify the clinical success of the therapy since it is dependent upon whether the treatment achieves a normalization of the pulse respiratory quotient or not.

During physical work, one ought to expect that the relationship of the pulse respiratory quotient, which is 4, is even more disturbed, yet the opposite is the case as Fig. 13 shows. As is well known, during work the pulse and breathing frequencies increase. Their relationship approaches the region 4 to 4.5:1.

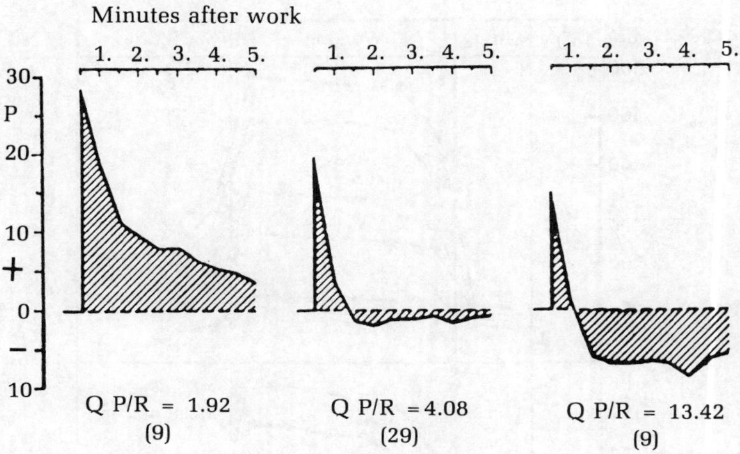

Fig. 12: Mean Pulse Frequency during the first 5 minutes of equal doses of incremented work-load. Three groups showing different rest values of the pulse respiratory quotient. Δ P = Deviation of the pulse frequency from rest value. The numbers in parenthesis show the group frequency, the Q P/R values show the group mean of pulse/respiration quotients at rest (according to Schaefer and Hildebrandt, *Arch. Physik. Ther.* 6 [1954], 375).

This frequency relationship remains relatively constant in this area in all stages of stress. One is dealing here during work with a remarkable approximation of the frequency relationship that is normal for the person lying at rest. Increasing evidence shows even more exactly, however, that in extreme stress and fatigue the value of 4 is striven for. In these cases the organism reaches back to the principle of optimal conditions that are most clearly given in the ratio of 4:1. This preference applies, however, not only to the relationship 4:1, but there is a clear preference for the simple, whole number relationships, a harmonic order of frequencies; the principle of whole number relationships dominates (see Fig. 14). There is also a strict preference for whole number relationships in animal studies.

It is significant that at the coupling of the phases of heart function and breathing, the heart rhythm is the leading factor. A coordination of phase exists, however, not only between

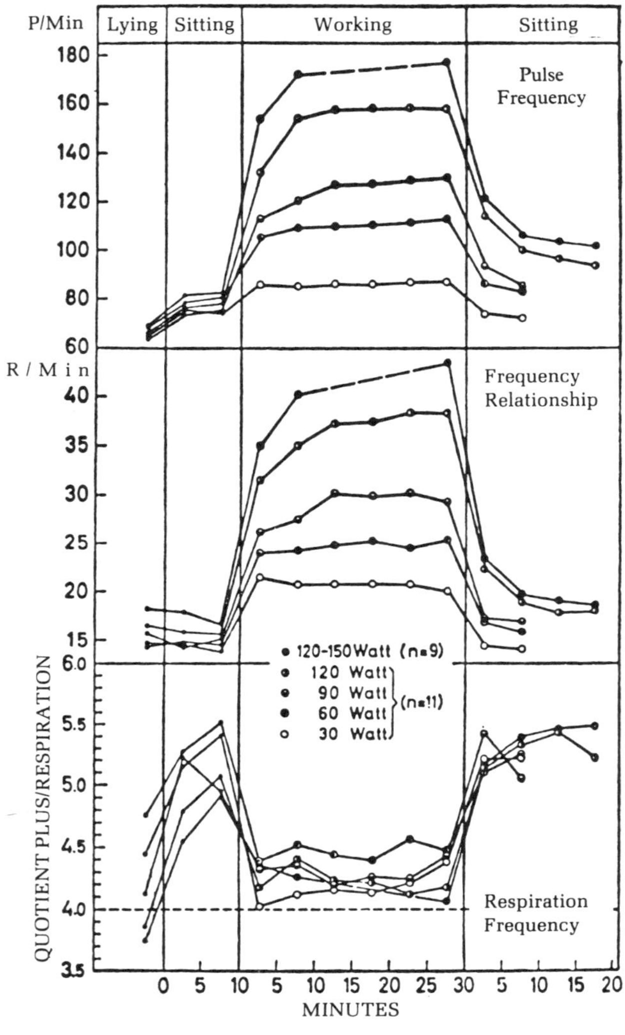

Fig. 13: Average progression of the five-minute average of pulse and respiration frequency and their mathematical relationship (pulse-respiration-quotient), lying down, sitting, during and after measured treadmill work. For the extreme stresses and pauses (120–150 Watts) only the first two 5-minute averages and the averages of the last five minutes of work before pausing are given. (From: Hildebrandt and Daumann, "Die Koordination von Puls und Atemrhythmus bei Arbeit," *Intern. Zeitschrift angew. Physiologie einschl. Arbeitsphys.* 2127, 1965).

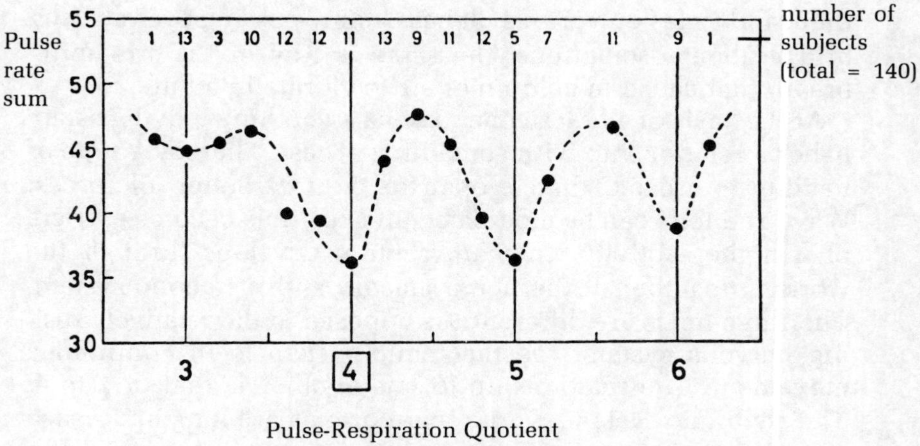

Fig. 14: Average of pulse rate sums (sums of the deviations of the pulse rate from the rate at rest, measured every ½ minute for 5 minutes) after work (climbing 3 steps six times in one minute at a given speed) plotted against the pulse-respiration quotient (measured at rest). From data collected by Hildebrandt, *Die rhythmische Funktionsordnung von Puls und Atmung*, Stuttgart, 1960.)

pulse beat and breathing, but also between breathing and the rhythms of the peripheral circulation such as the pulse pressure and other smooth muscle rhythms of the various organs.

Thus, an interrelationship of orders exists that have their own time relationships, a “rhythmical order of functions” (Hildebrandt), a “rhythmic system” (Rudolf Steiner). One is dealing here with an endogenous factor that encompasses the time structure of the human being. The life of man in time (his time-form) is, however, an expression of the working of the ether body. Yet the rhythm does not come about through it alone.

How does rhythm develop? When air passes over water, waves arise that show all the criteria of a rhythm: Every wave is similar to every other wave, but they are never the same. The same phenomenon occurs when water flows over sand. This, too, is rhythmically ordered.[12] This phenomenon is repeated a thousand times on various planes. A bow passing over a string brings about oscillations; the same is true of the streaming breath that causes a column of air to vibrate in a flute.

At the basis of all these phenomena something moving establishes a relationship with something at rest. Thereby a state of liability is created that is open to the interaction of forces. Wave and tone can be modulated and can thus become carriers of a higher activity. In man, rhythm develops through the working together of the nerve-sensory and metabolic system. Their dynamics are different. As opposed to the relatively resting nervous system, the metabolic system is in continuous movement. The relationship to one another is that of 1 to 4. The rhythmic system, whose main organs are lung and heart, stands as active mediator between the two.

The relative rest of the nervous system is meant here in a dynamic sense. This way of looking at things is not contradicted by the fact that the distribution within the rhythmic system is such that the more rapid frequencies are in the nervous system (EEG, "signal impulses," etc.) and the slower rhythms (daily rhythm-liver; monthly rhythm-uterus) can be found in the metabolic system.

Rhythm requires two contrasting conditions in order to come about, for example, rest and movement; it is itself the resultant third. It is not made up of the other two elements, however. It is rather an enhancement in the Goethean sense that can result from the tension of the polarities, through which something appears in a new form. The nature of the polarities consists in the fact that they both stem from a common origin. The tension ruling the contrast between them permits a third to unfold freely in this field and to utilize it.

Plato sensed something in the insertion of the heart between the polarities of nerve-sensory and metabolic systems when he called the heart the source of the blood, a guardroom standing in the middle between the head and the seat of desire. The interaction of lungs and heart is, on the one hand, an expression of the predominating tendency of one or the other system; on the other hand, the introduction of a new order also begins here. The rhythmic system is an indicator and healer at the same time. It gives man the possibility of psychological experience, and it also brings about the creation of new states of equilibrium.

The Physiology of the Heart

The activity of the heart has been thoroughly studied and is well-known. The extant concepts of the heart's circulatory functions have become common knowledge and it appears hardly possible to discover anything "new" in this field. The heart as motor, in the sense of a pressure or suction pump that drives the blood through a system of tubes, the hollow muscle that brings about the pressure, the valves that mechanically prevent the backflow, the streaming from places of higher pressure to places of lower pressure—all this clearly seems to speak for the heart as a mechanism, the task of which is to pump blood through the body. Nevertheless, this idea is relatively young, and is in no way in the form those who are considered its originators knew. Rudolf Steiner especially repeatedly and expressly pointed out that this idea does not correspond to the facts and that wrong ideas of this sort have destructive influences that penetrate right into the social environment.

William Harvey is generally considered to be the discoverer of the circulation of the blood and to be the one who established the ideas considered valid today. Prior to him, however, Miguel Servet, who was burned at the stake in 1553, described the small circulation exactly in a criticism of the Bible. In a chapter on the Holy Spirit, he describes an example of the working of Christ in the blood of the human heart. The breath of the creator working in the air of the earth, he says, penetrates by way of the small circulation into the blood of man.[13]

And how does Harvey himself speak of his discovery of the function of the heart and the significance of the circulation?[14]

> It is possible to call this movement a circulation in the same sense that Aristotle compared the weather and rain with a circular movement in the upper regions. For the moist earth warmed by the sun develops vapors; the rising vapors again densify to rain and fall downward again, moistening the earth.

> Here we have the circulation of the sun. In this and in similar manner through the movement of the sun, through its approach and retreat thunderstorms and other heavenly phenomena are brought about. So also it could possibly happen in the body that all parts are nourished, warmed, and vitalized by way of a warmed, perfect, vapor-like, spiritual and (if I may so express myself) nourishing blood, whereas the blood in the various parts of the body is cooled down, densified, and weakened and therefore returns to its origin, to the heart, its source, to the altar of the body (lar = protective spirit of a house; hearth) in order to regain its perfection. There, through the naturally powerful fiery warmth, this treasure of life (vitae thesauro), liquified anew, is impregnated with spirit and with balsam, as it were, and from here it is again distributed: and all that is dependent upon the beating movement of the heart. Thus is the heart the primal source of life and the sun of the small world (principium vitae et sol microcosmi), just as the sun in the same relationship deserves to be named the heart of the world. By virtue of this force and its beat the blood is moved, brought to perfection, nourished, and preserved from decay and disintegration. By nourishing, warming, and vitalizing, the heart in turn provides services to the entire body—this household god, the basis of life, the originator of all being. The heart is the root of the lives of living beings, the lord of them all, the sun of the small world upon which depends all life and from which radiates all freshness and all force.

In this work of Harvey's there is no talk of a mechanistic explanation. He makes no use of the concept of a pump, nor of any other technical analogies. He brings the heart into connection with the sun. This can also be found in ancient mystery wisdom, for example in the works of Aristotle.[15] The central position of the heart as the primordial source of life and protective god of the house is also clearly expressed. Harvey also writes that the transfer of the blood from the arteries into the veins takes place either directly through anastomoses or through porous places—a description that seems very modern, especially considering that the discovery of the capillary system by Malpighi did not take place until 1661, four years after Harvey's death.

The heart was only later considered to be mechanically active. Alfonso B. Borelli (1608–79) thought of the heart's activity as a mechanical process and used a pump as a model.[16] Johannes B. Bohn (1640–1718) said it even more clearly:

> What a hydraulic pump or piston achieves, the heart brings about in the living machine and the circulatory movement of all its liquids. Just as the former does with water, so the latter gives the blood its first impulse by driving it forward. When the pump and heart stop, the fluids of both also stand still.[17]

Quite a bit later it was seen that the movement of the blood need not necessarily be a consequence of the heart's action, but rather stems from another force. In 1793, C.F. Kielmeyer wrote:

> I use this term "propulsive force" without any special choice but simply because it came to me first. Another term might well be more suitable. It does express the phenomenon to be designated here that consists in a propulsion of fluid without the cause being known. For the time being it is designated by the word "force" until a reduction of the phenomenon has been made. That I was primarily thinking of plants when I defined the concept of the force of propulsion is clear.

He emphasized further that even "in animals that have hearts" one could not get along without such a concept.[18]

The "purely" mechanistic way of seeing things came to the fore only in the middle of the nineteenth century:

> If we take the process of the circulation of the blood with the greatest generality, then we are dealing with a movement of fluid through tubes, which, in a circular way, turn back into themselves, and with the course of this movement in a certain amount of time. This task is of a purely mechanical nature; nothing prevents the assumption that the heart pump, as a mechanical middle, is adequate to solve this task. The heart is a pump and possesses as such force enough to drive the mass of blood in a circulatory movement through the entire vascular system.[19]

However, further on we read: "Organic physics aspires to nothing more than to prove how the life principle utilizes physical means to achieve its ends."

Although this life principle is certainly only an abstraction, it is, nevertheless, considered to be of an order above the physical. In 1850, E. H. Weber expressed himself similarly: "The circulation of the blood in the living human being takes place through a system of tubes that run back on themselves, and that are supplied by two pumps."[20]

The fatal blow to the consideration of a certain inherent movement of the blood, of a propulsion force the cause of which was inadequately known, was struck by Johannes Müller:[21]

> Concerning the propulsive force unjustifiably attributed to the blood, an inherent force of the blood permitting it to move in circulation, a movement that is supposed to continue even when the force of the heart is no longer active . . . this hypothesis of Kielmeyer, Treviranus, Carus, Dellinger and Österreicher seemed most justified by the observation of Wolff and Pander that the blood of a chick embryo forms in the area vasculosa before the heart and that the blood in the peripheral area vasculosa streams toward the heart even before the blood pulsates.

Müller, however, could not establish the duration or persistence of the movement of the blood in severed parts and thus came to the conclusion:

> I deny, therefore, the curious force of propulsion and assume only the living interaction and attraction between substance and blood, which does not necessarily facilitate the circulation, but through which, under similar circumstances, a more enlivened part receives more blood than it otherwise might.

There are certainly also other voices, however. C. G. Carus says when he speaks about the circulation:

> In this matter we are confronting a primal phenomenon of animal and human life. Whoever does not open his eyes here in order to perceive and understand the extraordinarily curious events of the circulatory streaming of the embryonic blood will not understand it at all where it appears with all the infinite complications of the mature organism, not even with the help of various experiments and comparison to pumps. Just as it happens in the movements of the heavenly bodies in the cosmos and as the movement around axes and spiral movement is the

> original movement of the earth, so also do many earthly events still repeat manifold cosmic movements. We will never become aware of a definite organic polarity. The old comparisons of systole and diastole with a fire hose or pump certainly apply, but they do not encompass all of the processes. This mechanism alone is hardly sufficient to explain the living streaming of the blood in its circulatory vessels. Life certainly encompasses the mechanism and also the chemistry, electricity, etc., but the mechanism does not encompass life. The phenomenon of the continuously flowing blood in its curious path through day and night can never be explained only through the mechanism of the heart and arteries.[22]

Lorenz Oken wrote: "The heart beat is not the cause of the circulation; it is rather the reverse; the heart beat is the consequence of circulation."[23] And Goethe said: "The actual life is in the blood vessels, towards the outside. They are like a system of conduits and the heart is the point that determines the direction." Although later the mechanistic views of the heart gained increasing adherence and became commonly accepted, there were always those who questioned them or vigorously fought against them. Thus, Ottomar Rosenbach (1851–1907), an important clinician of his time, wrote:

> Under normal conditions the heart does not lift an amount corresponding to the quantity of blood; rather, it mediates only the transfer to completely formed and gradually enlarging capillary spaces, or it permits its content to be aspirated by using its force only for overcoming minimal frictional resistances. The essential part of the blood-moving force is not yielded by the heart but by the protoplasm of the organs—the skin and voluntary, including the respiratory, muscles.[24]

The data of Karl Hasebroek showed that there is movement in the circulation independent of the heart. According to him, the capillary flow is independent. The speed of its movement depends on the intensity of the life processes of the tissues, not on the size of the capillaries. In fact, the circulation persists for some time after the heart stops beating, and there is a similar independent flow in the veins. In any case, Hasebroek ascribed to the extra-cardio part of the vascular system a role as important as that of the heart.[25]

The well-known surgeon August Bier wrote in 1922:[26]

> It was repeatedly and triumphantly proclaimed that nothing in the living body was more wonderfully explained causal-mechanistically in all its details than the blood pressure. Harvey supposedly was the founder of the physics of life. I have shown, however, that vital influences on the movement of the blood also lie in the small vessels and are absolutely necessary, and that hemodynamics, in the crude form it was described to us, fails as soon as one places at the basis the natural conditions that are evident every day to us surgeons, instead of the crude, raw experiments on dead tubes and the large vessels of experimental animals.

In a paper published in 1928 entitled, "The Heart, A Secondary Organ," Martin Mendelsohn wrote concerning Harvey's theory of the circulation of the blood:

> Its dynamics could not be maintained, but one accepted it again and again as it was transmitted without paying attention to its impossibilities and incomprehensibilities. Those forces that bring about the coursing of the blood in the living organism are of an entirely different nature. That the heart alone is able to bring about such a mighty achievement is actually such an absurd thought that it is almost incomprehensible how it could remain valid for centuries. In the movement of the blood within the organism, the heart works primarily as a secondary, regulating and ordering organ.

For Mendelsohn the flow of the fluids is primary, the blood circulation is secondary. The primarily active force is the streaming brought about by "the living activity of the glands and the activity of the cells." Concerning the function of the heart, he comes to the conclusion:

> For a motor of considerable energy, the heart lacks virtually everything; not only is its force inadequate, but its entire structure is entirely unsuitable. It is most unsuitable as a machine to generate force. Thus, nothing is determined in the circulation by the heart, neither the force of movement nor the rhythm of the beats; the heart works in the circulation as a secondary organ. The heart is not a motor; the heart is a regulator.

Kurt Bergel and Ferdinand Ježek also speak along these lines.[27]

In 1936 Nishi advanced the thesis that the circulation does not depend entirely on the heart's activity but rather is much more an effect of the special property of the capillaries, which in accordance with the laws of physics bring about the movement of the blood by suction. He gives a detailed analysis of the problem of the circulation considered from the physical point of view.[28]

In the last few years Paul Vogler has decidedly expressed himself on the dominant views of the heart:[29]

> It is surprising how long physiology, despite all contradictory findings, has held on to this model with all its inadequacies, suggesting that it is a reality. Neither clinical observation as, for example, in the gradual progression of blood poisoning, nor the manifest physiological absurdities such as the 20,000 mkg achievement of the heart per day, make devoted scientists or an infinitely patient lay public doubtful. The dogma persisted for three centuries. Even our generation knows the combination of glass tube models that are used to clarify the circulation and its pumping station. It was accepted without thought that this small heart muscle is to drive a quantity of 6 to 8 litres of fluid with a specific weight of 1,060, a viscosity of 4.6 to 4.7, and a resulting strength of 20,000 mkg per day through a system of tubes of strongly fluctuating volumes.

He also speaks out in opposition to the concept of the circulation as a closed tube system—an assertion, in fact, which Harvey had never made (see above)! Modern tissue studies, histology and anatomy have shown that the circulation is open at the periphery, that there is a most active osmotic exchange, that a direct liquid and cell transport, and the intercellular substances of the connective tissue represent the structural and functional continuation of the capillary system. "Thus, as a final unit of the circulation, we no longer have the capillaries, but rather the tissue, the extravascular openings in the tissue. We know today that the heart is essentially a regulating organ."

Contemporary opinions and textbooks mention these presentations and contradictions either sparingly or not at all. The mechanistic view of the heart as a pump, the motor moving the blood, unfailingly dominates:

> The flow in the separate areas of the circulation is like the effective profusion pressure in an area divided by the resistance. . . . Two pumps are inserted in this path that maintain the flow: the left half of the heart between the lung and the body vascular system, and the right half between the body and the lung vascular system.[30]
>
> The blood . . . is pumped by the heart through the closed system of the blood vessels. The heart of warm-blooded beings consists, in contrast to the hearts of many lower animals, of two pumps connected in series.[31]
>
> The heart is a pulsative four-chambered pump composed of two atria and two ventricles. The ventricles supply the main force that propulses blood through the lungs and through the peripheral circulatory system.[32]

In the standard textbook of von Schütz,[33] in a reference to Mendelsohn and Havlicek, it is noted that "the heart is a pressure pump and is the central motor moving the blood."

As will be shown, it is not a question of denying the energetic achievement of the heart, but rather to recognize its position in the entire circulation in which this work has an entirely different meaning than that of moving the blood.

Rudolf Steiner, in a most decisive and comprehensive way, fought against the purely mechanistic conception of the heart and circulatory functions.[34] Among the multitude of comments Rudolf Steiner made on this theme are the following:

> Today, external theory makes the heart a pump, pumping the blood through the body. So one would have to see in the heart the organ that regulates the circulation. Actually, the reverse is true. The circulation is more original, and in its movements the heart gives a resounding of what goes on in the circulation. The blood drives the heart; not the heart the blood.[35]
>
> The activity of the heart is not a cause; rather, it is a consequence. The heart is essentially the organ that in its observable movement is an expression of the balancing of the equilibrium between above and below, the organ of perception that mediates between these two poles of the human organization.[36]
>
> The heart is not a pump. The heart is moved by the circulation of the blood; the circulation is not brought about by the heart-pump activity. The heart has as little to do with circula-

tory functions in man, as a thermometer has to do with external warmth and cold.[37]

These descriptions of the heart's function given by Rudolf Steiner can be characterized by two essential points:

1) The blood stream drives the heart, not the other way around.

2) The heart is not a pump; it is a sense organ and a "damming up" organ.

This view of the heart's function entirely contradicted everything that was presented by the physiologists of his time on the heart as the exclusive motor moving the blood by a pump mechanism.

On the basis of these seemingly irreconcilable, absolutely contrasting views the following questions can be raised:

1. What is the origin of the movement of the blood?
2. How does the heart function?
3. What task and significance does the heart have?

These questions are not asked today, let alone answered, since the heart has such obviously mechanical devices like the valves. A simply oppressive multitude of data shows the achievements of the heart, and the physiological function of the circulation seems to be no problem at all.

The Movement of the Blood

In order to settle the question of the movement of the blood, we must first study the various kinds of possible movement. A dead object can be moved only by external action. This process has been known since ancient times as *vis a tergo* (a force from behind). Its manner of action upon the object is determining, coercive. In the realm of the living, however, one is confronted by processes that go beyond that. The simple swelling of a seed is not "pushed from behind." Osmosis certainly plays a role, yet one must see that it is used by the ether body of the plant as a help and is not identical to it. The ether body of the plant must reach right into the physical. To do so it requires various instruments, mediators and given situations that are open to etheric activity as well as reaching into the physical. One of these processes is osmosis. Certainly this can also be studied "purely" physically. That, however, does not exclude the fact that such a process can be subjected to a super-ordinate lawfulness, in this case that of the ether body. In this process the salts definitely play a role. Often, then, one can clearly recognize how they are used by the members of man's being as an instrument, as for example the ether body uses potassium as a means of working in water.

Another way by which the etheric forces enter into relationship with physical substances is through the creation of surfaces. The etheric forces in their purest form appear in the plant. Thus, the plant's leaves create large surface areas, making it possible for the etheric forces to stream into the plant from the environment.[38]

The etheric forces of the environment are in a polar relationship with the forces emanating from the center of the earth that are connected with gravity. The etheric forces work from the environmental circumference in the sense of levity by removing the substance from the purely earthly laws. In the latter inertia and gravity, which are opposed by mobility and levity, apply.

The forces connected with the earth have been studied in great detail, which has led to mechanics, among other things. The other kind of forces, that of the circumference, namely levity, was neglected. This one-sidedness of research and methodology that goes back especially to Newton was indeed recognized: "He has explained to us—or that at least was the opinion at one time—what makes the apple fall. It did not occur to him, however, to explain an answer to the corresponding but infinitely more difficult question of how the apple first got up there" (Ruskin).[39]

How do the forces of the circumference and the center work together? This question comes significantly close to the question of how etheric forces work into substance. The significance of the surface has already been pointed to. This means, however, that through an increased working of the forces of the circumference, the earthly substance is freed from its subjection to gravity.

By enlarging a surface area it is possible to create targets for the peripheral forces and thereby to remove a substance from gravity. A simple example of this is dust. Tons of dust float in the air without seeming heaviness. The mass remains but the weight lessens the smaller the particles become, just as the weight decreases as the distance from the center of the earth increases. The particle is then no longer subjected exclusively to the forces of gravity but also to air flow, levity, electrical charges, etc. These can certainly be studied in detail physically. That these forces can work only in the realm of the smallest elements is decisive here. Certainly transitions depending on the size of the particles exist.

In the realm of fluids the same situation applies. Water in a vessel is subject to gravity. Yet, the same mass floats in the air in the form of small droplets as a cloud or fog and does not fall as long as a certain drop size is not exceeded. Then, however, the water can no longer be held in the air and descends as rain.

Cosmos	*Earth*
Plane	Point
Circumferential forces	Central forces
Lightness	Heaviness
Levity	Gravity
Mobility	Sluggishness [inertia]
Large surface	Small surface
Vortex	Drop
"Suction"	Pressure
Dispersion, atomization	Contraction into mass, condensation
Smallness of unit	Greatness
Qualitative action	"Quantifiability"
Action of Force	Action of Substance

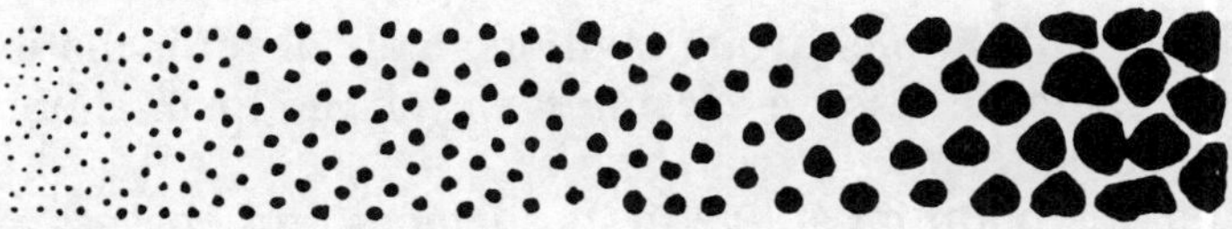

In principle, a similar phenomenon is present in the capillaries. In every capillary fluid rises against gravity, and moreso the smaller the capillary is. Certainly one is dealing here with physical forces of surface tension, adhesion, etc., of which accurate studies have been made. It is decisive that substances are more or less withdrawn from the activity of earthly forces in this way, and thus become accessible to the intervention of etheric forces. These utilize the capillary forces, increased surface area, etc., in order to intervene. These measurable forces are, however, not identical with the etheric forces but only prepare their way. They fit to one another as key to lock. There is the same relationship between them as between blossom and butterfly. They have a common origin yet one can only become active when the other is added.

"Suction" is the quality of etheric activity in contrast to that of the earthly forces, which are typically characterized by pressure. Suction is not meant here as an outer force, for this would be a *vis a tergo*. The suction that can be observed in the capillary region is the point of contact through which the etheric forces can become active. The same applies to a vortex in contrast to a self-contained drop.[40] The vortex is a picture of "flowing receptivity to stimuli"; like the drop, it is open to peripheral and central forces. Which force will predominate is dependent on size, surface area, milieu, etc.

The essential point is that living substance develops *between* the two polarities. Thus through the smaller units (capillaries, single cells) it is exposed more to the peripheral forces, while through the greater units (bones, accumulations of fluid) it is exposed more to the central forces and the corresponding effects.

Through a particular "smallness," then, the substance is in another realm of force activity—the etheric. This can become active only through conditions of smallness, that is, of a large surface area. In this cooperative working it is a question not of cancelling physical regulations but rather of the intervention of a higher principle through which a new order is made possible; for example, as in a crystal in which the form is not based on the substance.

Thus, the plant must live in its surfaces and possess a multitude of capillaries. On the other hand, it can here be realized that unicellular organisms, as well as cells, can never exceed a certain size. The cell's smallness is a precondition for its becoming a carrier and element of life. The large surface area made possible by the cell's smallness is indeed the very reason for its existence.

In the capillaries and cells, a living liquid flows. By virtue of the cell's smallness, this fluid or liquid is no longer subject to gravity or inertia. Rather, it is open to the working of the forces of the living environment, which are characterized by flowing and streaming, activity and movement. Thus, the cell plasma is in continuous movement as an expression of unfolding life. The "flow of juices is the primal phenomenon of life."[41]

Flowing movement is an eminently essential expression of life, of living fluidity. To "reduce" this to another—for example, mechanical—principle is methodologically as unjustifiable as the "explanation" of life through chemistry or physics, or of color through vibrations, etc.

One must see clearly, however, that this type of movement which is coupled to life is connected with the basic condition that the latter can establish a relationship with a suitable substance dispersed over sufficiently large surfaces. And this is the case in the capillaries. Only in them is the kind of movement possible which can be called *primary flowing.*[42] Primary flowing is thus bound to the capillaries or elements that do not exceed the size of approximately one cell. Certainly it is not possible to establish exactly determined boundaries, but these are smooth transitions, a gradual beginning and cessation, in arterioles and venules. The taking hold by the ether body reaches its maximum in the capillaries.

This streaming is primary and thus an expression of the inner mobility of a *living* fluid. It happens without an external driving force. In contrast to this, one can also bring about movement through pressure, for example, of a pump or also through the force of muscle. This would be secondary because it is caused by a push from behind (*vis a tergo*).

The primary flowing can be readily observed. In one-celled organisms like paramecia, for example, one can see lively streams that are often quite differentiated. Vacuoles fill and empty without the existence of specific contractile elements. The continuous movement of the blood can also be followed in the capillaries, for example, in the mesentery vessels of a frog or in the webs of its feet, and in the omenta of larger animals. The active penetration of cells through the capillary spaces also belongs to this movement. In earlier times the movement of living fluids was well known. It "was known that the internal juices of the human being have inner life, and thus that they move, that the heart is only a sense organ to perceive the movement of fluids in its manner."[43]

This primary flow is possible only in living fluids below a certain unit of size, as it is a direct expression of life. Above that level there is no path of entry for life, that is, for the ether body. Consequently, independent movement is not possible in large vessels. The observable and measurable capillary force makes it evident that in this realm the substance is, as it were, removed from the effects of certain earthly forces because of its absolute smallness and thus relatively great surface area, and is thereby opened to superordinate intervention: to the circumferential forces, or one could also say, to quality as opposed to quantity.

Expressed in a different way this means:

1. The phenomenon of primary flowing cannot be demonstrated with water, especially not in a dead vessel. The physical effects of capillarity are only the instrument, the starting point used by the ether body, the precondition necessary to make possible primary streaming. A method for making this expression of the formative forces visible is provided by the capillarity of filter paper, as this has been elaborated into the capillary dynamic blood test (*Steigbilder*). (See vol. I and related literature.)[44]

2. Primary streaming can never take place in collections of fluid in unformed spaces or vessels that exceed capillary size. This is connected with the laws of the etheric world that requires adequate circumstances in which to express itself.

To be sure, the shearing, gliding movements that occur in streaming fluids can imitate surfaces which provide opportunities for the engagement of formative forces (esp. in vortex formation). In the physical domain, this can be observed in the falling of a colored drop into water and the streak formation (drop formation method).

The limitations of size and surface are also connected with the nature of an organism, which maintains a specific, i.e. absolute, size made constant by these limitations. It must remain within these boundaries. Thus, in the organism of the elephant, governing principles work that apply only to its size. The same is true of a mouse. Therefore, an elephant the size of a mouse with a pulse of 25 to 46 beats a minute would be just as incapable of life as a normal sized elephant with the mouse's pulse of 1000 to 1320 beats per minute. Pulse and body weight stand in an inverse logarithmic relationship to one another. Similarly, the primary streaming is also bound to the *law of absolute size.*

The purest kind of primary flowing can be found in nature in the plants, in which the surface and capillaries predominate regardless of the size of the plant. This is true also of gigantic trees, whose capillary diameter remains constant.

In animals one can also find the principle of primary flowing since they, too, have ether bodies. But they also have muscles, a specialized organ for movement created by the astral body. In order for the astral body to reach into the physical by way of the ether body, it needs organs that are open to its intervention. Since this intervention is differentiated, there are particular organs for specific functions: the nervous system makes possible consciousness; the kidney transfers these impulses into anabolism, the thyroid gland makes possible the working of the astral body in the metabolic system, etc. Direct intervention of the astral body into the physical would be magic.

Correspondingly, a typical astral expression, movement, requires its own organ; this is the muscle. It is movement that has become an organ. The heart as a specific muscle has been created from movement for leading it further and enhancing it. Without these astral organs, which are certainly formed by the ether body, the functions mediated by them are not possible; that is, without nerves, there is no consciousness and without muscles no movement. In any other way these functions are just as impossible as to experience visual impressions without the eye.

The activity of the muscle is contraction, a shortening. It works thereby upon another object, such as bone or the intestinal contents, etc., which it moves from the outside. The movement impulse itself is external only to the moved object, but both are within the animal. The animal receives the impulse to move not from the outside but from within, from its astral body, which has created the muscles as an instrument of movement in order to work outwardly and inwardly, and to move such substances as the intestinal contents that are no longer subject to the primary flowing.

All these movements can be found, naturally, in man since he also possesses these members of being. His astral body, however, is ruled by an ego, which is why human movement is completely different from that of the animal. Man uses his muscles through his astral body, but he incorporates this possibility into a spiritually integrated form of movement. Summarizing, one can represent the movement impulses in the four realms of nature as follows:

Etheric forces require capillarity, cells, lightness—i.e. smallness, and the large surface area accompanying it—in order to bring about movement; primary flowing is an expression of the ether body.

Astral forces require muscles in order to overcome gravity. The astral body is above the ether body and takes hold of the arterial system; this becomes evident in the blood pressure. It lives in polarities that express themselves in narrowing, contraction, and expansion of vessels, hypotony or hypertony, etc.

The ego of man takes advantage of the totality of these processes, and in health they can be mastered.

The laws of one realm are encompassed and taken hold of by the others and its forces are used for other, higher goals and purposes. At the same time this is a problem of man's step-by-step emancipation from physical conditions, in which cause and effect and thus compulsion hold sway, to their utilization in freedom. Thus it is an example of the "physiology of freedom" (Friedrich Husemann).

	Force	*Type of Movement*
In the realm of man	Ego forces	Spiritually permeated form of movement
In the realm of the animal world	Astral	Muscle
In the realm of the living world	Etheric	Primary flowing
In the realm of the dead world	Physical	A force from behind (vis a tergo)

It was pointed out that in the realm of plants there can only be vessels of the order of capillaries. Only in these is primary flowing possible.

In man and animal there are, however, larger vessels that far exceed this realm. From what has been said so far it becomes evident that primary flowing of the blood cannot take place in the large vessels. Here the laws of gravity and inertia apply that require other measures which we will discuss later. Since in the blood we are dealing with a circulation however, it must be recognized that the driving force of the blood in the capillary region arises from the described innate force and in no way externally. This flow of blood in the capillaries is primary in the circulation of the adult as well as in the embryo and phylogenetically.

It is a well-known phenomenon that no vessel is formed without blood. What is original is the blood. From it the vessels are formed. It moves and slowly flows before the heart is formed as parts of the vasculature—a fact that has been known for a long time but has not been considered because there is no true understanding of it.

These relationships were also known to Harvey: "If, however, you observe the formation of the chick in the egg, there is, as I have said, at first only a little bubble—that is to say, an auricle, or a pulsating drop of blood. Only after growth has begun is the heart developed."

An experiment performed by Ph. Stöhr, Jr. is quite conclusive.[45] He turned the heart of young tadpoles by 180°. If the movement of the blood were initiated by the heart, it would now have to be reversed. The opposite is the case, however. "The turned heart structure is completely changed in its development by its environment, so that the arterial portion is transformed to the venous portion. An almost typically formed heart develops that pulsates in the normal direction as if it had not been rotated at all." Once the heart structure is determined in later stages, the experiment is no longer successful. "Accordingly, the heart turned by 180° would drive the blood in opposite directions. It does not appear possible, however, to turn the circulation completely around; consequently, the animal soon succumbs to edema."

Primary flowing without a heart can also be observed in the animal realm. It is well-known that mollusks—snails, for example—have an open circulation. How can the blood find its way back to the open venous system if it is supposed to be driven by the heart? Actually, this is an illusory problem because primary streaming that is subject to the laws of the ether body takes place in the periphery. There the blood is finely dispersed, a precondition for primary flow, while in the "larger" vessels a heart is necessary. According to the above-mentioned law of absolute size, an open circulation is not possible in larger animals.

Finally, there are also animals without a heart, like amphioxus. "The lancet fish actually lacks a heart, the blood vessels are all uniform and are not separated into arteries and veins. Their structures are most easily compared to the finest vessels of the higher vertebrates, the capillaries."[46]

This also says why this animal, which has only capillaries, does not need a heart. Only larger vessels would require a heart. A way of life is thus physiologically possible with capillaries alone but again only up to a certain size and development. Such an organism can survive only as a fish when the blood is carried by the water. On land it could not be active at all. It is almost at a plant-like stage and does not provide a basis for a differentiated astral body. Therefore, such a system must, to evolve further, add other systems—the larger vessels and heart. In contrast to the plant, to the extent the embryo grows, to that extent the vessels enlarge. As the vessels exceed a certain diameter, a new complex of problems develops because primary flowing is no longer possible. As the vessels increase in size, the blood is no longer subject to the forces of the circumference. This transition happens gradually. In the sense of the descriptions above, the blood certainly remains a living fluid. As such, however, it leaves the realm of the forces of the periphery and moves into that of the central forces and the realm of earthly laws. Thus, there is a transition or an alternating state that is described in Fig. 15.

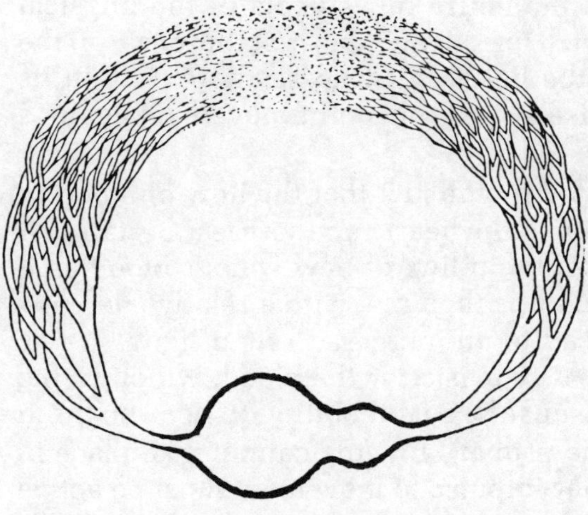

Fig. 15: Diagram of the Polarity in Blood Circulation

Periphery and center, circulation and heart, are a functional unity that mirrors a large world polarity. "What the earth has from the sun is mirrored again in what the blood must do with the heart."[47]

The larger the vessel, the more the living blood is subjected to the forces of gravity and earthly forces. These interactions are naturally greatest where the vascular diameter is largest, that is, in the heart. Approximately when it reaches the heart, the blood would have lost all the movement it had received from the capillaries. Because of the influx of the blood, it would certainly not come to a total standstill. Yet, it would flow slowly until it reached the capillaries again. In a favorable case, it could maintain biological life but not that of the soul. Human functions, especially, would be impossible. The stream of blood at least potentially coming to rest in the region of the heart is a constitutive factor of the heart. It lies primarily at the basis of every heart action. It is also valid, however, in relation to the initiation of heart formation. "At the point where the first initiated movement again comes to rest originated and developed the organ in the body that later, when it ceases its movement, also brings the entire movements of the physical body to rest—the heart. Here, from the first impulse of the movement, originates the heart, but it arises here only in its first primordium because also at this point movement again is brought to rest."[47]

This is not contradicted by the fact that the flow of blood in the vena cava on the way to the heart can increase. Certainly it becomes thicker through the influx of new venous blood as it approaches the heart. As it is then met with a relative narrowing, it would have to lead to an increased rate of flow.

In any case, the necessity exists for the blood, which in the large vessels gradually must lose its mobility, to be brought to the periphery. Since the primary flowing cannot take place in the large vessels, another impulse to movement must be active here. The large vessels are typical for man and animal. Their formative impulse stems from the astral body, which is why they do not occur in the plant realm. The large vessels are formed to give the astral body a specific focus for activity. The necessary impulse for the movement of the blood as it comes to rest can therefore come only from the astral body. Its organ of movement is the muscle. So, in this way, it works externally on the blood by way of the vascular system. It thus gives it a new impulse, a new movement. The necessary organ, the specific muscle that accomplishes this, is the heart. Its formation is thus necessary only because there are large vessels that man and animal need in order to incarnate the astral body. The heart has the physiological task of lifting up the blood, which is subject to gravity, so that it can again establish a relationship to the laws of the etheric prevailing in the capillarity. This can be brought about by no other means than through muscular force.

As for the blood supplying the tissues with oxygen, the problem could certainly be solved with a purely capillary system. It is actually realized in the animal realm. Then, however, there would be no point of contact for an astral body as possessed by higher animals and man, and also no possibility for higher consciousness. In other words, the existence of the heart is less a physiological and much more a soul-spiritual necessity, and it is created in such a way that the soul-spiritual can develop.

The origin of large vessels is connected with the separation of the arterial from the venous blood. This must be seen as a genuine polarity that goes back to a common source: the primary flowing in the earliest embryonic period. Though the vessels later do develop, during the entire embryonic period it is a mixed blood that flows in them, corresponding to the primordial state. The physically disposed polarity does not take effect until the separation into arterial and venous blood occurs, i.e. not until the first breath, at the moment when the soul-spiritual nature unites intimately with the body. (see chap. "Lung") The precondition for this is oxydative processes, i.e. an arterial system. Opposed to this, the venous system develops the vegetative side (V. Portae, liver). This polarity as well is embraced in the heart, not only in the sense of right = venous and left = arterial, but also in diastole – systole. From an organic point of view, in the heart there is a regulating and uniting of the etheric/vegetative process of the liver with the astral/soul process of the kidney.

	arterial	O_2	ensouled	nerve-sense system	systole
	/				
primary flowing					
	\				
	venous	CO_2	vegetative	metabolic system	diastole

The possibility for the development of blood pressure arises through the presence of the larger vessels. This is a direct expression of the working of the astral body. "Here it (the astral body) is in its very element: blood pressure. Here it engages itself very deeply."[48]

Blood pressure develops from the cooperation of heart and arterial vessels, whose tonus is just as essential as the action of the heart. In order to achieve the necessary blood pressure, the astral body utilizes the muscles, which are found in the wall of the arteries and, in their extreme development, in the heart. This suggests that the primary physiological task of the heart lies in the production of blood pressure, not in pump output.

In physiology one distinguishes between the work of pressure and the work of flow of the heart. The first is necesary in order to achieve blood pressure, that is to say, to overcome the already existing arterial pressure and to maintain it. The work of flow supposedly gives the driving impulse to the blood. The work of pressure is approximately a hundredfold greater than that of the flow, which is in reality actually zero since, as was shown above, the blood comes streaming to the heart but is not moved through it. Nevertheless, because of the pressure and the pressure alteration resulting from it, a movement comes about. This is actually an enhancement or acceleration of an *already existing* movement, hence is not of original, causative nature. The function of the heart, technologically expressed, could best be designated as that of an amplifier. The primary flow of the blood from the periphery is thus overriden in the heart and arterial system through the intervention of the astral body. It thereby undergoes both a qualitative change, in the form of pressure, as well as a quantitative change in the form of a ca. 20- to 30-fold acceleration. The arterial system also seems to take part in this: Though known since 1926 (Frank), it is a scarcely heeded fact that the systolic pulsatory pressure (not the *mean pressure*) increases towards the periphery up to the arterioles, along with a 140% increase in peripheral amplitude. In middle-sized peripheral arteries, the pulsatory pressure increase is accompanied by a definite decrease in diameter (!). On the basis of corresponding tests, Wehn postulated an accelerating activity of the arterioles.[49]

That the heart is not the point of initiation of the movement of the blood but rather the result of it can also be seen in the profusion of well-known physiological findings. If the venous inflow to the heart is increased, then as a consequence stroke volume is increased. If, however, the resistance in the arterial system is enhanced, then the earlier stroke volume is maintained under increased pressure. Both studies state, however, that the action of the heart is determined by the periphery: it reacts to the latter but does not determine it. Therefore, it is also possible in an animal that has been dead for days (rabbits, 112 hours, human corpses until 20 hours after death) to bring the heart to beat again by supplying the venous bloodstream.[50] In other words, the adequate stimulus for the heart's action is the venous supply, for which the heart has organs of perception.

It has recently been verified that the heart valves are richly innervated. Williams showed that "the valves function as receptors; they register how strongly the blood flows and relay this information to the brain."[51]

Older experiments taught that the sinus venosus—the right atrium—in lower animals plays an essential role here. If in frog's hearts the caval venous sinus is tied off from the atrium (first Stannius's ligature), then the separated heart does not move in diastole. Certainly the Keith-Flack sinus node is the primary center of stimulus formation, yet as a sense organ of the heart it is directed to the perception of the peripheral flowing blood. The autonomy of the heart says nothing about priority. The heart as an organ is clearly a self-contained organism. Yet it does not rule the blood, the periphery and the circulation, but rather is integrated into them.

The classic ideas of Starling-Straub see an increase in stroke volume caused exclusively by the increased venous pressure. There certainly is no doubt today that this is only "one of a number of equally important factors"[52] to which the arterial blood pressure, the heart frequency, the volume of the systolic rest, and the influence of the cardiac nerves and hormones must be added. The distensibility of the chamber and the contractility of the myocardium are also included as factors.[53]

These findings show that the heart is not a purely pressure passive organ but is in itself an organism despite its insertion into the circulation. "In this auto-regulative potential the heart, to a large extent, is comparable to the blood vessels and other abdominal organs. The auto-regulation is thus the basis of hetero-regulation. The heart is thus no longer merely the "plaything" of the central venous and arterial pressures, which it would have to maintain passively. Thus, it is the tonically activated auto-regulation of the heart that makes it into a feedback-free control element."[54]

The variable contractile diastolic heart muscle tonus is of essential significance for the heart action. The stroke volume is dependent upon the tone of the heart chamber. An optimal relationship of diastolic tone and systolic contractility is significant. These are in inverse relationship to one another, which is an expression of the polar processes in the heart that first make the rhythmic activity possible.

The sinus node thus stands as a mediator between the flow of blood and the heart function. "It is the point with the greatest rhythmic potency and can be designated as the coordinator of the entire heart. One is so captivated by the idea of the automatic nature of the heart brought about by the so-called pacemaker, the sinus node, that one forgets to take those conditions seriously that must first be fulfilled so that this sinus node can unfold its activity."[55] "One cannot justifiably call the sinus node 'the pacemaker,' but rather 'the perceiver.' "[56]

From these findings it is evident that the heart may well be a unified organism, but as such it has a highly sensitive perceptive capacity. In this sense, the heart is actually a sense organ. That it has still further functions beyond physiological perceptions will be described later.

The perception is handed over to the active, forceful side of the heart. "In that sense one could thus describe the heart as a three-membered being, with a perceiving and a forceful aspect. The rhythmic aspect manifests in the meeting of the polarities."[57]

Furthermore, almost every tissue is capable of perceiving the conditions of the blood. In this relationship we are reminded of the "blood sensation" of organs and extremities, as August Bier called it. In 1897 he published the results of experiments of which the following can be said: He amputated the leg of an anesthetized pig, except for the blood vessels, which were left intact. Upon occluding the artery, there occurred a lack of blood. After loosening the occlusion a reaction hyperemia occurred that can also be observed in normal organisms. Since the limb in this experiment was completely separated except for the vessels, the non-participation of the nervous system was proved. The stimulus for the increased blood supply thus emanates from the living tissue and not from the heart.

This principle is known in physical therapy as Bier's congestion. If one ties off a person's limb with an elastic bandage, an artificial ischemia is produced. When the bandage is loosened, a stronger permeation with blood occurs than before—an example of a meaningfully active response to a stimulus by the organism; this lies at the basis of homeopathy as a therapeutic principle.

With the knowledge and recognition of the primary flow in the capillary regions, the main difficulty for the customary views of the circulation, the so-called capillary resistance, also disappears. According to the law of Poiseuille, the volume of fluid that flows through a straight pipe is directly proportional to the pressure, the time and the fourth power of the radius. The diameter of the pipe thus influences the resistance to an especially high degree. A fifty percent decrease of the radius would increase the resistance sixteenfold and vice-versa, and it would follow that the primary resistance resides in the capillaries. There is no doubt that this law is absolutely valid for the sharply circumscribed, purely physical conditions under which it was developed. These are, however, conditions in the inorganic realm—a model of glass pipes, constant pressure, etc. The application of this law to physiology comes from the thinking of that time that attempted to explain life mechanically. More recently it was shown "that the elasticity of the path is a cardinal factor that excludes the direct application of Poiseuille's law to the circulation of the blood."[58]

It is a fact that these studies depend on the constancy of the driving pressure, which especially in the capillary realm does not apply. In the capillaries the pressure, in the sense of a push from behind (*vis a tergo*), is equal to zero. Therefore, the "expanded law of fluid dynamics of the circulation" (Wezler) that includes elasticity is valid also only in a system of larger vessels. The decisive issue, which prevents the attainment of concepts based in reality, is the idea of the effect of pressure as a driving force emanating from the heart and pushing from behind.

All calculations of the vascular resistance of the capillaries stem from the tacit presupposition that the conditions must be the same as in an inorganic system. In a living organism, however, such a capillary resistance does not exist, since there and only there in the small vessels the described laws of the etheric world, which cancel out gravity and inertia, are valid.

Nevertheless, one could conclude that an intact circulation can enhance the primary flow—and secondarily the venous pressure—with systolic blood pressure, but only in the sense of an enhanced stimulus, similar to how the filling of the heart is the necessary factor for a greater rate of flow.

Since periphery and center form a unity, and the movement of the blood stemming from the periphery determines the center, the heart, it can be assumed that the periphery is also attuned to the behavior of the heart, the blood pressure, etc., in the sense of a unity of the processes in the circulatory system. This does not alter the fact that the point of origin of the blood's movement is the periphery, not the heart.

The return of the venous blood can no more be explained by the suction power of the right ventricle than by the venous valves. For this reason a "peripheral heart" was postulated already quite some time ago. In accordance with the way of thinking prevalent today, this is sought in some form of "pump mechanism," for example an arteriovenous coupling (Schade, Liebau)—i.e. a mechanical pressure transfer of the arterial pulse wave onto the venous wall. It is not significant if or to what extent this also plays a part. What is critical is that the primary flowing, as the cause of blood movement, does not occur mechanically and therefore cannot be grasped through mechanistic conceptions. Its action is felt well into the venous regions, decreasing as the diameter increases. The fact that from this point on—i.e. starting in the venous region—mechanical forces must also take effect, ought to be understandable from what has been set forth. Of these forces, muscular contraction ("muscular pump") is the primary one which in conjunction with the venous valves effects an additional promotion of flow and with it a lowering of the venous pressure. This mechanical promotion must necessarily complement the primary flow coming from the periphery. Even when it is absent—at absolute rest in a sitting posture, for example—the reflux takes place, though with more difficulty; and this is a result of the primary streaming, which now acts as a *vis a tergo* itself and, in a healthy person, can even to an extent overcome the weight of the blood, at least to heart level. The weight is true of lymph flow.

From these points of view several physiological peculiarities of the heart also become comprehensible. In contrast to skeletal muscles, the type of muscle present in the heart can be assigned a place between the voluntary skeletal musculature and the involuntary smooth musculature. Only the former is fatigable, while the latter is indefatigable [!]. Here again the heart occupies a middle position, though one of a special nature, being both fatigable as well as indefatigable: It possesses an absolute refractory stage in relation to stimuli. This explains the impossibility of tetanizing the heart muscle. This absolute rest is polar to the all-or-nothing-law. These two extremes of the function can only be understood from the nature of rhythm and its inclusion in the great polarity of nerve-sensory and metabolic systems. Their dynamics are of an opposing nature. Systole corresponds to the contracting dynamic of the nerve-sensory system, diastole to the expanding tendency of the metabolic system. The heart's function alternates between them. It is decisive that the heart is completely and entirely opened first to one and then to the other impulse. Thus, maximal work work alternates with absolute rest. At the same time this signifies a maximal amplitude of frequency. The refractory stage (diastole) corresponds to extremely deep sleep, the always maximal contraction to intense work.

Here is the secret of health and the seeming indefatigability of the heart. It is not ceaselessly active without rest, but rather, after every activity an absolute rest is necessarily inserted at the optimal moment. It is only for that reason that the subsequent performance is possible. Not indefatigability, but rather guided rest alternating with intensive activity, that is, a strict rhythm makes lifelong function possible and thus shows the archetypal picture of health.

The further significance of the all-or-nothing-law will be discussed later on.

Summary

The blood is moving, not resting, when circulation begins. The heart is not a motor moving the blood, nor is it in principle a pump.

The movement of the blood in the circulation emanates from the periphery, not from the heart. The heart is created from movement for movement, in the way Goethe explained of the eye that "it is formed by light for light." The heart's activity is inserted into the flow, effecting a rhythmization of it, that is, the alternation of systole and diastole, of perceiving activity and force exertion. Thereby an enhancement of the blood's movement comes about in the form of acceleration and blood pressure.

Only through the uniqueness of these relationships can the heart mediate higher spiritual functions, because these reach from the spiritual down into the physical-mechanical element.

The heart is the primal image of all balancing processes. It stands as an active mediator between the most varied polar functions of the human organism. It is the central organ of the rhythmic system on whose balancing, mediating dynamics the primary image of healing is based.

In the preceding considerations the conditions of the circulation as an independent flow that works upon the heart activity were developed from insight into the laws of the etheric world and its interworking with the physical. The results of experiments demonstrates this. In the last two decades, particularly the Polish cardiac surgeon Leon Manteuffel-Szoege investigated these problems experimentally.[59] He writes:

> The starting point of our experiments were the studies done by Thompson in 1948.[60] He injected heparin into dogs, anesthetized them intratracheally with curare, and put them into

> mechanical respirators. During this time the oxygen saturation of the arterial and venous blood in the animals was measured. After the observations, the respirator was turned off until asphyxia developed. A half-hour after cessation of the heart beat, artificial respiration was again initiated. After asphyxia, the oxygen content of the arterial blood had dropped to the level of the venous blood. After re-initiating artificial respiration, it rose again within ten minutes to 100 percent. In this experiment radioactive sodium and fluorecein were injected intravenously. It was determined that the respiratory activity is adequate, without the accompanying activity of the heart, to support the persistence of the blood circulation—not necessarily enough to maintain life but still worthy of note. According to Thompson, the rhythmic inflation and deflation of the lungs works as an effective pump.

In order to exclude the mechanical influence, Manteuffel-Szoege modified the experimental conditions. After asphyxia and ten to fifteen minutes after cessation of the heart beat, oxygen was insufflated through the endotracheal tube without rhythmic respiratory movements in the lungs. After continual insufflation of oxygen into the lungs, the oxygen content of the blood rose from 20 to 30 percent, then to 85 percent and after artificial respiration, to 100 percent. In contrast to the normal circulation of the blood during rest of 15 seconds, this circulatory period was 20 to 30 times longer.

These experiments show that in the dog, after cessation of the heart's activity through acute anoxia, the blood circulation still persists for some time (under conditions of adequate oxygen saturation). It was observed that the circulation persisted even two hours after cessation of the heart beat if an adequate supply of oxygen was provided to the blood. Manteuffel-Szoege concluded that the blood has its own movement energy, which proves to be a fundamental factor of hemodynamics, and "that the blood has a specific spontaneous capacity for movement within the circulatory system that does not depend on the heart's activity."

From experiments on chick embryos the following developed: "After removal of the heart, one can observe the blood flowing from the coronary sinus, while the coronary arteries remain wide and empty and do not bleed. The same picture of bleeding veins and wide open, empty arteries can also be noted after removing the kidneys, spleen, or liver." If arterial pressure is the point at which the movement of the blood begins, then the artery would bleed, but not the vein. In fact, the reverse is the case.

> After removal of organs such as the kidneys, heart, spleen, etc., the blood continues to flow drop by drop from the veins. The arteries do not bleed. The points of incision are empty, and deep within one can observe a concave disc that gradually withdraws and becomes invisible.
>
> In operations on humans, as well as in experiments on dogs, we have observed that after eliminating the heart, the blood continues to flow through the veins. The following facts have verified this. It is evident in man and animals that the vena cavae expand when they are occluded at the point of transition into the right atrium; after the aorta and the pulmonary artery are occluded, the animal heart expands so much in two minutes that its circumference is doubled.
>
> Furthermore, in our cases there was increased venous pressure. Frequently, it rose up to 20 mm hg while the arterial pressure dropped to zero, in many cases even below zero. Thus, a reversal of the pressure drop took place in that the venous pressure rose over the arterial.

Thus, when the heart is excluded, a circulation persists although in a significantly lesser degree. This even leads to pressure in the venous system. The persistence of a circulation even without heart function is actually known. Houssay wrote in 1955:

> If the pulsation of the heart weakens or ceases, the venous circulation does not immediately cease, nor does it cease if the arterial pressure drops to zero. This is observed when the heart is stopped by stimulating the vagus nerve and also by atrial fibrillation. In both cases the heart increasingly expands since its contents continually increase, and the veins become remarkably congested in its vicinity.[61]

Here, too, the phenomenon should be familiar today. No attention is paid to it, however, since an understanding of it through customary thinking, seeing the point of impulse as coming from the heart, is lacking.

The question as to how the movement of the blood develops is wrong in principle. Rather, it should be stated as follows: How does rest come about in the blood stream? Ontogenetically and phylogenetically, it is flowing, not resting fluid that stands at the beginning. However, the customary mode of thought is programmed otherwise today.

The Function of the Heart

It has been described above how the circulation can function without the heart and how it is not a motor moving the blood but that through its activity pressure develops in the arterial system causing an increase in the circulatory flow. It is expressly emphasized, however, that a circulation without a heart is tied to certain conditions, and in humans and higher animals it would not be adequate even for minimal life. The fact that the heart is essential for life is not based on its bringing the circulation into movement, but rather on its bringing the peripheral circulation into such a form that a higher life (astral body and ego) becomes possible. Through the heart's action there is thus a transforming, an enhancing, of something that already exists.

It is natural to look for a mechanical comparison to the heart's activity. In this connection Rudolf Steiner pointed to the hydraulic ram, which he designated as "a hopeful beginning, at least to look at this mechanical basis of the heart's activity—nothing more to be sure."[62] He mentioned K. Schmid[63] who in 1892 made a beginning with this comparison. Later, the idea that the activity of the heart corresponds to that of a hydraulic ram was also presented by Havlicek,[64] F. and G. Husemann,[65] and Manteuffel-Szoege.[59] Other authors also discussed the heart's function and the movement of the blood.[66]

Rudolf Steiner commented on the treatise by Schmid that the latter noted in his medical practice that "one does not actually have a heart that works as a pump but rather one that is active as a damming up apparatus. Schmid thinks the whole process of the movement and impulse of the heart is like the activity of a hydraulic ram, which is brought into movement by flowing fluid. Therein lies the inherent truth in the discussions of Dr. Schmid."[62]

The hydraulic ram is a mechanical construction that can be inserted into a continuous flow of fluid. The stream drives the ram and through its speed determines the ram's action. The ram cannot function without the driving stream. Here lies its decisive difference from a pump, whose activity, as is well-known, is completely independent of the supply of water. Through the hydraulic ram an evenly flowing fluid is rhythmically interrupted; at the expense of the energy of movement of a larger quantity of freely flowing water, a small quantity of water is transported.

The ram corresponds to the heart's function in that both are inserted into a flowing stream; they are brought into directed activity by the flow. Neither heart nor ram are motors of movement; they are rather merely inserted into it. The flowing movement itself is primary. Furthermore, through the activity of the heart and ram, a continuous flow is rhythmically interrupted.

Certainly such a mechanical model is only conditionally applicable to an organic process. In contrast to the hydraulic ram, in the heart the same quantity of blood exists before and after its activity since it is a closed system. In the ram, however, the higher pressure is produced at the expense of the water that leaves the system. In the ram the flow and pressure rise to exceptionally high values until a valve is closed; that makes its function possible. In the circulation of the blood, however, the pressure and energy of movement continuously decline as it approaches the heart. As was shown above, this is an essential necessity. From pressure measurements by Manteuffel-Szoege, the venous pressure can rise to 20 mm hg; more frequently it is lower. At times, as is well-known, there can even be a negative pressure in the veins. The end diastolic ventricular pressure is approximately 2 to 4 mm hg on the left and 1 to 2 mm hg on the right, while in cases of pulmonary and aortic stenosis, the pressure was noted to be greater than 20 mm hg in the corresponding chambers.

The pressure differences before the heart, as with the ram, vary extremely. The ram transforms movement energy directly into pressure energy. However, the movement energy of the blood arriving at the heart is very weak as was shown by Manteuffel-Szoege and, according to the considerations above, must even stop. It is therefore meaningless to talk of a transformation of the venous movement energy into arterial pressure. Rather, a new, radically different impulse is required to take hold of the blood. This is an astral impulse, which with an organ specifically created for it, the muscle, grants the flowing blood a new impulse.

The weak energy of movement of the flowing blood at the heart can just as little transform itself into pressure as astral forces can develop "out of etheric forces." The flow of the blood is a result of the ether body; to it something entirely different—the blood pressure as an expression of the astral body—must be added. This is not a phenomenon of transformation but rather of superimposition with all necessary criteria of astral activity. Finally, the etheric forces are not withdrawn from the blood through such a transformation, as happens in the thinking process.

What function then does the stream of blood, although weak, have? As was described, it encounters the heart as a sense organ, which specifically perceives this streaming and reacts to it. For this purpose extremely small energies are adequate, the same as generally in the region of the senses. Sense impressions that are insignificant in terms of energy, a tone or light signal, can prompt a human being to an activity that, in the bodily realm, is dependent on muscle function. Then the signal is a stimulus but not the source of energy. The movement energy of the resulting activity originates from the muscle that was specifically created for that purpose. In the same way the blood stream arriving at the heart occasions the heart's activity, but it does not provide the energy for blood pressure. The guiding, impulse giving function of the moved blood has no connection with the aspect of the energetic pressure of the circulation. The former is primary and predominates, the latter has only implementing character, as is valid for every muscle. Certainly a person is able to stand erect with the help of the muscles in his legs, but the impulse does not arise from the muscles. It is rather an expression of the ego force that uses the musculature.

The "Mechanical Basis of the Heart's Activity"

The eye is built in such a way that optical processes make vision possible. The heart is also an organ that in spite of or because of the highest spiritual activities connected with it requires a corresponding physical correlate. It was already described above how especially at the point of the greatest vascular diameter, where the heart is situated, earthly laws rule in a most remarkable way. How does the heart deal with these forces? It cannot be denied that the structure of the heart resembles a pump: The two valves on each side, contraction in the way of a piston, etc. This analogy is so handy that it has a suggestive effect and no further questions arise. Therefore, one overlooks the fact that this idea that stems from the structure fails immediately when considered in relation to function.

As is well-known, a pump works the better the more it operates "circularly" so that the lift and suction phases are as much as possible of equal length, begin gradually and move smoothly over into one another. The opposite is the case in the function of the heart, however. In systole, corresponding to the push, there is always a maximum contraction. The all-or-nothing-law states that the heart muscle, in contrast to skeletal muscle, does not contract gradually but always completely and maximally. That brings about the heart beat rather than a gradual pressing out of the blood. This beating is so typical that it has been used as a designation for the heart's activity ever since ancient times in almost all languages. If one were to drive a pump according to this principle and perform a maximal beat each time, then this would lead to extreme wear and tear on the material of the pump and it would be a highly wasteful use of work. It is significant that this remarkable difference between the function of the pump and that of the heart is not seen and thus not discussed. Apart from that, the pump's capacity is autonomous, which means that it is completely independent of what is offered to it. As is well-known, this does not apply to the heart, because its activity is directed by the venous inflow.

This most obvious discrepancy between the functions of the pump and the heart certainly was noticed by various researchers, and Rudolf Steiner, too, repeatedly and expressly pointed out that the heart is not a pump. Yet, it remained for Liebau[67] to trace this aspect of the function of the heart into the mechanical process and to discover a new and special principle (1954).

Many physicians, including Mendelsohn and Manteuffel, observed that there are persons with cardiac illnesses who continue to live despite almost complete loss of both valves on one side. If the heart were a pump in which the work output is what matters, then life would be impossible with these defects, because without valves there would be no work put out.

Liebau constructed a model made of tubes that had a larger incoming (venous) vessel and an outflowing, somewhat narrower (arterial) vessel.[68] When this model was compressed, the fluid merely moved back and forth. When, however, the contractions occurred as beats over a brief period of time, then a clearly directed flow passed from the larger into the narrower vessel. Here, the quality of contraction is decisive, not the quantity. It is functional only with a brief contraction in the beat. This device marks the discovery of something that was hitherto unknown in hydrodynamics, that is, the "valveless outflow" principle, as Liebau originally called it,[69] according to which the valves are not supposed to be necessary. The direction of the flow is determined by vortices that work like a hydrodynamic vent.

There are valves, however. What tasks do they have if they are essentially "unnecessary"? Without doubt, the vortex movements do originate through the beating of the heart and the pressure of the encounter of the beating heart with the blood. If the valves are placed exactly where the flow of blood and the back stroke of the heart contraction encounter each other, then the mechanical need for them would indeed be minimal. The valves would then only have to withstand a relatively low pressure, and it would be their primary task to direct the stream of blood and support the existing vortex formations. This would be optimal for the work of the heart. Thus, the valves would present the same effects in hydrodynamics as the spicules in the bones. These are always distributed and placed along lines of force so that optimal support is achieved with the use of minimal material. Correspondingly, the valves of the heart can be placed exactly where in accordance with fluid dynamics their stress is least; they guide and optimize the vortex formation. The organism is formed based on function; not function on the basis of what previously exists. Novalis coined the maxim: "Our body is a formed stream." For example, the placement of the fibers of the heart muscle and the septum show a picture that corresponds to congealed streams.[70]

Liebau's model undergoes a modification with the notion of the "suction thrust siphon" (Hildebrandt), which takes into account the adsuction movement of the plane of the valvular rings of the heart. The latter are lowered with a sudden motion during ventricular systole. This produces an acceleration of venous blood return, which leads to an elevation of pressure in the ventricle.[71] According to this view, "the kinetic energy needed for the reaction effect is exerted by the systolic adsuction movement of the valvular ring plane itself. The heart, however, amplifies the pressure elevation in the ventricle through a responsive reflex ventricular systole, and so draws the valvular ring plane down over the congested fluid segment. Then, upon the diastolic raising of the valvular ring plane, it shifts this fluid segment in an arterial direction in favor of the renewed forceful filling of the ventricle."

The question remains as to why the above-mentioned principle, which was completely unknown before 1954 and which is based on the brief contraction in the nature of the beat, is realized in the heart. If what mattered was only the work of outflow or elevation of the blood pressure, etc., then this could also be achieved with the principle of a pump. In every case an exceptionally uneconomic principle is noticeable. During every contraction the blood stream is stopped and moved anew. An enhancement of movement or pressure would certainly be technically possible without stopping the blood stream. A peristaltic wave would prevent the uneconomical and brief cessatoin of this stream of blood. This principle is realized in the animal, for example, in the fishes. In the pump and also in the hydraulic ram, however, the inevitable cessation of movement takes place, which only the circular pump and the turbine circumvent.

Rudolf Steiner expressly pointed to the heart as a damming up apparatus. Evidently, a damming function is necessary for the heart. It must be emphasized that this damming up is strongest in the Liebau principle. The beat to which the blood is subjected brings about a far stronger reaction effect than a pump or even a ram. In the Liebau principle the damming up is brought about by the mechanical valve; in the heart it comes about through the beat of the muscle upon the flowing blood, which is thereby slowed down on one side and speeded up on the other. What purpose does this uneconomical damming event have for which there is physiologically no necessity? It can only be concerned with higher functions that use physiological functions. This happens in a twofold way.

A continuous flow cannot be the foundation of rhythmical events, which are based on an interacton of contrasts, as was shown. Without the alternating opening to the resting nervous system and to the moving metabolic pole shortly thereafter, rhythm would not be possible, and the heart would not be the central organ of the rhythmic system with all the previously described functions based on it. The continuous primary flowing is typical of the plant world in which processes of consciousness do not play a role. An element of consciousness is connected with the interruption of a continuity; every continuously even procedure works soporifically and fatiguingly. Thus, it is not quiet that brings about sleep, but rather a singing monotone, a lecture, an evenly rocking movement, etc. A sudden interruption, not its gradual stopping, brings about an awakening process by addressing the subconscious. It is the half-conscious region of feeling with which the rhythmic system is connected; conscious thinking is connected with the nervesensory system and willing with the metabolic system.

The lulling effect of monotony need not lead to outright sleep; taking effect by way of the feeling, it leads primarily to an alteration or *partial* elimination or influencing of consciousness from the region of the subconscious. This fact is most effectively put into practice through the incessant showering of noises, through so-called background music (in restaurants, department stores, etc.). The damming up function of the heart is thus preconditional to the possibility of a perceptive function in the semi-conscious realm, in the region of feeling. To what does the perception apply?

The Heart as the Soul-Spiritual Organ

As presented above, the existence of the heart is primarily soul-spiritually based; that is, the astral body and ego need the greater vessels, the blood pressure and the heart in order to actively experience and work in the human organism.

Further, the physiological activity of the heart as a sense organ was described. In addition, the heart fulfills other functions, namely, the sensing of the relationship that the nervous system has to the metabolic system. This relationship is expressed in the pulse-respiratory quotient. In an extended sense, however, the heart not only perceives the impulses brought with the blood from the periphery, but also their immersion in earthly laws; in other words, the relation of the cosmos to the earth is sensed in the heart. This is the greatest of all existing polarities. What is the significance of its half-conscious perception? It is the relationship of spirit to earthly experience, the maintaining or denying of the spiritual kernel of man's being in his earthly deeds. This he experiences as an unconscious "weighing out," as *conscience*, which also "beats" like the heart. It happens on the level of the emotions arising from the subconscious, yet it requires an organ of perception that can weigh deeds in relation to the archetypal spiritual image of man. That organ is the heart, which is able to fulfill its task because it is perceptive and directed to the impulses emanating from the nerve-sensory system and also from the metabolic system, from the cosmos and from the earth. To these it must be connected. Because of the special position of the rhythmic system, the contents of perception, the voice of conscience, are not compelling as is the logic of the nerve-sensory system, but they "speak" in the subconscious, maintaining the space of freedom. "The pangs of conscience radiating into our consciousness are what is reflected of our experiences by the heart."[72]

Ordered as the heart is in the position between above and below, left and right, etc., this middle position also applies in its higher functions and polarities. An enhancement in the Goethean sense is possible through this inclusion in polarities, such as a continuation of the field of tension on a higher plane or utilization of the given possibilities in an integrative way. It has already been pointed out that this position is not passive, but mediates actively and in a controlling manner. This is, however, always an ego function. The ego works by integrating, perceiving, and encompassing. The heart can take a central position since it is a profound expression of the *entire* human being. It is the organ of destiny. This feeling lies at the basis of innumerable expressions that can be found in all languages in which the heart is considered equivalent to individuality. "To take something to heart" means to unite it with the personal impulse, with the ego.

No other organ emerges as directly from or expresses as fully the blood as does the heart. For that reason, everything that lives in the blood can be perceived by it, especially the spiritual forces streaming toward it from the cosmos. Similarly, no other organ is as closely connected with the earth. Certainly the skeletal system is the result of earthly forces and the lungs the organ that makes them active and rules them; the heart, however, perceives the earthly forces; it makes possible *earthly consciousness*.

How could it do this if nothing adequate to the task existed in it? Precisely through the fact that the "deepest" point is in the heart in which the blood is completely exposed to the forces of gravity can a consciousness of the earthly forces develop. The living blood would, at least potentially, come to rest at this deepest, most earthly point of circulation if the heart were not exactly here to grant it a new impulse to overcome the earthly forces. For that, however, the heart needs a mechanical basis that is not given in the periphery. To perceive and overcome the earthly forces is an expression of the interweaving of the heart into the central part of the human being and of its activity.

Expressed differently, what the heart perceives is the life stream of the blood, which is endowed on the periphery with cosmic forces; it then comes under earthly laws. They are overcome through the activity of the heart. It is the passage of the life stream through the earth to a new development as higher life that is based organically in the heart.

On this basis, the soul-spiritual faculties can develop and their deviations be understood. Man can experience heaviness too strongly, and its overcoming too little. In this case he experiences a depressive mood, which is an expression of the excessive perception of earthly forces, of feeling overcome by them. This can also be called a lack of lightness, hence of light forces. The heart is set as mediator into this polarity of heaviness and light.

In principle, the same situation can express itself as a feeling of the fear of death. This is typically based on the heart and is an expression of the fact that the heart experiences the earthly forces, which are related to the forces of death, too strongly. The feeling of death or extinction that typically arises in cases of angina pectoris or myocardial infarction occurs on the level of feeling. It is independent of the actual proximity to death, and it can also be distinguished from a death phobia. It is the perceived relationship of death and life that is expressed in the heart.

On the other hand, the human being can also inadequately perceive heaviness. Out of a deficiency of earthly consciousness, he then places himself beyond earthly conditions, which leads to an excitatory state as seen in mania. The heart in all these cases is the experiential basis for the described polar soul sensations. In the fear of death and the feeling of extinction, it also plays a role in the cause of those experiences. The depressive mood, however, is perceived only by the heart. Its actual basis is formed by the hepatobiliary system. To express it another way: this patient feels a loosening of the ether body in the heart region.

In the activity of the heart, the human being experiences heaviness within his organism and the overcoming of it. But that is also the organic basis of the development of true courage and enthusiasm. The working of the spirit in matter, the enspiriting that lies at the basis of enthusiasm, is a typically human function—an ego activity that can develop from the foundation of warmth as its ego carrier, and in which the human being can be actively creative. In the same sense, the heart is the organ that rules the warmth organism just as the kidneys rule the air organism or the liver the water organism.

Courage and enthusiasm in the true sense can develop only if earthly objects are taken as completely real and the path to surmount them is seen. Otherwise, it would be either a case of foolhardiness or of dreaming or reverie. For that reason a healthy heart function mediates the proper relationship between levity and gravity, between light and darkness, past and future, cosmos and earth.

But the heart also takes a middle position in relation to time. The nerve-sensory system is shaped from the forces of the past. In the metabolic system lives the future. The heart weaves between both the present. It is the organ of man's destiny from which the question of transformation is posed. Also from this aspect the typical fear of death of those with cardiac illnesses is understandable.

Finally, there is the power of love, which man can develop because he has a heart. Similarly, perceiving belongs to it as do the transformation and selfless action, an activity emanating from the ego, but which has overcome egoism.

The Pathology of the Heart

Only the presentation of points of view that are based on physiology and through which pathological phenomena are made comprehensible can be of concern here. Function, not the pathological anatomical end state, such as a valvular defect or an insufficiency, can be a guide here.

A pathological anatomic modification of an organ is the consequence of a preceding disturbed function. Certainly the organic change in turn can also bring about a disturbed function; this, however, is the third stage that has come to the fore, and it may require immediate treatment. It is thus necessary to recognize in the change the dynamics that led to the problem.

In view of previous considerations, the heart is the archetypal image of all healing processes. The obvious question is, why can this organ even get sick? Actually, the typical heart diseases do not originate in the heart. The heart was described in its active role of mediation between the nerve-sensory and metabolic systems, from which tendencies of sclerosis and inflammation emanate. The heart is alternately open to the dynamics of the one or the other system and lives in their balancing. If it is too much given over to one or the other, it is taken over by those dynamics and overcome. It was described how the result of the dynamics of the nervous system is systole, that of the metabolic system is diastole. Therefore, corresponding to the two polar tendencies of illness, there are also two kinds of cardiac arrest: the tonic systolic kind that is brought about, for example, by cardiac glycosides or calcium, and the atonic diastolic kind brought about by potassium or cardiac muscular insufficiency. One or the other impulse can lead to cardiac death. In the genesis of heart disease and its therapy it is essential to discover the origin and the kind of impulses that bring about the illness. In this sense one can distinguish three groups of cardiac illnesses.

Inflammatory Diseases of the Heart

The tendency toward inflammation stems from the metabolic system. It is frequently less a predominantly quantitative disturbance than a more qualitative one. These relationships were presented in detail in vol. I. In inflammation a "demixing" is present, a dissolving of form, that is a precondition for all regeneration and growth. If the ordering principle is lacking here, an inadequate or insufficient buildup results, which can in turn be the basis for bacterial colonization.

Mostly for that reason the actual inflammatory heart diseases (endocarditis, myocarditis, pericarditis) are resulting conditions of other illnesses, especially of infectious diseases such as scarlet fever or polyarthritis. Polyarthritis can be preceded by tonsillitis; dental problems can also initiate the whole disease process and maintain it. In every case we are thus dealing with a metabolic process that has not been mastered and that finally takes hold of and damages the heart. There is a predominance of the inflammatory, form-dissolving tendency in contrast to the formative principle that emanates from the nerve-sensory system. This shift is frequently constitutional, or the preceding illness is not healed in the acute phase so that a chronic inflammation persists. This must be judged differently from an acute inflammation. Unlike in fever, the ego is here no longer actively engaged in these organic processes. The direction for proper protein build up is also lacking. In this situation, therefore, one finds paraprotein, dysproteinemia, increased sedimentation rate, etc. Finally, the muscle fibers of the heart can be damaged with subsequent functional disorders. This development finally leads to degenerative transformations, myodegeneration of the heart, myocardosis and finally cardiac insufficiency.

The expression myodegeneration of the heart is considered obsolete and inexact today; it had to yield to "more exact" diagnoses. Yet in accordance with the manner of thought of that time, it relates more to the general, i.e. superordinate occurrence—the degenerative deterioration of the heart muscle. Such all-embracing concepts are often closer to the actual dynamics involved than are descriptive names for a given state, e.g. hypertrophic or dilatative cardiomyopathy. Although insufficiency is not of an outright inflammatory character at all, it still belongs to the basically inflammatory diseases, all of which stem from the metabolic system. This is why adrenalin and its derivatives have an intensifying effect on the contraction. Adrenalin and contraction are both an expression of the action of the nerve-sense dynamics.

Other pathological factors of the muscle fibers of the heart include toxic damages caused by barbituate poisoning, anesthetics, alcohol, asphyxia, etc. All these cases are primarily disorders of the metabolism. Also to be considered in the development of these myocardial changes is that the pathological anatomical findings are often preceded by a long period of latency. That is generally the case in chronic metabolic disorders. It is for this reason that it is so difficult to discover the genesis of the diseases, in this case the primary inflammatory disease process stemming from the metabolic system.

Certainly between all these phases there are transitions. Often signs of inflammation may be absent. This does not contradict the original inflammatory genesis of the entire process. The absence of several signs of the inflammation is especially typical for the chronically persistent process that passes into degeneration and is for that reason frequently overlooked. A chronic myocarditis is more frequent than generally assumed and often is not diagnosed during life.

It is characteristic of disorders stemming from the metabolism that they hardly enter consciousness. Thus they and the ensuing defects often proceed without pain. Often fatigue and decreased vitality are the only symptoms. Only later do arrhythmias, valvular defects, or insufficiency develop. An increased pulse rate, often noticed only during stress periods, can frequently be an early clue to the process. It is a sign that the increase in stroke volume is no longer adequate and the heart has only a limited reserve capacity.

These conditions ask that attention be paid to "slight" early symptoms and also that preceding illnesses really be brought to a thorough healing rather than simply causing them to disappear through symptomatic therapy. The same applies to heart therapy. Especially the early states are absolutely accessible to a proper healing process. The more defects (myocardial changes, fatty degeneration, micronecroses) exist, however, the more one will have to utilize "cardiac supports." With the proper indications, these, such as the application of cardiac glycosides, are certainly justified, but this does not signify a healing of the diseased heart process. Early initiation of these supports may indeed bring about a momentary improvement of the patient's life situation, but it will not alter the basic pathological situation or the life expectancy. The ultimate origin of the inflammatory heart diseases—and insufficiency is among them—must be sought in the metabolic system. The involvement of the liver here ought to be evident, and is known from physiological and clinical experience; and yet therapeutically it is scarcely heeded. In the future it will be necessary to investigate the causative involvement of other organs as well (especially kidney, lung, and spleen) and turn it to therapeutic use.

Primary Sclerotic Illnesses of the Heart

The nerve-sensory system has a contracting character, in contrast to the expanding tendency of the metabolic system. The contracting dynamics are also the foundation for a possible premature excretion, that is, sedimentation and thus also a sclerotic tendency. This can manifest, for example, in a coronary sclerosis. Independent of the deposits there can be inadequate circulation, regardless of its genesis. The dynamics behind it are decisive; they are in contrast to the blood pole.

Angina pectoris is the classic picture of the dynamics working from the nerve-sensory system into the heart area. This tendency toward contracting, awakening, and breakdown can be sensed directly. Pain is enhanced consciousness. The highest expression of the disintegrating character of these dynamics is experienced in the pronounced feeling of impending doom and fear of death. During these phases there is an increased acidity, which is an expression of the astral body working excessively into the metabolism in a catabolic manner. In any case, the sensation of stenocardia, of constriction is the direct and proper expression of the contracting dynamics emanating from the nerve-sensory system and overpowering the heart.

Where the dynamics takes hold is secondary. However, contemporary research sees only the organic events without considering the reality of forces standing behind them. Thus there are contrasting points of view concerning the genesis of angina pectoris, that is to say, of myocardial infarction. In the framework of the views presented here, this discrepancy is secondary, but naturally interesting and significant. The two possibilities of development, however, are not mutually exclusive. A high degree of sclerosis of the coronary arteries exists as well as a primary inadequate metabolic situation of the myocardia.

The customary and generally accepted view arises from the

findings that by virtue of changes in the intima, the lumen of the coronary vessels is narrowed. Thus ischemia develops in the heart muscle area. The end stage of this process would be a coronary infarction. Supposedly underlying this is coronary sclerosis or even repeated spasms, a theory that Heberden, the creator of the concept angina pectoris, presented. The paradigm of cardiac infarction set forth in textbooks since the thirties, has revealed so many anomalies since then that it has long been inadequate to explain all the related phenomena:

1. A rise of only 2 percent in the incidence of athero-arteriosclerosis occurred in the same time span in which the frequency of myocardial infarct increased thirtyfold (3000 percent).[73]

2. Arteriosclerosis increases after the sixty year threshold; infarcts, however, decrease.[73]

3. If an arteriosclerotic change were at fault, then infarcts would have to appear with much greater frequency in other extracardial areas; above all, at least the right side of the heart would have to show the same frequency as the left. Ninety-nine percent of all infarcts, however, are found in the left heart.[73]

As is well-known, the findings in autopsies of healthy war dead of the Korean War, 1950–53, raised considerable interest. It was shown that young American men from 20 to 25 years old had high-grade arteriosclerotic occlusions of their coronary vessels without having had cardiac illnesses, corresponding disorders, or having died of a myocardial infarction.

Against the customary teaching there are the results of essentially two significant researchers:

1. The pathologist Richard Thoma (published in Virchow's Archiv in 1880–1923) showed that, based on 10,000 pathoanatomical preparations, atheromatous deposits only develop where there is a prior vascular distension. These begin characteristically as a loss of elasticity of the media, which, as is well-known, receives the main impulse of the vessel's pressure. Only in the preformed enlargement of the vessel, in which a vortex of the flow would appear, is the fatty atheroma placed. The distension remains outward and prominent during life. The vas-

cular collapse at death, with lumen reduction to one-twentieth of normal, gives the impression of the vessel having been already occluded during life by the atheroma. Thoma, to prove this hypothesis, made vascular preparations with fluid paraffin under pressures existing during life and was always able to prove that the atheromas were outwardly, not inwardly, prominent.

The drawings of cross-sections of an atheromatous vessel, familiar from textbooks, do not exist in nature. The studies of Thoma were confirmed in 1953[74] and 1971.[75] After these studies, customary atheromas (developed from fat-like substances, lipids, etc.) cannot be said to lead to vascular occlusions during life. Thus an infarct cannot develop through atheromas.

2. The pathological anatomist Giorgio Baroldi[76] from Milan has shown with 5,000 pathological preparations that the myocardium is so rich in anastomoses between the coronary arteries and their branches that a full supply of blood to the entire myocardium is always possible. (This was previously doubted because Cohnheim maintained in 1881, on the basis of questionable experiments, that the coronary branches were end arteries and therefore did not supply neighboring tissue through anastomoses.) A full supply can still be possible even with several intramural vascular occlusions.

A result of these studies is that an occlusion can never lead to an infarct because of the anatomical conditions existing in the heart muscle wall. Baroldi suggests that what was hitherto designated as myocardial infarction should be called "idiopathic heart muscle necrosis."

Kern's pathogenetic model[77] starts from the basic question, why do myocardial infarctions develop almost exclusively in the left heart? In searching for an explanation he encountered a phenomenon that has been known at least since 1879; it may well have adorned various textbooks as a side issue, but it has actually never had any significance in medicine. What we are talking about is the fact published by Landois that the inner layers of the left heart during systole, previously described as lasting significantly longer than diastole, are always bloodless and are compressed completely white. Blood flows through the inner layers of the left heart only for 0.2 seconds per heart beat. The inner layers of the left heart are thus supplied with blood only for one-fifth of the entire human life!

Besides this situation of the blood supply, there is an essential anatomical difference between the right and left chamber walls of the heart. Right and left chamber walls have essentially the same number of muscle fibers, which, like nerve cells, are incapable of regeneration. The left chamber wall, compared to the right, is twice as thick only because the fibers are twice as big in diameter as those on the right.

These two basic facts, the systolic stoppage of blood flow on the one hand, and the endogenous basic hypertrophy of the left chamber on the other, cause the left inner layers to benefit from only about one-sixth of the metabolic exchange that the maximal capacity of the coronary system would permit under different conditions. In addition, every left ventricular, myocardial fiber still has to effect several times the energy and metabolic exchange of a right fiber, five times that of every right ventricular fiber, and ten times that of every atrial fiber, even though it has relatively less metabolic exchange for that function.[78]

Throughout life the myocardial regions of the left inner layers are subject to an especially unfavorable metabolic condition which is expressed in the usually increased acidity of this area compared to other areas of the body. The pH of this area is normally quite acid at 6.7, while the remaining tissue's is 7 to 7.2. The energy of the heart muscle is basically gained by aerobic metabolism. Aerobic processes occur maximally at a pH of 7 to 7.2. If, on the basis of the anomalies of the left heart, a switching of anaerobic lactic acid fermentation is necessary, the pH drops and a pH of 6.7 is normal here. When it drops lower, local cell death occurs at pH 6.2.

Everything damaging to the heart muscle—infections, metabolic disturbances (hyperglycemia, hyperuricemia), adrenalin incrases (under stress or nicotine consumption), dystrophy related to starvation, overworking, liver or kidney insufficiency—works so that the acid metabolic situation of the inner layers of the heart leads to local cell death, to local necroses. These can grow together confluently. The capillaries flowing through such areas react by swelling the walls. Through increase and further confluence, larger and larger areas of the muscle are included. Finally, a chemical erosion process arises that develops into a transmural infarct and through the more or less sudden activation of lysoenzymes (lysoenzymal tissue destruction chain reaction), thromboses occurring at some time within this sequence of events are an ascending result of the myocardial process, not its descending cause (Meadows, Zollinger, Baroldi, Erhardt).

Ernst Edens pointed the direction for the results of this cardiological research. Based on his therapeutic observations, he came to the conclusion that "coronary heart disease" consists "to a large extent of patients with over-burdened left hearts who have hypertension with a consequent clear diminution of cardiac work capacity. All suffered from more pronounced dyscardias. There were almost daily stenocardias brought on by slight effort, angina pectoris attacks, etc., and approximately a third of the patients had suffered one or several clinically verified left heart infarcts. These patients were persistently and often seriously ill and had been unable for a long time to work at their professions. Thus, many of them had had prolonged clinical treatments, even without infarct but regularly without strophanthin. . . . They all received strophanthin from Edens, in part rectally and in part intravenously. No other measures were undertaken."[78]

"In a short time, all these patients noted the disappearance of the stenocardia and angina pectoris attacks. This occurred after a rapid improvement from day to day, often on the fifth or at the latest on the fifteenth day. Of these, all remained healthy, unchanged and free of infarcts as long as they were supplied with strophanthin. However, they all experienced such surprising improvement only with strophanthin. A later change from strophanthin to digitalis proved to be a mistake in every case since the attacks recurred immediately."[79] Edens' survival rate, when myocardial infarcations were treated with strophanthin, was approximately 96 percent.

Kern writes that "the myocardial infarct is essentially a myocardial phenomenon and not so much the coronary phenomenon it was considered to be as long as one was accustomed to interpret the dyscardias (such as angina pectoris) prior to the discovery of the left side chronic myocardial insufficiency only as a sign of coronary insufficiency.[79]

It has already been pointed out that pain is an enhanced process of consciousness elicited by the excessively strong dynamics of the nerve-sensory system. The same applies for the feeling of constriction. In the same sense the verified shifting of the metabolic situation into the acid pH range must be understood; this is an indication of an excessively strong activity of the astral body. There certainly is agreement on the metabolic insufficiency of the cardiac muscle if not on the question of how it came about. Clearly the shifting of the balance is expressed here, that is, the pushing back of the metabolic pole, which is also qualitatively changed, in favor of the nerve-sensory pole. The well-known increase in myocardial infarctions in winter—the maximum is in January, the minimum in summer—shows clearly the dynamics of contraction corresponding to winter. In the human organism these emanate from the nerve-sensory system.

The risk factors that can lead to angina pectoris or to myocardial infarction are well-known. Through these risk factors it is to some extent possible to recognize those in danger of infarction. Here one is primarily dealing with hypertension, smoking, overweight, overeating, increased cholesterol values, gout, tachycardia, a sedentary life style with restricted movement, stress, emotional factors, among others. It is not known what exactly these risk factors elicit. They certainly play a significant role and have been obtained in collective studies from which individual reactions cannot be predicted as they are determined by the soul and spirit, the higher members of man's being.

Despite the obvious relationship between the increase in fatal myocardial infarcts, and angina pectoris and the modern life style, this connection receives much too little attention. Rather, isolated factors are played up, such as the above-mentioned risk factors. Even stress is put aside as a factor since it is difficult to verify it as a laboratory value. Nevertheless, there is no doubt that the pace of modern life, the "angina temporis," is one of the factors that favors this illness. The pressure under which humans live today, a more or less unconscious stress situation in which as achievement-oriented modern people they find themselves, obsessions, etc. all are only an expression of the previously mentioned dynamics of the astral body. It presses into the rhythmic area of the heart via the nervous system. The risk factors only support these events.

These dynamics must be considered as real in order to really understand this illness; the dynamics are primary, the way they develop is secondary. A typical expression of this are the catecholamines (adrenalin, the sympathomimetic substances). Their catabolic, astral character is unmistakable. They are directly and indirectly involved in the process of myocardial infarction. Their occurrence after emotional or physical stress is an expression of the enhancement of the characterized dynamics; their increased formation in the anoxemic situation of an infarct is understandable because of the decrease of oxidative de-amination. Thus, a vicious circle arises. An overly strong breakdown tendency produces catecholamines. These damage the tissue. Their physiological breakdown is thereby decreased and their further development favored. It is a fact, however, that they, as well as the underlying impulse—the astral basis—are to some extent necessary for the contraction of the heart. Therefore, their decrease or therapeutic exclusion by β-blockers brings about a decrease of the contractility of the myocardium. For the same reason the use of catecholamines or an increase of the impulse underlying them is contraindicated in acute situations. (On the other hand, in insufficiency the noradrenalin concentration in the heart is significantly decreased. The administration of appropriate derivatives acts like a whip in improving contractions in the failing myocardium.)

These risk factors thus favor the infarct without actually causing it. Yet, it is justifiable to decrease these risk factors. However, these isolated measures are significantly over valued and thus draw attention away from the central event. A "correction" of increased blood values—for example of hypercholesterolemia—is merely cosmetic and, as has been shown by extensive studies, has only a minimal or no effect on the mortality due to coronary disease. Certainly it is senseless to thoroughly exclude one risk factor and to neglect the others. We discussed the "problem" of cholesterol in different connections. Here it need only be mentioned that the capacity of the organism to rule the lipid metabolism is much more significant than the exogenous supply. If the lipid metabolism is undisturbed, the organism will easily be able to deal with the relatively small fraction of cholesterol coming from the food in a reasonable meal.

The issue is not to avoid cholesterol but to overcome it, that is, to carry it further through breakdown, which is a function of the astral body in the metabolism or of its correct interaction with the ether body (see vol. I).

It is obvious that there are more cases of myocardial infarction in males than in females, since it is well-known that women, prior to menopause, hardly ever have myocardial infarctions. This can certainly be traced to the hormonal balance, but that only shifts the problem. It contributes nothing to an understanding of the illness. It has been repeatedly shown that men are united more deeply with their bodies and live more out of the nerve-sensory system than do women. This, however, favors especially the sclerotic illnesses and the pathological dynamics discussed here.

Ultimately, the disturbed dynamics are revealed once again *ex juvantibus* (from the treatments): The use of analgesics, sedatives, tranquilizers, β-blockers, (β-receptor-inhibitors), etc., is an attempt to quiet the situation, which is certainly justified in acute cases. Through these measures the activity of the astral body is inhibited, "blocked." The β-blockers set to work on the lowest level; hence they are the most effective in the acute conditions. Tranquilizers and sedatives have a somewhat "higher" point of attack. Nevertheless, these are only symptomatic effects, which do not touch the cause of disease. This shows that the efficacy of an acute measure says nothing about its healing effect in the sense of an overcoming of the disease.

One of the best prophylactics is still regular physical work that is intended to divert the astral body from the nervous system and incarnate it more in the metabolic system.

To a certain degree, this same myocardial degeneration can be caused by the chronic working of inflammatory as well as sclerotic processes. In principle, however, it makes no difference whether the destruction of the myocardium occurs through toxins, inflammations, micronecroses, or hyperacidity. The end state is often unsuited to make it possible to recognize the dynamic that caused it. Just as in the physiological state the impulses of the nerve-sensory and metabolic systems alternately meet in the heart, so both can lead to the destruction of the heart but along different paths. It is secondary whether this happens slowly as in a chronic inflammatory state, or more rapidly as in an infarct. It is certain, however, that the therapeutic points of attack are different in each case.

Thus, despite all known risk factors, the question is still open as to what lies at the basis of the infarct itself. There is no doubt that the exclusion of the risk factors is necessary and the customary therapy today is effective in acute cases. Yet, coronary dilatation, β-blockers, etc. achieve in the most favorable cases only symptomatic effects that do not address the actual process of illness.

To look at these matters only from physiological and pathological-anatomical considerations cannot yield satisfactory insight into the pathological processes involving the heart since such illness is not a purely scientific problem. Especially the heart is, as described, a soul-spiritual organ and cannot be understood when this connection is ignored. It has been mentioned how the connection of the soul with the heart is still alive in language and how even in the pathological realm the wisdom of speech still addresses connections that are hardly touched upon today. One can lose one's heart in a matter; one can take something to heart; one can die of a broken heart, etc. The specific connections of the heart to the being of man, to his soul-spiritual path, can be sensed directly.

Just as it is uncontested today that an unresolved psychological stress can lead to a ventricular ulcer, to a duodenal ulcer, or to kidney damage, so there are still other soul-spiritual experiences that one takes to heart and that can damage it organically if they are not managed on a soul-spiritual plane. Whoever unites himself with his whole being—that is, with his heart—with a problem to make it his own, lives in it; but he subjects himself organically to the problem if he cannot adequately handle it. For example, responsibilities, or more exactly a long-lasting conflict of conscience, which includes everything that has to do with the destiny of man on earth, with his task and life goals, may demand too much of him. Here the pathological influences establish contact with those that arise from stress situations, from an excessive active astral body; this often leads to hypertension.

However, he who takes nothing to heart because he has "a heart of stone" and is indifferent to everything, is not touched by soul-spiritual problems as decisions of conscience. His heart remains organically healthy because it is insensitive to the function of the higher senses. It is unable to sense and receive soul-spiritual ego impulses.

From this, three fundamental possibilities for therapy will be mentioned here.

1. The patient becomes dull and apathetic; he does not participate; (let everybody do what they want, just care about your own health, "learn to turn off," etc.). Medicinally, this is achieved through tranquilizers that supposedly calm down the life of feeling, but actually deaden or dull it.

2. A true relief is attempted (giving up part of one's excessive responsibility, regular periods of rest and recovery, bodily training, diet, exclusion of risk factors, etc.). Medicinally, we will mention only the specific heart therapy by which one generally means almost exclusively digitalization, lowering of blood pressure, and coronary dilatation.

3. Other possibilities are hardly taken into consideration today or are mentioned only peripherally, such as a rational lifestyle or psychotherapeutic guidance. Every over-load is a problem of balance between innate capacities and demands. If

the demands are met with a corresponding counterbalance—an appropriate soul-spiritual hygiene, for example—then the ego and soul can withstand the stresses, even mature and become stronger from the task. This is possible when a situation has been understood and the problems consciously solved. (This is not to say that objectively things can always be solved.) Here, too, it is not resignation but rather a trust in the guidance of destiny that indicates the path. The working through and mastering on a soul-spiritual plane prevents and even makes it unnecessary for one to take the matter too much to heart, that is, that it overcomes the patient, sinks down into the organic and makes his heart ill. These influences are especially applicable in the heart as a spiritual organ.

For the patient, this does not mean that he no longer should "take to heart" what is oppressing him. It means that he will learn to work through these things in *equanimity* and *calm*. This naturally takes time, but it is a specific indication for the heart.

The acclaimed method of "turning off," relaxing, etc., despite its basic correctness, often allows the patient to fall into a vacuum, and there his or her soul-spiritual aimlessness can only emerge all the more clearly. Positive measures must create the conditions for being creative in a completely *different* way, in the artistic domain for example, or in *measured*, reasonable physical activity as a relief of the head, and also in working with nature and one's environment with loving attention.

Instead of a cold, sober intellectual life, a rich soul and spiritual life that takes the reality of the spirit just as seriously as bodily hygiene, which today is almost exclusively considered, is part and parcel of soul-spiritual hygiene. Added to this are eurythmy and curative eurythmy, as well as special exercises that expand the soul and strengthen the ego.

It is understandable that the third path is exactly the opposite of the first, which is a road backward that brings about a weakening of the soul-spiritual existence. It is all a problem of the development of the consciousness soul. To this extent, an illness such as myocardial infarction is a cultural illness whose background can be understood from the cultural milieu and nature of the human being. Surely the risk factors should be added to this, and they may even stand in the foreground.

These measures, taken as a way of dealing with problems, are addressed to the basis of the illness. They can be supported by medicines that are conceptualized from a comprehensive insight into the nature of the heart and its function.

Disorders of Rhythm

The heart is the archetypal rhythmic organ. Rhythm is an integrated part of its function. Therefore, a loss of rhythm in the heart is of much deeper significance than it is in any other organ. The "loss of the middle" is worked out in the realm of art, "which in accordance with its nature stands between the spirit and the senses."[80] This loss signifies the loss of man's being and is justifiably seen as a spiritual and human problem of our time. On an organic plane it attacks specifically the heart as the organ of the middle.

It was described above how rhythm represents a principle of the middle and how two polar deviations are possible—beat and arrhythmia. By beat, we mean an unchanging action that can no longer adapt to demands; thus, rigid regulation results. This doubtlessly pathological deviation is noticed much less today than is arrhythmia; indeed, its pathological significance is hardly seen. What it means in reality is that the heart is unable to take in actively the excessively one-sided effects from either the nerve-sensory or the metabolic systems. It is unable to limit and transform all these activities, and it is thus overcome by the dynamics under consideration; thus the development of the previously described sclerotic or inflammatory illness is encouraged.

The polarity of heart and circulation can also be disturbed in their harmonious relation to one another. For example, the heart can no longer deal with the demands of the circulation because it either perceives incorrectly or reacts falsely, or not at all. If this condition persists, the heart is overcome and weakened by the flow of blood. One then finds an initially latent followed by a manifest insufficiency. (Initially, insufficiency under stress, later also at rest.) The heart is overburdened by erroneous, inappropriate functions. Preceding this condition, however, is a wider disturbance of the rhythmic relationship. The resulting insufficiency is an end state that ought not to be the point at which deliberations and considerations begin. Here other therapeutic considerations are also valid.

The other deviations from the active physiological rhythm are the incomparably better known rhythmic disturbances in the narrower sense, including absolute arrhythmia.

It has been described how the heart is an organ whose rhythmic activity is an expression of the alternation between and of the complete surrender to impulses from the nerve-sensory system (systole) and the metabolic system (diastole). These polar impulses are joined—congealed, so to speak—in the heart, so that an independent rhythmic activity appears as an organ. This is most concentrated in the "stimulus conducting" system that only seemingly "directs" the heart's action autonomously. Actually, it is an organ for perception of the above-mentioned polar impulses and of the movement of the blood; these flow together in the heart action in a somewhat independent way as stimulus formation and stimulus conduction.

In a certain sense the rhythmicity of the heart has become independent and a separate organ in the stimulus conduction system. Within one organ we have a situation similar to that of the relationship of the entire organism to a single organ. Just as the ether body uses the liver for its metabolic tasks and the astral body the kidneys, so the rhythmic system forms a rhythmic organ within the heart, the stimulatory system with its centers, the nodes. The corresponding functions can be comprehended only through the formative impulse.

It is thus understandable that this system is exceptionally sensitive as a perceptive organ, especially to nervous (vagotonic and sympathicotonic), psychic, chemical, and even mechanical influences. It can be clearly seen here how the actual muscle tissue is gradually transformed into a tissue that is neither completely muscle nor yet nerve. With its Purkinje muscle fibers the stimulatory system presents an *organon sui generis* that is not closed off in itself, however, but is rather highly sensitive to influences outside the heart. Because of its unique origin, any structural damage to the cardiac muscle can also affect the stimulatory system. This is a direct expression of the heart and its functions and proceeds from its dynamics. Here is an example of how the dynamics, the force relationships, structure the organ and differentiate it, but can also change it in a pathological one-sidedness.

Corresponding to this sensitivity, the possibilities for disorders are manifold. Disorders of stimulatory conduction can give rise to a total AV block. This can be fatal if not enough organic substrate has been retained or has been developed that can take over this function (secondary or tertiary chamber rhythms; so-called replacement automaticity).

In summary of heart pathology, one can say that the heart does not fall ill of itself but through pathogenic influences from the metabolic system, which ultimately lead to insufficiency, or through predominant influences from the nerve-sense system causing angina pectoris or myocardial infarction. Even if these disease tendencies stand as polar opposites, behind both of them there lies a life problem in the form of a loss of, or disregard for, rhythm as life in time. The deviations from rhythm move in the direction either of rigidification, toward beat, or of loss, toward arrhythmia. The organ ultimately affected—in some cases after decades of latency—is the organ of the mean, the organ of rhythm, the heart.

Heart Therapy

The more ill a heart is, the more necessary and effective the treatment. This, as a self-evident statement of fact, leads to an evaluation of the effectiveness of a treatment especially in cases of serious insufficiency. It is an end state, however, and it is in its nature that it can be most rapidly and effectively addressed with a symptomatic therapy. This situation, however, leads to a lopsided displacement in judging cardiac therapy in that it is understood to be almost identical with use of glycosides and these in turn with digitalization. This will therefore be discussed first.

Glycoside Therapy

The use of glycosides goes back to a folk knowledge of the specific plants that have been used since ancient times. Rudolf Steiner pointed out that Paracelsus still had the capacity to follow organs and plants back to their common origins. "He knew that Digitalis purpura developed when the human heart developed."[81]

The cardiac plant remedies are still a necessary constituent of cardiac therapy. The principle has remained the same, yet today the plant extracts are standardized according to their active substances, or the latter are semi-synthetically processed. One must be clear about the fact that in using cardiac glycosides one is practicing only symptomatic therapy even if it is often live-saving or at least life-prolonging.

The fundamental questions were dealt with in detail before. The indications, however, are not arrived at on the basis of the effectiveness of the substances, but rather from a comprehension of the process of the illness and the ideal of causal therapy, that is the healing to be striven for.

It is quite revealing that most of the cardiac plant remedies form a relatively unified substance despite variable origins and ways of growth (for example, Digitalis, Scilla maritima, Convallaria, Strophanthus). This unified substance is combined under the term cardiac glycosides. In their chemical structure, there is a steroid skeleton with an unsaturated lactone ring and ether-like fixed sugars. The steroids were discussed in detail in vol. I. The impulses underlying all steroids, despite extremely variable effects, were characterized as mediators for the astral function in common. This is also applicable to the cardiac glycosides.

Their specific affinity to the heart is achieved by a bond with sugar that cannot be found in other steroids. (The sugar-free aglycones lose their cardiac activity to a large degree. They cannot be fixed to the heart.) The significance of sugar is obviously to direct the activity of the steroids to the heart and to anchor it there. Why it is especially sugar that establishes the connection to the heart can be understood from the nature of sugar and that of the heart. Sugar was described as the carrier of the ego-organization, thus as the carrier of the spiritual organization underlying the human being. The heart is, however, the spiritual organ, through which man is deeply bound to his being, his *I*. In principle, therefore, only a substance like sugar is in a position to direct into the heart the constructive astral impulses which are within the ether body. (Besides glucose there are still other specific sugars, such as digitoxose to be found among the heart glycosides, which shows the modification of the fundamental impulse through the plant.)

It must be emphasized once again that the effect of the heart glycosides is symptomatic. They replace the activity of the members of the human being, or, after the latter are loosened, they draw them again into the organism, more specifically into the heart, in such a way that a relatively healthy function is the result. This, however, ceases again as soon as the effect of the glycosides has worn off.

One could also designate the effect of cardiac glycosides as substitution therapy. Earlier, on the basis of various experiments, a "cardiac hormone" was postulated (Haberlandt, Asher, Rein, among others) which was, interestingly enough, to have originated in the liver. In any case, the experimental exclusion of the liver brings about a functional disorder of the cardiac muscle within minutes. This disturbance can be relieved by reinsertion of the liver as well as by strophanthin.[82] Here, the spleen appears to play a significant role. It was tempting to think of a steroid hormone—or a strophanthin-like bodily substance—but at that time it could not be isolated. Later studies showed that in the heart, NNR-like substances (aldosterone-18-monoacetate) could be found.[83] It is certainly possible that someday a bodily cardiac hormone of a steroid character, possibly even a glycoside, will be found. It is also well-known that the poisons of toads, which are also steroids, cause a strong cardiac activity. To this extent one can speak of a transition to a substitution therapy.

There is no doubt about the special connection of the glycosides with the heart. Yet their anabolic effect extends also to other areas. Digitalis in vitro encourages plant growth, and when applied locally, it improves local regeneration and organ function. Thus, it is also used externally. This application even seems to have been the original one, for digitalis was used for centuries as a component in healing ointments. (Only quite recently has this come into practice again.) It was not until much later that Withering (1741–99) introduced the use of digitalis as a remedy for dropsy (monograph 1785). Its effect on the heart muscle was still unknown to him. Digitalis glycosides show a tonic effect upon the venous vascular system and are thus also indicated for local application in varicosities, venous ulcers, thrombophlebitis, etc. In addition, there is a positive effect and partially rapid relief of pain in arthroses and other degenerative illnesses. Digitalis is also used in eyedrops to vitalize the function of the eyes. The effect is evident from the description above.

An obstacle to a differentiated cardiac therapy is the still "valid" view that all heart glycosides always affect the hemodynamics in a qualitatively similar way. For that reason, glycosides are considered synonymous with digitalis, although that is not exactly true. This equivalence is actually true when one considers only the symptomatic effect of the economizing heart activity in the case of insufficiency. But through this one-sided conceptual fixation on a single parameter as a measure of function, all other factors are excluded; thus a standardization necessarily comes about. The differentiation occurs merely *within* this pharmacological effect concerning absorption, rapidity of action and duration, degree of saturation and decline of activity, all of which have been studied in great detail. Methodically, this had to lead to a preference for the "hardest" glycoside, digitoxin, which has an absorption quota of approximately 100% in contrast to scilla with 5–20%, or strophanthin, of which there is almost no absorption at all. Thus, digitoxin had to be considered preferable without even considering the greater adhesion and other data that express a greater intensity. The methodical aspect of this kind of study was described in Chapter 1 of this volume.

The contemporary preference for the most "effective" glycoside, digitoxin, is a result of the medical thinking of today to which the most intensively active substance must also be "the best." The use of these substances is not only a question of dose but also one of method. Typical of these methodological procedures is the "rapid saturation" preferred by American clinicians and the occasionally practiced view that considers optimal digitalization to be achieved only when toxic symptoms occur. For decades, digitalis was too highly dosed, even if indicated.

It cannot be ignored that, despite these well-known and recognized differences within the hemodynamic effects of the cardiac glycosides, the opinions regarding the optimal therapeutic application are quite divergent. Thus, in Germany strophanthin therapy finds wide application while in the United States digitalis is used almost exclusively. The preference for strophanthin or digitalis prior to or after a myocardial infarction has been just as heatedly discussed as the absorption quota of strophanthin.

The dispute that has simmered for decades concerning the adsorption of orally applied strophanthin—against which primarily pharmacological measurements, and to a lesser extent clinical experience speak—cannot be discussed here. It must be remembered, however, that the first successful application of strophanthin occurred in 1855 in the form of a tincture. For a long time after that, this therapy held a favorite place. The intravenous application followed only twenty years later.

The more or less generally propagated early digitalization deserves special mention. It can be easily shown, however, that in a so-called stress insufficiency—a latent insufficiency that is still compensated and frequently occurs in older persons—there is a diminished capacity for bodily work. If these patients are digitalized, the capacity for work definitely increases, thus it seems to be proved that they require glycosides.

Without doubt, the latent insufficiency can gradually or rapidly become manifest with increasing stress, and then go over into decompensation. For this reason these patients require *treatment* but not necessarily glycosides. The disastrous error consists in thinking that this treatment must be by digitalization. It was pointed out above that it is not justified to consider glycosides or heart therapy as equivalent to digitalis. Its effect is symptomatic and does not change anything of the cause of the developing insufficiency. Certainly an "improvement" of the heart function occurs, which patients frequently experience. To evaluate this effect as an indication is, however, erroneous. Rather, the time ought to be used for a true and not only a symptomatic therapy. Since symptomatic therapy does not fundamentally change an illness but only covers it up, physician and patients feel a false and deceptive security that allows the favorable time for healing to slip by. As a result, after a short time early digitalization must go over into permanent digitalization. The illness process as such is not stopped but in favorable cases only delayed. Finally, it appears as a definite insufficiency—an end state for which a symptomatic or substitution therapy is then justifiable and necessary. Since other possibilities besides glycosides (and the exclusive focus on digitalis among them) are hardly noticed and certainly not applied because of methodological narrowmindedness, appropriate different therapy is not realized. This will be described in more detail below.

First, the differences within the cardiac glycosides will be discussed. In general, a kind of spectrum is recognized at one end of which is strophanthin and at the other digitoxin. The differences between these extremes are considered to be the rapid but brief action of strophanthin as opposed to the longer and more intensive action, the cumulative effects, etc., of digitoxin. This is the difference between the so-called "soft" and "hard" glycosides. The remaining glycosides take a middle position. It is, however, easy to note that beyond the well-known, exclusively considered parameters the general effects are variable. Thus strophanthin shows a general stimulating effect that is especially expressed in the nerve-sensory system. It was also suggested for use in the treatment of certain forms of headaches, transitory cerebral ischemia, and even for trigeminal neuralgia, especially if it is brought on by a stress on the circulation. The effect extends far beyond that of the known energizing component on the heart and an increased blood supply, and it cannot be achieved with "harder" glycosides. According to Rudolf Steiner, strophanthin is indicated in order to balance the damaging influences of contemporary civilization. He certainly did not mean isolated active substances but rather the active principle of the plant or the seeds. A special preparation of strophanthin is the fatty oil of strophanthus, Oleum strophanthi, which is available in capsules and ampules from Weleda.

The vitalizing component of all steroids, which in the glycosides is directed at the heart, is directed in strophanthin at the dynamics proceeding from the nerve-sense system. These dynamics are caught and actually answered in a countereffect by the blood stream, as can be recognized from the abovementioned vitalizing, anabolic action in the head region. To this extent, there is a situation here that is similar to that in the kidney system, which turns the catabolic impulses of the nerve-sensory system into the anabolic impulses.

The general effects are different with digitalis; the "toxic" component—i.e. the one directed at the metabolism—predominates. In the nerve-sensory system there is not a vitalizing effect as with strophanthin. Instead, there are visual disturbances, nausea, states of confusion, and apathy, among others, especially in overdoses. Thus there arises an intensification of the forces of the nerve-sense system, without its receiving better circulation or vitalization. This also brings with it a strengthening of contraction, for contraction is based on these dynamics. The domain of digitalis is serious insufficiency, decompensation, especially tachyarrhythmic (R-V) insufficiency. From the existing weakness and cardiac dilatation, the attempt arises to somehow live up to the required performance by means of tachycardia, but the outcome is often absolute arrhythmia.

The lengthening of the conduction time by digitalis is most characteristic and relieves the heart; thus, digitalis is irreplaceable in these conditions. However, the actual inadequate metabolic activity of the heart is not addressed. With digitoxin there is greater potassium depletion than with the softer glycosides since the former increases the performance but less so the regeneration. This can be understood from the description of the significance of potassium and its antagonism to calcium.

The application of digitalis, then, ought to be saved primarily for end states, tachycardias and absolute arrhythmias; in no case should it be used early. Because of the previously described therapeutic guidelines it ought to be used primarily with these indications, which actually require intensive treatment. Fundamentally, it is necessary that a therapy should be as gentle as possible and as intensive as necessary. By gentle we must not only understand the possible toxic damage, but also the therapeutic effect; namely that—apart from transition states—a symptomatic therapy should be applied only when it is no longer possible to stimulate the forces of regeneration and thus effect healing.

The early states of cardiac muscle weakness require "nourishment" of the heart, a stimulation of regeneration and regulation of the heart muscle metabolism. This is made possible by the soft glycosides. The most useful is strophanthin, the "milk of the aged," which among the glycosides is quite in contrast to digitoxin; yet this series can still be expanded and continued beyond strophanthin.

Here we will mention a few glycosides that are close to strophanthin but are still in part softer and have a more extensive activity that is hardly noticed today. Adonis vernalis, a ranunculaceous spring plant, stands completely on the anabolic side of the course of the year and possesses a strong vitalizing component that is indicated especially in early myocardial diseases. The same applies to Convallaria, which is also indicated particularly for stenocardic difficulties and arrhythmias. Oleander has a similar action, especially in tachycardia. Scilla maritima, the sea onion, works similarly to strophanthin and is indicated in bradycardia and edemas. Its diuretic effect is ten times that of digitalis. All of these glycosides have low toxicity. Following this group are the lanataglycosides (lanatocide C), including the purpureaglycosides among which digitoxin stands at the other end of the series.

It is significant that most of the glycoside-plants also contain saponins. It is characteristic of them to bring astral working into the etheric, as has been repeatedly pointed out. Even if they do not have pronounced "cardiac effects," the saponins nevertheless act in accordance with the fundamental tendency of these plants, rounding out and expanding the picture, making the total extracts far better than the isolated substances. Considered as method, this total working is certainly neglected when only one parameter is evaluated.

The So-Called "Small Heart Therapy"

In addition to the activity of strophanthin and related substances there are other cardiac remedies that contain no glycosides as active substances and therefore must appear insignificant to thinking that is oriented only to substances. First in line here is Crataegus oxyacantha, which in general improves myocardiac metabolism (seen, for example, in the lowering of the lactic acid and BTS levels). It encourages cardiac circulation and nourishes the myocardium through the formation of favorable energy. For that reason Crataegus is the basic remedy at the beginning of cardiac insufficiency, especially in older persons. The active substances of the plant have been studied in detail, but they seem to be insignificant. It is not possible to make manifest their dynamics as isolated substances, as was attempted above for the cardiac glycosides.

A healing plant for cardiac disorders hardly noted today is Leonurus cardiaca, a labiata that has an exceptional rhythmic structure. It is indicated when excessively strong astral influences act upon the function of the heart (tachycardic reactions in hyperthyroidism, cardiac rhythm disorders, and cor nervosum).

The necessary vitalizing component can be achieved generally through Prunus spinosa, which, according to an indication given by Rudolf Steiner, can be used also in cases of heart insufficiency, "internally very strongly."[84]

These healing plants and also the softer glycosides are usually designated as "small heart therapy"; this fails to recognize the active principle and constitutes a methodological failure of judgment based on the preference for symptomatic and strong effects. In reality, the so-called small heart therapy is the actual heart therapy; it maintains the function by favoring the formation of energy, whereas glycosides with their necessarily toxic components bring about a release of energy, but in conjunction with this the necessary anabolism is not necessarily addressed. This is exactly the difficulty with digitoxin. The formation and release of energy cannot be entirely separated. Both exist with all glycosides. The first, energy formation, predominates in the soft glycosides, while energy release predominates in digitalis. To a certain extent this also works in a vitalizing way, but under certain circumstances the formation of energy is inadequate to the energy released. This can be seen from the potassium depletion. As has been described, there are always all kinds of transitions between those remedies just mentioned; when considering the entire range, strophanthin is in the middle. The group of healing plants mentioned last works exclusively in an anabolic way and less by freeing energy. This, however, is no standard for evaluating their effect, which is achieved only through supporting the metabolism, etc., for a longer time.

Other Remedies for Heart Therapy

Cardiodoron

Cardiodoron is a comprehensive remedy for the cardiac circulatory system. It goes back to indications given by Rudolf Steiner and is one of the remedies for typical illnesses. It consists of the plants Primula, Onopordon and Hyoscyamus, which are processed by a special procedure. None of these plants was known to have an effect on the heart or circulation. An understanding of their effect thus does not result from knowledge of the substances they contain but only from the conception of them arising from spiritual research. Accordingly, Cardiodoron represents the archetypal image of the cardiac circulatory function. An attempt will be made here to point out these correspondences. What is described as a way of growth, etc., must not be understood to be a “proof,” but rather as grounds to penetrate to the nature of the plants and to grasp them in pictorial form.

Primula officinalis is definitely a spring plant that thrives on moist, cool meadows. It is a direct expression of the forces that are active during the period when the forces of life that have withdrawn during winter begin again to appear with the rising sun. Life stems from the cosmos and moves into the earth again in the springtime. The wild primrose, which unfolds fully during this time, is like an indicator of a place through which forces stream into the moist, cold element and fill it again with life. Ancient wisdom is still evident in the old uses of language and so its folk name "Key of Heaven" can be understood in the way that through this plant the heavens are unlocked, letting its forces stream again into the earth. The plant contains saponins, among other substances. This class of substances has already been mentioned several times. They make possible the mixing of air and water, which is the essence of foam formation. Here, it signifies the leading over of cosmic astral forces into the working of the watery etheric so that organized life can become manifest. In the organism, the periphery of the circulation corresponds to it; of the former we said above that in it peripheral cosmic forces are active. Through the primrose "the life force" is gathered and led via the periphery into the living blood of the organism. In man, it stimulates this process relative to the blood and its movement.

In relation to outer form and place of growth, Onopordon acanthium, the donkey or Scotch thistle, is the exact opposite of the primrose. It grows on sparse, dry wasteland. Its home is the plains of the European southeast, the Great Hungarian Plain. In the first year this biennial forms a strong tap root that then forms a rosette lying close to the earth, and the following spring the imposing plant grows from this; it then unfolds its greatest growth as a large thistle in summer. Where do thistles grow? A characteristic of their growth is that they thrive where other plants are unable to live, for example, at the edge of a desert, where it is hot and dry. They are pioneer plants, preparing the earth in such a way that a living layer can develop and be maintained. Thistles overcome the forces of the earth, which they can do only because they partake of the earth and yet are not subject to it. To overcome the earth other, mainly cosmic, forces are required. These are the forces of silica that are active in this plant family and are evident in the thorns. The nature of silica always manifests in a radiating structure.

Onopordon, a plant that tastes bitter, goes deeply into the earth to unite with it. Then, however, it responds by growing up to 2.5 meters tall, demonstrating its mastery of the earthly forces in its life.

Just as Onopordon is in its way almost the exact opposite of the primrose, its field of activity also extends to the polar side: No longer to the periphery but to the heart, the deepest point of the circulation where the blood is most exposed to earthly forces and where it must receive a new impulse to be brought back again to the peripheral cosmos. This overcoming of earthly forces is demonstrated by Onopordon in nature, by the heart in the human organism. It is therefore not surprising that pharmacological research on Onopordon led to repeated reports of its stimulating effects on the activity of the heart.[85] There are also studies of the phytochemistry of its blossoms.[86]

Primula and Onopordon are opposites in nature. Primula leads cosmic life into the earth; Onopordon overcomes the earth and unites earth and cosmos in a new way. In the organism these relationships correspond to the peripheral circulation and the heart.

A mediating element—Hyoscyamus niger or henbane—is necessary for active cooperation. Like all Solanaceae it is a poisonous plant. It can be seen in the alkaloids how the astral element of the earth, which should only touch the blossom, is pressed into the plant. There, it works in the metabolism with nitrogenous substances and produces a substance that is an expression of astral activity. This is particularly strongly developed in the Solanaceae. Within this family Hyoscyamus shows a most rhythmic structure. Its field of activity is also more in the rhythmic system (whereas the related Belladonna works more in the nerve-sensory system). The botanical characteristics of both plants are described in volume I.

Through Hyoscyamus the connections between the activities of Primula and Onopordon are established and harmonized. In the organism this is the area between the periphery and the heart, the region of the arterial vasculature that was described as a place of the astral body's activity. This is addressed through Hyoscyamus, a strongly rhythmic and astralized plant. It is understandable here that only a small amount of Hyoscyamus can be used; the other two plant constituents are "mixed with a trace of Hyoscyamus" in the preparation of Cardiodoron.[87]

Cardiodoron thus can be considered a remedy for any disorder that arises from an altered heart and circulatory function. Like all remedies for typical illnesses, it is not directed against any particular disease but rather represents the healthy function "for purposes of orientation," thereby enabling it to be re-established and maintained. Cardiodoron is not a cardiac remedy in the usual sense, nor does it stimulate the circulation, but rather it stimulates the physiological functions of both. By reason of this harmonizing character, it is also indicated in opposing illnesses—for example, hyper- and hypotension, cardiac insufficiency, angina pectoris, etc. These effects are reported in experimental and clinical publications.[88]

However, it would be entirely amiss to think that Cardiodoron could replace digitalis or other specific cardiac medicaments although it could certainly support other therapies and also help to decrease the dosage of glycosides. That, however, is less the purpose of its use than the fact that its target and way of working is completely different than that of usual medicines. Through Cardiodoron a re-establishment and healing of the disturbed function is striven for, whereas the glycosides represent a symptomatic effect and are merely a cardiac support. That these different working principles are in no way mutually exclusive but can meaningfully supplement one another has been mentioned repeatedly.

Aurum

Aurum is the most comprehensive remedy for the heart. The formative impulse for the organs stems from cosmic effects, which also underlie the metals. Thus, the formation of the heart arises from impulses that go back to the sun and also appear in gold. As the sun is the mid-point of the planetary system, so the heart stands in the center of the human organism. Therefore, Aurum can also work specifically on the heart. It appeals to the formative processes and is indicated in all disorders that cause damage to the cardiac muscle. Particularly in the phase of regeneration after infarct, Aurum also stimulates the maintenance and re-establishment of the tissue. The application at the beginning of therapy is thus started with Primulum aurum cordicum 1%, later, Aurum D6–8, and for stabilization and longer application, Aurum D10.

A particularly effective combination is that of Aurum with Stibium, both for cardiac insufficiency as well as for regeneration after infarction. Stibium (see section on minerals) allows the forming force of the higher members of being to take effect. It has an inner organizing action on the protein metabolism; by means of Aurum, the action is guided to the heart region. This combination finds its ideal complement in Hyoscyamus (Aurum/Hyoscyamus comp.).

Other Remedies

The application of organ preparations consisting of heart substances in extracts as well as in potentized form (Cor D3–4) is also most meaningful. The potentized form is most effective combined with Arnica (particularly after treatment of an infarction) or with Aurum as a mixed ampule, through which its activity is directed to the heart.

Sugar must also be mentioned in relation to the anabolic heart therapy. Its relationship to the heart has been described. The intravenous application of glucose may have been overvalued in earlier days. In any case, from the points of view indicated it has its justification. Also the positive effect of honey on patients with heart disease has been known since ancient times (intravenous preparation M2 Woelm).

The Mineral Metabolism of the Heart

The point of attack of the glycosides in the heart is a secondary problem. They liberate calcium, which means they give the astral body a point of attack since it requires calcium in order to work in the metabolism. Thereby the force and dynamics of contractions are increased with appropriate consequences (positive inotropic effect). Because of this synergism of calcium and glycosides, their simultaneous application almost constitutes malpractice.

A significant but entirely contrasting role is played by potassium. It is a carrier of the etheric forces that are directed into the water organism. Thus, it forms the etheric foundation for contraction, which, as a movement impulse, is a function of the astral body and supported by calcium. The middle third of the ventricular septum, the "center" of the heart, is particularly rich in potassium. Through contraction, potassium is used up, and the etheric basis is transformed into the extracellular space, depolarization). Thus, it can be understood why the heart especially requires and retains potassium. An excessive decline in the potassium level is an expression of the fact that the ether body has become loosened from the organ, which in the case of the heart is fatal. The EKG gives an indication of the potassium content of the cardiac muscle cells. A flattening of the T wave with a simultaneous increase of the U wave indicates a potassium deficiency and vice versa.

The application of glycoside brings about an enhancement of contractility but also a decrease of potassium in the myocardium. This is most notably so with digitoxin, much less so with strophanthin and the soft cardiac glycosides. A low potassium level increases the toxicity of the glycosides (which can lead to danger of atrial fibrillation). This is an expression of the fact that the astral body fails to take hold properly and works directly into the physical, causing a cramp if the ether body is too weak to perform its work. Since just as in the gall bladder, the bronchi, etc., a cramp is not possible in the heart because of the refractory time, it is expressed in the form of ventricular tachycardia or atrial fibrillations. Therefore, in therapy using cardiac glycosides an adequate etheric "basis" must be supplied in the form of potassium.

Sodium is the specific opposite to potassium in relation to the water organism. The old demand for limiting sodium consumption in inflammatory cardiac diseases and insufficiency—not only in hypertension—is therefore justified. Today attempts are frequently made to solve this problem with saline diuretics.

The physiological opponent of calcium is magnesium. Like potassium, magnesium is also an expression of the activity of the ether body. Magnesium forms the basis for the working of calcium (the membrane-ATP-ase is activated by magnesium), and just as with potassium, the glycoside sensitivity is increased by an insufficiency of magnesium. In contrast to that of potassium, the effect does not lie in the watery region but "higher," in the light ether at the cell membrane. Its antispasmodic effect is characteristic and is directed against the excessively strong working of the astral body when it is active with the dynamics of the nerve-sensory system. This is the situation in angina pectoris and it leads to cardiac or myocardial infarction. Thus, magnesium is indicated here; the form in which it is given is secondary. Rudolf Steiner suggested Magnesium phosphoricum D3 (together with Cardiodoron). An injection of Magnesium phosphoricum D6 with Nicotiana D10 is particularly effective. If magnesium is given in non-potentized form, it must be given in such a way that it "arrives" and is used in an organic bond with an organic compound. The easily soluble magnesium sulfate works upon the gall bladder and also as a laxative and so is not useful in cardiac therapy. (Organic magnesium compounds are, for example, magnesium diasporal, magnesium ascorbinate, magnesium orotate.) When properly indicated, one can be easily convinced of the strong effectiveness of every kind of the described magnesium therapy. Nevertheless, this therapy today is still not given its proper place. This is prevented by the almost reflex thought that heart therapy is equivalent to the use of digitalis glycosides.

Summary

It has been frequently said that the heart cannot become ill from its own dynamics but rather through influences that result from the quantitative or qualitative predominance of the nervous or metabolic systems. The influences of the participating organs must be discovered in the process of diagnosis, which then has direct therapeutic consequences.

One must point to the liver as one of the main organs significantly influencing the cardiac function. It was known as early as 1880 that the liver, when excluded experimentally, soon brought about a rapidly progressive, fatal cardiac insufficiency. Today it is known that the spleen and liver form a functional system, whose decisive significance can be seen in protecting the organism from oxygen insufficiency. Especially in acute hepatitis there are strong effects on the heart, while in hepatic cirrhosis, as long as there is still functional tissue, the cardiac manifestations decrease again. These findings can be understood from the essential nature of the organs, since the liver is the main organ of the ether body and thus forms, substantially speaking, the living basis for the other organs. Not every cardiac muscle weakness must be hepatogenic, yet an inadequate liver function can initiate a cardiac muscle weakness and maintain or promote it. Thus, one must also think of the functions of other organs, namely, the kidneys and lungs, which together with the liver and heart, represent the four protein forming organs.

In the future, it will be necessary to direct one's view beyond the heart as the end organ in the disease process and more to the influences that work on it, and to differentiate therapy by including other organs and the diverse workings of the various cardiac remedial plants.

Blood Pressure Disorders

The development of blood pressure was described as an expression of the activity of the astral body. This requires the arterial vasculature to incarnate in the water organism. The mediating substance here is sodium. The two deviations from the normal physiological blood pressure are hyper- and hypotension.

Hypertension

Hypertension is considered to be the most widespread illness. It causes no discomfort at first; on the contrary, it is the hypotensive person who does not feel well. The hypertensive person feels fine. The illness is often discovered only when organ damage has become evident. Here, in the consequent stages, lies the significance of the illness and also the need for its early recognition. The increased blood pressure promotes diseases of the kidneys, the heart—in which it causes especially insufficiency but also infarcts—as well as the vasculature, such as arteriosclerosis, with the consequent states of cerebral and eye vascular seizures or attacks, and hemorrhages.

In what follows we will discuss primary, genuine, essential hypertension. Secondary hypertension is based on a primary disease of the kidneys, where chronic pyelonephritis increases in significance and also renovascular stenosis and endocrine abnormalities, such as pheochromocytoma and primary aldosteronism (Conn's syndrome) among others. These require special diagnosis and treatment.

What was said about cardiac illnesses in general also applies to essential hypertension. A number of risk factors is generally known; however, the causes of the pathological and permanent elevation of blood pressure are not known. One of the main risk factors is salt. Through its relation to water and the astral body, sodium gives the astral body a greater point of attack, allowing it to unite more intensively with the arterial vascular system. Salt reduction is therefore the simplest and, dietetically speaking, the most important therapeutic measure in treating hypertension.

Another risk factor is smoking. Nicotine is a well-known vascular toxin that can bring about acute and chronic vascular narrowing and wall damage. To be overweight shows an excess of unmanaged metabolism that binds the higher members of man's being too strongly and inappropriately to the metabolic system instead of permitting them to be free. These two risk factors also must be considered prior to and in conjunction with drug therapy.

Today the possibility of treating these three risk factors with drugs certainly exists. Through diuretics the avoidance of cooking salt becomes "expendable"; through peripheral vasodilation, vasoconstriction can be relieved, and overweight can be approached with various drugs. The patient is seemingly helped by the early application of such medication. The development of the illness, however, is in no way addressed, since again one is dealing only with purely symptomatic effects. The same applies for the β-blockers and other adrenolytic substances. With such medication it is possible for the patient to lead a "normal life" without giving up any of its "enjoyments," but he must continue taking this medication for the duration of his life. A thorough understanding of the pathogenesis, however, will lead to the recognition that it is these conveniences that increase the tendency to the illness. It was pointed out that in the blood pressure one can recognize the taking hold by the astral body of the arterial vascular system, and it can even be measured. In the hypertensive person this happens too intensively and with dynamics that work by way of the nerve-sensory system, the contracting, awakening character of which has been frequently mentioned. Therefore, everything that addresses the astral body in the characterized dynamics increases the blood pressure. Every stimulation can be clearly seen in the elevation of blood pressure. This subsides again when the stimulation decreases. If, however, the stimulation of the astral body is not relieved, then the consequence is constitutional, essential hypertension. It can be a matter of constant stress and also of an unconscious, unrelaxing tension. It goes without saying that contemporary life is such that the astral body of man is addressed incomparably stronger than in earlier times. We need mention only the stimulative overload of the senses, the labor system that fails to recognize biological or individual necessities, the awakening of desires and wishes for various stimulants, etc., all of which originate only in the astral body.

Through these constant appeals to the astral body it becomes increasingly difficult for man to rule the astral body with his ego, which is here the basic principle of therapy. That is, however, primarily a soul-spiritual problem. Only when the astral body is no longer ruled on this plane does it express itself on a lower stage, in the organic; it can then no longer be reached by the ego, but rather works independently with its own dynamics. It thus changes the entire organism and a fixed hypertension develops, whereby the typical astral organ, the kidneys, become victimized and are unable to fulfill their task of switching these catabolic impulses over into anabolic impulses (see the chapter on the kidneys). But other organs also show the effect of the catabolic one-sided character of the astral body.

A causal therapy will strive to balance this improper relationship between the ego and an overpowering astral body. This is certainly possible, and to some degree even necessary, through a symptomatic diminution of stress and exclusion of risk factors. In the course of further therapy, the attempt will be made to create a new equilibrium by strengthening the ego as against the astral body. This is possible through practicing and learning the mastery of one's wishes, desires, irritations, etc. The conscious avoidance, for example, of salt, smoking, gourmandizing, etc., is the actual therapy in which the risk factors are excluded and the illness tendency standing behind them is mastered. It is understood that such measures are not popular with patients, and physicians also tend to follow the faster, comfortable and "successful" symptomatic medicinal way. This help, however, is not only superficial but even inhibiting to the spiritual life of the patient. In no way should the patient be commanded to exclude or limit the risk factors because this would bypass his ego, causing him to seek substitute satisfactions in a most forceful way. Rather, this ought to arise from insight and would then result in a voluntary renunciation; thus the first step toward a true therapy would be taken.

The conscious control of thoughts and soul experiences belongs here, too. This is made possible through exercises in which the temporary cessation of the customary course of the day is attempted, and one tries to fill the soul with other, more spiritual contents. Certainly here, too, an ordered, regulated course of life must be mentioned in which rhythm is essential. The exclusion of the impulses stimulating the astral body also belongs to a successful therapy. Many of these influences are well-known today, but one is resigned to them because their excitation is considered exogenous and taken for granted, especially since one now has an effective therapy. In the excitation, however, what matters is not the external factor but rather the inner reaction, which is not necessarily determined by these outer factors but which can be controlled through practice.

The situation is different with fixed hypertension. As described here, the astral body is already locked so deeply in the organic sphere that it is hardly accessible anymore to the free rule of the ego. This is the beginning of the end state in which symptomatic therapy is unavoidable. There are, however, all kinds of transitions up to a pronounced nephrosclerosis. Drug therapy is determined by the phase of the illness. For beginning hypertensions, Belladonna is almost specific. This plant shows, as do all Solanaceae, a strong astralizing impulse, which is, however, balanced by a counterflowing etheric stream. Belladonna is indicated in these tendencies of hardening and facilitates the loosening of the excessively intervening astral body. Low potencies, D5–6, as well as higher ones, D20 and 30, are used. In the image of its activity Belladonna stands close to Cuprum, a metal related to the kidneys. Belladonna therapy, due to its antispasmodic, receptive effect, can continue, but it is indicated not just in renal hypertension. Used here are Chamomillam cuprum cult., Cuprum sulphuricum D4–6, Cuprum prep. D6–30, Cuprum/ren D4, 6 and others.

Plumbum is used as Scleron. Its original indication—"loss of memory, weakness of the kidneys"—indicates its relationship with the kidney system. Through Plumbum the catabolic process is brought to the corresponding physiological place where the nervous system and other organs, particularly the kidneys, are relieved of these dynamics of the astral body, through which water and salt excretion is also stimulated. The application occurs as Scleron, or Plumbum mellitum D20, Plumbum silicium D20. As always with lead, this medication should be given only for a few weeks, after which there should be a rest period. In this interval it is advisable to give Belladonna or Copper as well as Aurum. Gold represents the "middle" and has the primary relationship to the heart and vascular system. It is used here in D10–30. The remedies mentioned can supplement each other and can also be used in combination. In addition, Rauwolfia stands at the border between the various therapeutic starting points presented. It takes hold of the illness process in a comprehensive way and justifiably holds a favorite place in the therapy of hypertension.

The goal of the therapy outlined here is to limit the overly strong intervention of the astral body and to bring it back to its physiologically appropriate limit. As mentioned, this is sometimes no longer possible, particularly when hypertension is fixed, and it is impossible to do without so-called symptomatic therapy. This preference for isolated, immediate effects is in accordance with contemporary thinking; it is, however, a departure from the actual therapeutic principle of healing. To this extent, we have here the same conditions as in the therapy for cardiac illnesses.

Just because the blood pressure can be successfully lowered with symptomatic effects, the danger exists of overcompensating or bringing it down to "normal values." It is well-known that certain patients experience difficulties when the blood pressure is decreased too rapidly. It is also well-known that some patients require hypertension, and "normal values" could leave them unable to work. Blood pressure is one way in which the individual deals with his astral body, a lesser or stronger intervention of which the ego requires. It is the task of therapy to limit the excess and to make adjustments suitable to the individuality of the patient.

Hypotension

In hypotension we have the opposite conditions. The astral body does not unite adequately with the vascular system so that the entire organism appears hypotonic, adynamic. The therapy is almost a mirror image of that for hypertension. The basic remedy here is iron, the incarnation metal, and its plant form, Urtica dioecea. One can begin therapy with Ferrum per urticam 1% and continue it with Glandula suprarenalis/Solutio ferri. This therapy brings about an enhancement of the kidney radiation, which to a large extent is the basis of hypotension. Since the astral body is addressed through arsenic, it is its combination with iron as Scorodit that is especially effective (D4, 6). Still more comprehensive is the activity of Levico, which contains iron, arsenic, and copper in an ideal combination and is best used as a cure at a spa.

Hypotension is not only a problem of the astral body, however, but also of an ego that does not adequately unite with the body. This ego-warmth relationship is most clearly addressed with Rosemary, which is effective internally (10%, D2) but is also effective in supporting physical therapy when added to a bath. Such baths, given as partially cold washings, Kneipp applications, etc., work directly on the vascular system in a tonic way and generally activate it. There are also comprehensive symptomatic possibilities of therapy in hypotension that include adrenalin derivatives and NNR-active substances. Through them the astral body is drawn into the kidney system. This can be understood from the presentation of the substances under consideration. Certainly the effect remains symptomatic. Coffee (caffeine), too, is an active remedy in hypotension, but it is often followed by a negative counter-swing.

Since hypotension, in contrast to hypertension, does not bring about organ damage, it is certainly possible to avoid symptomatic therapy here. A more or less forced elevation of blood pressure in a patient with a constitution for which this is not suitable, signifies an unjustifiable intrusion into his personality. In some cases the latter ought to remain for a longer period of time in a relative "rest" period, in order to find—possibly only in later years—the tasks appropriate to the individual destiny. This would have been rendered impossible by a relatively premature incarnation of the astral body. The reverse, an excessively strong drop of the blood pressure in a case of hypertension could potentially prevent the fulfillment of life's tasks because the necessary instrument has thereby been made too weak. To sense the individually "correct" measure is the task of the physician's art. It is also part of this art to protect people from damage and make it possible for them to pursue the path of their destiny in accordance with their spirit.

The Lungs and Their Diseases

Physiology and Function of the Lungs

The lungs are the portal of the air organism. Through breathing, man is intensively connected with the environment. One part of the air of the environment becomes the inner world for a moment and is taken into the organism. This contact with the environment is even more intensive, but also more ephemeral, than the interaction with the nourishment in the gastrointestinal tract. The lungs are actually a surface open to the environment and are protected by the respiratory passages from excessively severe influences.

Invagination, the forming of hollow spaces, is the archetypal phenomenon of the lung formation. Structurally, they are tubular alveolar glands. It has been said repeatedly that one can recognize an astral principle in invagination, the forming of a hollow space. To this extent, the lungs are typically astral organs. With the help of the respiratory process the astral body incarnates via the lungs.

Today breathing is considered to be merely a means of supplying the organism with oxygen and expelling carbon dioxide. If this were the only purpose of the lungs' function, one would have to designate them as exceptionally inefficient organs. The gaseous exchange in the gills of fishes is much more effective than that in man. The physiological process, however, is only one side of the matter. A higher function and task is of necessity connected with this. As is well-known, human and animal respiration represents exactly the reverse of plant respiration; it is an oxidation process in contrast to a reduction. Through respiration man forms "air," i.e. carbon dioxide, from the substance of his body, i.e. from "earth." Thereby imponderables are freed; life is transformed through breathing into light and warmth.

The meaning of this "irrational" structure of the lungs cannot be based on physiology. This seeming unsuitability has a deeper meaning. Through this structural principle a damming up takes place. The alternation of in- and outbreathing, out- and inbreathing, in each case produces a brief cessation of the stream of breath. Exactly the same principle, however, is also present in the heart; the continual stream of peripheral blood is interrupted in the heart. In the chapter on the heart it was described how this damming up is a problem of consciousness that occurs in the realm of semi-consciousness in the realm of feeling. However, the rhythmical system is the basis for feeling, just as the nervous system is the basis for thinking and the metabolic system the basis for willing. Through the damming up process, soul movements can be perceived.

The coupling of elements of feeling with the rhythm of breathing has, of course, been known for a long time, but it has never been studied adequately. The change in breathing rate with inner excitation or fear can easily be observed, as can taking a "deep breath" during the release of tension and depression. But the breathing times of prolonged or shortened inspiration or expiration also give indications of the person's soul state.

The formative impulses of the lungs must be looked for in the Mercury sphere. Mercury is the messenger of the gods, the mediator between heaven and earth. In the mineral realm this cosmic impulse corresponds to the metal mercury, and in the human realm, to the lungs. Their task, which is to unite the soul-spiritual being of man with the earth, has been described. The activity of mercury can be followed right into the lungs' microscopic structure in that the alveoli correspond in their fine bubble-like formation to the dispersal of a drop of quicksilver.

The breathing process itself, however, is deeply connected with iron. The intake and exchange of oxygen are functions of the hemoglobin in which iron is active. But ultimately the entire process of incarnation is supported by the iron process. It continually mediates between spirit and matter, between the ego and the body throughout life. Iron is *the* incarnation metal and in this function it is the "true mercury," as Rudolf Steiner called it. Such considerations can also make the therapeutic application of these metals comprehensible.

The seemingly opposite behavior of breakdown, oxidation, and excretion on the one side and buildup of body substance and growth on the other is encompassed by the breathing and lung process. A picture for this is in- and outbreathing. Through this kind of metabolism the ego of man enters into a connection with the physical world. At the same time, however, an experiencing of the spirit becomes possible. The polarity of in- and outbreathing signifies an awakening in the physical world, but also an awakening in the spirit. The possibility of both is evident in the physiological processes.

The connection with the earth that is given through the lungs signifies an individualization, which is an earthly problem. The grasping of, and entry into the earth that occurs through the limbs is also a breathing problem. Thus, the development of the limbs is connected with the development of the lungs and the breathing process. The development of the lungs from ontogenetic and phylogenetic points of view was discussed in the chapter on the heart.

In life, the catabolic process must be balanced with its opposing anabolic process. It is characteristic that these contrary processes are dependent upon one another. Certainly there must first be something that can be broken down through the breathing process. On the other hand, substance cannot be newly formed if the new formation was not preceded by a breakdown. This is the same phenomenon we encountered in metabolism. Only when food has been completely broken down can the formation of body substance begin. As an archetypal image this phenomenon makes its appearance in the first breath, and is justifiably considered to be the beginning of life on earth. Nevertheless, this taking into the lungs of the first breath is an oxidation, a breakdown, a catabolic process. The temporary decrease of the body weight after birth can also be understood in this way. The breakdown is a precondition to a new buildup. The "old," still largely motherly body substance is breathed out, excreted (CO_2 formation), and creates thereby the basis for the building up of new individual body substance. The uniting element in these two polar processes is warmth. It originates through the dissolving and combustion of the body substance, and then, since it is the carrier of the ego, provides the basis for a stronger interaction of the ego with corporeality.

As organs, the lungs thus to a large extent rule the dissolution and densification of substance, that is, the connection of man as a soul-spiritual being to his corporeality. The process of man's incarnation takes place through respiration. The higher members of man enter the body via this path. Thus, it is a fact that not birth but rather the first breath is the beginning of man's path on earth. (In forensic medicine this distinction still plays a large role.)

The life that begins with the first breath is naturally not the vegetative life that originates in the ether body of the embryo prior to birth. It is only oxidative breathing that makes possible a higher life, which is bound to the higher members of being, the ego and astral body; in this way, they come to activity in the organism. Thus, the structuring of the lungs is a direct expression of the incarnation process of the astral body. It has been described above how the tendency of the astral body to incorporate can be seen in the vital capacity.

Thus, the lungs are *the* organs of incarnation by way of which the soul-spiritual being of man enters the body and thus into a connection with the earth. In relation to the elements the lungs are an earthly organ. They regulate the relationship to the physical organism, just as the liver regulates the relationship to the water organism, etc. That makes the constitution and the soul configuration of the "lung man" comprehensible. These relationships are described in detail in vol. III.

The relation of the lungs to the heart and kidney is of special significance. The structure of the lungs represents an organ that is to the highest degree shaped to the last detail. In the formative forces that are expressed here, the astral body and the dynamics of the nervous system are recognizable. In the middle man the breathing and blood processes encounter each other in the interaction of the lungs and heart; this dynamic relationship is expressed in the quotient of respiration to pulse that was described in detail in the chapter on the heart. One can see from their anatomical positions and functions that the lungs are oriented more toward the nerve-sensory pole, whereas the heart and the blood system are oriented more toward the metabolic system.

The kidneys were described as the organs that regulate the breathing through of the organism. Lungs, like kidneys, are astral organs. Hereby, the lungs are the performing and the kidneys the ruling, organ of breathing. Lungs and kidneys are from an inner point of view considered to be as close as the liver and heart. These things are of greatest significance in therapy; this becomes especially clear in asthma.

The typical illnesses of the lungs can be understood from the organ picture and its significance for man. A few will now be discussed.

Lung Diseases

Pneumonia

Classic lobar croupous pneumonia has almost disappeared in the last few years. Today broncho- or lobular pneumonia, which in earlier times was typical of childhood, predominates. Although the differences between these two forms are clear, nevertheless a common process underlies them, and so we will discuss them together since the therapy is practically the same.

Incidentally, it is another question whether the developmental tendency toward decreasing occurrence, which is noted as an average, will continue, or whether one day circumstances might bring about a counteraction with a consequent increase of the pneumonias. The occurrence of viral pneumonias points absolutely in this direction: with the help of viruses, the same condition is achieved.

Pneumonia is an illness with a typically inflammatory character. The inflammatory process of, for example, hepatitis, myocarditis, nephritis, etc. is comparatively slight when compared to the dramatic processes going on in a pulmonary infection. Pneumonia can be designated as a prototype of the inflammatory febrile illnesses.

During pneumonia an infiltration of the lungs and a displacement of air occurs; it manifests in an increase of watery processes or a predominance of the blood process. Thus, metabolic processes arise in a place which ought to be subject more to the dynamics of the upper man. The air organism is prevented by the blood pole pressing forward from taking hold, and finally the lungs are permeated with substance causing hepatization. In the course of a high grade hyperemia, the air spaces are filled with a liquid consisting of blood cells and serum that excludes air. After a few days, a loosening, at times in the form of a crisis, is achieved, during which the exudate is liquified, resorbed, and transported away.

A prominent symptom in pneumonia is fever as an expression of the high grade inflammation. According to the points of view described elsewhere (see vol. I), one can see here an exceptionally meaningful measure taken by the organism. The fever is the expression of the fact that the ego attempts to unite more strongly with the organism. A new incarnation process takes place in the incarnation organ, the lungs, in an especially intensive manner. As a consequence of the special significance of the lungs, their inflammation, more than any other factor, leads man to a new decision concerning his relationship to the earth and to his corporeality. Therefore, pneumonia can be of incisive significance for the entire life of a person.

Not infrequently a constitutional change can be observed in the patient after overcoming this illness. It is, in particular, a demand to bring about a transformation and a new beginning. But the difficulties that pneumonia creates for the heart and circulation can also be understood. Through the predominance of the metabolic element, especially in the realm of the rhythmic system, the heart as the actual organ of balance between the upper and lower person is taken hold of and overwhelmed by the metabolism. Thus, the necessity arises for an additional heart therapy when one treats pneumonia. Also a phlebotomy at the beginning of the pulmonary edema ought not to be understood merely as a mechanical relief of the circulatory conditions. It signifies a relief of the entire blood, which is to say, the metabolic system.

As is well-known, the incidence and mortality of pneumonia have declined in the last few decades. This is often presented as a consequence of sulfonamide and antibiotic treatment. As

Fig. 1 shows, however, a decrease of mortality from pneumonia has been observed at least since the turn of the century, long before the introduction of the therapeutic measures to which

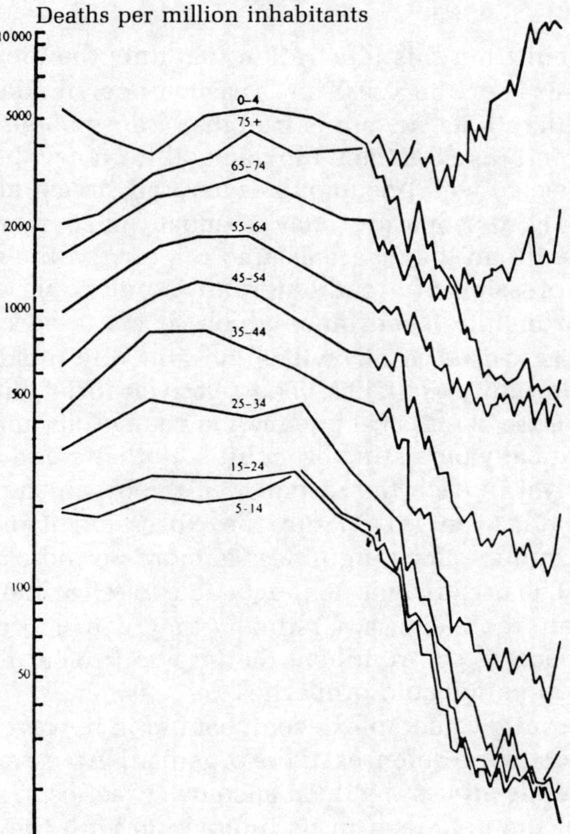

Mortality per Million Inhabitants

Fig. 1: Pneumonia mortality according to age groups in the years 1861–1969. The fluctuations in the curve from 1931 on are based on the fact that yearly quotas were recorded, while prior to that the averages of decades were given. (From *Pneumonia in Decline*, 1969, cited by O. Gsell, "Infektionskrankheiten" in *Pathomorphosis*, No. 1, 1969.)

alone one today attributes this effect. The decrease is much more a factor that is based in the illness process as such, namely, in the general decrease of the febrile illnesses. This is a problem of evolution, which has been discussed in detail in the chapter on infectious diseases. (See also the section on lung cancer.)

It is evident from this illustration that only the mortality of older persons is on the rise. This is easily understandable from these considerations since it is true that older people begin to excarnate, and thus for them the demand for a new beginning that is connected with pneumonia is naturally much more difficult. Middle-aged people are today essentially much more strongly incarnated than they were around the turn of the century.

As an expression of a pathomorphosis one could also consider the bronchitic syndrome, which seems to spread more and more as a disease of civilization and now holds fourth place in morbidity statistics. The relatively brief but highly dramatic course of classical pneumonia changes its appearance into a chronically persisting bronchitis. Both are of a bacterial nature and yet in each the response of the organism is different. A dramatic event is by nature the expression of an activity, while a creeping, persisting illness is more an indication of a weakness. The organism is no longer able to "clear the table"; it must tolerate the bacteria. Gradually they gain more ground until they become so prominent that previously harmless bacteria develop pathogenic properties.

This is certainly a complex event; behind it, however, stands the weakness in the defenses of the organism. An essential role is played in this process by the inadequate practice, from childhood on, of the organism in its interaction with the environment. It is basic to contemporary therapeutic thinking that the organism must be protected from "stresses." Through the so-called protective immunizations, illnesses are prevented. They no longer arise acutely but rather subliminally and as chronic disturbances (see the chapter on infectious illnesses in vol. III). But even in an acute case, the organism is spared defensive action by an immediate and almost exclusive antibiotic therapy that in principle does not consider the organism at all. Problems of this kind of therapy are already partially recognized in that "through destroying the pathogenic agents the immunization processes of the involved organism is to a large extent, or almost completely, brought to cessation; because of the missing antigen stimulus this then leads to an irregular course of the repair processes that are necessary to overcome an illness."

"From this point of view it is evident that pulmonary fibrosis, which was earlier practically unknown but has been increasing in the age of antibiotics, has its origin in the exclusion of the pathogenic agent which inhibits the immunization effect and switches the course of the healing process into proliferative, intermittent episodes of inflammation. In other words, pulmonary fibrosis is based on a cumulative, diffuse increase of the interstitial connective tissue as a consequence of repair and disease defense that has become irregular following the therapeutic destruction of pathogenic agents."[1]

Thus, to a large extent, we are dealing here with consequences of suppressive reactions of inappropriate iatrogenic measures. They are the result of a view of illness that lacks the sense for the purposefulness of a reaction. The general weakness of defense that can proceed to an anergic disease situation is, however, not only a consequence of the characterized inappropriate therapeutic measures, but also an expression of the described shifting of human disease tendencies. The world wide decrease of febrile illnesses corresponds to the constitutional displacement of the incarnation tendency from the metabolism to the nervous system. Modern man lives more and more in his nervous system and from this stem the hardening, inhibiting impulses.

A therapy for these conditions may not be limited to the treatment of bronchitis, but rather it must take hold of the constitution and transform it through stimulating defense, attempts at "reattunement," change of milieu and the attempt to bring a chronic state over into an acute state, a regressive metamorphosis, may become necessary. For orientation, only the following can be mentioned: hot baths, change of climate, application of Echinacea, iron in different forms, application of sulphur, mustard plaster, etc., in addition to the individual constitutional therapy are helpful.

Therapy of Pneumonia

If the organic interrelationships are truly known, treatment of pneumonia will not merely strive to kill off the bacteria that find an ideal nutrient soil in the uncontrolled and excessive metabolic and blood processes. Rather, the attempt will be made to so stimulate the organism that it is enabled to permeate the blood processes with formative activity. Iron comes primarily into consideration here since it has a most special connection to the entire function of the lungs. As is well-known, the entire respiratory process is coupled to iron through hemoglobin; without this metal the respiratory lung function would not be possible. Furthermore, iron has, as *the* incarnation metal, the task of leading the soul-spiritual of man into the corporeal. It mediates as "the true mercury" between the spiritual and physical.

In addition, one can be still more specific in addressing the different processes of pneumonia therapeutically. To a certain extent, Aconitum napellus represents a special effect of the iron process because it enhances the organizing activity of the warmth organism. As a Ranunculaceae it has, in addition, a special relationship to the watery realm. It is always indicated when the fever is still rising and until there is sweating during the crisis, in which the reorientation of the members of being comes to expression. In its excessively strong root formation, Byronia represents the forces of the nerve-sensory system (salt pole), which in pneumonia need to be stimulated so that the metabolic processes can be pressed back. Of the mineral remedies, phosphorus must be mentioned. Through its application one leads the ego more into the corporeality, thus conforming to what should be the basic tendency in the treatment of pneumonia. Here one meets the striving of the organism, making the disease reactions superfluous and depriving them of their foundation. The excessive protein processes can be specifically addressed with antimony. It stands in a position polar to the albuminizing forces and dampens their pressing upward from the metaboic region. It has proved to be especially useful in its organic compound as Tartarus stibiatus.

A combination of these remedies is found in Pneumodoron 1 and 2. Certainly the constituents can be used separately if one wants to address different phases of the process—for example, Bryonia to structure the warmth organism and Tartarus stibiatus to master the protein process, which through resorption, expectoration, and excretion is normalized and again led over into the normal structure. The applications of Pneumodoron 1 and 2 alternate hourly; iron is best used as Ferrum prep. D10 or Ferrum phosphoricum D6, 8 or 10 as a daily injection. In influenza pneumonias one ought also to think of injections of the patient's blood. If empyema develops, then Erysidoron 1 and 2 in which Belladonna D3 and Apis D3, or Sulphur D2 and Carbo betul. 5% are combined, and also injections of Argentum prep. D30 and Mercurius vivus naturalis D10–D30 are indicated.

Pneumonia that does not resolve requires a stimulation of the dissolving processes, actually an enhancement of the inflammation in the proper form. This can be achieved with mustard plasters but also through the internal administration of a sulphuric substance, preferably Hepar sulfuris calc. D4. Besides physical therapy (fresh air, eucalyptus spray, moist compresses), one must always pay attention in pneumonia to the heart and circulation, to which the pressing into the foreground of the lower metabolic processes presents an increased stress. Here Cardiodoron and 01. camphoratum 20% i.m., or Camphora D3 dil. have proved to be of value.

Frequently, pleuritis can be discovered adjacent to or over the involved lobe of the lung. It always develops if there is a disturbed excretion or an inadequate tin process. Excretion is stimulated with a mere sweat pack. The necessary permeation of the form of the unorganized water is achieved with Bryonia D3–6 (dil. and sc.), as well as with horseradish compresses. To stimulate the Stannum process one can give injections of Stannum prep. D8, D10, together with Equisetum D10, D15 or Bryonia. Furthermore, in pneumonia as well as in pleuritis, diuresis must be stimulated because excretion has been displaced from below upward. As a matter of course, intestinal excretion must also be stimulated—with enemas, for example.

Tuberculosis of the Lungs

Pulmonary tuberculosis has decreased so remarkably in the last few decades that a detailed discussion no longer seems justified. Nevertheless, tuberculosis is a typical disease of the lungs and in its occurrence, course, etc., one can see the fundamental aspects of its development and therapy. Thus, this consideration will be in somewhat more detail than the frequency of the illness might warrant.

If one accepts only the concept of infection, one can say that persons with a certain constitution are preferentially infected with tuberculosis. That, however, does not permit one to understand why the lungs are by far the preferentially susceptible organ and 85% of all tubercular infections involve the lungs. Such understanding is possible only from a knowledge of the inner nature of the organ.

It is not possible to trace the infection of the lungs to the inhalation of tubercle bacilli because in an active process there are always more bacteria in mucous that is swallowed without an infection of the esophagus or stomach developing. In order for the stomach to become infected, for example, it would require six times as many bacteria. Similarly, it is known that if the possibility of an infection exists, not every exposed person is infected, and those who are susceptible do not succumb or get infected at all times in the same way. Relative to the healthy person's constitution and disposition, one must recognize a specific deviation of force relationships that prepares the predisposed person as a soil for the tubercle bacilli. It is explained in more detail in the chapter on infectious illnesses how without exceptions, the infection is not the beginning of an illness; rather, it only makes the illness manifest. It is preceded by a shift of force relationships that makes the infection possible in the first place.

Relative to tuberculosis, we will here mention only what is

required for the lungs and therapy. According to a presentation by Rudolf Steiner, the predisposition to tuberculosis arises through a displacement of processes localized in the upper and lower organism.[2] If the person lives too much in the dynamics of the nerve-sensory system, and if this makes strong demands on him, then the foundation for neurasthenia is laid. If, on the contrary, the situation is such that there is an excessive autonomy of the metabolic processes with an excessively weak upper organism, then we have the phenotype of hysteria. It is understandable that the individual metabolic organs can be considered to be clinically absolutely healthy. Consequently, the manifestation of the illness is primarily noted in the psychological realm. If, however, the excessive and predominating metabolic processes rise into the middle man, especially into the area of the lungs where the dynamics of the nervous system, the head forces, should predominate, then the predisposition to tuberculosis is given. It is, as it were, an excessive rising upward of the lower processes. These then provide the living foundation, the nutrient soil, for the tubercle bacilli to flourish.

From this point of view a number of findings becomes comprehensible. For example, it is known that women have tuberculosis more frequently than men. As has been said repeatedly, men in general are more deeply incarnated than women and have a more form-permeated corporeality. In them, the nerve-sensory system predominates. In women, however, it is more the metabolic or rhythmic system that prevails. Thus, men tend more to abstract thinking, women more to art and imagination. In women the possibility of predominant dissolving tendencies of the metabolism is greater than in men.

Many findings show a clear polarity between tuberculosis and silica. Thus, the lungs, which have the strongest susceptibility to tuberculosis, have a low silica content. Even within the lungs the susceptibility is in an inverse relationship to the presence of silica. The right lung, which has a smaller concentration of silica, succumbs more frequently. The most infrequently affected inner organ is the pancreas, which shows the highest concentration of silica. In contrast, when a person has progressive tuberculosis, the silica content in the pancreas is decreased. Silica is the representative of the formative forces that emanate from the head pole. As mentioned above, in tuberculosis these forces are too weak and are thus forced back. The disturbed force relationships can be directly seen in these findings.

Among the organs below the diaphragm, the adrenal glands are most frequently affected. Through the kidney system the catabolic forces of the nervous system, which we connected with silica, are limited in their activity and transformed into opposing buildup processes. To a certain extent, therefore, the predominance of the anabolic processes in the adrenals is physiological. It thus stands to reason that this organ in particular is the first to be exposed to the consequences of these excessive metabolic activities. Furthermore, the adrenals participate most strongly in the metabolism of light, upon the disturbance of which, according to an indication of Rudolf Steiner, tuberculosis is ultimately based. In the section on light metabolism in vol. I these relationships are presented in greater detail. Another essential aspect of the anabolic processes is their dissolving effect. This is physiological in the metabolic region. In tuberculosis, however, it leads to the dissolution even of the organ tissue and finally to the destruction of the lungs. One is reminded here of the exudative form of tuberculosis, to which the present description is primarily applicable, and in which the inflammatory changes predominate.

In the indurative, productive form of tuberculosis there is rather the opposite, namely, a hardening tendency that always goes out from the nerve-sensory pole. In this case the lung strives to "become too much head," as Rudolf Steiner expresses it.[3]

Connected with this is an unhealthy nerve-sensory activity. Man unites too strongly with earthly conditions and is diverted from the sun, space, and cosmos. One can think here of the impoverished living conditions of earlier times, whose influence on the development of tuberculosis remains uncontested. As conditions changed, the basis for this form of tubercular illness also disappeared.

It was described above how the lungs as earthly organs rule

over the connection of the soul-spiritual being with the corporeality, and thus the soul-spiritual state of consciousness is also established. If this organ is disturbed through a disease process, one loses the organic basis for the higher members to live together with the corporeality in a healthy, balanced harmony. That again results in the psychological peculiarity of the person suffering from tuberculosis. He is usually very imaginative, but not an abstract thinker. This thinking mainly requires an intensive activity of the nervous system, an excessive formative force of crystallization. However, this element in particular is lacking in those with tuberculosis. The rise of the uncontrolled metabolism is experienced as a feeling of "vital discomfort." On the other hand, these patients easily live in a kind of euphoria that is often crassly contradictory to their physical health. This is an expression of the weak connection to their being with the body. They do not really communicate anymore since the organ for that has been damaged. They actually float somewhat over their corporeality and the realities of the world. Especially this state (among others) provides the foundation for artistic productive activity.

Gradually, the organism can be disconnected still further so that the latter can hardly be built up at all. The withdrawal of these forces and the disappearance of structure and substance correspond to the name "pulmonary consumption," which denotes the nature of this illness much better than "tuberculosis"—a term that stems from the pathologic-anatomical findings. Tuberculosis thus shows in the body and frequently in psychological behavior an inadequate connection with the corporeality or the earth—at times even a certain tendency to fly away from the earth.

The two described types also have correspondences in the psychological realm. The more dissolving inflammatory character of the exudative form corresponds to an illusory, euphoric soul mood. The hardening, productive form corresponds more to a psychic constriction such as in compulsive phenomena. In both cases the healthy balance of above and below is displaced; the organ of the middle, the lung, is disturbed, and the establishment of balance is made more difficult.

In regard to morbidity and mortality, one finds relationships

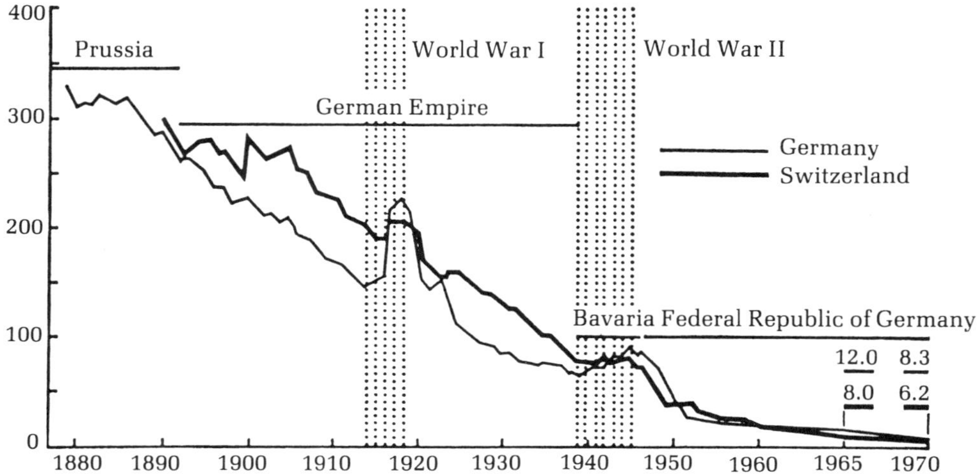

Fig. 2: Incidence of Tuberculosis (all forms) Deaths per 100,000 People. (From O. Gsell, "Die Infektionskrankheiten," in *Pathomorphosis*, No. 1, 1969.)

similar to those of pneumonia in tuberculosis. As Fig. 2 shows, there has been a continuous decline, at least since the turn of the century. Without doubt, chemotherapy has shortened the illness and has also saved lives in isolated cases. The decisive decline of this scourge occurred, however, many years before. The determining influences were an improved public hygiene and, in recent decades the progressively stronger connection of man with the earth in civilized areas.

The Therapy of Pulmonary Tuberculosis

An understanding of the nature of the illness leads to the basis for a rational therapy. The significance of iron as the metal of incarnation was mentioned above. It is in a position to enhance the connection of the members of man's being with the corporeality, and it can therefore address the fundamental disturbance in a specific way. It is given in the form of Ferrum prep. Hematite, Ferrum phosphoricum, Ferrum chlorat. comp., Meteoric iron, or Ferrum rosatum with graphite. (Ferrum rosatum is prepared from red rose leaves and meteoric iron.)

Through the combination with graphite, the lungs as organs of the earth are addressed. Furthermore, the polarity of silica and the susceptibility to tuberculosis was pointed out. By administering quartz, particularly plant silicic acid—for example, through Equisetum among other things—one stimulates the formative structural forces. By salt rubbings one can "work against the hardening processes that form from within." They are thus indicated in the proliferative, indurational form. Phosphorus, which intervenes or takes hold of the light metabolism by way of the ego-organization, must also be mentioned. In the use of phosphorus, care must be exercised in the inflammatory exudative processes because of the possibility of hemoptysis. Here it may be better to give phosphorus in the form of Apatite (calcium phosphate).

Also Mercury D6–10 is indicated. It works in a mediating, regulating, uniting way and is the metal that orders the formation of the lungs. The medication, however, must be varied according to the stages of the illness and particularly according to the individual situation. Attention must be paid especially to the unburdening of the metabolism; for example, by treatment of the liver to stimulate detoxification, or by enhancing excretion by way of the kidneys and intestines.

Especially in tuberculosis, however, the remedies present only one aspect of therapy. It will also be necessary to pay attention to the entire lifestyle, the training of intensive thought activity, and the working for concrete thought forms; mathematics, for example, will prove to be essential for those suffering from tuberculosis since through such an activity the formative forces are enhanced. To be added here is a comprehensive stimulation of the sensory functions directed toward the outer world in order to strengthen the ego activity. These examples should show the direct development of therapy from pathology.

Bronchial Asthma

Shortness of breath, gasping inspiration, and increased difficulty in expiration are the unmistakable signs of an asthmatic attack. One finds a spasm of the smooth musculature of the small and smallest bronchials as well as a swelling and forming of secretions in this area. The attacks occur most frequently at night. A spastic bronchitis still frequently persists between attacks.

The consideration of cramping, a phenomenon of the astral body, opens the way toward understanding. In the realm of the nerve-sensory system the astral body works in a concentrating, formative way that is the precondition to being able to follow a sequence of thoughts. In the region of the rhythmic system, however, no firm or solid form may develop. An in- and out-breathing must take place as a fluctuating rhythm. If now the astral body penetrates too deeply into the rhythmic system with the dynamics of the nerve-sensory system, a cramp develops that tends to hold the air. The pathological formative tendency goes so far that there are outpourings of secretions from the bronchials, the so-called Curschmann's spirals. The formation can proceed to mineralization and a material densification in Charcot-Leyden's crystals. These consist of octahedric fatty acids that stem from the granules of the disintegrating eosinophilic leukocytes. In extreme cases, even calcium salts can develop.

The secret of how mineral substance develops from organic substance through the death forces and formative forces emanating from the head pole is revealed in these processes as an archetypal phenomenon. Cramps that develop through the one-sided working of the astral body with the dynamics of the nervous system and without the mediation of the ether body "hook themselves" into the lung areas, as Rudolf Steiner said, but can in turn be a secondary phenomenon, namely, an attempt to secrete substances, as is also the case in renal colic or gall bladder colic in which the organism attempts to excrete a stone. Thus, it may happen that pathological metabolic processes precede the spasmodic events. This would mean, however, that here metabolic and nervous systems meet directly, which is always a pathological state. The encounter is healthy only if the rhythmic system stands between them as a mediator, making the free in- and outbreathing possible.

Histamine and the allergens show that it is true that metabolic products or pathological substances can bring about an asthmatic attack. Among them are primarily animal products (feathers, hair) and pollens. In all these substances the relationship to the astral body is obvious. Therefore, asthma is in most cases considered to be allergen dependent, which is perfectly justified. It has already been said that the allergic phenomenon is based on the fact that foreign substances unjustifiably penetrate the organism, which then attempts to protect itself from the foreign intrusion by an allergic reaction. The entire event is a form of self-maintenance that proceeds on the wrong plane or overshoots the goal. To this extent, one has the same conditions in an asthmatic attack as in an anaphylactic shock. Both could end fatally. It is, however, essential to recognize the meaning behind these reactions.

Asthma is an instructional example of how strongly the psychic and organic planes are connected in the region of the lungs. An attack can be set off by allergens of which often the most miniscule, hardly detectable quantities are sufficient, but also even by merely thinking about the allergen. The latter, however, occurs only when the organism is already "primed."

The asthmatic generally appears to be an extremely sensitive and conscientious person. This enhanced sensitivity is the same on a psychological level as that on the organic level toward the allergen, so one can thus speak of a "psychological allergy." The sensitivity is also a protection of the self from foreign intrusions since the astral body is always in a posture of defense, and the smallest physical or psychological allergens are sufficient to bring it into wrong activity. The encapsulation, the cutting off that then ends in cramps, can happen on the soul plane as well as on the organic. It is characteristic of the lung region that bodily and psychological influences, and the reactions to them cannot be separated. There is, therefore, a purely allergic asthma as well as a purely psychogenic type and between them innumerable transitions.

As was pointed out by Rudolf Steiner, this special configuration of the members of being can also be caused by shock experiences. During such events there is a partial loosening of the ether body, which can then no longer integrate itself properly. In this situation the astral body works unjustifiably with the one-sided dynamics emanating from the head pole; this then leads to a cramp or spasm.

According to an indication given by Rudolf Steiner, the disposition for asthma may be traced not only to outer changes, but sometimes also to shock experiences suffered by the mother that were transmitted to the patient during his embryonic life. Provided shock experiences are found in the case history, a corresponding treatment of shock with Oxalis and Argentum is indicated.

It was described above how in asthma the metabolic and nervous systems meet directly without mediation. It is the task of the rhythmic system, which in this case has been overcome, to hold them apart. Thus, on the one hand, there is a disorder of the metabolic system, which either forms pathological substances or permits foreign protein to penetrate the organism. On the other hand, there is an over-sensitivity of the astral body that takes hold of the metabolism in an improper way. To insert the astral body into the metabolism in the right way, so that it is not active with the dynamics of the nervous system but rather structures the substances and is properly active in the anabolic functions, is a task of the kidney system. We have discussed how the penetrative structuring of the air organism and of respiration is a task of the kidney system. For that reason, the actual cause of asthmatic illnesses lies here. *Asthma is a functional disease of the kidney system, and the lung is here a secondary organ.*

Asthma Therapy

In asthma as in all illnesses in which cramps or spasms occur, the goal of therapy and healing is the transformation of the basic situation. In separate attacks or in status, a symptomatic treatment may be absolutely necessary. The fundamental illness, however, is not influenced by such symptomatic treatment. The justification of symptomatic therapy in breaking through a state of illness was discussed.

The customary treatment today in a severe status asthmaticus is the use of corticosteroids. "It is surprising in a pharmacology of the glucocorticoids in asthma that under experimental conditions a spasmolytic effect cannot be verified; this is difficult to reconcile with clinical experience."[4] The application of glucocorticoids does not have a direct effect but rather a stimulating one; it acts as substitute for the kidney system in which the cause of asthma lies. Also, a spasmolytic therapy practiced earlier with adrenalin derivatives is, fundamentally speaking, a therapy by way of the kidney system, as was described before. One prescribes the finished product, however. The effect thus remains symptomatic and is, in the best of cases, merely a substitution therapy.

The goal of healing is to change the asthmatic constitution as it has been described. For this the following has proved to be of help. These suggestions go back to Rudolf Steiner and are given here as a schema:

1) Prunus spinosa D3 or D5 inj. in the neck region;

2) Nicotiana tabac. D6 or D10 in the kidney area;

3) Gencydo 1%, 3% between the shoulder blades. These injections should be given daily, or each of them once a week.

Prunus spinosa (blackthorn or sloe) is a plant that is strongly able to concentrate the etheric formative forces. It is one of the first plants to blossom in the spring, and the fruit ripens at the end of the year. Fruit formation is thus (in contrast, say, to the cherry) extended over the entire year. In addition, it is able especially to take into itself and concentrate the entire vegetative period. This contracting activity, which is indicated in the fruit, can be experienced in a most telling way when the fruit is eaten. The vitalizing effect of the plant is even communicated to the environment and soil. As a preparation, Prunus can be used to bring these strong formative forces to the patient. In this case, a vitalization is achieved in the head area to counterbalance the excessive catabolic tendencies of the astral body. It is thus effective to give the injection at the hairline of the neck region.

Nicotiana tabacum, the tobacco plant, is poisonous because it has taken up too much astrality. It was discussed in detail in vol. I. Therapeutically, it is administered in potentized form to regulate the activity of the astral body and to balance deformations. Gencydo is used in particular in the treatment of hay fever; it works primarily on the water organism and is discussed in more detail later.

In a further treatment of asthma one can use preparations made from oak bark and Veronica. Quercus 10% is given in the morning and Veronica 10% in the evening. In many cases a concentration of D3 is quite adequate. Oak bark is distinguished by a high content of tannic acid and calcium. With it one can stimulate the astral body in such a way that it works in a more structuring way on the ether body and releases the nerve-sensory system. Veronica officinalis or speedwell, a Scrofularia, is a tender plant. One stimulates the ether body with it and thus addresses the process from "another side."

This fundamental therapy can provide the basis for nearly all treatments of asthma. However, in asthenic, "dry" constitutional types it is advisable, instead of Gencydo, to use a corresponding constitutional remedy—for example, Argentum nitr. D20 or an appropriate copper preparation.

A further basic medicament is copper. From previous discussions and from the significance of the kidney system, the rationale for the use of copper should be evident, especially since it is actually always indicated in spasmodic or cramped states. Of proven value is Cuprum aceticum D3, D4, which is particularly indicated in spastic bronchitis and whooping cough, that is, in an early stage or another form of spasmodic illness in the lung region.

A specific effect can be achieved with Cuprum/ren. The principle of these metal-organ preparations was described before. In this case, we have a copper-nitrogen complex. Through the nitrogen the astral body is specifically addressed, and through being directly processed with the kidneys it is directed into their region. Besides having been helpful in kidney illnesses, Cuprum/ren has also been useful in asthma.

As external measures, carbonic acid baths are indicated. They work to make the astral body more active from below. In general, the application of acids in suitable form (Gencydo, Prunus, Formic acid, Carbonic acid) is indicated here.

Furthermore, especially in the therapy of asthma, the constitutional type is decisive. If the entire appearance is "dry" so that the agonizing, glutinous secretions are difficult to bring up, then one must support the ether body as a counterbalance to the drying action of the astral body. This can be achieved by giving fluids, which may have to be alkalized (by adding sodium bicarbonate) since alkaline substances give the ether body a foundation, whereas acids correspond to the working of the astral body. A liquification of the secretion is just as necessary as overcoming the acidic tendency that develops through the astral body. Especially in children these measures are often necessary. However, there are also constitutional types who are too "watery" with excessive secretions, in whom drying out measures are indicated (limitation of fluid and salt consumption). In an acute case, phlebotomy can be most rapidly helpful, particularly with congestion as in cor pulmonale. This constitutional type can be encountered more frequently in transition from hay fever.

This fundamental therapy can naturally be modified or supplemented in accordance with the individual requirements. Thus, in asthma in childhood the application of Quercus in the morning can be replaced by Phosphorus D5 or D6; in the evening Cuprum per melissam or Quartz D12 to D20 can work better than Veronica. Finally, Belladonna stands quite close to copper. It is indicated as a preparation of copper therapy, and it may occasionally work more strongly but not as persistently as copper. If there are strong hardening processes, then sulphur baths could be necessary. Also Formica D6, 10, 15, or 30 work in a dissolving and vitalizing manner (injections in increasing potencies appear to be most effective, two to four injections of every potency, and higher potencies less frequently). Often preparations from the homeopathic pharmacopœia are extraordinarily useful. The basic therapy described above and a suitable homeopathic therapy in no way exclude one another but can complement each other effectively.

In childhood asthma attempts at therapy have been made by increasing respiration by counting, humming, and by voice exercises. Furthermore, diaphragmatic or abdominal breathing is consciously practiced, which activates the personality in the specific area of respiration. By this means immediate help and healing can be achieved, but it naturally demands considerable participation by the patient, the physician, and the parents. Because of the comfortable and immediate effects of symptomatic therapy, these therapeutic measures have been neglected unjustifiably. Especially in childhood asthma there are concrete possibilities of avoiding the danger of a long course of steroid therapy. One can also refer to nutritional change as an essential therapeutic factor. Here, the measures discussed in hay fever can be considered.

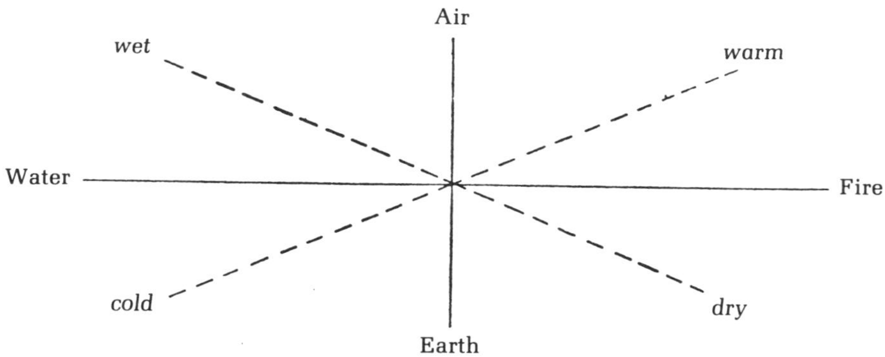

An essential factor of the pathogenesis and therapy in asthma is the climate, which, of course, has an intense influence on the condition of the air. Thus, one can intervene in the illness process by this road. One is dealing here, however, with the four classical elements, namely, earth, water, air and fire, through whose interaction the specific climate of a place develops. The significance of the resulting qualities for, among other things, the healing plants and their application was known in ancient times and used until the Middle Ages. The descriptions given at that time were not taken seriously anymore and must be developed anew. In order to understand the meteorological principle that is significant here, the following diagram may provide assistance.

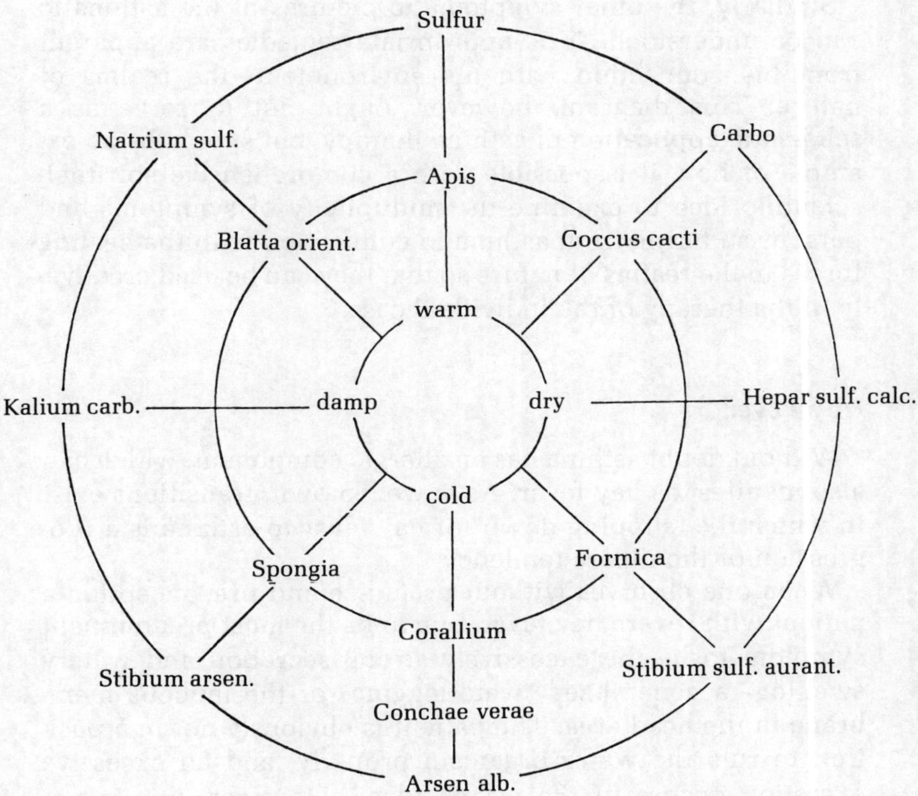

These qualities play a significant role for the asthmatic. It is not a matter of indifference whether he lives in and inhales dry, moist, warm, or cold air. Here are clear individual differentiations that are given by the members of being and the organizations—warmth, air, water, physical organism—ruled by them. The predominant organization determines a specific constitution which then produces a particular temperament. If, for example, the water organism predominates, meaning that the fluidity of the body is not properly permeated and taken hold of, then one must make the access to water possible. This is possible through Kalium carbonicum, which was described in detail in the chapter on the hepato-biliary system.

Similarly, the other symptomatic pictures of the asthmatic can be understood. "The appropriate remedies are apparent from his connection with his environment—the realms of nature. This diagram, however, ought not to serve as a schematic application of asthma therapy, but should be an example of how it is possible with a comprehensive spiritual-scientific idea to examine the multiplicity of symptoms and persons suffering from asthma in connection with the healing forces in the realms of nature so that they can be used creatively in the therapy of the individual case."[5]

Hay Fever

Without doubt asthma has an allergic component, which can also manifest as hay fever. As is well-known, transitions exist in which the "slipping down" of hay fever to asthma is a progression of the illness tendency.

When one observes without prejudice and preconception a patient with severe hay fever, one finds the most predominant symptom to be the excessively strong secretion and watery swelling—a generalized "waterlogging" of the mucous membrane in the head area. The patient is obviously not in a position to rule the water organism properly, and an excessive excretion occurs in the wrong place. However, this is not primary but is an absolutely purposeful reaction. It is preceded by the intrusion of the allergen—in this case, pollens, etc. Through secretion the foreign body is mechanically removed or floated out. On the other hand, in every inflammation there is also a catabolic process. Thus, here the attempt is made to break down inappropriately penetrated foreign substances somewhat later than would normally have taken place. In hay fever, there are two disorders which are certainly connected but are yet of different natures.

1) There is an incapacity to rule the water organism. It is seen from experience that most hay fever patients have a watery (hydropic) constitution and suffer from an exudative diathesis. This alone, however, is not sufficient to cause the development

of hay fever. It is also treated differently, for example, with Kalium carbonicum.

2) On this basis the actual allergic phenomenon comes to expression. It consists in the fact that the nasal mucous membranes are too easily permeated by the pollens of grasses, etc. These penetrate untransformed through the mucous membranes and provide the foundation for the allergic reaction. Thus, there is an increased permeability. The organism cannot appropriately or at the right time defend itself or prevent the penetration by foreign life, and so must do it in the blood. For that reason, hay fever is not a local, but a total, illness. The delayed defense and the inflammatory reactions are connected with the formation of histamine.

Once this path of development became known, one sought for substances that prevent histamine release and block the reaction. This is possible by using antihistamines. Certainly this procedure takes its point of attack only at the very last phase of the illness process and is only symptomatic. It is possible with corticosteroids to intervene much earlier in the process since they attack the inflammatory components. Aside from side-effects that accompany this therapy, the purpose of the inflammatory events is negated. The self-defense against being overcome by foreign substances, which underlies allergies, is thus blocked. In the last analysis, the door is opened for foreign life processes to enter the organism, which is neither seen nor considered when the "successes" of this treatment are extolled. This displacement in the balance of forces—which can, under certain circumstances, arise after a latency of many years—can be understood from the descriptions in the chapter on inflammation and sclerosis (vol. I).

A causal therapy will strive to address the displacement of the members of being standing behind the symptoms and will attempt to harmonize them. Here, it is an unformed water organism and an inflammation that ideally are to be addressed together. The problem is a qualitatively altered predominance of the ether body; the astral body cannot properly penetrate and form it, and the former thus becomes excessively sensitive and works differently. Fundamentally speaking, it is the same disturbance as in asthma; however, here the water organism predominates. The therapy must thus be modified. In order to withdraw the astral body from above and to integrate it into the water organism, Rudolf Steiner suggested "fruits that have leathery rinds" for therapy. "In such fruits it is evident how formative forces working from outside inward are especially active." Thereby a "stimulation of the astral body in the direction of ether body is achieved."[6] The healing principle thus does not begin with the predominating ether body; rather one wants to "send a similar process from a polar opposite direction against it."[7] "Thus, the excessive centrifugally active forces are opposed by others that work strongly in a centripetal direction."[8]

Nevertheless, this battle against the excessive metabolic forces does not simply occur through an inhibition of inflammation. The ideal remedy must be addressed to both disorders, to the excessive, predominating water organism and to the inflammation. This exists in principle in nature in those fruits that have leathery rinds. This applies mostly to the lemon, Citrus medica. In it the double effect is united; that the contracting effect is found in the juice of the lemon requires no further verification since it can be experienced directly. In addition, citrus fruits contain a substance that in a series of tests showed a highly anti-inflammatory effect. It is 4½ times more effective than hydrocortisone and sixty to two hundred times stronger than phenylbutazone."[9]

In the course of the study of active substances and their isolation, the substance citral, which also occurs in other oils, was shown to be in lemon oil. It was shown to have a strong antihistaminic effect.[10] In a spasmolysis test, a specific antagonism between citral and histamine as well as a calming effect were discovered.[11] Furthermore, citral works in a strongly bacteriostatic way[12] and also has a regenerative, epithelizative effect.[13] One can here see in an exemplary way how in nature various principles can be encompassed in one plant or in one part of a plant, such as the fruit. Certainly active ingredients can be isolated that actually have special effects. However, these work only on symptoms and do not take hold of the unity of the disturbance. They are, then, no longer remedies.

Yet, even the isolated substance citral shows an extensive spectrum of activities that almost specifically fits the symptoms of hay fever. Much more comprehensive, naturally, is the lemon itself, which corresponds in its nature to the illness process. Fundamentally, one can only address one aspect of the process of an illness when a substance is isolated from its natural interconnections. Only the natural process corresponds properly to the illness process. The physician, through his effort and intuition, must find the process. The preservation or even enhancement of it is a pharmaceutical task.

In the preparation Gencydo an attempt is made to grasp this activity of the lemon; furthermore, the quince, which is similar, is also used in this remedy. Gencydo is best used prior to the occurrence of the symptoms, initially in a 1% form, later in a 3 to 5% form as injection, preferably between the shoulder blades. The stronger injections burn somewhat when injected. This can be avoided through intramuscular and slow injections. One can then go up to 7%. Depending upon the symptoms, the injections are initially given one to two times a week, later even daily. The inhalation of the vaporized ampule preparation (3%) appears to be even more effective (particle size 1 μ).[14] This is a basic treatment that in some cases achieves the goal; it may not always be sufficient by itself, however. In the future, greater effectiveness should be achieved by improving the preparation.

From the description of this illness process, one sees that it can also be addressed from various other sides. A possible way to delimit the excessive life is with the therapeutic application of lead. The catabolic death forces in the organism correspond to lead. This can be clearly seen in lead intoxication with the premature aging process, etc. It brings about the transition of a living substance to a mineral. At the same time, however, a border or enclosure is provided in relation to the outer world. In hay fever, however, there is not only excessive life, but also an inadequate enclosure of the mucous membranes. These factors can be specifically addressed with lead. Initially it is best used as Plumbum met. prep. D8 or D6 as injection, not more than once or twice a week, especially if one is dealing with the metabolic type. It is not indicated in patients who show premature aging. With them it could even be that through the hay fever a certain vitalization occurs in the head, so that the hay fever in itself would be only secondary. In this case, Argentum nitric. D20 is indicated.

One can also work on the water organism, however. The specific remedy to bring it under control is Kalium carbonicum, which can be used in D6 to D10 as dilution, also as Stannum trit. and injection.

As has been said, one can directly address the astral body with arsenic. The secretion can be rapidly limited with Arsenicum album D10 or D12, every fifteen to thirty minutes, but it does not bring about healing.

Dietetic measures can also therapeutically influence the water organism and the allergic phenomena. The oldest and most simple means of limiting the predominating water organism is the reduction of fluid intake. In this simple way one can experience an essential relief of any kind of "sniffles" or runny nose. Overcoming thirst, however, presents a psychological challenge that is not popular with patients today. Since all movements of water in the organism are connected with salt, the limitation of it is the most certain and simplest means of reducing the predominating water processes.

The allergic phenomena can also be similarly influenced by limiting protein consumption. Histamine originates, as do all biogenic amines, from protein metabolism. Increased protein consumption enhances not only inflammation but also favors the possibility of pathological breakdown paths. These dietetic measures intend the relief of the organism, which comes about through limiting water, salt, and protein consumption.

The qualitative aspects of protein also play an important role. The more differentiated a protein is, the more it is astralized—this applies to meat and especially to pork—and the more it has the tendency to support inflammatory reactions of the organism or to work as an allergen.

Finally, attention must be directed to the function of the intestines, and not only to constipation. The catabolic processes in the intestines serve not only as detoxification, but if they proceed pathologically, they can also form significant toxins. The typical pathological metabolic products such as indican, etc., originate also in the protein metabolism. A normalization of the intestinal activity, particularly of the intestinal flora, is a precondition to effective healing.

In such uncomfortable, but not life-threatening illnesses, it is necessary to completely heal them or at least to treat them, with that goal in mind. A "rapid improvement" can be deceptive and the sign of a displacement in which a progressive metamorphosis may occur, allowing the basic illness to appear, for example, as asthma, or in an even deeper displacement as a disposition to carcinoma. To verify displacements of this kind is not a question of statistical studies but rather of the insight into the process of illness and the meaning of the reactions.

Bronchial Carcinoma

Carcinoma in the region of the lungs is today the most frequent cancer in the male. In the Federal Republic of Germany in 1965, twice as many people died of bronchial carcinoma than in 1952. In Switzerland the deaths due to bronchial carcimona from 1931 to 1972 increased by 1,237% in men and by 623% in women. The overall deaths from cancer in that same period hardly doubled. In more recent times this rapid rise is still continuing and demands that one actively concern oneself with this illness.

The first pulmonary carcinoma was described in 1805; in Virchow's studies in the middle of the last century, not a single bronchial carcinoma is mentioned. In 1912, only 374 cases were described in world literature; today, it is the most frequent carcinoma in men.

Without doubt, smoking is an essential factor in the genesis of pulmonary carcinoma. 85 to 95% of the men who develop bronchial carcinoma smoke, but it also affects nonsmokers.

That the increase cannot be attributed exclusively to smoking is shown by the fact that people also smoked in earlier times, although not as much, and they smoked pipes more than cigarettes. The risk factor of smoking is, however, essentially more serious in men than in women. There is a specific sex difference in that ten times as many men as women develop bronchial carcinoma. The gender ratio is still shifting, however. In 1901 to 1925 it was three to one; in 1926 through 1950 it was five to one; now, however, it is ten to one. In this clear preference of this illness for the male organism, one can recognize a key for understanding it. As has been said repeatedly, men are more intensively united with their bodies and the earth than women. That this uniting became ever more solid and firm is a problem of the evolution of humanity. It leads of necessity to a solidification and hardening of the organism that can manifest pathologically as an increase in the sclerotic illnesses; with this increase there is a decline of the inflammatory illnesses. Since inflammation and sclerosis are a true polarity, a displacement toward one side must have consequences for the other. Because of the decline of inflammatory illnesses, an increase of the sclerotic and carcinomic illnesses would occur. But why pulmonary carcinoma predominates can be understood only on the basis of the nature of the lung as an earthly and incarnation organ and of the present position of humanity.

It was said initially that the most intensive connection with the outer world takes place by way of the air and lungs. Therefore, *all* inhaled foreign substances, not only carcinogens, are active as outer world within the organism—a permeation with substance which has not been transformed. The body's defense is the allergic reaction, which here may be taken as an attempt at healing.

To observe only the carcinoma illuminates only one aspect of reality. Only when one looks at it together with its opponent, with fever (or its absence)—in this instance, with pneumonia—can the partial phenomenon be understood. A connection of bronchial carcinoma with pneumonia is certainly to be taken into consideration today.[15] The increase of pulmonary carcinoma is not linear. A clear rise can be noticed since the thirties of this century. A second clear increase of bronchial tumors since 1945 coincides with the introduction of antibiotics. That pneumonia is an early symptom of carcinoma is certainly being discussed; however, one does not see in it an attempt at self-healing by the organism. Connected with this is something of great practical significance, namely, the demand not to get rid of pneumonia as rapidly as possible but rather to guide it, permitting it to heal according to the considerations mentioned above. Because of the described polaric displacement, fewer and fewer people are allowed to even produce pneumonia. They are in an anergic phase for a long time, and therefore they are exposed to the carcinoma processes.

In this connection it is interesting that not only the well-known carcinogenic substances like arsenic, asbestos, nickel, and organic substances can produce pulmonary carcinoma after inhalation, but that workers who handle chrome are also endangered. This finding is only understandable when the nature of chrome is understood. In many ways it is close to iron; however, like the entire chrome group (chrome, vanadium, and manganese) it has a much stronger connection with the earth. Its hardness, high melting point and other characteristics are related factors. Iron also has a strong connection with the earth, but it has also much of the cosmic in it (for example, light, which is visible in the sparks). This aspect is lacking in chrome, whereas iron is harmonious within itself.

Those forces of iron that are related to its connection with the earth are, so to speak, isolated in chrome. For that reason it also has a special effect on the earth organ, the lungs. It even appears that not only in chrome workers but also in all patients with pulmonary carcinoma the chrome level in the blood is elevated.

The zinc levels in patients with pulmonary carcinoma are extremely low. Zinc is, however, an opponent of iron in the organism to the extent that it protects the life processes against intervention of the ego. The "tree of life" must be maintained without damage. The individual life may not penetrate into the deepest vital layer because it can work only destructively. To prevent this is the task of zinc. Exactly this situation, this excessively strong working into the organism, the excessively strong connection of the higher members of being to the body is present in pulmonary carcinoma. The protective wall that should be formed by zinc is destroyed.

In literature the therapeutic prognosis after a "radical operation" for bronchial carcinoma is given as a 20–25% permanent cure. The diagnosis is generally made so late, however, that only approximately 10% of all patients can be operated. Thus, the curative rate is reduced to at most 2%.

Through the use of Iscador, Salzer could clearly lower the mortality. Of a control group, 21% survived, which corresponded to the international average, but in the Iscador group 60% survived.[16]

Also, Gaubatz reports that treatment with mistletoe "leads to survival rates that have hitherto not been attained through the use of the well-known cytostatics in bronchial carcinoma."[17]

Cancerous illnesses as such, and a comprehensive therapy that grasps the entire condition of the patient, is discussed in detail in the chapter on the causes and treatment of carcinoma in volume III.

Notes and References

Chapter I. Anamnesis and Diagnosis

1. R. Gross, *Medizinische Diagnostik—Grundlagen und Praxis.* Berlin, New York, 1969.
2. Schaefer, H. *Plaedoyer fuer eine "neue Medizin".*
3. See especially his *An Outline of Occult Science, Theosophy, Knowledge of the Higher Worlds and Its Attainment,* and *A Path to Self-Knowledge,* all available in the United States from the Anthroposophic Press.

Chapter II. Aspects of Therapy

1. Steiner, R., *Spiritual Science and Medicine.* London, 1948. Available from the Anthroposophic Press, Hudson, NY.
2. Jores, *Die Medizin in der Krise unserer Zeit.* Bern, 1961.
3. Steiner, Rudolf, *Universe, Earth and Man.* London, 1941. Available from the Anthroposophic Press, Hudson, NY.
4. Steiner, Rudolf, *Knowledge of the Higher Worlds and Its Attainment.* Anthroposophic Press, NY, 1982. See also his *An Outline of Occult Science.*
5. Steiner, Rudolf, *Hygiene as a Social Problem.* Spring Valley, NY. Available from the Anthroposophic Press.

Chapter III. Drug Therapy

1. By '*physis,*' the Greeks understood the living body, whereas the dead body, the corpse, was called '*soma.*' Only later, with Euripides, did '*soma*' come to denote the entire person—a change full of significance for the cultural and spiritual development.
2. Steiner, R., *Anthroposophische Menschenerkenntnis und Medizin,* lecture given on July 24, 1924. Dornach, Switzerland, 1971.
3. Steiner, R., *Cosmic Working in Earth and Man,* lecture given on January 19, 1924. London, 1952.
4. See Wolff/Brachmann, *Korrespondenzblätter f. Ärzte* (Weleda), 83/1973.

Chapter IV. Physical Therapy

1. Steiner, R., *Heileurythmie*. Dornach, Switzerland, 1966; M. Kirchner-Bockholt, *Fundamental Principles of Curative Eurythmy*. London, 1978.
2. Steiner, R., *Heileurythmie*, Lecture 2.
3. Aschenbrenner, M., *Die Sprache als Kunstwerk*, Vol. II, Schaffhausen, 1975.
4. Steiner, R., *Eurythmy as Visible Speech*, London, 1956.
5. Steiner, R., *Eurythmy as Visible Speech*.
6. Steiner, R., *Heileurythmie*.
7. Steiner, R., *Das Hereinwirken geistiger Wesenheiten in den Menschen*. A lecture given in 1908. Dornach, Switzerland, 1974.
8. See Ernst Bindel, *Die Zahlengrundlagen der Musik im Wandel der Zeiten*. Stuttgart, 1950. Günther Wachsmuth, *Erde und Mensch—ihre Bilderkräfte, Rhythmen und Lebensprozesse*. Dornach, 1965.
9. Hauschka, Margarethe, *Rhythmical Massage as Indicated by Dr. Ita Wegman*. Rudolf Steiner Press, London, 1979.

Chapter V. Remedies

1. Steiner, R. and I. Wegman, *Fundamentals of Therapy*.
2. Vorenkov, Zelchan, and Lukewitz, *Silizium und Leben*. East Berlin, 1975.
3. Vorenkov, Zelchan, and Lukewitz, *Silizium und Leben*.
4. R. Steiner, lecture of 8.28.24.
5. Steiner, R. and I. Wegman, *Fundamentals of Therapy*.
6. Steiner, R. and I. Wegman, *Fundamentals of Therapy*.
7. Steiner, R., *Geisteswissenschaftliche Gesichtspunkte zur Therapie*, 5th lecture. Dornach, 1963.
8. Steiner, R. and I. Wegman, *Fundamentals of Therapy*, Chapter 16.
9. Steiner, R., *Menschenerkenntnis und Medizin*, lecture given on August 28, 1923.
10. Steiner, R. and I. Wegman, *Fundamentals of Therapy*.
11. Steiner, R., *Spiritual Science and Medicine*, Lecture 19, London, 1948.
12. Steiner, R., *Spiritual Science and Medicine*.

13. Steiner, R., *Spiritual Science and Medicine.*
14. A detailed statement on this subject by O. Wolff is to be found in *Beitr. Erw. Heilkst.*, 1955, p. 94.
15. See Bindel, E., *Die geistigen Grundlagen der Zahlen.* Stuttgart, 1977.
16. With contributions from the discussion of Friedrich Husemann and Rudolf Treichler published in the first edition.
17. Pelikan, W., *The Secrets of Metals.* Anthroposophic Press, Spring Valley, NY, 1975.
18. Wolff, O., *Beitr. Erw. Heilkst*, p. 175, 1954.
19. Steiner, R., *Anthroposophische Menschenerkenntnis und Medizin*, a lecture given in Arnheim, July 24, 1924. Dornach, 1971.
20. Steiner, R., *Physiologisch-Therapeutisches auf Grundlage der Geisteswissenschaft.* Dornach, 1975.
21. Wolff, O., in *Beitr. Erw. Heilkst*, p. 182. 1954.
22. Steiner, R. and I. Wegman, *Fundamentals of Therapy*, chapt. 20.
23. See also Husemann, G., *Erdengebärde und Menschengestalt*, "Das Zinn in Erde und Mensch." Stuttgart, 1962, and Selawry, A., *Zinn und Zinntherapie.* Ulm, 1963.
24. See also Holtzapfel, W., "Der Kupferprozess in der kindlichen Entwicklung." *Beitr. Erw. Heilkst.* 1955, p. 77.
25. Wolff, O., in *Beitr. Erw. Heilkst.* 1955, p. 26.
26. zur Linden, W., in *Beitr. Erw. Heilkst.*, vol. 6/7, p. 25, 1947.
27. See Wolff, O., in *Beitr. Erw. Heilkst.* 1955, p. 15.
28. Poppelbaum, H., *Tier-Wesenskunde.* Dornach, 1954; *Mensch und Tier, Fünf Einblicke in ihren Wesensunterschied.* Dornach, 1975. W. Schad, *Säugetiere und Mensch; Zur Gestaltbiologie.* Stuttgart, 1971. F.H. Julius, *Das Tier zwischen Mensch und Kosmos.* Stuttgart, 1970. Kipp, F., *Die Evolution des Menschen im Hinblick auf seine lange Jugendzeit*, Stuttgart, 1980.
29. A detailed presentation of the epiphysis from the spiritual scientific standpoint can be found in D. Boie, *Das erste Auge.* Stuttgart, 1968.
30. Steiner, R., *Mystery Knowledge and Mystery Centers*, lecture 13. London, 1973; *Nine Lectures on Bees*, lectures 8

and 9. Spring Valley, 1970; *Fundamentals of Therapy*, chapter 17. Spring Valley, 1938.
31. Steiner, R., *Spiritual Science and Medicine.*
32. Steiner, R., a lecture given in Berlin, October 22, 1904.
33. See Simonis, W. Chr., in *Beitr. Erw. Heilkst.* 1953, p. 260.
34. Boie, D., in *Beitr. Erw. d. Heilkst.* 1960, p. 193, and 1966, p. 213.

Chapter VI. The Fourfold Organ System

1. Steiner, R., *An Outline of Occult Science.*

Chapter VII. The Liver-Gall System and Its Diseases

1. Steiner, R., *Hereinwirken geistiger Wesenheiten in den Menschen*, 1908.
2. Ponfick, cited by F. Eichholtz, *Lehrbuch der Pharmakologie*, 9th ed., Berlin/Göttingen/Heidelberg, 1957.
3. Wannagat-Wollheim, *Leber, Endocrinium und Wasserhaushalt*, Stuttgart, 1969.
4. Steiner, R., *Entsprechungen zwischen Mikrokosmos und Makrokosmos*, April 23, 1920.
5. Steiner, R., *Spiritual Science and Medicine*, 11th lecture.
6. Steiner, R., *Geistige Zusammenhänge in der Gestaltung des menschlichen Organismus.* Lecture given on February 22, 1922. R.S. Nachlassverwaltung, Dornach, Switzerland, 1976.
7. Steiner, R., *Die Erkenntnis des Menschenwesens nach Leib, Seele und Geist.* Lecture given September 9, 1922. Nachlassverwaltung, Dornach, Switzerland, 1976.
8. See G. Wachsmuth, *Erde und Mensch*, 3rd printing, 1965.
9. Steiner, R., *Curative Education.* Rudolf Steiner Press, London, 1972.
10. *Spiritual Science and Medicine*, lecture 13.
11. Wolff in *Beitr. Erw. d. Heilk.* 7, 1954, p. 175.
12. Grohman, G., *The Plant.* Vol. 1. Rudolf Steiner Press, London, 1974.
13. Husemann, F. and O. Wolff in *Beitr. z. Substanzforschg.* Vol. 1, 1952, p. 180.

14. Steiner, R., *Welche Bedeutung hat die okkulte Entwicklung des Menschen für seine Hüllen und sein Selbst?* A lecture given in 1913, included in *Wie erwirbt man sich Verständnis für die geistige Welt?* Rudolf Steiner Verlag, Dornach, Switzerland, 1973. See also G. Schmidt, "Zur Alkoholfrage," in *Der Beitrag der Geisteswissenschaft zur Erweiterung der Heilkunst. Anthrop.-mediz. Jahrbuch* II, p. 165. Stuttgart, 1951.
15. Steiner, R., A lecture given on September 9, 1922, included in *Die Erkenntnis des Menschenwesens nach Leib, Seele und Geist.* R.S. Verlag, Dornach, Switzerland, 1976.
16. Blond, Caspar, *Liver Damage as Cause of Cancer.* 2nd printing, Bristol, 1960.
17. In the Anglo-American language area there is a mnemotic device summarizing the characteristics through alliteration: female, fat, forty, fertile, fair, four children.
18. Grötzinger, *Die mediz. Welt* 20, 1969, p. 391.
19. Cited by Fromm, *Niedersächs. Ärzteblatt* 47, 1974, p. 816.
20. Steiner, R., *Mystery Knowledge and Mystery Centres.* Rudolf Steiner Press, London, 1973.
21. Steiner, R., *Fundamentals of Therapy.* Chapt. 17.

Chapter VIII. The Renal System and Its Diseases

1. Portmann, A., *Einführung in die vergleichende Morphologie der Wirbeltiere.* Basel/Stuttgart, 1969, p. 320.
2. Steiner, Rudolf, *Anthroposophische Grundlagen für die Arzneikunst*, a lecture given on October 27/28, 1922, in *Physiologisch-Therapeutisches auf Grundlage der Geisteswissenschaft.* Dornach, 1975.
3. Wolff, O., *Beiträge zur Erweiterung der Heilkunst* 7, 175 (1954).
4. Wiehmeyer and Bock, *Internist. Prax.* 13, 695 (1973).
5. Steiner, R., A lecture given on July 28, 1923, included in *Rhythmen im Kosmos und im Menschenwesen.* Dornach, 1962.
6. Steiner, R., *What Can the Art of Healing Gain through Spiritual Science?* London, 1950.
7. Walb, L. & I., "Die Hay'sche Trennkost." Ulm, 1961.

8. R. Steiner, *Welt der Sinne und Welt des Geistes*, 6 lectures, 1912.
9. Olbing, *Monatsschrift für Kinderheilkunde*, 122: 69 (1974).
10. R. Steiner/I. Wegmann, *Fundamentals of Therapy*. London, 1983.

Chapter IX. The Cardiovascular System and Its Diseases

1. Steiner, R., *Karmic Relationships*, Vol. V. Lecture given on March 30, 1924, London, 1966.
2. Ekman, *Roux Archiv* 116 (1929); Copenhaver, *Anat. Rec.* 31 (1925); Stöhr Ph. jr., *Roux Arch.* 102, 103, 106, 112.
3. See F. Kipp, *Hoeherentwicklung und Menschwerdung*. Stuttgart, 1948. 2nd Edition is entitled: *Die Evolution des Menschen im Hinblick auf seine lange Jugendzeit*. Stuttgart, 1980.
4. See Poppelbaum, H., *Tier-Wesenkunde*. Dornach, 1954.
5. Heinemann, H. and Pflug, B. (ed.), "Rhythmusprobleme in der Psychiatrie." *Aktuelle Psychiatrie*, Fischer, Stuttgart, 1978. Hildebrandt, G. (ed.), *Biologische Rhythmen und Arbeit*. Heidelberg/Wien/New York, 1976. Pengelly (ed.), *Circannuel clocks*. New York/London, 1974.
6. Steiner, Rudolf, *Anthroposophical Leading Thoughts*. London, 1973.
7. Steiner, Rudolf, *Geisteswissenschaftliche Menschenkunde*, Lecture 21. Dornach, 1973.
8. See Bühler, W., *Das bewegliche Osterfest*. Tübingen, 1965.
9. Steiner, Rudolf, *Geisteswissenschaftliche Menschenkunde*, Lecture 12.
10. Steiner, R., *Erziehung und Unterricht aus Menschenerkenntnis*, lecture given on October 16, 1923. Dornach, 1972.
11. "Rhythm. Funct. Order and Man's Emancipation from Time Factor," in: Schaefer, K.E. (ed.), *Basis of Indiv. Physiology*, Mount Kisco, N.Y. Hildebrandt (ed.), *Biologische Rhythmen und Arbeit*, Springer, Vienna/N.Y., 1976. (Survey of lit. up to 1963 in *Beitr. Erw. Heilkst.* 1964, 107).
12. Schwenk, Th., *Sensitive Chaos*. Rudolf Steiner Press, London, 1965.
13. See Wedepohl, *Beitr. Erw. Heilkst.* 1964, p. 149.

14. Harvey, William, *On the Movement of the Heart and Blood in Animals, (De motu cordis et sanguinis in animalibus)*, 1628.
15. Kolisko, E., "Thomas v. Aquin über die Bewegung des Herzens." *Natura* 1926/27, p. 168.
16. Borelli, *De motu animalium*. Rome, 1681.
17. Bohn, *Circulus anatomico-physiologicus seu oeconomia corporis animalis*. Leipzig, 1697. Cited in Simonia, *Beitr. Erw. Heilkst.* 1966, p. 78.
18. Kielmeyer, C.F., *Ges. Schriften I–III*. Berlin, 1938.
19. Volkmann, A.W., *Die Hämodynamik*, 1855.
20. Weber, E.H., *Anwendung der Wellenlehre auf die Lehre vom Kreislauf des Blutes und insbesondere auf die Pulslehre*, 1850.
21. Müller, Joh., *Handbuch der Physiologie d. Menschen*. Koblenz, 1833, Vol. I, p. 139.
22. Carus, C.G., *System der Physiologie*. Dresden & Leipzig, 1838–40.
23. Oken, Lorenz, *Naturphilosophie*. In *Beitr. Erw. Heilkst.*, 1964, p. 175.
24. Rosenbach, O., *Die Krankheiten des Herzens und ihre Behandlung*. Vienna, 1893–97, and *Grundriss der Pathologie und Therapie der Herzkrankheiten*. Vienna, 1899.
25. Hasebroek, Karl, *Über den extrakardialen Kreislauf des Blutes*. Jena, 1914.
26. *MMW* 1922, No. 23. Cited in Kolisko.
27. In Wolff, "Das Herz—ein sekundäres Organ," *Beitr. Erw. Heilkst.*, 1977.
28. Nishi, K., *Nishi System of Health Engineering*. Cited by Manteuffel-Szoege, *Über die Bewegung des Blutes*. Stuttgart, 1977.
29. Vogler, P., *Neue Anthropologie*, vol. I, Stuttgart, 1972.
30. Wetter, E., in Keidel, *Kurzes Lehrbuch der Physiologie*. 1973, p. 510.
31. Ganong, *Lehrbuch der medizin. Physiologie*. 1974, p. 435.
32. Guyton, Arthur C., *Textbook of Medical Physiology*. 5th ed., p. 160, Philadelphia/London/Toronto, 1976.
33. Schütz, Ed., *Physiologie des Herzens*. Berlin/Heidelberg/Göttingen, 1958, p. 377.

34. A review of this problem in Rudolf Steiner's works is to be found in Sieweke, H., *Beitr. Erw. Heilkst.* 1948, 24, and W. Ch. Simonis, *Die wahre Herzaktion.* Freiburg, 1974; W. Bühler, W., *Die Sonne als Weltenherz.* Stuttgart, 1966.
35. *Welche Bedeutung hat die okkulte Entwicklung des Menschen für seine Hüllen . . . und sein Selbst?* 2nd lecture, GA 145, 4th ed. 1975.
36. *Spiritual Science and Medicine,* 2nd lecture, GA 312, 1961.
37. *Geisteswissenschaftliche Gesichtspunkte zur Therapie.* 1963.
38. George Adams, *Physical and Ethereal Spaces.* Rudolf Steiner Press, London, 1978. George Adams and Olive Whicher, *The Plant Between Sun and Earth.* Rudolf Steiner Press, London, 1980.
39. Quoted in Lehrs, E. *Mensch und Materie.* 2nd ed. Frankfurt, 1966.
40. See Schneider, P., *Beitr. Erw. Heilkst.* 1977, 37.
41. Kolisko, E., *Beitr. Erw. Heilkst.* 1964, 169.
42. Wolff, O., "Zur Physiologie der Herz- und Kreislauffunktion," *Beitr. Erw. Heilkst.* 1966, 25.
43. R. Steiner, *Origins of Natural Science.* Lecture VI, Jan. 1, 1923. Anthroposophic Press, 1985.
44. A. Fyfe, *Die Signatur des Mondes im Pflanzenreich,* Stuttgart. *Die Signatur des Merkurs im Pflanzenreich,* Stuttgart. *Die Signatur der Venus im Pflanzenreich,* Stuttgart. *Die Signatur des Uranus im Pflanzenreich,* Stuttgart.
45. *Kli. Wo.* 1925, I, 1005.
46. Portmann, A., *Einführung in die vergleichende Morphologie der Wirbeltiere.* Basel-Stuttgart, 1969, p. 213.
47. Steiner, Rudolf, *The Spiritual Hierarchies and their Reflection in the Physical World.* (Lectures of April 12–18, 1909). Anthroposophic Press, 1983.
48. Steiner, R., *Rhythmen im Kosmos und im Menschenwesen.* Dornach, 1962.
49. Wehn, P.S., *Bibliotheca Anatom.* Vol. 1, 336 (1961) and Wehn, P.S., "Pulsatory activity of peripheral Arteries" Oslo, 1957.
50. Schütz, E., *Lehrbuch der Physiologie des Herzens.* Berlin/Göttingen/Heidelberg, 1958.

51. Cited in *Beitr. Erw. Heilkst.* 1970, 35.
52. Katz, U.M., in *Circulat. Res.* 3, 588 (1955), cited in Wezler, *Vehr. dt. Ges. Inn. Med.*, 70. Kongress 1964, p. 22.
53. Rushmer, in *Physiol. Rev.* 35, 138 (1955), cited by Wezler.
54. Wezler, Die ärztliche Fortbildung, *Regensburger Colloquium* Bd. XVII, 1969.
55. Appenzeller, K., Blutkreislauf und Herzfunktion, *Beitr. Erw. Heilkst.* 1960, p. 99.
56. Wedepohl, in *Anthroposophie und Medizin.* Dornach, 1963, p. 113.
57. Mees, *Beitr. Erw. Heilkst.* 1975, 89 and 98.
58. Wezler, K. and W. Sinn, *Das Strömungsgesetz des Blutkreislaufes.* Aulendorf, 1953.
59. Manteuffel-Szoege, L., *Über die Bewegung des Blutes.* Stuttgart, 1977.
60. Thompson, S.A., "Effect of pulmonary inflation and deflation upon circulation," *Jour. Thoracic Surg.*, 17, 328 (1948).
61. Houssay, B.A., *Human Physiology.* New York, 1955.
62. Steiner, R., *Spiritual Science and Medicine.*
63. Schmid, K., *Wiener Mediz. Wochenschr.* 1892, No. 15, 16, 17; s. *Beitr. Erw. Heilkst.* 1974, 93.
64. Havlicek, H., *Arch. f. Kreislaufforschung. I.* (1937), 188.
65. Husemann, F. & G., *Beitr. Erw. Heilkst.* 1974, 115.
66. Among other authors (*Beitr. Erw. Heilkst.*): Faber 1972, 130; Bubenzer 1973, 102; Paede 1948, 39; Simonis 1966, 88; Weissenborn 1974, 45; Weckenmann 1966, 173. Basfeld, *Beitr. Erw. Heilk.* 1982, 1; Bibliographie der Widder-Literatur, see *Beitr. Erw. Heilk.* 1982, 132.
67. Liebau, G., in *Naturwissenschaften* 41, 327 (1954); 42, 339 (1955); *Zeitschr. f. ges. experim. Medizin* 123 (1954); 125, 494 (1955). Pestel and Liebau: *Phänomen der pulsierenden Strömung im Blutkreislauf*, Bd. I. *Hochschulskripten* Nr. 738/738a, Mannheim, 1970.
68. Liebau, G., *op. cit.* and Wolff, *Beitr. Erw. Heilkst.* 1966, 25.
69. Otherwise Liebau holds to the idea of the "heart force as the only source of energy for the movement of the blood." He uses the principle described here to explain the move-

ment of the blood in the periphery in purely mechanical terms.

70. Schwenk, Th. *Sensitive Chaos.* Rudolf Steiner Press, London, 1965.
71. Hildebrandt, *Beitr. Erw. Heilk.* 1980, 143.
72. Steiner, R., *Weltenwerden Weltenseele Weltengeist,* lecture given on July 2, 1921. Dornach, 1967.
73. Kern, B. and Rothmund, W., *Die Verhütung von Myokardinfarkten durch Myokard-Euthetisierung.* 1967.
74. Crawford, T., and Levene, C.I., "Medial Thinning in Atheroma." *Jour. Path. Bact.* 66 (1953), p. 19ff.
75. Kreinsen, U., *Herzinfarkt aus myozytogenen Ursachen.* Diss. Heidelberg, 1971.
76. Baroldi, G., and Scomazzoni, G., "Myocardial circulation in the normal and pathological heart," 1967; "Lack of correlation between coronary thrombosis and myocardial infarction or sudden "coronary" heart death," *Ann. N.Y. Acad. Sci.* 156 (1969), pp. 504–25; "Coronary heart disease: Significance of the morphological lesions," *Am. Heart Jour.* 85, (1973), pp. 1–5; "Function morphology of the anastomotic circulation in human cardiac pathology," *Meth. Achievm. Exp. Path.*, 5 (1972), pp. 438–73; "Human myocardial infarction: Coronarogenic or non-coronarogenic coagulation necrosis?" In E. Bajusz and G. Rona, *Myocardiology*, 1972, pp. 399–413.
77. Kern, B., *Der Myokard-Infarkt.* Stuttgart, 1974.
78. Edens, E., *Digitalisfibel*, 3, 1948.
79. Kern, B., *Die Linksinsuffizienz.* 1949.
80. Sedlmayr, H., *Verlust der Mitte.* 2nd edition, Salzburg, 1948, p. 150.
81. Steiner, R., *Grundelemente der Esoterik*, lectures given on September 26 and October 31, 1905. Dornach, 1976.
82. Schütz, E., *Lehrbuch der Physiologie des Herzens.* Berlin, Heidelberg, 1958, pp. 44, 455.
83. Lockett, Knox, *Jour. Endocr.* 43 (1969), 315; Lockett, *Jour. Physiol.* 202 (1969), 671.
84. *Krankengeschichten*, edited by Degenaar, No. 3.

85. Alijew and Rachimova, Ceskoslov, In: *Farmacija 10* (1961), 464. Zizin, *Atlas der Arzneipflanzen der USSR*, Moscow, 1962. Donev, *Farmacija*, Sofia 17 (1967), 31. Müller-Dietz, "Arzneipflanzen," *Berichte d. Ost-europa-Inst. FU Berlin, Reihe Medizin* (1968).
86. Karl, Müller, Pedersen, in *Dt. Apothekerzeitung* 116 (1976), 57.
87. This indication comes from Rudolf Steiner. The effects of Cardiodoron are described from various points of view by the following authors: W. Wedepohl, *Anthroposophie und Medizin*, Dornach, 1963, p. 115. Basold, *Heilmittel für typische Krankheiten*. 1959, p. 49. W.C. Simonis, *Beiträge zur Erweiterung der Heilkunst*, 1955, p. 186.
88. Weckenmann, in *Therapie über das Nervensystem*, Bd. 11, *Hypo- und Hypertonie*. Hrsg. Gross, Stgt., 1973, p. 190. Weckenmann, *28. Internat. Kingr. f. Homöop. Medizin. Kongressberichte*. Wien, 1973.

Chapter X. The Lungs and Their Diseases

1. Clauberg, K.W., *Deutsches Ärzteblatt* 40, 2763 (1975) and *Chemotherapie* I, No. 3 (1960).
2. *Geisteswissenschaft und Medizin*, 1920. GA 312, 2nd Lecture.
3. *Geisteswissenschaftliche Gesichtspunkte zur Therapie* (1921), lecture 6.
4. Gerdes, H., *Internist* 12, 512 (1971).
5. Diagram and quotation from A. Rust in *Das Bild des Menschen als Grundlage der Heilkunst*. 1st ed. Stuttgart, 1956.
6. Steiner, R., *Fundamentals of Therapy*. (1925). 4th edition, Rudolf Steiner Press, London, 1983.
7. Steiner, R., *Anthroposophische Menschenerkenntnis und Medizin*. Lecture 15.
8. Steiner, R., a lecture given on July 24, 1924.
9. *Präparat. Pharmazie* 3, 79 (1967).
10. Dobromylsky, *Nachr. Oto/Rhino-Laryngologie* (Russian), 10, 6, 57 (1948); 1950 II, 1108.

11. Wagner and Sprinkmeyer, *Dtsch. Apoth. Zeitg.* 113, 1159 (1973).
12. Möse and Lukas, *Arzneim. Forsch.* 7, 687 (1957).
13. Rochlin, *Sowj. Medizin* 8, 1949 *Ref in Pharm. Zentralh.* 89, 211 (1950).
14. Belart, W., *Ars medici*, 68, Vol 3 (1978).
15. Watson, in *Zeitschr. f. Krebsforschung* 57, 199 (1950).
16. Salzer, G., in *Z. Erkr. Atm.* 142, 127 (1975).
17. *Pneumatologie* 148, 79 (1975).